**The Technology
of Ecological Building**

The Technology
of Ecological Building

Basic Principles and Measures,
Examples and Ideas

Klaus Daniels

English translation by
Elizabeth Schwaiger

Birkhäuser Verlag
Basel · Boston · Berlin

Table of Contents

■
For Thomas, Mark, Philip, Oliver –
you are the future

Ecology (Greek)

The study of the interaction of living organisms
with their inanimate (e.g. climate, soil) and
their animate environment, as well as the study of
resource and energy management in the biosphere and its sub-categories.

Ecological Building,
a movement in contemporary architecture.

This movement aims to create environmentally
friendly, energy-efficient buildings and developments by effectively managing natural resources.
This entails passively and actively harnessing solar
energy and using materials which, in their manufacture, application, and disposal, do the least
possible damage to the so-called 'free resources'
water, ground, and air.

Meyers Neues Lexikon, 1994

What is the Technology of Ecological Building?

'Environmental crisis', 'ozone hole', 'acid rain', 'dying forests', these are only some of the problems facing us that make immediate action imperative. Politicians are responding to public opinion and have come to see the need for legislative action to safeguard the future. But why wait for pressure from above? It is up to each individual to take action, face the dangers, and create an environment worth living in for our children and future generations.

This book is perhaps the most comprehensive analysis to date, ranging from global prognoses and projected risk potentials to specific measures for preventing these risks. More and more clients and investors recognize the need for architectural innovation that will render buildings less vulnerable to crises. Here, climate, exterior design, and the immediate environment play as large a role as does designing buildings that will utilize environmental resources. The book shows, for example, that deep-plan and very tall buildings are as suited to natural ventilation as are standard two-axis buildings of moderate height.

Ecological building means applying technical aids sparingly and making the most of all passive means provided by the building's fabric. Here, developments in structural engineering and construction in urban areas, building form, and orientation play important roles. To help better understand certain climatic, aerophysical, and technical processes and functions, the basic principles of these fields are made easily accessible, laying a foundation of information with which to begin drafting new designs. The measures employed in ecological building are complex and derive from several specialized disciplines – from urban planning, architecture, construction, and façade design to active technical building services and their applications. Planted surfaces, indoor and outdoor, fresh air, soil, water, and rainwater all contribute to an integrated design, as does the management of building services and utilities that use the abundant resources of the environment.

Everybody talks about ecological building. Yet few architects, construction engineers, and building services engineers are truly able to deal with these issues; their training has usually not prepared them. This book aims to close the information gap by presenting and explaining the basic principles and practice of ecological building – including the surrounding space – and by illustrating these issues with examples and design concepts.

Zurich / Munich
August 1995
Prof. Klaus Daniels, B.Eng.

1

Human beings should live in harmony with
nature – what can we learn from our ancestors
about this topic?
A quick overview offers insight into the evolution
of mankind and its environment: From life in
wide open landscapes to modern life in crowded
urban centers.

1.
Introduction

Until a few hundred years ago the relationship between human beings and their environment was characterized by their willingness to adapt to the environment and to live in harmony with it. The comfort requirements were very different in the past and cannot be compared to today's demands, since people were unable to tame nature to the degree to which it is possible now. The global population was much smaller and groups had ample space, finding in nature all they needed for survival.

Small populations and modest requirements for energy utilization meant low emissions, mainly related to combustion processes (open fires). The waste products of past centuries were readily recyclable and bio-degradable and posed no threat to the environment. All waste could be returned to the natural cycle.

In the past, buildings were characterized by:
- small windows,
- building masses with high storage capacities,
- and low standards for heating and sanitary systems.

The small window units allowed little daylight to penetrate into rooms. The main function of windows was to provide visual contact with the outside world. Small windows also resulted in minimal heat gains from the outside to the inside, and therefore in minimal cooling loads. Hence, the problem of compensating for thermal loads never presented itself: knights did not experience problems associated with cooling.

In winter, these small windows created only insignificant heat losses and the heating requirements for rooms in these buildings were generally no higher than they are in modern, well-insulated buildings.

The thermal storage masses of very old buildings were large in relation to the square footage – high storage capacity is the current term – and were usually unfinished (natural stone walls), so that thermal energy coming from the outside or released in the room was almost completely absorbed by the building masses. Due to the minimal loads and the high storage capacity such buildings remained cool even on hot summer days and tended to be uncomfortably cold in winter. Thermal transfer through the non-insulated building mass lead to low, internal surface temperatures which would be unacceptable to modern comfort requirements. Furthermore, these very high storage buildings exhibited a sluggish regulatory behaviour: In other words, room temperature changes as a result of thermal gain or loss were slow and minimal. The consequence for day-to-day life was that in winter occupants gathered around an open fireplace to warm themselves by the heat radiating from it.

The citadel Alcazar in Segovia (Figure 1) is a perfect example of this type of building. Warm water heating systems and sanitary installations were still in the distant future and the inhabitants accepted standards which would be unthinkable today. Firepits for heating and open cloacae are hardly compatible with our ideas on living standards or comfort.

As the use of building materials continued to evolve together with demands for comfort and better hygiene, the form of buildings changed: They became more open. The Glücksburg, a moated castle (Figure 2), illustrates this tendency in architecture in comparison to the citadel Alcazar. A first glance reveals that the windows are much larger, allowing more daylight to fall into the rooms, thereby improving the lighting. At the same time thermal gains from the outside increased in summer, as did heat losses in winter.

However, high storage buildings were still constructed with natural materials and greater heat gains in summer did not create over-heated rooms but merely improved the comfort level. Tile stoves came into use between the 15th and 18th centuries; they could heat not only one but several rooms through shafts. This system improved comfort overall and satisfied the increased heat requirements created by the larger windows. What is more: comfort was improved without any threat to the environment. While wood combustion increased the emission of dust to a small degree, the waste products were not damaging to the environment.

The moat surrounding castle Glücksburg was created for safety and protection and not for ecological reasons. Nevertheless, the inhabitants of the building benefitted from this interesting feature with regard to comfort. On the one hand water reflects additional light towards the windows and on the other hand the evaporation occuring at the water's surface cools the surrounding air, improving conditions in summer and, finally, at night the water mass cools less slowly than the surrounding air, improving the climate near the building. The end result was an ecologically fascinating, albeit unintended, overall solution.

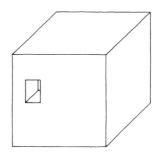

Basic building principle of old citadels and castles: body with massive walls and small openings

Figure 1
Citadel Alcazar
in Segovia

Figure 2
Water castle
Glücksburg

Contrast to these examples of buildings in temperate zones, the development of building forms in hot climate zones was quite different. The tendency in those areas was to locate living areas underground to utilize the coolness of the earth and to create ventilation through buoyancy, thus improving thermal comfort. Figure 3 is a schematic sketch of such earth covered buildings in Libya and a similar building type in China.

In the Middle Ages, as buildings grew taller, they were as solid and massive in the hot zones as they were in Central Europe. Small window openings and roof elements allowed very little light into the building and minimized the heat transmitted from the outside (Figure 4). The sketch illustrates the principle of natural ventilation and internal air movement: Proof of how earlier generations reacted intelligently to the influences of nature, utilizing physical properties to achieve thermal comfort in their homes.

The dawn of the industrial age at the beginning of the 19th century precipitated the well-documented migration of an ever increasing population from rural areas to urban centers where workers were needed. Industrialization and rapid advances in technology increased the demands for energy which were mostly met through the use of coal and, in part, of natural gas. The sharp increase in emissions was generally ignored and no effort undertaken to act against the environmental threat posed by dust, soot and other polluting materials. Yet another environmental pressure existed through the dumping of untreated waste water from residential as well as industrial areas into rivers and lakes. This was the beginning of an environmental calamity with which we struggle even today: Water, a valuable natural resource, was, and continues to be, polluted, leading to serious environmental destruction.

Figure 3
Earth house in Gharian, Libya (Sketch based on drawing by B.Eng. H. Hooss)

Warm air rises in the large inner courtyard drawing air through the cool access tunnel into the courtyard. A constant cool breeze blows near the entrance to the courtyard.

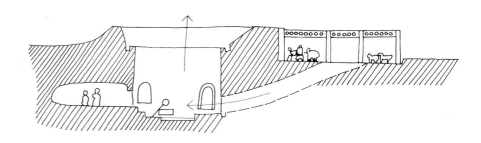

Figure 4
Typical building configuration in warm climate zones, Gadhames, Libya (Sketch based on drawing by B.Eng. H. Hooss)

The access and entrance areas are usually covered by buildings. This creates the impression that one enters through the basement. Warm air rises through ventilation shafts to the roof and suction draws fresh air from the entrance areas, thereby cooling the building.

to Figure 3
Aerial view of earth houses
in China

to Figure 4
View of Skoura, Morocco,
and above view into a typical
lane in the region, showing
the location of doorways into
buildings.

In the 20th century progress continued to advance at a frantic pace, especially in industry; increased urbanization followed and with it the concentration of labour in cities, a trend which has continued right up to the present time and has triggered the tendencies of the post-industrial age with which we are all too familiar. Its main characteristics are:

– the concentration of workplaces in small areas,
– the shortening of distances for communication and information,
– the maximized utilization of available space.

Figure 5 shows a dense urban centre which pays no heed to ecological concerns: The architecture and the technology that goes hand in hand with it does not focus on energy consumption and the environment. To build skyscrapers in diverse architectural forms and to provide maximum housing on minimum space, architects abandoned the previous standards of natural ventilation, and building services switched to fully automated climate control. By the thirties the technology applied to the majority of these buildings supplied them mechanically with fresh air as well as sufficient cooling and heating energy. The skyscrapers built in Manhattan approximately 30 years ago have hermetically sealed façades, incapable of responding to environmental influences such as wind, smog, external temperatures, and humidity. Yet, there were some architects who strove to design buildings with at least some relation to their natural environment. One example is the well-known office building of the Ford Foundation in Manhattan, New York, where the architects integrated a planted courtyard into the building design (Figure 6).

Figure 5
Manhattan is a prime example of a dense urban environment demonstrating how necessary it has become to think ecologically.

The energy crises, beginning in 1973, led to a renewed search for simpler solutions, above all with regard to ventilation and air conditioning systems. The main characteristics, some new, some familiar, were:

- the opening of façades for natural ventilation,
- the creation of climate buffer zones (halls and atria),
- improved heat insulation and sun protection,
- the implementation of energy recovery systems.

This was also the time when engineers, architects and clients began to discuss how building concepts could be modified to create buildings with room depths amenable to natural ventilation and lighting, giving rise to a new wave of thought focussed on ecological building design. At issue were not only energy efficiency and savings in reaction to a possible reduction in energy resources, but more importantly environmental protection, since we are faced not so much with an energy crisis as with an environmental crisis. In other words and more to the point: we are already in the middle of it.

Figure 6
Ford Foundation in New York, view from street and courtyard (Architects: Roche & Dinkeloo, 1965)

Basic Principles of
Ecological Building

2

The population explosion, the proportionately
increased demand for energy, and the simultaneous destruction of CO_2 diminishing forest
regions of the earth, are all factors which contribute to the greenhouse effect. A worldwide
climate catastrophe seems inevitable.
We must counter the threat of a very real environmental crisis, far exceeding a medium-term
energy crisis, with appropriate measures. In our
need to lessen the burden on the environment
the motto 'less is more' has never been more
pertinent.

2.
The Status Quo – Global Prognoses

Mankind, aided by technology, is well on the way to reversing, within the course of a few centuries, a process of 500 million years. We are consuming oil and coal reserves at a rate two million times faster than these reserves took to grow, and we are living far beyond our means, at the expense of nature. We should all be aware that our activities are tantamount to a global climate experiment with a largely uncertain outcome and we must be prepared for global temperature changes far beyond anything experienced in the past two million years. We know furthermore that our very lives, as well as our economic base, are dependent upon the world's climate. Nevertheless we behave as laid back as if these problems were still remote. Many people, however, realize that the current population explosion (Figure 7), together with the environmental damage which goes hand in hand with population growth, virtually guarantees a pre-programmed human tragedy on a scale not only immeasurable but also, and perhaps more importantly, inexcusable. No one knows today how such a population can be fed and given a sustainable environment to survive in when, at the same time, rainforests are being destroyed. Rich soil is being eroded, turning into steppes, or slowly but surely becoming saturated with toxins. Oceans and lakes are being polluted. And climate zones are shifting within short periods across various borders.

According to prognoses issued in 1992 by the IPCC (Intergovernmental Panel of Climate Change), the global mean temperature will surpass the 1990 average by approx. 1.8–4.2 K by the end of the 21st century. This prognosis is based on the assumption that the atmospheric CO_2 content, currently approx. 360 ppm (1992), will rise to double the preindustrial rate, i.e. to 560 ppm, and will then remain constant at that level.

A rise of this magnitude in the earth's mean temperature would lead to increased evaporation rates for the world's oceans, which in turn might cause important changes in the water cycle. Several consequences are likely: Low, compact cumulus clouds could increase, reflecting a portion of the sun's radiation and thus having a negative humidifying impact on the greenhouse effect, which causes them in the first place. On the other hand, there could be more and more high storm clouds (cumulus nimbus), which operate like huge atmospheric pumps, transporting steam into the higher troposphere. This type of process is conducive to the formation of high-lying, veil-like clouds, which are too 'heavy and opaque' for heat radiation, thereby further worsening the greenhouse effect.

Other, little-known cause and effect relationships, whose forces cannot yet be measured or guessed at, will also play a role. A vital and critical process relates to hypolimetric water production. Infinitesimal variations in density due to different salt contents as well as different temperatures will result in a lowering of the sea level in the North Atlantic, transferring approx. 1/3 of excess heat, caused by the greenhouse effect, into the deep sea (approx. 42 million m^3/s). This water volume corresponds to a layer 3.2 m deep across the world's ocean surface, sinking yearly and resulting in a vertical mixing of all oceans in approx. 1,190 years, based on an average ocean depth of 3,800 m. Thus, in the initial phases, about one-third of the anthropogenic greenhouse effect will be absorbed by the deep sea during one millennium. However, if the vertical mixing of oceans does not take place, then the expected rise in temperature would increase by 50 %, i.e. to approx. 4–6 K.

Current models show a paucity of critical values and cyclical processes and are thus unable to simulate sudden changes or significant variations or other complex changes (e.g. the real comparison to global climate behaviour in the past 150,000 years). We must therefore be prepared for surprises all over the world, including the possibility, among others, that the polar ice cap may melt completely, leading to an increase of 60 m in sea level. Such a process typically requires many millennia, during which the polar ice caps are renewed approx. every 5,000 years.

The sea level has been rising at a rate of approx. 15 cm per century since 1930, a rise unrelated to the melting of the polar ice cap by this time. The erosion of the Greenland ice shield by approx. 6 cm per century contrasts with the current increase of the arctic ice shield, thus having an equalizing effect. The reasons for this phenomenon, only partially known, can be explained somewhat by the increase in oceanic surface temperatures and the decrease of mountain glaciers.

Melting processes have very slow reaction times. Hence, one can safely assume that the sea level will continue to rise over the course of several centuries, even if CO_2 emissions were to be cut back significantly and immediately. A rise in sea level by several metres is thus already a given for future generations. It is equally certain that the extreme weather events of recent years (Figure 8) are a result of climatic shifts (rainfall, wind force, storms, cyclones, droughts, etc.).

Many scientists believe that a temperature rise of approx. 1 K per century is tolerable. To achieve this balance, global CO_2 emissions would have to decrease immediately by approx. 1 % per annum, which seems an unrealistic expectation.

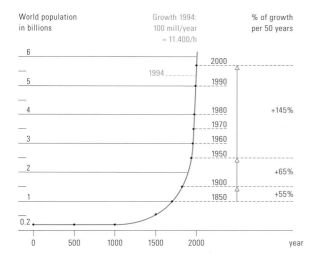

Figure 7
Population explosion leads to overpopulation on a global scale with unpredictable consequences.

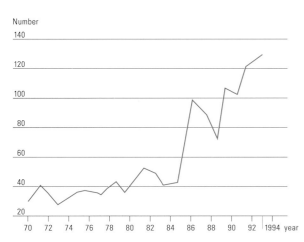

Figure 8
Increase in natural catastrophes from 1970–1993

19

Furthermore, global warming could reduce some (climatic) anomalies, e.g. the frequency of extremely low temperatures, a change that is not necessarily for the better, since low temperatures inhibit the survival of many bacteria and insects (diseases and parasites). In other words, less frequent low temperatures may automatically result in an increase of undesirable populations. Unlike global prognoses, local assessments are very difficult to make, and for some regions of the earth it is virtually impossible to make any predictions.

Since behavioural change in mankind is usually linked to considerable evidence of (potential) suffering and since policymakers and legislators are not implementing such changes, we must, at least at this point, assume that harmful emissions, especially CO_2 emissions, will not be curtailed unless individual measures succeed, in the medium term, in developing a new consciousness.

Yet the years 1990 and 1991 seem to testify to an approaching potential climate catastrophe. These years were the warmest on record, a record which has been kept for 200 years. The eruption of Mount Pinatubo in the Philippines resulted in a global cooling of 0.1–0.2 K. The aerosols projected into the stratosphere as a result of the eruption and the subsequent diminished solar radiation must surely affect the coming years. In Europe, there hasn't been a string of six summers in one decade with above-average temperatures since 1500, nor have three such mild winters as 1988–1990 been recorded in Switzerland since 1250. This is indeed food for thought. Almost every year, precipitation levels and storms registered in Europe and in India approach ever higher readings, singular for this century.

2.1
Energy Consumption and Energy Reserves

83 % of global primary energy is consumed by only 25 % of the world's population, leaving a mere 17 % of global energy consumption at the disposal of the remaining 75 % of the world's population. (Figure 9)

South America, Africa, India, China, and Asia are far below the global average as regards per capita energy consumption. The high per capita energy consumption in the former Eastern Bloc countries and the former USSR can be attributed to inefficient use.

The global average of per capita energy consumption is 1.9 tonnes UBC (units of bituminous coal). Any interpretation of this figure must take into consideration that each person requires approx. 0.4 tonnes UBC to cover the basic needs of food, clothing, and shelter per annum. When other needs, such as health care and education, are added, the figure rises to 1.2–1.4 tonnes UBC per capita per annum.

Figure 10 illustrates our current knowledge of global energy reserves as well as the rise in energy consumption, forecast to the year 2020. While oil stocks in their current form (crude oil production) will be drastically reduced, considerable reserves remain which can be extracted in an economically viable manner. Hence, massive cost increases for fuels will become a reality at the earliest in 20–30 years.

Judging by the average global consumption of individual primary energy sources from 1978 to 1987, we can ascertain the following secured timeframes of supply for all fossil energy stocks worldwide (secured/estimated resources) as shown in Figure 11:

– petroleum up to approx. 40 years
– natural gas up to approx. 80–100 years
– coal up to approx. 230 years

In addition to fossil fuels, a secured, extractable reserve of uranium exists which is the equivalent of approx. 80 billion tonnes of UBC. This reserve could stretch the overall stock of fossil fuel considerably, provided reactor technology is used. Therefore, the finiteness of energy reserves is not a decisive factor when considering necessary economies in consumption of primary fossil energy sources, even if other estimates are considerably below those presented here.

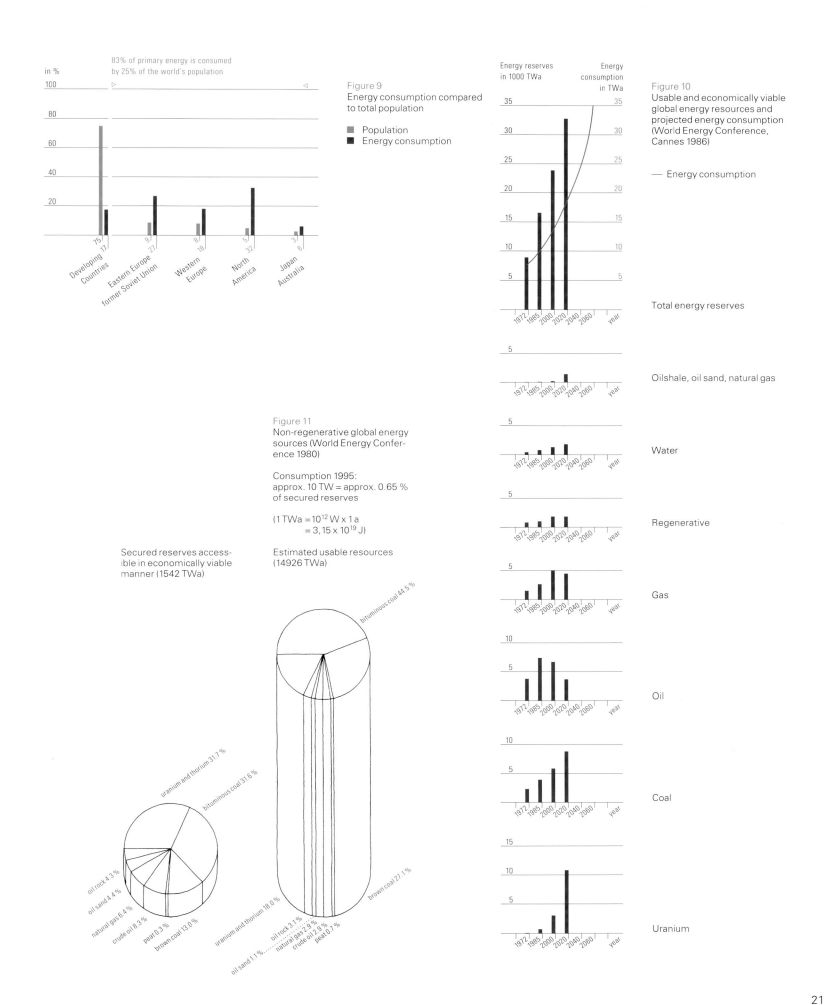

in %

83% of primary energy is consumed
by 25% of the world's population

100

80

60

40

20

75 17   9 27   8 18   5 32   3 6

Developing Countries
Eastern Europe former Soviet Union
Western Europe
North America
Japan Australia

Figure 9
Energy consumption compared
to total population

Population
Energy consumption

Figure 11
Non-regenerative global energy
sources (World Energy Conference 1980)

Consumption 1995:
approx. 10 TW = approx. 0.65 %
of secured reserves

$$(1\,TWa = 10^{12}\,W \times 1\,a = 3,15 \times 10^{19}\,J)$$

Secured reserves access-
ible in economically viable
manner (1542 TWa)

Estimated usable resources
(14926 TWa)

bituminous coal 44.5 %

uranium and thorium 31.7 %

bituminous coal 31.6 %

oil rock 4.3 %
oil sand 4.4 %
natural gas 6.4 %
crude oil 8.3 %
peat 0.3 %
brown coal 13.0 %

uranium and thorium 18.0 %

oil sand 1.1 %
oil rock 3.1 %
natural gas 2.9 %
crude oil 2.9 %
peat 0.7 %

brown coal 27.1 %

Energy reserves
in 1000 TWa

Energy
consumption
in TWa

35

30

25

20

15

10

5

1972 1985 2000 2020 2040 2060 year

Figure 10
Usable and economically viable
global energy resources and
projected energy consumption
(World Energy Conference,
Cannes 1986)

— Energy consumption

Total energy reserves

5

1972 1985 2000 2020 2040 2060 year

Oilshale, oil sand, natural gas

5

1972 1985 2000 2020 2040 2060 year

Water

5

1972 1985 2000 2020 2040 2060 year

Regenerative

5

1972 1985 2000 2020 2040 2060 year

Gas

10

5

1972 1985 2000 2020 2040 2060 year

Oil

10

5

1972 1985 2000 2020 2040 2060 year

Coal

15

10

5

1972 1985 2000 2020 2040 2060 year

Uranium

2.2
Environmental Protection and the CO_2 Problem

In view of the global prognosis for the Earth's climate, as outlined on the previous pages, we must meet these dangerous developments with a deescalation, i.e. a reduction of emission rates, especially of CO_2. The reduction of other toxins, such as CO, SO_2, NO_x, dust, etc., must be given equal consideration. Yet these toxins can be reduced by technical means. CO_2 emissions, on the other hand, can be reduced by various means in the short and medium term.

Short-term means include, above all, the reduction of energy consumption, a switch from oil and coal to natural gas and, finally, higher efficiency in the transformation and utilization of energy.

Today's 12 kW per capita consumption in the United States could easily be reduced to the European average of 6 kW without undue hardship. This would, in turn, reduce the current CO_2 emission of 1.3 Gt/a to approx. 0.6 Gt/a.

When coal is burned, each unit of bituminous coal releases 2.68 t CO_2, while natural gas results in only 1.54 t CO_2. In other words, a reduction by half. Medium-term means include requisite support and disposal technologies, nuclear energy having new importance as an alternative to fossil energy sources.

Should an even higher CO_2 content (Figure 12), singly or in combination with other tracer gases, result within the next decades in an even higher atmospheric temperature (Figure 13) and increasing climatic instability, our objective would have to be the complete elimination of CO_2 emissions in the burning of fossil fuels, even if all potential energy savings were achievable in other ways as well. For it is clear that neither industrialized countries nor third-world countries will be able to switch completely from fossil energy sources to other CO_2-free energy sources.

Figure 12
CO_2 concentration in atmosphere (top) and global temperature change (bottom) over the course of the past millennia to the present. Based on data of a ice drilling core at the Vostock station in the Antartic.

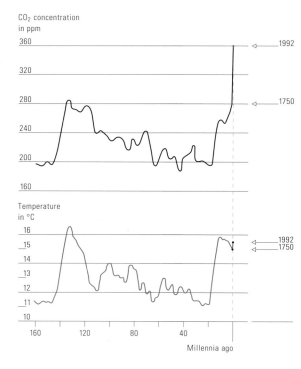

Figure 13
Development of observed air temperature (1850–1980) with and without (presumed) CO_2 increase

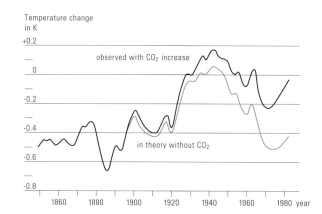

Figures 14.1 and 14.2 (30 TW strategy) illustrate what would happen when switching from fossil energies to nuclear and solar energies and simultaneously reducing worldwide energy consumption to 30 TW, as well as the resulting estimated CO_2 emissions and temperature shifts worldwide.

The reciprocity of atmosphere and biosphere has not been fully explained and is probably barely explicable. Nevertheless, certain trends can be seen, even today. Additional information about this very complex cause and effect relationship can be gathered by including in our observations the transformation of town and urban development.

2.3
Potential Savings

A careful and rational husbandry of energy use and a broad application of regenerative energy sources are essential to any plan for the future. The use of natural resources and regenerative energy sources, far from being an alternative, has become an imperative if we wish to meet the challenges of the future.

Solar radiation energy has a very special place in these considerations, since this energy source is globally and, even on a national scale, abundantly available. Furthermore, there are so many methods and technologies for utilizing this energy source that its application spectrum is by far the greatest among all regenerative energy sources. Potential savings can be gained not only by activating specific technologies but also through the planning of urban environments and individual buildings: all natural resources found in the environment should be integrated into planning, and buildings should then be conceived in such a way that their form and location as well as their structure permit energy savings. Hence, when an urban area or a building is being planned and developed, all passive measures must be exhausted before active measures in building technology can intelligently develop. Of utmost importance are the high energy coefficients of any primary energy sources.

Savings in energy consumption and environmental protection do not begin with 1:100 scale drawings. Integrated design means planning natural ventilation of urban areas, creating planted surfaces and humid areas for the purpose of evaporative cooling, creating shaded areas for the summer months, designing buildings with buffer zones for the utilization of passive solar energy in winter, creating surrounding environments for the use of earth heat and rain water. The list goes on and on. Urban areas planned with these factors in mind are noteworthy for requiring, from the onset, 50 % less heat energy than conventionally planned, well insulated projects.

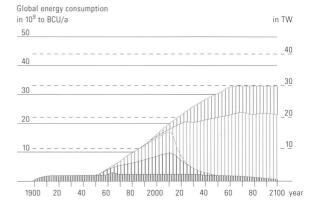

Figure 14.1
30 TW energy strategy with solar and nuclear energy

III solar
III nuclear
III gas
III oil
IIIII coal

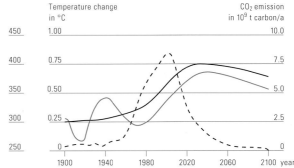

Figure 14.2
Simulated CO_2 effect with 30 TW solar and nuclear energy application

— CO_2 concentration in atmosphere
--- CO_2 emission
— Temperature change

23

2.4
Ethics and Ecology – a New Trend

Many investors are no longer indifferent to how they achieve their financial growth. Increasingly, ethics and ecology are given as much importance as simple considerations of financial return. This trend means that investors show a preference for companies and projects conceived with a view to ecology and a sustainable future. Furthermore, ecologically smart building projects are far easier to market, especially in a period of rising energy costs, since they offer a favourable ratio of rent to operating costs.

We are all responsible not only to ourselves but especially to future generations and must therefore face the major challenges of the future. Insofar as this is true, whenever we assess the life cycle of a project, we must ask whether and to what degree this project is crisis-proof, i.e. whether it will survive the future energy crisis which it is now reasonable to expect. Hence, an ideal building would be self-reliant with respect to energy utilization and would mostly service itself through environmental energy and resources taken from its immediate surroundings. It is interesting to note that in the United States 'ethical' and ecological investment funds are being offered with great success. Naturally, the investor is hard-pressed, at times, to evaluate the ethics and ecology of an investment vehicle. Hence the current discussion about creating a rational basis for organizing and evaluating relevant ecological technologies according to not only ecological, but economical principles. Environmental sustainability in construction,

upkeep, and recycling is of primary importance as an ecological criterion, as are the environmental savings which may be expected from large-scale application of the relevant technologies.

The environmental relief of a product, so long as there is complete environmental compatibility, can best be quantified through the annual CO_2 volume, produced by the technology which the product replaces or substitutes. The following values are recommended for technical installations:

– mean efficiency coefficient for relevant primary energy = 87 %

– average CO_2 emission per primary energy transfer = 0.35 kg/kWh

– average efficiency coefficient of fossil-fuelled systems = 80 %

– average efficiency coefficient of electrical energy production = min. 35 %

The embodied energy of a product is often only calculable with a high error margin. The term itself has not yet been clearly defined. Even with relatively simple production of, for instance, building materials, we can acquire only widely varying data, depending upon whether the process evaluated is purely one of construction or manufacturing or, for instance, the energy consumed by office machines or of lighting is taken into consideration as well. Total Quality Management (TQM) is another concept, used to award certificates to buildings and technologies in the same categories. We need to more clearly define and classify these terms.

In the UK, the BREEAM label is used to certify buildings. Introduced to the industry at the EUREKA technology conference on 15th July 1994 by Paul Bartlett and Alan Yates of the BRE (British Research Establishment), BREEAM (Building Research Establishment Environmental Assessment Method) is a certificate awarded to environmentally responsive buildings. Financed by the BRE and several sponsors, it is intended to encourage voluntary self-monitoring, and was initiated for office buildings in 1991. In the meantime, the ecology label is awarded to supermarkets and private homes as well.

BREEAM 5/93 evaluates office and industrial buildings according to the following criteria:

Global Evaluation and Resource Utilization

- CO_2 emissions caused by primary energy consumption
- acid rain
- ozone depletion potential, caused by CFC's and HCFC's
- natural resources and recycled materials
- integration of renewable materials
- longevity

Local Evaluation

- transportation means and transformation
- water management
- noise
- local wind-force strain
- shading provided by neighbouring buildings and properties
- reuse of existing building substances or contaminated soil
- ecological value of building site

Interior Evaluation

- dangerous materials
- natural light
- artificial light
- thermal comfort and overheating
- ventilation

The projects are assessed as being "quite good", "very good", or "excellent".

The following effects and goals are attributed to the label:

- Image enhancement
  Client demand (architects, contractors) was high despite a cost of £1,500–£4,000. It seems that 24 % of clients would be willing to pay higher rents for 'green buildings'.

- Better marketability
  BREEAM specifically intends to achieve commercial advantages for the construction industry by addressing the environmentally aware customer and further stimulate and support environmentally friendly solutions in construction.

- Higher environmental sustainability
  Since the inception of BREEAM, awareness is growing that 'green buildings' protect the health and well-being of their residents.

BREEAM is the first approach of its kind in the world. Comparable models are being developed in other European countries.

Confirming the necessity of ecological planning concepts, Figure 15 illustrates once more the single influential factors which will play a major role in the design of future buildings, not only to proof them against energy crises but also to make them interesting, in the long term, for their users.

Figure 15
Integrated design –
an obligation in the future

Developer

User

Market saturation
Energy cost increase
(utilities)

Environmental protection

Energy cost increase
(utilities)
Reusage
(renting)

Marketability

Utilization of new primary energy sources

Economic sustainability
cost/utilization

More nature – less technology
More quality – less quantity

More integration
More innovation

In the urban environment
In the building
In the work and living space

3

Buildings must be in harmony with their environment, i.e. 'live' in and with the environment.
For the various regions of the Earth this means a variety of bioclimatic building designs.
The climatological conditions in Central Europe provide an environment which should be utilized for the purposes of thermal, hygienic and visual comfort.

3.
Buildings of the Future – Requirements

'Less is more' is the motto for all future buildings with regard to ecological demands. Past and modern designs as well as state-of-the-art materials and technologies should be adopted to minimize energy demand and thus actively protect the environment.

In his book Bioclimatic Skyscrapers, the architect Ken Yeang (Kuala Lumpur, Malaysia) has convincingly described his philosophy of building in various climate zones. He strives to do justice to local climate influences by focusing on design, orientation and location, and glazing aspects, as well as integrating planted surfaces, terraces, and shading elements into the design of his buildings.

3.1
Climate and Building Form –
A Global Perspective

For Ken Yeang, climate zones and precipitation regions determine the development of building designs and the detailed modelling of the fabric of a tall building, with ecological demands always being kept in mind.

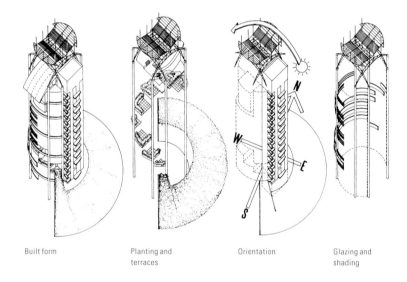

Built form

Planting and
terraces

Orientation

Glazing and
shading

Figure 16 shows the four main climate zones, tropical, arid, temperate and cold, and the distribution of climate conditions across the world. Each climatological characteristic was analyzed as to its influence on traditional building forms, implementation, and typical characteristics of various building components in that zone.

Shading and solar heating, as well as wind stress factors upon buildings, play an important role in this analysis. Other aspects include the relative external humidity and the quantity of rainfall at a specific location (Figure 17). In hot and arid zones, water is a matter of life and death. This is even more evident when one considers that only 25 mm of the annual average global rainfall of 86 mm falls in hot and arid regions of the earth. In addition to very unreliable rainfall, these regions are affected by high evaporation rates due to the high temperatures prevailing there.

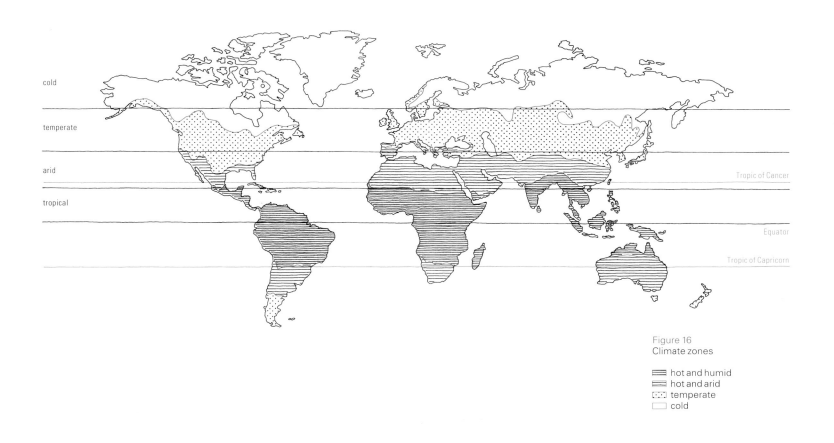

cold

temperate

arid

tropical

Tropic of Cancer

Equator

Tropic of Capricorn

Figure 16
Climate zones

≡ hot and humid
≡ hot and arid
⦂⦂ temperate
☐ cold

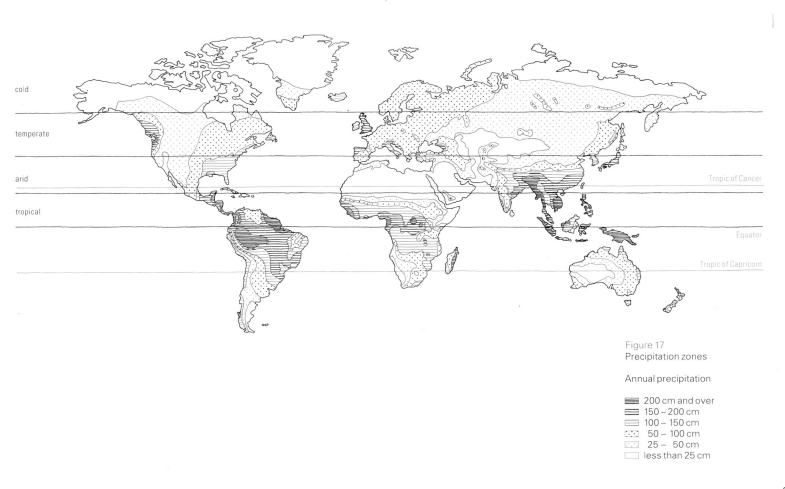

cold

temperate

arid

tropical

Tropic of Cancer

Equator

Tropic of Capricorn

Figure 17
Precipitation zones

Annual precipitation

≣ 200 cm and over
≡ 150 – 200 cm
☰ 100 – 150 cm
⦂⦂ 50 – 100 cm
☷ 25 – 50 cm
☐ less than 25 cm

Figure 18 includes five diagrams giving a comparative overview of the specific climatic characteristics in the four climate zones.

Diagram 1 illustrates the annual requirement for solar shading and solar heating. Beginning at the Equator and moving north, the need for solar heating increases (white range), while the need for solar shading (hatched range) follows the opposite course.

Diagram 2 gives information about the annual requirement for wind screening. The darkly hatched area represents the percentage of wind screening required; the more lightly hatched area indicates the percentage of breezes needed over the course of a year for comfortable conditions; the white area (in the middle) represents a happy medium, where natural conditions are so favourable as to require neither additional breezes nor wind screening. It is apparent that the lower latitudes (tropical zone) require wind for cooling almost the whole year round, while the higher latitudes require wind screening almost constantly. The measure to which naturally favourable conditions exist in each zone is relatively small.

Diagram 3 shows the annual average level of relative humidity in the four climate zones. In the arid zone, the low level of humidity can be beneficial for evaporative cooling (adiabatic cooling). The high level of humidity in the tropical zone, however, leads to very uncomfortable climatic conditions.

The annual average quantity of rainfall, indicated in Diagram 4, is directly related to the humidity levels.

The distance of the diagonal line (in Diagram 5) from the vertical represents the annual seasonal variations in each of the four zones. High latitudes, as well as the cold and temperate zones, have pronounced seasonal variations; the lower latitudes have constant climates throughout the year.

The four diagrams in Figure 19 provide an overview of the sun's influence on local climates. The shading requirement (Diagram 1) depends upon the sunpath in each season. In the lower latitudes, there is a danger of total overheating related to undesirable solar gain (darkly hatched range), whereas, in the higher latitudes, overheating only occurs during the summer months. The hatched sections indicate the sunpath as observed in each climate zone.

Diagram 2 indicates the optimum location of vertical sun shading (solid line), shielding buildings from low sun angles in the morning and evening, and of horizontal sun shading (broken line), blocking the high midday sun. Tropical zones require both types of shading throughout the year. In higher latitudes, horizontal and vertical shading is only needed during the summer and during transitional seasons along east-, west-, and south-facing sides of buildings.

Diagram 3 represents the shape of the sunpath in each climate zone. The sun or solar path becomes more southerly as one moves north, changing from a 'bow tie' pattern near the equator to a 'heart' shape in the temperate zones.

Near the equator, seasonal variations are minimal and the need for solar heating is low, whereas, in higher latitudes, this need increases during the winter (Diagram 4).

Figure 20 shows the traditional types of low-rise dwellings in various regions and makes clear the relationship between climate, built form and materials.

Heavy timber construction or heavily insulated exterior walls in cold zones ensure higher heat absorption in winter, as do the low pitched roofs. These characteristics also increase radiation absorption in summer and reduce heat by loss of radiation, conduction, and evaporation.

1
Traditional regional dwelling types

a   heavy timber construction
b   wall more protective than roof
c   stone or clay walls support roof
d   timber frame, roof more important than walls

2
Typical indigenous roof types

a   low pitch allows snow to remain, acting as insulation from chilling winds
b   medium pitch allows rain run-off
c   flat roof, rain reservoir
d   high-pitch roof allows drainage and ventilation

Figure 20
Typical, traditional dwelling and roof types in different climate regions

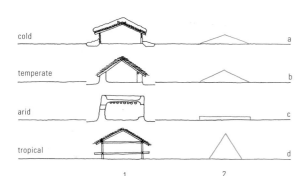

cold
temperate
arid
tropical

1   2

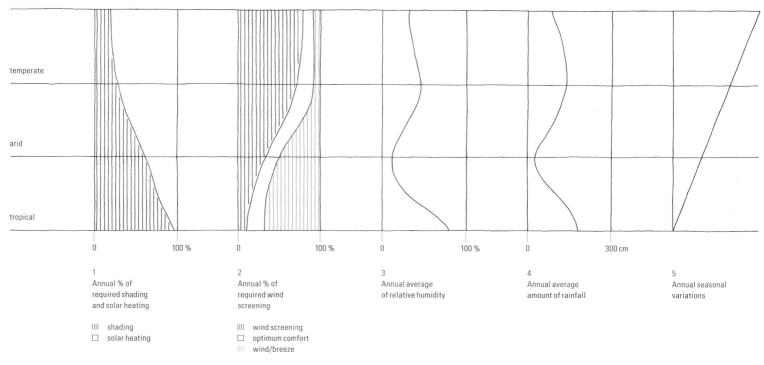

cold
temperate
arid
tropical

0   100 %   0   100 %   0   100 %   0   300 cm

1
Annual % of
required shading
and solar heating

2
Annual % of
required wind
screening

3
Annual average
of relative humidity

4
Annual average
amount of rainfall

5
Annual seasonal
variations

|||| shading
☐   solar heating

|||| wind screening
☐   optimum comfort
|||| wind/breeze

Figure 18
Climatic characteristics

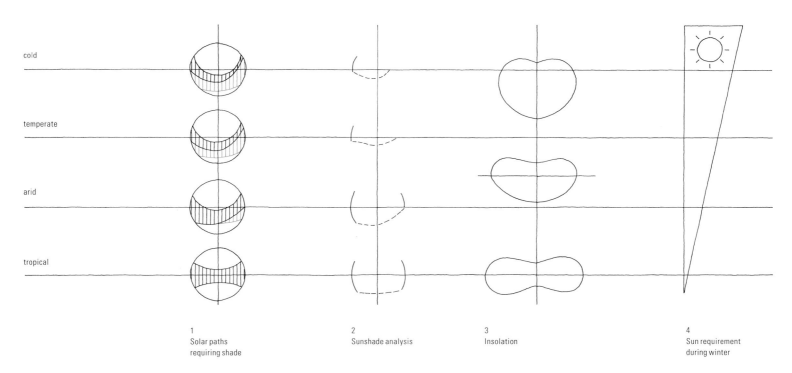

cold
temperate
arid
tropical

1
Solar paths
requiring shade

2
Sunshade analysis

3
Insolation

4
Sun requirement
during winter

Figure 19
Insolation

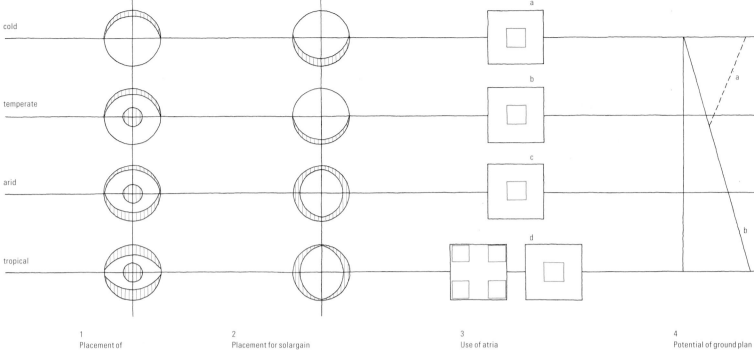

Figure 21
Climate influences
on built form

1
Placement of
transitional spaces
(e.g. hallways, stairs
and lobbies)

2
Placement for solargain
In the arid and tropical zones these areas
must be shaded.

3
Use of atria
a centre of building for
   light and heat
b centre of building for
   light and heat
c centre of building for
   cool shading
d to provide ventilation

4
Potential of ground plan
useable as atrium space

a atrium as heat buffer
   (solar 'trap')
b atrium as 'cool' zone
   (roof and shade)

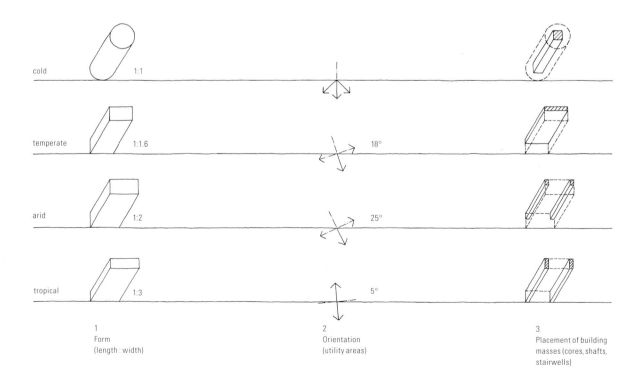

Figure 22
Climate influences on built
form and orientation and mass
distribution

1
Form
(length : width)

2
Orientation
(utility areas)

3
Placement of building
masses (cores, shafts,
stairwells)

In temperate zones, well insulated, medium pitch roofs, allowing rain run-off, establish a balance between reduction and promotion of seasonal heat absorption, radiation and appropriate convection effects.

In arid zones, where the flat roof is both sun protection and rainwater reservoir, the built form itself regulates heat production, reduction or promotion of radiation loss, and reduction of conduction gain, and promotes evaporative cooling.

In tropical zones, open building designs and high pitch roofs reduce convective and radiation gains and promote evaporation loss for cooling (rainy seasons).

Figures 21 and 22 illustrate the influences of climate upon built form and the areas where these factors can be utilized for heat energy, and the use of atria in various climate zones.

The lightly hatched sections in Diagram 1 (Figure 21) indicate the traditional placement of lobbies, stairs, hallways, and other annexed areas. These areas do not require total climatic control and natural ventilation is usually sufficient. In tropical and arid zones, the transitional spaces are often located on the north and south sides of a building, where the sun doesn't penetrate too far into the rooms. Atria can also be used as transitional shaded spaces. In temperate and cold zones, the transitional spaces are located on the north side of the building, acting as buffer zones.

The lightly hatched sections in Diagram 2 indicate the location of spaces that can be used for solar heat gain. The location follows the sunpath in each climate zone. In the tropical and arid zones, these are on the east- and west-facing sides; and in the temperate and cold zones, they are on the south-facing side.

Diagram 3 shows the optimum position for atria in all building forms in each climate zone. In the tropical zone, the atrium should be placed as shown, to ensure ventilation; in arid zones, it should be located at the centre of the building, for cooling and shading; in cold and temperate zones, the atrium should also be located at the centre, to gain heat and provide light.

Roof and ground plane can be designed as potential useable exterior space; a less feasible option the farther north we move from the equator (Diagram 4). In tropical and arid climates, the potential to make use of all external spaces is high, while, in northern regions, these same spaces have to be covered to be used.

Figure 22 shows the optimum aspect ratios of buildings in each climate zone, the best orientation of main façades, and the distribution of primary mass to achieve maximum solar shading or solar gain respectively.

Looking at the aspect ratios (Diagram 1), we see that lower latitudes require an elongated form, to minimize the east and west exposure. This form gradually evolves into a 1:1 ratio, i.e. to a cylindrical form, as we reach the higher latitudes in the north, where the surface capable of utilizing solar gain should be as large as possible.

The optimum orientation of a building and the placement of the main façades become clear when we study Diagram 2 in relation to Diagram 3 (optimum location of primary mass). Orientation is an important factor in 'bioclimatic planning', since directional emphasis can help keep heat in or out of a building (see Section 4.2.2).

In tropical zones, the closed or protected primary mass, the core, should be located on the east and west sides of a building, to ensure that it is shaded in daytime against the low sun. In arid zones, the mass should also be located on the east and west side; shading is primarily needed in summer. In temperate zones, it is best to place the primary mass on the north side, so as to leave south-facing sides available for solar gain in winter. Buildings in cold zones should ideally have open perimeters, to maximize heat penetration and solar heat gain. Therefore, core components (primary mass) should be concentrated at the centre of the building, allowing sun rays to fall into the building and the heat to be retained.

These principles should be generally applied in each local region, to further the bioclimatically correct orientation of buildings.

3.2
Local Meteorological Conditions

On these pages, Figures 23 to 28 show the basic meteorological conditions and design parameters for buildings and their services. They are the basis for further deliberations on how to construct ecologically viable buildings.

The isothermic chart (Figure 23), upon which all calculations for heat requirement are based, indicates the lowest diurnal temperatures (average over a period of two days) for various locations and thus yields data about the insulation levels required for each region. It also identifies those regions exposed to strong winds.

The chart in Figure 24 indicates wind directions, their percentages, and their distribution across the map. This information is valuable for natural ventilation of buildings and cities.

Figure 25 indicates the summer climate zones according to VDI 2078 (cooling calculation rules, Association of German Engineers), a basis for investigating external temperatures in summer and, hence, for calculating cooling requirements during that period.

Figure 26 identifies all insolation zones across Germany – in other words, the solar energy radiated onto one square metre per annum. The map clearly shows the variation in solar radiation from region to region. Hence, location has a large influence on the selection of useful alternative technologies. The graphs above this map track the annual variation in the average daily total insolation outside and inside a double-glazed façade

Figure 25
Summer climate zones
from VDI 2078
(Assoc. of Germ. Eng.)

|||| T_{max} = 29°C
☐ T_{max} = 32°C

Figure 23
Isothermal chart:
lowest temperature in °C
(2 day average)
according to DIN 4701

numbers = temperatures
in corresponding regions

W = strong winds

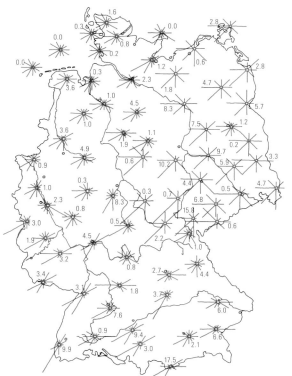

Figure 24
Average annual percentage
distributions of wind direction
at selected locations in Germany;
German Weather Service,
report 147

100 % = 30mm
numbers = % of windstill days

to Figure 26
Annual curve of daily mean
values of total insolation outside and inside double glazing
with various orientation at the
50th latitude

Glazing: external surface

— horizontal
— East/West
— South
— North

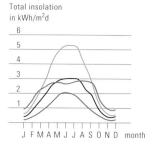

Total insolation
in kWh/m²d

Glazing: internal surface

— East/West
— South
— North

with varying orientation along the 50th latitude.
This comparison illustrates how (building) materials affect the utilization of environmental energy
sources.

Figure 27 shows the same map, this time illustrating average annual precipitation at various
locations in Germany. This map can be a planning
tool whenever rainwater is to be used as utility or
cooling water in buildings.

Figure 28 represents an intensity-of-illumination
curve with overcast skies and diurnal, as well as
annual, variations with regard to daylight. This is
vital information for lighting-technological calculations. The curves clearly show that even with
overcast skies, there is sufficient light (more than
500 lx) for use as natural lighting in buildings.

Figure 26
Average annual total insolation
in Germany in kWh/m²a;
German Weather Service

░	900 – 950
▥	950 – 1000
▧	1000 – 1050
▨	1050 – 1100
▥	1100 – 1150
▨	1150 – 1200

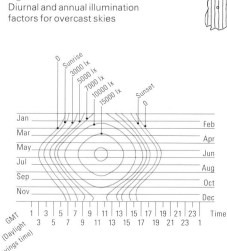

Figure 28
Diurnal and annual illumination
factors for overcast skies

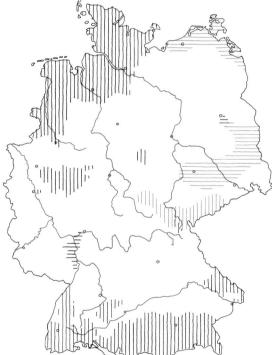

Figure 27
Rain chart of average quantity
of annual precipitation
(DIN 4108 part 3)

▭	Annual precipitation below 600 mm
▭	Annual precipitation 600 to 800 mm
▥	Annual precipitation above 800 mm (in northern coastal region of Germany (strong winds) above 700 mm)

3.3
Comfort Zones –
Thermal, Hygienic, Visual Requirements

Thermal Comfort

Buildings are environments for people. In the case of office and work environments, productivity levels are very important, and all steps should be taken to optimize ambient conditions and thermal comfort. Figure 29 is an overview of the results of some experiments regarding the influence of room or ambient temperature upon accident frequency and performance levels during tasks carried out while sitting. As the figure shows, thermal comfort exists only within a relatively small range in temperature fluctuation, this range being at the same time the optimum thermal condition for intellectual performance. However, this presumes that other important factors are ideal (air temperature, air velocity, humidity, surface temperatures, clothing, health, age, degree of activity).

Thermal comfort is achieved when the occupants find the temperature, humidity, air movement, and heat radiation in their environment to be ideal and don't wish the room air to be warmer or cooler, drier or more humid.

Thermal comfort and air quality in rooms are influenced by

the occupants, depending on:

– activity,
– clothing,
– time spent in room,
– thermal and chemical density,
– number of occupants;

the room itself, depending on:

– surface temperatures,
– air temperature distribution,
– heat sources,
– contaminant sources;

ventilation and air-conditioning systems, depending on:

– air temperature,
– air velocity,
– air humidity,
– air change rate,
– air purity,
– air distribution.

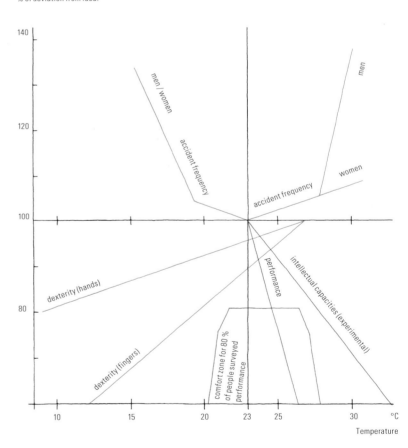

% of deviation from ideal

Figure 29
Experimental studies on accident frequency, human performance and comfort dependent on room temperature during tasks performed while sitting (1 met) and in light clothing (0.6 clo) accord. to D.P. Wyon

Air-conditioning systems influence the air temperature, air velocity, and relative air humidity of a building. The design and form of a building should protect against direct sun radiation, since ventilation and air-conditioning systems have no influence on it.

Other important influences upon physical as well as psychological comfort can be found in acoustic and light conditions as well as in the colours of a room. In areas where people spend a lot of time, one must take into consideration the combined ratio of air temperature t_{ou} and radiation temperature of surrounding surfaces t_τ. The local temperature is called perceived temperature or, sometimes, operative room temperature t_o; it was not sufficiently considered in the past. The perceived room temperature can be calculated with the approximation formula:

$t_o = 0.5 (t_{ou} + t_\tau)$

Perceived temperatures should be measured at 0.1 m, 1.1 m, and 1.7 m above floor level, whereby surface temperature and surface factors are weighted according to their irradiation zones when calculating local radiation temperatures. In Figure 30 operative i.e. perceived room temperatures are shown in relation to outside temperatures. A rise in perceived temperature (red hatching) is acceptable during high summer temperatures and for short periods.

The cooling requirement for rooms is frequently defined less by outside temperatures than by interior thermal loads. If these loads are short-term, the perceived room temperature may rise to 26°C with outside temperatures below 29°C (black hatching in Figure 30). Perceived room temperatures ranging from 20°C to 22°C (blue hatching in Figure 30) are acceptable with certain ventilation systems (e.g. floor to ceiling ventilation, displacement ventilation).

The vertical temperature coefficient is another important factor for thermal comfort. This coefficient must not exceed 2 K per metre of room height. The room temperature at 0.1 m above floor level should be no less than 21°C to avoid discomfort (heat demand at ankle point). One-sided warming or cooling of the human body through uneven temperatures in the surrounding areas can lead to thermal discomfort.

For evaluation purposes, the room should be divided into two sections and radiation temperature should be calculated or measured in each section. The top and bottom limits in temperature variation for thermal comfort are:

– for warm ceiling surfaces $(t_{\tau H_1} - t_{\tau H_2}) \leq 3.5\ K$

– for cold wall surfaces $(t_{\tau H_1} - t_{\tau H_2}) \leq 8\ K$

– for cooled ceiling surfaces $(t_{\tau H_1} - t_{\tau H_2}) \leq 17\ K$

– for warm wall surfaces $(t_{\tau H_1} - t_{\tau H_2}) \leq 19\ K$

These limits apply to perceived room temperature within the comfort zone and for persons wearing light to medium clothing who are performing activities while sitting. There is insufficient information at this time for thermal comfort limits under different conditions.

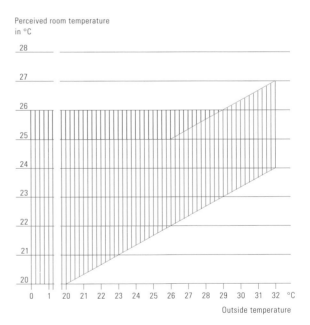

Perceived room temperature in °C

Outside temperature

Figure 30
Range of perceived temperatures (according to DIN 1946 part 2)

Prerequisites:
Activity levels I and II
Light to medium clothing

III Acceptable during short-term additional cooling loads
III Recommended range
III Acceptable e.g. for displacement ventilation

Thermal comfort is greatly influenced by air movement within a space. The limits for air movement in the comfort zone depend upon the air temperature and the turbulence quotient of the air flow, as shown in Figure 31. Perceived room temperatures ranging from 20°C to 22°C – with the exception of induced ventilation (broken line) – still provide thermal comfort if the air velocities indicated in the figure are not exceeded. The three curves each represent the limits of velocities measured over a given period of time for each degree of turbulence. Minimal air movement is necessary for convective heat and molecular transport. It occurs (naturally) as a result of free convection at a heat source.

The upper limit for moisture content in the air, while maintaining overall comfort, is 11.5 g water/kg dry air and 65 % relative air humidity. There are no proven data with relation to the lower limit for relative air humidity. A comfort limit may be established at 30 % humidity, some short-term deviation to even lower values being acceptable.

Hygienic Comfort
(Air Quality)

The air quality in a room is determined, on the one hand, by the quality of intake air and, on the other hand, by air-contaminating factors such as room usage. Intake air consists mostly of outer (or surrounding) air, possibly of recirculated air, whose quality must also be taken into consideration. Recirculated air should be avoided whenever possible and be used, if at all, only in situations with low pollution factors or, if necessary, due to thermal loads. Outside air intake should ensure sufficient ventilation of pollutants. Furthermore, it is important to note that circulated air flow can contaminate the surfaces of air ducts. It is therefore advisable to avoid circulated air completely or to use only air recirculated back into the same room.

Air pollution consists of organic and inorganic elements, such as:

- gases and vapours (CO, CO_2, SO_2, NO_X, O_3, radon, formaldehyde, carbon-hydrogen),

- odours (e.g. microbial byproducts of organic material, human, animal and plant odours, evaporation from building materials and work processes),

- aerosols (e.g. inorganic dust such as fibres and heavy metals, organic dust such as carbon-hydrogen compound and pollen),

- viruses,

- bacteria and spores (legionella, anaerobic gas-forming organism, i.e. gas-gangrene bacillus),

- fungi and fungal spores (e.g. germs causing humidifier fever, humidifier lung).

Intake air should have outside air quality, unless, of course, the outside air is especially polluted. In areas where work materials are not a decisive factor, the recirculated air ratio should not exceed the limits established as hygienic. As regards concentration of air pollutants in work areas, official guidelines (threshold limit value or lower toxic limit) must be adhered to.

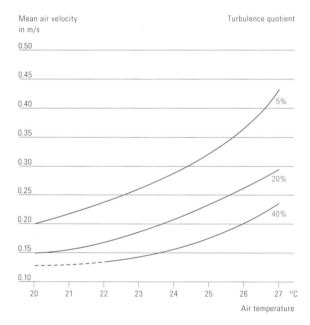

Figure 31
Comfortable average air velocities as function of temperature and turbulence quotient in air: Values apply to activity level I and heat transmission resistance of clothing of approx. 0.12 m² K/W. With higher activity levels and heat transmission resistances the boundary values can be taken e.g. from VDI (Assoc. of German Engineers) 2083 Form 5 (currently draft form). The 40 % curve applies also to turbulence quotients > 40 %.

Air flow in rooms should be maximized to ensure the most efficient and effective exchange of room air and intake air, as well as the removal of air pollutants and odours. Ventilation efficiency is a key factor when it comes to clearing pollutants out of naturally ventilated rooms or ventilation systems.

Ideal mixed flow :　　　ventilation efficiency = 1
Displacement flow :　　ventilation efficiency > 1

Calculation of outside air flow, necessary to balance the air quality in a room, is based upon the number of people using the room, the surface of the room, or the air pollutants present in the space. Pollutants must be divided into those created in manufacturing environments and others, or into industrial contaminants and pollutants or odours. The necessary outside air flow rates are:

– approx. 40 to 60 m^3/h per person for offices,

– approx. 20 m^3/h per person for meeting rooms,

– approx. 20 to 30 m^3/h per person for lecture rooms,

– approx. 20 to 30 m^3/h per person for public areas.

Visual Comfort

Visual comfort exists when the perceptive faculties in the human brain can operate without any interference. Incorrect distribution of light density in a room, glare, poor colour matching, and inappropriate interior design all inhibit perception. On the other hand, when perception is in no way inhibited, the basic senses of the eye, such as vision, speed, and contrast sensitivity, are optimized. Optimal working conditions can be achieved by harmonizing the light density conditions in the working environment (surrounding light density), starting with the light density conditions at the workstation (interior field light density). A stable perception field for workstations where vision is especially important (e.g. office stations with PCs) should include contrast sensitivity as a criterion.

Visual comfort also depends on sufficient light in the area of visual focus and the avoidance of glare, be it direct, indirect (reflex glare), or daylight glare. The colour and temperature of light are additional criteria. Light hue defines the type of colour this light casts and is divided into three groups for general lighting purposes:

– colour temperature below 3300 K (warm white light),

– colour temperature from 3300 K to 5000 K (neutral white light),

– colour temperature above 5000 K (daylight white light).

Colour temperatures below 3300 K are generated by incandescent lamps, halogen lamps, fluorescent lamps, and discharge lamps with a high red light contribution. Colour temperatures ranging from 3300 K to 5000 K are generated by daylight fluorescent tubes and electric discharge lamps. Colour temperatures above 5000 K are created with special fluorescent and electric discharge lamps. Incandescent and halogen lamps are most agreeable in low light densities. Higher densities (e.g. in offices or showrooms) call for whiter light hues with a greater blue contribution (colour temperature approx. 4000 K).

Visual comfort includes not only light, colour, and density but also sufficient shade (to increase the plasticity and three-dimensionality of objects and surfaces). Shade is estimated according to the relation between cylindrical and horizontal illumination. This relation should be no less than 0.3, if hard-edge shade is to be avoided.

Last but not least, visual comfort means visual contact from the inside out and the outside in.

Figure 32 is an overview and summary of possible active/passive measures for improving comfort and accommodating changing conditions. It illustrates the many influencing factors.

Figure 32
Overview and flow chart of
possible active/passive
measures for load compen-
sation

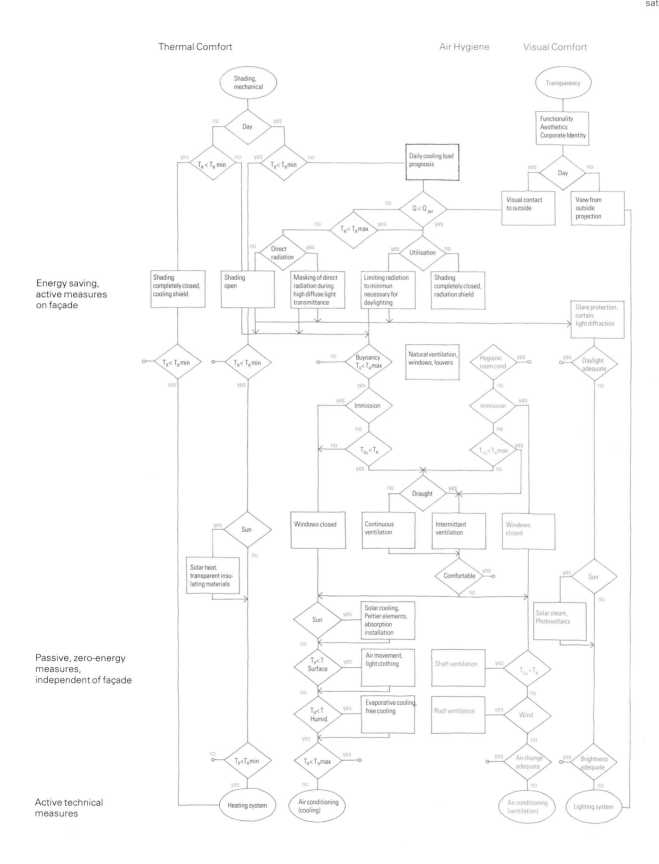

Thermal Comfort

Air Hygiene

Visual Comfort

Energy saving,
active measures
on façade

Passive, zero-energy
measures,
independent of façade

Active technical
measures

3.4
The Sick Building Syndrome – a Challenge

According to Dr. P. König's definitions, Sick Building Syndrome reveals itself in various SBS-related symptoms and their possible causes. The individual manifestations and their possible causes are listed in Table 1.

These are:

– excessive air velocity or turbulent air flow in a room,

– symptoms arising from microbial allergens or cell toxins,

– malfunction of thermal regulation due to excessively high or low temperatures (poor stimulus climate)

– problems arising from low-frequency sound (< 100 Hz),

– noxious smell resulting from poorly maintained installations.

These problems can be avoided by ensuring draught-free air supply into rooms, whereby the velocity of air flow should be slowed sufficiently (< 0.12 m/s) to no longer be perceived as uncomfortable, especially in rooms where persons spend any length of time.

Microbial allergens and cell toxins can be prevented through regular maintenance of humidifiers and filter installations, for instance by using high-performance filters which can remove a number of pollutants from the air. A filter installation developed by Prof. Dr. R. Detzer (Kessler Tech GmbH) is just such a high-performance device, available under the name Human-Air-Filter (Figure 33). The performance table of this particular air filter shows that not only pollutants are removed but bacteria and particles as well, thereby considerably improving the air quality.

All buildings should, in principle, have openable windows and operate efficiently without ventilation and air-conditioning systems. Likewise, windowless rooms should not be used as areas where people spend any length of time. The window area to façade ratio should be at least 50 %, given sufficient sun protection and a large storage mass to prevent overheating of rooms. The temperatures must always be kept at a com-

Figure 33
High performance filter (Human Air, KesslerTech GmbH) with filter characteristics listed to the right

Table 1

SBS symptoms	Possible causes
draught tendency to colds rheumatism	excessive air velocity, excessive turbulence, insufficient air intake, intake air temperature too low
irritation of mucous membrane in upper respiratory tract and eyes, feeling of dryness	microbial allergens (from air conditioners), dust, mites (broadloom)
fever, difficulty of breathing, ache in joints, fatigue	microbial cell toxins (endotoxins, cytotoxins) from humidifier water, filters and intake air units
fatigue lack of concentration numbness, headache	irregularities in thermoregulation: – temperatures > 23 °C, – non-physiological diurnal course of temperature, – excessive relative humidity, – lack of window ventilation, low frequency sound (< 100 Hz), allergens, endotoxins, cytotoxins, insufficiency of: – shading (missing/indoor), – window surfaces (too large), – storing masses (too small), air-conditioning performance/ maintenance
poor air quality	odour from air conditioners: -- technical (material, filter), – microbiological, insufficient effective air change

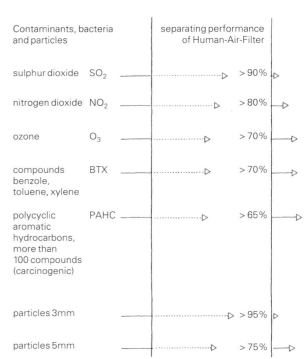

Contaminants, bacteria and particles		separating performance of Human-Air-Filter
sulphur dioxide	SO$_2$	> 90%
nitrogen dioxide	NO$_2$	> 80%
ozone	O$_3$	> 70%
compounds benzole, toluene, xylene	BTX	> 70%
polycyclic aromatic hydrocarbons, more than 100 compounds (carcinogenic)	PAHC	> 65%
particles 3mm		> 95%
particles 5mm		> 75%

fortable level, as indicated in Figure 30.
22°C ± 1 K is recommended by experts in industrial medicine as the base temperature for optimum thermal comfort, requiring thermostats in each room and the option of switching off air-conditioning or ventilation when opening windows.

Humidification should only be considered when the relative humidity falls below 30%. Indoor plants are a good method of additional humidification.

The water used in mechanical humidifiers must be physically sterilized (UV, ozone, silver) as must humid sections of ventilation and air-conditioning installations. Preference is given to circulated spray humidification with water of potable quality.

All sections in ventilation and air-conditioning installations susceptible of transmitting micro-organisms to humans must be serviced and cleansed on a regular basis, to eliminate legionella, other pathogenic germs, and any micro-organisms thought to trigger allergic reactions (humidifier fever, humidifier lung etc.).

3.5
Buildings of the Future – Utilization of Environmental Energy

Buildings of the future will turn more and more to passive and active measures for reducing energy demand and consumption while protecting the environment. Passive energy gain from the environment (indirect utilization) is illustrated in Figure 34, with notes about the technologies which may be used. Energy can be gained from:

– the sun,
– water,
– soil,
– air,
– fauna (conditional),
– flora (conditional).

The first four items in this list play a major role. The use of plants inside and around buildings is of particular psychological significance.

Figure 34
Energy gained from environment

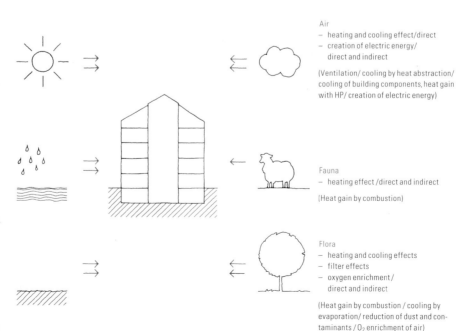

Sun
– heating and cooling effects/ direct and indirect
– creation of electric energy/ direct and indirect

(Solar heat gain active and passive*/ cooling by heat energy, absorber technique/ photovoltaic/solar furnace/TIM façades)

* solar installations, winter gardens

Water
– heating and cooling effect/ direct and indirect

(Groundwater for cooling or heating with heat pumps (HP)/surface water for cooling, recycled cooling or heating with HP/ rainwater for heating with HP)

Soil
– heating and cooling effect/ direct and indirect

(Cooling by 'air well'/storage of heating or cooling energy in aquifer storage)

Air
– heating and cooling effect/direct
– creation of electric energy/ direct and indirect

(Ventilation/ cooling by heat abstraction/ cooling of building components, heat gain with HP/ creation of electric energy)

Fauna
– heating effect /direct and indirect

(Heat gain by combustion)

Flora
– heating and cooling effects
– filter effects
– oxygen enrichment/ direct and indirect

(Heat gain by combustion / cooling by evaporation/ reduction of dust and contaminants / O_2 enrichment of air)

Figure 35 shows a hypothetical office building taking a number of ecological measures, passive and active. This illustrates the options available with current technology. The winter garden plays a special role, since it not only serves as energy reservoir as a greenhouse, but it also provides an enhanced working environment as a secondary office space. The extent to which such options can be employed differs from case to case and must be decided jointly by the architect, the client and the engineer, because neither the architect nor the engineer can make these choices alone. The engineer is required to take a long-term approach and to find, together with the architect, a satisfying solution for the client and the future occupants of the building. In short, planning and design today require: a good knowledge of all the factors playing a role in and around the building and a better analysis and implementation of the users' express desires.

Figure 35
Model for application
of ecological measures
on a building

Passive measures

1   TIM façade
2   passive solar utilization /
    evaporative cooling
    in winter garden (plants)
3   natural ventilation
4   natural lighting
    (daylight quotient)
5   cooling load reduction
    through storage masses
    (supported ventilation)
6   'air well'
7   planted roof surface
8   rainwater utilization
    (greywater)

Active measures

 9 photovoltaic units
10 solar collectors
11 absorber surfaces
12 wind generators
13 low temperature heating
14 cooling towers
15 chilled ceiling
16 chiller as heat pump (HP)
17 absorption installation
    ('refrigeration energy as
    heating energy')
18 combined heat and power
    station (CHP)
19 filter installation for surface
    or groundwater heating (HP)
20 ice water storage
21 heat accumulator (storage)
22 aquifer storage
    (HP operated)

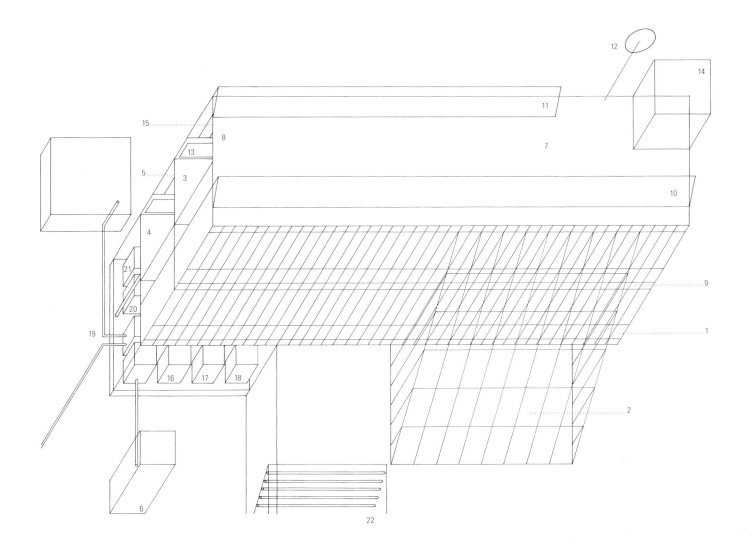

4

The ecological circle shows the many possibilities for utilizing surrounding air, soil, groundwater, surface water, and rainwater, as well as planted surfaces. In this circle, sustainable and efficient urban planning is given as much consideration as the location and form of individual buildings. Ecological building begins not with the application to existing structures of measures for utilizing renewable energy sources but, rather, with conceptual urban design and landscaping.

4.
Design Principles – the Ecological Circle

In future, building design and development must take into consideration the interactions and dependencies illustrated in the ecological circle (Figure 36). This figure clearly identifies the crucial topics, such as exterior space, stuctural fabric, and technology, and their respective sub-topics. The overview further illustrates how many options for savings exist: in technical investment, operation and upkeep, and possibly even construction costs. However, to achieve this, one must go beyond the current practice of superimposing individual approaches onto existing buildings and, instead, aim for true integration. Each aspect must be given equal weight during the planning phase, e.g. air, soil or earth, water surfaces, halls and atria, construction, façades, and roofs, as well as the various technological installations and systems. Figure 36 illustrates these interactions for the aspect of cooling. Such topics as natural ventilation, groundwater cooling energy, greywater, surface/lake water, evaporative cooling, night cooling with surrounding air, storage masses in façades and construction, and more, can all come into play. In each case, at the initial planning phase, the relevant links should be established under each topic heading; engineers and architects should decide which of the main topics listed above will be taken into consideration. Many of these topics overlap, and it is fair to say that integration of all aspects into the overall scope is too great a task for any individual planner, whether architect or engineer. Developing relevant ecological concepts is a matter of teamwork. In other words, henceforth all participants in the planning of such projects must be brought to the table early on and work towards achieving a symbiosis of the respective individual aspects.

to Figure 36
The ecological circle illustrates the interactions between environment, building and building technology – the factors which influence building design. The connections marked in this figure are those pertinent to the aspect of cooling.

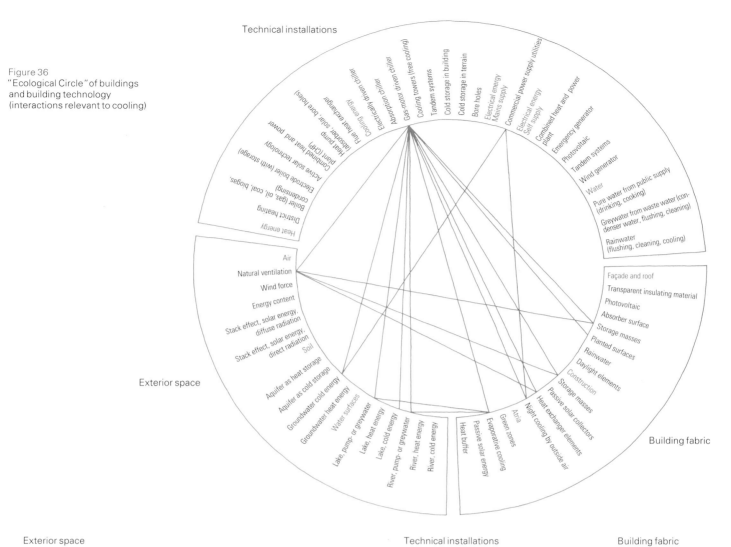

Figure 36
"Ecological Circle" of buildings
and building technology
(interactions relevant to cooling)

Exterior space

Air
Free air
    Natural ventilation
    Wind force
    Energy content
Stack effect
    Solar energy, diffuse radiation
    Solar energy, direct radiation

Soil
Aquifer
    Heat storage
    Cold storage
Groundwater
    Cold energy
    Heat energy
Earth/rock
    Geothermal cooling
    Heat energy

Water surfaces
Lake
    Pump water or greywater
    Heat energy
    Cold energy
River
    Pump water or greywater
    Heat energy
    Cold energy

Technical installations

Heat energy
Direct
    District heating
    Boiler (gas, oil, coal, biogas, condensing)
    Electrode boiler (with storage)
Indirect
    Active solar technology
    Combined heat and power plant (CHP)
    Heat pump (absorber, solar, bore holes)
    Flue heat exchanger

Cooling energy
Direct
    Electrically driven chiller
    Absorption chiller
    Gas-motor driven chiller
    Cooling towers (free cooling)
    Tandem systems
Indirect
    Cold storage in building
    Cold storage in terrain
    Bore holes

Electrical energy
Mains supply
    Commercial power supply utilities
Self supply
    Combined heat and power plant
    Emergency generator
    Photovoltaic
    Tandem system
    Wind generator

Water
Pure water
    Public supply (drinking, cooking)
Greywater
    Waste water (condenser water, flushing, cleaning)
Rainwater
    Flushing, cleaning, cooling

Building fabric

Façade and roof
Transparent insulating material
Photovoltaic
Absorber surface
Storage masses
Planted surfaces
Rainwater
Daylight elements
Collectors

Construction
Storage masses
Passive solar absorber
Heat exchanger elements
Night cooling by outside air

Atria
Green zones
Evaporative cooling
Passive solar energy
Heat buffer

4.1
Exterior Space

In any design of buildings and their technical installations, the surrounding or exterior space is especially important and should be considered an essential part of the design phase. The exterior space – consisting of air, soil, water, and plants – is rich in possibilities for minimizing the use of technical installations while saving energy and operating costs. A major factor in heat and cooling supply, it forms an integral part of the kind of comprehensive ecological thinking desirable for buildings in the future.

Figure 37
Time curve of wind
velocities measured at three
different heights

— 153 m
— 64 m
— 12 m

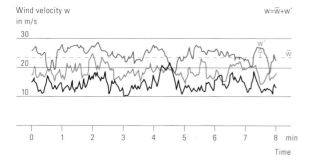

4.1.1
Wind
(Ludwig Ilg)

Fresh air is an interesting starting point for developing ecological concepts, because of the potential of wind-induced and buoyant forces as well as the energy content of wind. The energy content will be discussed further on under technological measures; this section will concentrate mainly on building-related air flow with relation to natural ventilation.

The Physics of Wind-Induced Air Flow near Buildings

Wind close to the ground is gusty: its velocity and direction are prone to great spatial and temporal variation. Usually these winds are characterized as a highly turbulent flow field and can be described by the time-dependent velocity components and the time-dependent static pressure in each point of space. These values appear to be random and are thus difficult to calculate for natural ventilation applications. Hence, it is acceptable, and necessary, to separate the flow field for the calculation and description of some problems. It is then treated as superposed of a time-averaged flow field and a time-dependent field of fluctuating deviations.

Figure 37 depicts recorded wind velocity at various heights over the course of several minutes. The time-averaged value $\overline{w}$ and the time deviation from the mean value (w') are plotted on the curve. With the help of this separation, it is possible to pinpoint a number of aerodynamics problems around buildings using averaged values for velocity and direction and turbulence intensities.

Figure 38 shows an example of the air flow fields near a building. Figure 39, on the other hand, divides the flow field near a building into four regions and relates these to flow dynamics observed around an airfoil section or a building model in a wind tunnel. The four regions are:

– the unimpeded flow,
  which can be calculated with the methods of potential theory (assuming there is no friction effect),

– the boundary layer close to solid walls,
  to which one can, in certain cases, apply the boundary layer theory for the calculation of a velocity profile,

– recirculation areas,
  whose range and structure have been investigated by empirical means for a number of geometries (considerable mathematical effort is needed for calculation of this type of flow),

– free shear layers,
  separating the undisturbed surrounding air flow from e.g. the zones of recirculation.

The arrows are streamlines of a flow field averaged over a given period. Streamlines always point parallel to the flow at any given location and any instance of time.

In the case of air flow around an airfoil section, the actual course of the flow is sufficiently indicated by defining a time-calculated field; when applied to buildings, the same approach may lead to completely erroneous results. The cause for this deviation lies in the time frame involved in wind flow processes. To achieve a stable streamline image, one would have to capture and evaluate the flow during several minutes. If a great number of wind flags were to be set up in the vicinity of a building, one would have to use an exposure time of close to an hour in order to achieve a reproducible image. As an illustration, Figure 39 includes (bottom left) a simulated image sketched as if a camera were following the main flow.

The topology of aerodynamic fields near buildings can be made visible and determined through the use of smoke in model experiments in wind tunnels. The pressure forces upon the enclosure of buildings can then be estimated with the continuity equation (to determine mass) and Bernoulli's theorem (to determine energy).

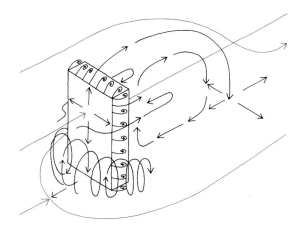

Figure 38
Turbulent air flow field near building has very complex structures which are difficult to calculate

Figure 39
Comparison of flow field observed around airfoil section or a building model

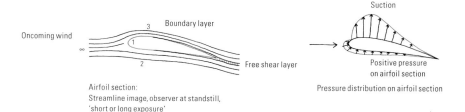

Oncoming wind

Boundary layer

Free shear layer

Airfoil section:
Streamline image, observer at standstill, 'short or long exposure'

Suction

Positive pressure on airfoil section

Pressure distribution on airfoil section

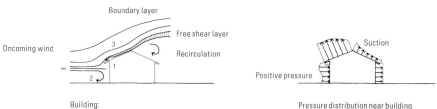

Oncoming wind

Boundary layer

Free shear layer

Recirculation

Building:
Streamline schematic, observer at standstill, 'long exposure'

Suction

Positive pressure

Pressure distribution near building

Streamline image, camera follows medium wind velocity, 'short exposure'.

∞: Main flow:

Bernoulli's theorem applicable:
$$p_\infty + \frac{\rho}{2} \cdot w_\infty^2 = \text{constant}$$
along a streamline

1: Stagnation point:

flow reaches standstill, maximum pressure
$$p_1 = p_\infty + \frac{\rho}{2} \cdot w_\infty^2$$

2: Decelerated flow:

$w_2 < w_\infty$,
positive pressure compared to surroundings
$$p_2 = p_1 - \frac{\rho}{2} \cdot w_2^2$$

3: Accelerated flow:

$w_3 > w_\infty$,
negative pressure compared to surroundings
$$p_3 = p_1 - \frac{\rho}{2} \cdot w_3^2$$

The continuity equation states that the influx mass flow entering a duct limited by fixed boundaries also exits at the other end. Since the stream dynamics hardly change the air density at these low velocities, the same equation can be applied to volume, i.e. the product of velocity and cross-sectional area. Where streamlines get closer, the flow accelerates; where streamlines move apart, the flow decelerates.

Bernoulli's theorem is used as a simple means of estimating pressure in the stream field. It is assumed, for this purpose, that the only forms of energy relevant to air flow around buildings are pressure and kinetic. Along a streamline, energy is transformed between these two types of energy only owing to the aerodynamic processes. As a result, pressure drops in areas with higher velocity and rises in areas with decelerated flow. The highest pressure along a streamline occurs where the motion comes to a complete stop: at the stagnation point. Figure 39 also illustrates the conclusions which may be drawn from a qualitative interpretation of the visualized flow field. For one part of the flow field, 'dead air' i.e. recirculation areas, it is impossible to draw streamlines. The medium pressure in these areas is balanced. It can be estimated as the mean value of the pressures existing along the free shearing layer, forming the border of this area.

Figure 41
Global circulation patterns result in typical regional winds near the ground.

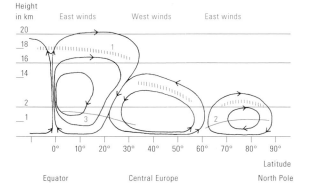

Figure 40
Varying solar irradiation creates temperature differences on the Earth's surface. The resulting air movements partially equalize these differences.

1   Tropopause
2   Polar inversion
3   Tradewind inversion

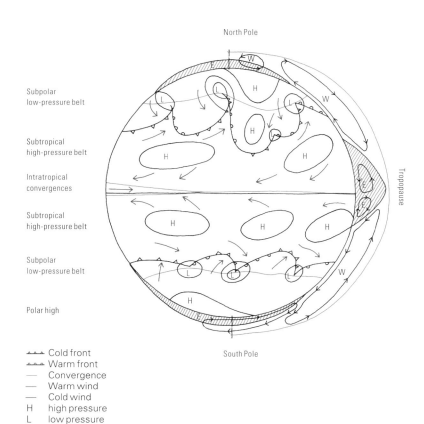

≜≜≜ Cold front
≜≜≜ Warm front
—   Convergence
—   Warm wind
—   Cold wind
H   high pressure
L   low pressure
W   westerly winds
E   easterly winds

Natural Winds (Close to the Ground)

Air movements in the atmosphere are a result of solar irradiation. At the equator, where the Earth's surface is warmest, heated air masses rise into the tropopause to a height of approx. 18 km and begin to flow towards the poles. To the north and south of the equator, the air, which has begun to cool again, sinks to the ground. At around the so-called horse latitudes (approx. 30th latitude), sub-tropical high-pressure areas form, from which the air flows back to the equatorial low-pressure belt in layers near the ground (Figure 40).

Air movements in the atmosphere, driven by pressure differences, not only follow the direction of the air pressure gradients, they are also influenced by the Coriolis force. Resulting from the Earth's rotation, it diverts air currents along the north/south axis to the right in the northern hemisphere. Hence, geostrophic wind is approximately parallel to isobars, the curves along which air pressure is constant. This gradient wind is not directly influenced by ground surface (Figure 41). Its annual mean velocity at the upper edge of the boundary layer is approx. 10 to 15 m/s in European latitudes and can easily be derived from the distribution of air pressure (isobars) seen in weather charts.

The predictable maximum velocities are a result of the frequency distribution of the wind velocities (probability of occurrence). In this, there are noticeable deviations from region to region. Statistically, geostrophic wind reaches velocities of 50 m/s every 50 years; even velocities of more than 100 m/s have been recorded.

Atmospheric Boundary Layer

By approaching the ground, wind velocity decreases due to surface friction, while turbulence increases due to disruptive surface interference. The boundary layer, where the slowdown occurs, is approx. 300 to 1000 m thick and characterized by a lively, vertical exchange of air masses and energy (Figure 42). The combined effect of friction, inertia, buoyancy and pressure forces in the boundary layer creates a complex vortex structure, which, for practical reasons, can only be described by statistical methods.

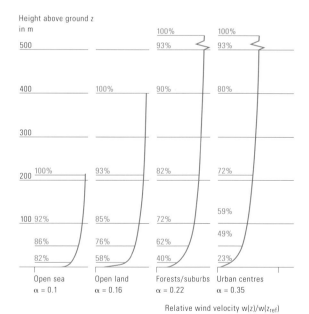

Figure 42
Wind velocity increases proportionately with height above water or flat ground. Above built environments, velocities decrease; the boundary layer begins at a greater height.

$$w(z) = w(z_{ref}) \, (z/z_{ref})^{\alpha}$$

$w(z)$ — wind velocity
$w(z_{ref})$ — gradient velocity = 100 %
z_{ref} — reference height
α — profile exponent

The largest eddies, which recur constantly, have a depth identical to that of the boundary layer (Figure 43). They disintegrate in cascades into smaller and smaller vortices, rotating in space, until finally only heat remains of the residual variational energy. The greatest proportion of variational energy is found in eddies with a diameter of approx. one-tenth of the boundary layer depth, i.e. 30 to 60 m (Figure 44).

Gust is measured by the turbulence intensity, i.e. the range of variation in velocity in relation to the mean wind velocity. Close to the ground, it is approx. 10 % to 20 %, depending on building density (Figure 45). Near and around buildings, it can reach values of 100 % and more, for instance in the rebound or recirculation flow.

The variational energy contained in the gust of wind close to the ground covers a wide range (comparable to acoustic noise) of frequencies from approx. 0.001 to 0.3 Hz (Figure 46). The greatest variational energy in atmospheric turbulence is found in frequencies close to 0.015 Hz: these are variations in the minute range, which relate to eddy formations of approx. 50 m for average wind velocities.

Figure 43
Wind near the ground is characterized by a variety of eddies, which are experienced as gust near the ground. The upper schematic illustrates the path balloons take when released at different heights.
The lower schematic illustrates the wind movement's paths.

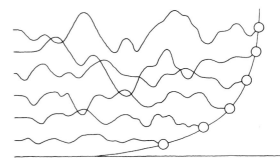

Long exposure

Short exposure (split second)

Figure 44
The average diameter of eddies in the boundary layer increases with height. Close to the ground, the most energetic eddies have dimensions corresponding to typical measurements of larger buildings. The largest eddies have a depth identical to that of the boundary layer.

Figure 45
Gust strength of wind diminishes with decreasing height. The turbulence quotient is an indicator of the variation ratio of wind velocity to mean wind velocity. Top gust velocities are approx. 3.5 times the variation range above the mean value.

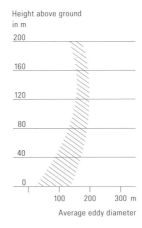

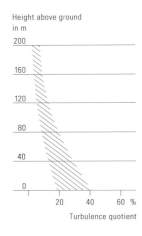

Figure 46
Even large weather systems can be viewed as turbulences which, however, unfold along different time and length dimensions. The curve of the energy spectrum shows a gap between the two areas. It enables us to separately treat the two processes.

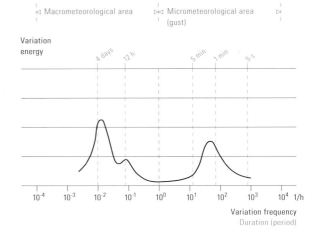

Influence of Local Landscape on Wind

Landscape factors and their combinations, such as coasts and shores, hills, mountains and valleys, city and country, influence the wind system in so many ways that only a few, simplified examples can be mentioned here.

Thermally caused, local wind systems can develop when the global weather system leads to weak winds. By convention, land and sea winds are named according to the direction from which they originate. A land wind, for instance, develops on clear nights if the air above water is warmer than the air above land (Figure 47). In stormy weather conditions, such local wind systems cannot occur.

This is also true for katabatic winds and down draughts (mountain and valley breezes). They are generated by the differences in heat created by solar irradiation, which are manifest at different times of the day along slopes and valley floors with different orientation (Figure 48).

Day

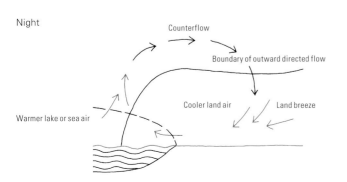

Night

Figure 48
Upward currents form on sunny slopes. Ascending valley breezes form along sunny, ascending valley floors. When the surfaces cool overnight, downward currents so form on the slopes that the mountain breeze flows down valley.

Different orientation of valley in relation to the solar path creates complex wind systems.

Sunrise
(mountain breeze and upward current on slope)

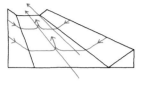

Sunset
(valley breeze and downward current)

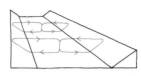

Late morning
(upward current on slope)

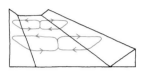

Night onset (dusk)
(downward current)

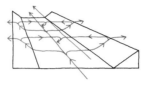

Noon
(upward current and valley breeze)

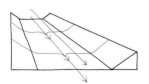

Middle of night
(downward current and mountain breeze)

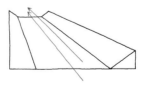

Late afternoon
(valley breeze)

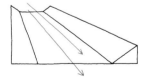

Early morning, before sunrise
(mountain breeze)

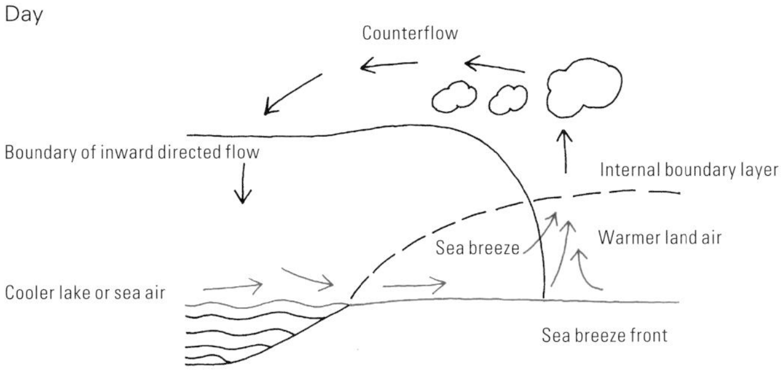

Figure 47
Sea and land breeze: Due to good mixing the surface of large bodies of water is warmed very slowly by insolation. Evaporation also cools the air above water. The air rising above land surface, warming quickly, falls or descends above water. During the night this process is reversed.

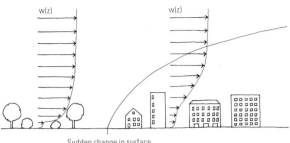

Sudden change in surface

Figure 49
Influence of change in ground
roughness on wind profile

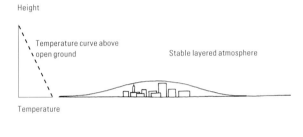

Temperature curve above
open ground

Stable layered atmosphere

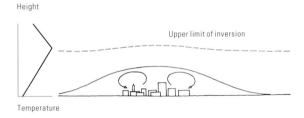

Upper limit of inversion

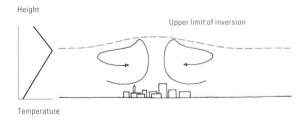

Upper limit of inversion

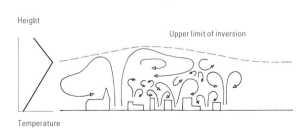

Upper limit of inversion

Figure 51
Weak winds result in complicated flow fields and layer conditions especially above urban
centres, which may result in poor
air quality. (Fig. after Hertig)

Figure 50
Thermal layering in the
atmosphere near the
ground leads to strong deviations in the vertical structure of the boundary layer.

Compared to the natural
temperature (black, broken)
line, created solely by
decreasing air pressure at
increasing height (dry adia-
bate), various other typical
temperature lines (red) and
their corresponding wind
velocities are shown.

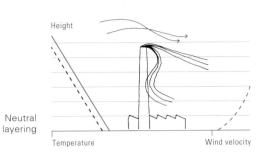

Neutral
layering

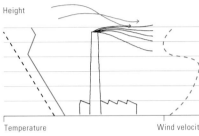

Height inversion

Ground inversion

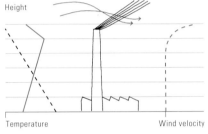

Unstable layering

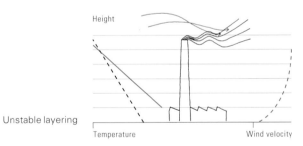

Boundary layer
between unstable and
stable layering

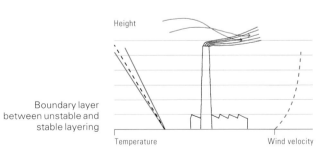

Stable layering

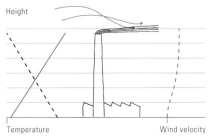

Ground roughness is especially important, causing deviations from the above mentioned empirical vertical velocity profile. Seen from the windward side of a change in roughness, a new boundary layer develops, underlying the incoming boundary layer (Figure 49).

Vertical distribution of air temperature in the atmosphere is another important factor. Figures 50 and 51 illustrate these relationships qualitatively.

4.1.2
Earth and Groundwater

In the past, untreated groundwater could be used for the cooling of buildings; today, this is mostly prohibited. In the future, we must therefore access thermal heat indirectly through earth coils and bore holes, as well as through air-ventilated pipes or thermal labyrinths.

Thermal energy rises vertically from the centre of the earth to the surface (approx. 0.08 W/m²); conversely, solar heat penetrates the soil. Depending upon soil consistency, up to 70 % of global radiation penetrates the surface and stabilizes the soil temperature. Rainwater seepage also contributes significantly to the influence of atmospheric temperature upon the soil. Earth and groundwater temperatures range from 8°C to 12°C (Figure 52).

Figure 53 depicts the soil temperature profile, measured immediately before a heating period, for a bore hole installation in Elgg (Switzerland). The graph clearly shows how noticeably temperatures rise in the areas close to the surface (0 to 10 m), due to solar heat.

Heat flow into and within soil is dependent upon the heat transfer coefficients, the soil density, and the soil's specific heat content. The values in Table 2 are approximate, since relevant readings of the physical soil characteristics are very difficult to take. Low soil temperatures can be utilized directly for cooling a house, whereas accessing thermal heat usually requires secondary heat pump systems.

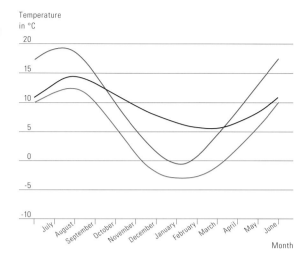

Figure 52
Approximate course of earth temperature at 1.5 m depth and air temperature

— Air
— Soil undisturbed
— Soil with heat extraction

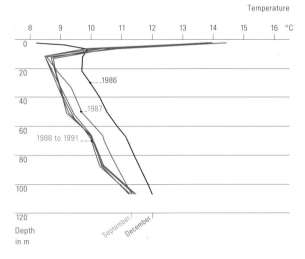

Figure 53
Temperature profile in soil taken immediately before start of a new heating period (September) at 50 cm distance from bore hole in Elgg (Switzerland). The curve 'December 1986' defines the steady state condition before the heating system was activated.

Table 2
Reference earth types according to Jäger

Ground-type	Soil	$\lambda\,[W/m \cdot K]$	$\rho\,[kg/m^3]$	$c\,[J/kg \cdot K]$	$a=\frac{\lambda}{\rho \cdot c}\,[10^{-7}\,m^2/s]$
1	Sand (dry)	0.7	1.5	921.6	5.064
2	Sand (water-saturated)	1.88	1.5	1198.8	10.455
3	Clay (moist)	1.45	1.8	1339.2	6.015
4	Clay (water-saturated)	2.9	1.8	1591.2	10.125

4.1.3
Water (Rain- and Surface Water)

Fresh water is one of our most precious resources; there is no adequate replacement. Water supply enterprises produce it at considerable expense and market it to consumers under stringent hygienic quality controls. We don't realize, for the most part, how much of this valuable resource is being literally flushed down the toilet in residential housing (approx. 33 %). Cleaning, car washing, and plant watering consume needlessly large amounts of drinking water. Figure 54 shows water requirements for private households and areas where water of potable water quality and water of rainwater quality can be used respectively. In other words, approx. 50 % of drinking water could be replaced with rainwater – an enormous savings potential. Only 3 % of drinking water is normally used for food preparation or consumed. Rainwater is generally considered a safe and hygienic alternative for laundry water, with the additional advantage of needing less detergent, since rainwater is naturally softer than sterilized or treated water. This leaves food preparation, dish washing, and personal hygiene as the only tasks for which drinking water is necessary (approx. 44 %), while all other requirements can be met by rainwater.

Water surfaces near buildings considerably improve the microclimate and can be used accordingly. Water moats, small lakes, or large water basins are appropriate environmental formations for creating evaporative cooling near buildings. Water and its specific potentials are elaborated on in Section 13.

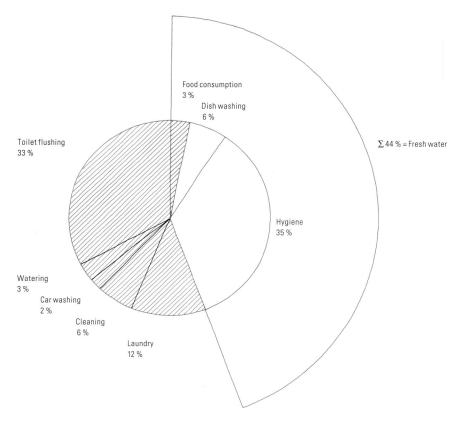

Food consumption
3 %

Dish washing
6 %

Toilet flushing
33 %

Σ 44 % = Fresh water

Hygiene
35 %

Watering
3 %

Car washing
2 %

Cleaning
6 %

Laundry
12 %

Figure 54
Water requirements in private household: 56 % of potable water consumed in private households could be replaced with greywater.

One example of outstanding utilization of water and waste water is to be found in the Kreuzberg district in Berlin (Figure 55). Here, during the 1980s, as part of the International Construction Exhibition (IBA), Öko Inc. designed and built a project called "Block 6 – integrated water concept". This project, the first to fully implement an urban decentralized water cycle, led to potable water savings of approx. 50 % and put to the test a new ecological approach to urban water management.

The 106 apartments in the complex were equipped with every available water-efficient plumbing installation: toilets flushing with 4 and 6 l of water, sanitary fittings equipped with flow regulators, warm- and cold-water meters in each appartment for billing per consumption.

Furthermore, a heat pump installation can recycle most of the energy gained from warm waste water for heating water. The waste water is cleansed sufficiently in a biological treatment plant, located in the central courtyard of the complex, that it can be recycled to flush the toilets and to water the planted areas around the buildings. The biological treatment plant is surrounded by a rainwater pond, where rainwater is gathered from the block, and also from partially planted rooftops, and used by children in the neighbourhood for swimming. Overflow rainwater and cleansed waste water is returned to the groundwater by seepage.

Figure 55
View of courtyard in Block 6,
Kreuzberg district of Berlin,
with biological treatment plant
and rainwater ponds

4.1.4
Planted Surfaces (Shading and Wind Protection)

Carefully designed planted surfaces provide natural shading for outer walls exposed to the summer sun, thus ensuring that the surfaces do not overheat and reducing the cooling load. Planted areas should be designed to shed their foliage in autumn, to enable passive solar energy usage in winter. Evergreen areas are, therefore, not desirable, since they only provide a positive effect in summer. Planted areas also reduce the brightness on exterior walls of offices, a must, especially for offices with PC work-stations. Figure 56 illustrates a residential building in Garching near Munich, designed to these specifications.
The technical headquarters of the Savings Bank, Munich, are shown in Figure 57. This building was erected near high volume traffic streets. In architects Kochta and Obersteiner's concept, tall glass walls offer protection against noise pollution. The courtyards created by this design were densely planted, not only improving the microclimate, but also, and more importantly, creating transitional spaces, often used by the employees working in the building. Trees, shrubs, and groundcover create a green environment around the pavilion-style building of HLTechnik AG, improve the

Figure 56
Werner-Heisenberg House,
Garching (near Munich).
Residence for visiting scientists
of Max Planck Institute
(Architects: Adam and Associates, Munich)

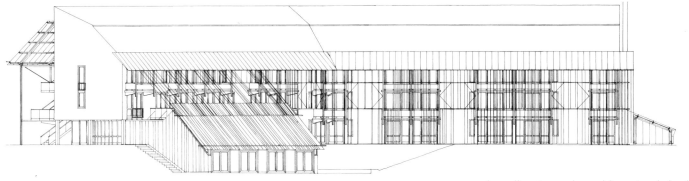

microclimate, and provide natural shading of the building fabric itself (Figure 58). The fabric of this pavilion had to be erected on piles to preserve the 80-year-old trees and to prevent damage to the roots. This demonstrates how the building form itself must react and adapt to the given environment, in this case, planted areas.

Figure 57
Savings Bank, Munich:
isometric drawing and view of
courtyards
(Architects: Kochta and Obersteiner, Munich)

To enable the offices in this
building located near busy
streets to be naturally ventilated, planted courtyards were
integrated into the design and
separated from the street by
a noise buffer.

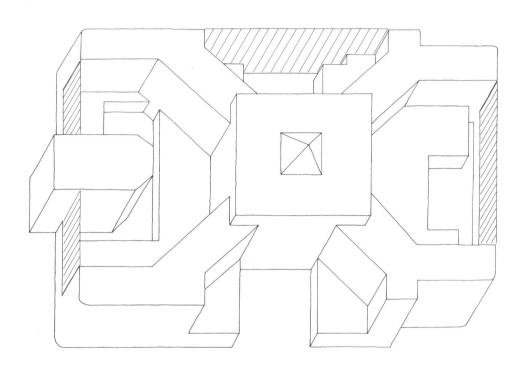

Figure 58
Natural shading by deciduous
trees of the pavilion-style
building of HL Technik AG,
Munich
(Architects: PFP Planung
Fahr + Partners, Munich)

As well as the advantages already mentioned, trees and shrubs offer wind protection and are thus not only shading elements but also heat shields. Figures 59.1 and 59.2 depict typical characteristics of wind forces acting upon a windbreak consisting of trees and the percentages of wind-velocity reduction of these forces behind the trees both with and without foliage. Planted windshield belts are sometimes deliberately used in urban planning to protect buildings from cold winds or to direct cool summer winds through built structures. As an example, Figure 60 illustrates planted windbreak areas in an urban neighbourhood in New Jersey, used to protect apartment buildings from cold winter winds.

Figure 59.1
Flow characteristics in wind shield belt

H height of wind shield

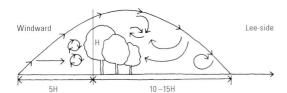

Windward · Lee-side

5H · 10–15H

Wind velocity
%

Dense foliage

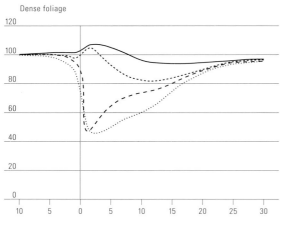

Figure 59.2
Effect of wind shield at different heights

······ 1/2 H
– – 1 H
– – – 1 1/2 H
— 2 1/2 H

No foliage

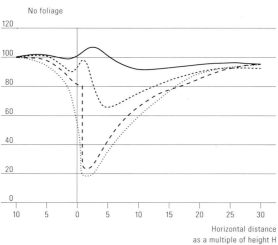

Horizontal distance
as a multiple of height H

Cold winter wind

Wind shield (planted) ·················

Town centre ·················
Residential area ·················

Cool summer wind

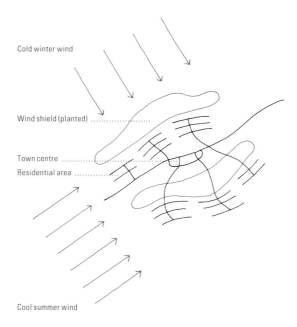

Figure 60
Wind shield planting in New Jersey for protection against winter winds

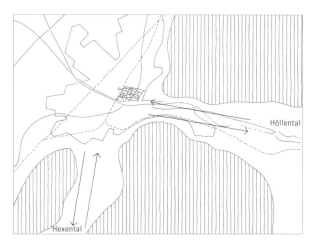

Figure 61.1
Example of local, thermally
caused wind system: Freiburg
in Breisgau district, Germany

Figure 61.2
— mountain breeze, night to
  early morning
— valley breeze, noon to late
  afternoon

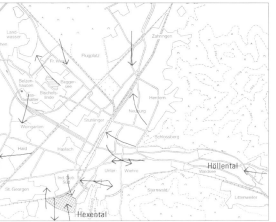

Figure 61.3
— mountain breeze
— valley breeze

4.2
Urban Space and Building Location

Urban planning and development must take several
aspects into account in order to achieve an ecologically beneficial overall solution. The form and orientation of buildings are important, as are the design of
building structures and the location of individual
buildings for optimum ventilation of the built environment, reducing heating and cooling requirements.

4.2.1
Building Form and Orientation

Urban concepts should be developed that include
essential ecological aspects, above all the natural
ventilation of the urban area and, conversely, a
minimization of urban (over-) heating. Figure 61 illustrates how orientation was used in urban planning in
Freiburg/Breisgau (design: Prof. G. Pfeifer, Lörrach),
utilizing the typical wind currents in this region during the night and in the morning and/or afternoon to
ventilate the area and to allow the prevailing winds
to reach the town centre.

Figure 61.4
Urban design
(Architect: Prof. Pfeifer,
Lörrach, Germany)

Enhancing natural ventilation of buildings and natural night-time cooling by storage masses, means incorporating this aspect into urban planning and developing an urban concept open to useful options (in the future). Figures 62.1 and 62.2 illustrate the effect of building orientation upon heat requirements in winter and heat gain in summer, respectively, with modified floorplans (length to width). Figure 62.2 also shows the effect of building form upon transmission heat requirements.

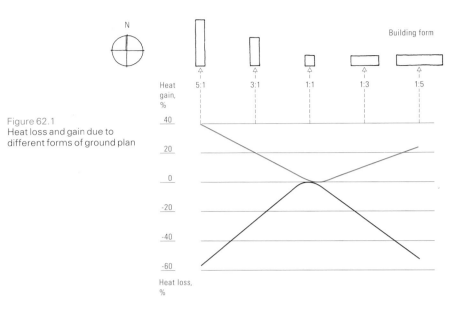

Figure 62.1
Heat loss and gain due to different forms of ground plan

Figure 62.2
Change in transmission heat loss dependent on building form and surface-to-volume ratio

$k_{m,K+F}$ = 1.75 W/m^{2}K
k_D = 0.45 W/m^{2}K
k_G = 0.80 W/m^{2}K

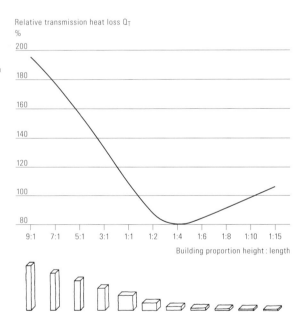

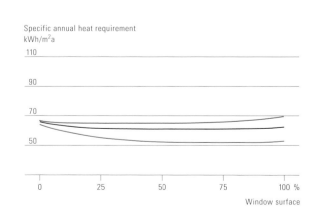

4.2.2
Reduction of Heating and Cooling Requirements

Reducing heating requirements, as shown, begins with the orientation of a building and the surface-to-volume ratio. Figure 63 demonstrates the change of solar irradiation in relation to building orientation and makes visible the considerable differences with regard to potential passive use of solar energy.

Reducing the heating requirements, i.e. optimizing incoming heat, is, however, not simply a matter of building orientation; it is also influenced by the form of the building and the ratio of volume to surface. The reciprocal relationship between building form and heat requirement is shown in Figure 64 with simple geometric shapes and the dissection of a cube. These relationships must be taken into consideration to save both construction and upkeep costs; they must be incorporated into any integrated planning. The relationship between window surfaces, orientation, and specific annual heating requirement is shown in Figure 65 as a further aspect in the design of façades and windows. This figure clearly illustrates that, in the past and even in the development of heat requirement guidelines, this aspect was treated with insufficient differentiation and that a blanket approach of, for instance, minimizing window surfaces to reduce heating requirements is, per se, simply not acceptable.

Figure 65
Annual heating requirement of basic room with excellent window design and various window surfaces and orientation

— North
— East/West
— South

Figure 63
Insolation and building orientation

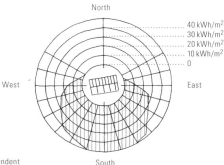

Solar annual reading dependent on direction of insolation
Window orientation 170° (SSE)
The solar annual reading is 255.9 kWh/m² of window surface.

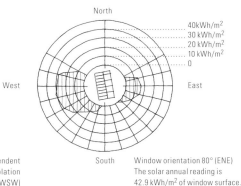

Solar annual reading dependent on direction of insolation
Window orientation 260° (WSW)
The solar annual reading is 88.9 kWh/m² of window surface.

Window orientation 80° (ENE)
The solar annual reading is 42.9 kWh/m² of window surface.

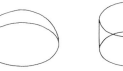

96 %   98 %   100 %   112 %

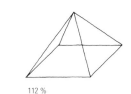

Figure 64
Percentages of change in heating requirement for different building types and separation of comparable total building mass

100 %

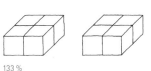

133 %

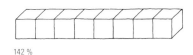

142 %

200 %

**Buildings of Tomorrow:
Examples and Ideas**

5

Buoyancy and wind, used correctly, can help us
naturally ventilate even the tallest and lowest
buildings.
As the examples show, natural ventilation does
not limit the scope of architectural design;
instead, it may lead to interesting new solutions,
possibly even to a new architectural language.

5.
Natural Ventilation of Buildings
(Ludwig Ilg)

In the context of Sick Building Syndrome, we have already mentioned the benefits of partial natural ventilation of buildings. J. Röben has studied 44 buildings for symptoms occurring in fully air-conditioned, naturally ventilated, or partially-mechanically ventilated buildings. The results of his investigation (Figure 66) show that naturally or partially-naturally ventilated buildings have the lowest occurrence of problems and symptoms.

This chapter, however, is not exclusively devoted to discussing natural ventilation; it attempts a much more balanced assessment of the topic, since natural ventilation also has some disadvantages. These are:

– a significantly increased heating requirement,
– below-acceptable humidity values in winter,
– above-acceptable room temperatures in summer,
– periodic strong draughts due to forceful oncoming winds,
– periodic poor extraction of contaminants during windstill days.

The resulting building type, developed over the last few years, allows occupants to choose between openable windows and air-conditioning or humidifiers in summer or winter, respectively, as the need arises.

How can, should, or must wind be considered in building design (Figure 67)? To answer this question, we must first understand the influences of wind upon built structures. In the process, positive and negative characteristics emerge, some of which argue for openable windows and others for a closed building.

Observation of nature and analysis of traditional building forms show that humans and animals alike have always carefully adapted their habitation to the local microclimate.

Prairie dogs are a wonderful example. They dig burrows below mounds of earth with two exits, instinctively aligning them with the prevailing wind and adapting them to the pressure differences created by buoyancy (Figure 68). Termites achieve the same result with a completely different design (Figure 69).

Both inhabit arid climate zones. To best protect their homes against enemies and adverse weather conditions, the covering is made as hard and/or massive as possible, limiting the number and size of openings. However, the interior of these habitats is liable to become overheated from both solar radiation and the body heat of entire families of warm-blooded animals, or thousands of insects; furthermore, their exhalations must be exhausted. To deal with these complications, the animals have developed very clever ventilation systems.

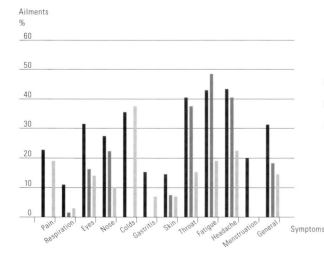

Ailments
%

Figure 66
Results of the SBS study
by J. Röben

■ fully air-conditioned building
■ mechanically ventilated building
■ naturally ventilated building

Figure 67
Leonardo da Vinci's study of air movement around buildings, modelled with water

Overheating was rarely a concern in the temperate climate zones of Central Europe in pre-industrial times. Climate, settlement and trade patterns allowed for small units, generally characterized by a well-balanced management of heat and air. Moreover, there are still, today, traditional building forms in North Africa and Asia which imitate the examples mentioned on the previous page. The dominant form is a solid construction, which protects against storms and temperature variations, combined with building elements (such as a wind-catch or 'malqaf') which capture a welcome, cooling breeze (Figures 70, page 70) and make deliberate use of buoyancy (Figure 71).

Figures 69
The structures built by termites are oriented to wind direction and solar radiation.

In hot zones termites construct their highly developed structures along principles of natural ventilation, thermal storage and evaporative cooling (right).

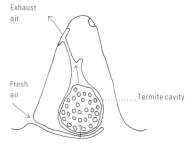

Exhaust air

Fresh air

Termite cavity

Ground water

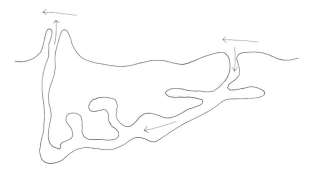

Figure 68
The prairie dog utilizes wind to naturally ventilate its burrow.

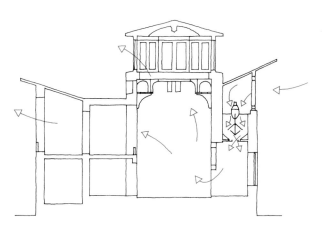

Figure 71
Traditional architecture in North Africa utilizes wind in combination with evaporative cooling to cool buildings.

Little is known of how competent in air ventilation the master builders of ancient civilizations might have been. An analysis of the reconstructed plans of pre-historic settlements demonstrates that they could integrate local climate characteristics into their design, at times even better than in modern design practice (Figure 72). Wind load stress was not a particular problem. The dead weight of building materials created direct stress exceeding wind loads generated by even the greatest storms (Figure 73).

Ancient Rome featured sophisticated heating and ventilation systems, described in detail by the engineer and architect Vitruvius. Adapted essentially from examples in nature, they were laid out on an empirical basis, the physics or proven methods of calculation being then unavailable.

Figure 73
Modern building technology and materials reduce pressure on buildings created by the dead weight of the materials. These pressures, in modern lightweight construction, are below maximum wind pressures. (from Hertig).

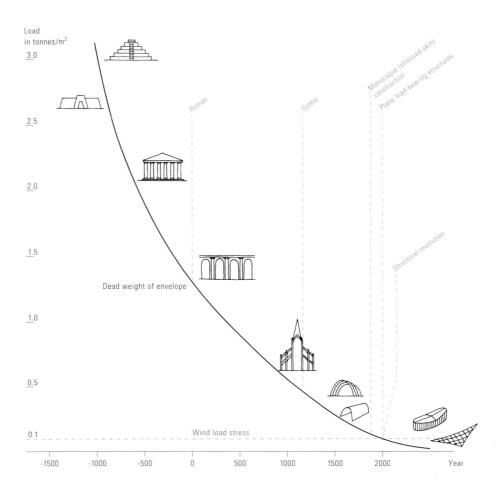

Figure 72
The layout of Kahun in Egypt around 2000 B.C. was more advantageous for the upper class with regard to protection from hot desert winds and utilization of cool breezes from the north.

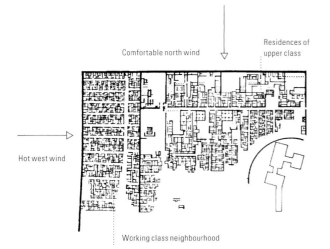

New discoveries about basic ventilation techniques weren't made until the beginning of the eighteenth century. Large buildings constructed before then were always designed so that fresh air naturally replaced used air. This called for sufficient height and appropriate dimensions for openings close to the ground and near the roof (Figure 74).

With industrialization came the demand for more meeting halls, theatres, barracks, and hospitals, and with the construction of these buildings, also, a greater need for and interest in information about effective ventilation systems. By the end of the eighteenth century, the air supply in mines and the evacuation of noxious gases produced by industry posed further challenges.

Several inventions in this field were conceived at the beginning of the nineteenth century. The ventilation system of the House of Commons in London is very well documented. It was designed by the chemist David Boswell Reid during the period 1835–1845 (Figure 75).

In 1858, Max Joseph von Pettenkofer was able to prove that, clinically and hygienically, a minimum fresh-air rate of approx. 60 m³/h per person is required. It was now clear that natural ventilation principles were too limited. Henceforth, research would focus on mechanical air-control systems and the development of effective technical installations.

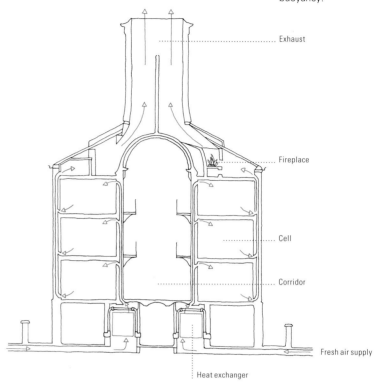

Figure 74
In 1844 Joshua Jebb achieved an air change rate of 3 ac/h in this prison building in England exclusively with natural buoyancy.

Exhaust

Fireplace

Cell

Corridor

Fresh air supply

Heat exchanger

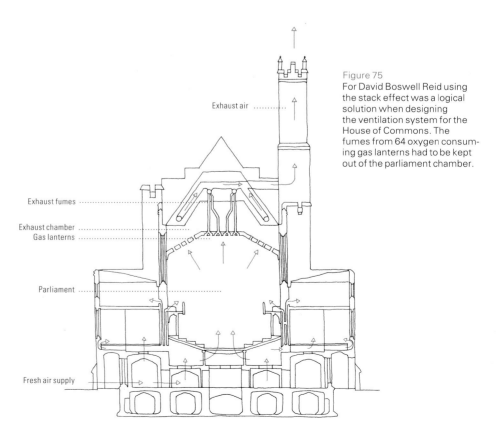

Figure 75
For David Boswell Reid using the stack effect was a logical solution when designing the ventilation system for the House of Commons. The fumes from 64 oxygen consuming gas lanterns had to be kept out of the parliament chamber.

Exhaust air

Exhaust fumes

Exhaust chamber
Gas lanterns

Parliament

Fresh air supply

Figures 70
Wind towers in Heyderabad
and the Tomigaya Tower
project

The wind towers of Heyderabad
show how simple means can
successfully create natural
ventilation.
The Tomigaya Tower project
(R. Rogers) provides a modern
example of the many uses of
wind.

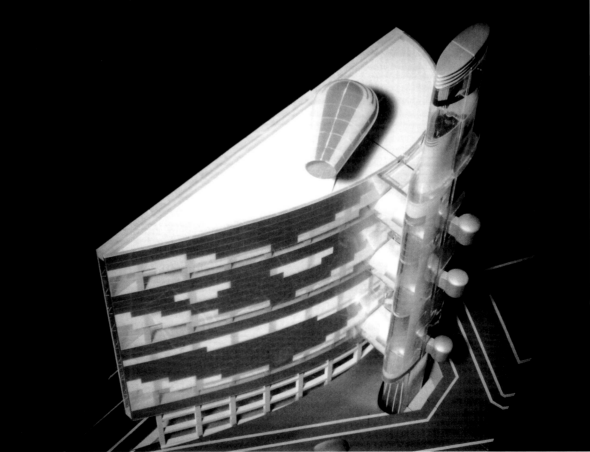

Ventilation of Buildings

Increasingly, modern buildings with high heating requirements, e.g. residential buildings, are being constructed with a completely (hermetically) closed envelope and designed to use only mechanical ventilation systems in combination with heat-recovery installations. Office building façades make other demands. While heating energy requirements have fallen due to increased interior loads and improved insulation, the requirements for ventilation and for cooling have risen. The need remains, nevertheless, for natural ventilation and energy-efficient night cooling in summer and some part of the transitional seasons.

Pressure differentials at the built envelope (steady-state and turbulence-induced fluctuating differentials), caused by wind and thermals, can become the chief means for meeting this need. Several manufacturers offer complicated façade systems which are supposed to do the job with special constructions. The optimum system, however, is not yet available, since flow conditions on and in façades depend very much on design factors and building location. Layout must take into account not only aerodynamics but also acoustics, fire safety regulations and emissions. This makes for a very complex situation.

In recent years, advances in computer technology have made possible the simulation of internal air movement given known boundary conditions. This method is not applicable to air movement on façades (e.g. double-leaf) in cases where pressure differentials caused by natural wind at openings and joints are the decisive factors. The flow action is also greatly influenced by the surface and texture of the surrounding terrain and the structure of the built environment. Neighbouring buildings completely change the pressure, velocity, and turbulence fields near a building.

Similar to the nature of problems encountered in weather forecasting, geometric details such as parapets, roof overhangs, and roof pitch, as well as small differences in wind direction, can significantly change the course of flow at façades. Currently, there are no economically viable calculation procedures for accurate and detailed prediction of the velocity field, the pressure field, and the transport of contaminants near buildings.

Atmospheric Boundary Layer

As outlined in Chapter 4.1.1, velocity decreases the closer wind gets to the ground, due to surface friction, while turbulence and gust increase. The boundary layer where this deceleration occurs is approx. 300 to 1,000 m high and is characterized by a brisk vertical change in air masses and energy. Friction, stagnation, buoyancy, and pressure forces within the boundary layer create a complex eddy structure which can only be described statistically. Eddies, continually forming anew, have a diameter identical to that of the boundary layer itself and gradually dissolve in cascades until smaller and smaller eddies, turning in space, are so reduced that, of the contained variational energy, only heat remains. The turbulence quotient – in other words, the extent of variation in actual wind velocities in relation to the mean wind velocity – is approx. 10 % to 20 % close to the ground, depending upon the density of the built environment; near buildings, e.g. in the recirculation area, it can reach values of 100 % and more.

Wind Load Stress on Façade Components

Wind loads on a building fluctuate in time and space. They act directly upon the exterior surfaces of closed buildings and indirectly, because of the permeability of the building envelope, upon the interior walls. Any interpretations must consider not only statistical wind load stresses but also the dynamic wind effect of turbulence differentials. The gustiness of natural winds, the recirculation turbulence of neighbouring buildings, or the periodical eddy change at the structure itself may produce vibrations in the structure or in building components. This may cause self-initiated sway (e.g. in bridges) which can be understood as a reciprocal force between movement in the structure and oncoming wind.

Static Wind Load Stress

Static wind loads are forces released by the effect of wind which elicit some torsion but little or negligible motion from a built structure. They are especially important in the measurement of structures not susceptible to sway. The static wind load upon a façade element is the sum of all active pressure and friction forces. In most cases, the friction forces are negligible. For dimensioning purposes, all loads applied to buildings or building elements are indexed to the dynamic or impact pressure, a comparative pressure proportionate to the square of the wind velocity. The dynamic pressure is a reference for the pressure coefficient c_p, wherein positive coefficients correspond to positive pressure in the environment, and negative coefficients correspond to negative pressure.

The positive or negative pressures acting upon a building surface are calculated as the product of the local pressure coefficient and the dynamic pressure. The force upon a single element or upon an entire building can be determined by multiplying all partial pressures of all sectional surfaces by the corresponding surface and by adding all resulting pressure forces with regard to their direction. It is important to note that positive or negative pressures also result inside the building and that for some components (e.g. windows and interior walls) the pressure differentials at opposite walls govern. For practical measurement purposes, typical coefficients are gathered from existing wind-load norms (e.g. SIA 160, DIN 1055, Part 4, Euronorm CN/TC 250/SC 1) (Table 3). Cases departing from the norm are measured in wind-tunnel model experiments. The dimensioning can be further supplemented by calculating the location-dependent dynamic pressure. This may occur only once every 50 years of a building's lifespan or during a gust (or squall). It is dependent upon distance from the ground and is either taken from the norm reading or calculated according to the methods of peak value statistics.

Dynamic Wind Load Stress

The spectrum of variational energy contained in gusts covers frequencies ranging from approx. 0.001 to 0.3 Hz, and the cyclones resulting from it usually exert aperiodic and random pressure variations on a building. The natural frequency of oscillation, or resonant frequency, of most buildings far exceeds the frequencies mentioned above, thus limiting the risk of resonance phenomena on large-surface support structures, bridges, or tall, narrow buildings.

In the interpretation of these forces, the resonant frequency of the façade element should be as far removed as possible from the frequency range where atmospheric turbulence displays the highest variational energy. One must, therefore, ensure that the structure in this frequency range is sufficiently dampened. Experiments and calculations for large-scale elements made of glass or aluminum have shown that these disruptive forces originating from oncoming winds tend to be impervious to resonance phenomena. Corresponding relationships occur, for instance, at the windward side of free-standing buildings, where the building elements simply follow the deviations created by the fluctuating, wind-induced pressure forces because of their resonant frequency, which is higher than 3 Hz.

Table 3
Wind loads for individual building components

h = height
a = depth

The boundary area is the area along the edge of the building with a depth of a/8.

Wind loads for individual building components on geometric fabric from DIN 1055 Part 4		Normal range $h/a \geqq 0.5$	Normal range $h/a \leqq 0.25$	Boundary area
Pressure coefficient c_∞ for pressure		1.00	1.00	1.00
Pressure coefficient c_∞ for suction		-0.70	-0.50	-2.00
Height and dynamic pressure		Wind pressure $W_P = c_\infty \cdot q \left[kN/m^2 \right]$		
		Wind suction $W_S = c_\infty \cdot q \left[kN/m^2 \right]$		
$h \leqq 8m$ $q = 0.50 \, kN/m^2$	W_P	0.50 kN/m²	0.50 kN/m²	0.50 kN/m²
	W_S	-0.35 kN/m²	-0.25 kN/m²	-1.00 kN/m²
$8m < h \leqq 20m$ $q = 0.80 \, kN/m^2$	W_P	0.80 kN/m²	0.80 kN/m²	0.80 kN/m²
	W_S	-0.56 kN/m²	-0.40 kN/m²	-1.60 kN/m²
$20m < h \leqq 100m$ $q = 1.10 \, kN/m^2$	W_P	1.10 kN/m²	1.10 kN/m²	1.10 kN/m²
	W_S	-0.77 kN/m²	-0.55 kN/m²	-2.20 kN/m²
$h > 100m$ $q = 1.30 \, kN/m^2$	W_P	1.30 kN/m²	1.30 kN/m²	1.30 kN/m²
	W_S	-0.91 kN/m²	-0.65 kN/m²	-2.60 kN/m²

Recirculation Turbulence

The recirculation around neighbouring buildings or on the lee-side of a building exhibits very different phenomena. There, one may find additional, subordinate, or periodic eddies at the façade, and the frequency of such secondary cyclones created by the separation of the flow may closely resemble the resonant frequencies of the building elements. Typical frequencies and cyclone measurements depend greatly upon corresponding geometric relationships.

Wind Comfort and Ventilation Efficiency

The phenomena described above primarily affect buildings which are much higher than the surrounding built environment or others which are in close proximity to such a tall building. The higher wind velocities at roof level may be guided along the façade to the ground (pedestrian zones). There, they may become uncomfortable or even dangerous to pedestrians. One indication is the gust speed in pedestrian areas. The speed and frequency of gusts help categorize the utility of such a space (e.g. shopping area, window display, sidewalk cafés, parks, schoolyards, etc.). When new buildings are being planned, it is often interesting to make a 'before and after' comparison of these dynamics. Comparative wind-tunnel studies are used to calculate gust speed and to evaluate these dynamics with regard to the values before the new structure was built. Wind-tunnel experiments are thus useful for the prevention of undesired draughts through the evaluation or development of corresponding architectural elements or building measures.

The ventilation efficiency of naturally or partially-naturally ventilated buildings is greatly dependent upon atmospheric influences. It is derived from the distribution of averaged pressures and the distribution of size, frequency, and correlation of pressure variations on the built envelope. The ventilation efficiency is therefore dependent on:

– wind direction,
– building geometry,
– built environment,
– inner and outer temperatures (buoyancy),
– type and degree of envelope permeability.

The pressure coefficient (wind-induced pressure) c_p can be used to roughly evaluate the quality of ventilation.

The pressure coefficient is derived as follows:

$$c_{pi} = \frac{p - p_{ref}}{\frac{\rho}{2} w_{ref}^2}$$

Where:

p = local static pressure
ρ = air density
w_{ref} = reference wind velocity
  (e.g. at roof height)
p_{ref} = reference air pressure
  (e.g. barometric air pressure)

The difference between local inner pressure and outside induced pressure is crucial for air infiltration into a building. The pressure differential within the building created by buoyancy (or thermal lift) must be taken into consideration. The pressure differential with regard to infiltration, assuming a constant inner temperature, is:

$$\delta p_i = \left(c_{pou} - c_{pi} \right) \cdot \frac{\rho}{2} w_{ref}^2 - \rho_{oi} \, g \left(z - z_o \right) \left(\frac{T_i}{T_e} - 1 \right)$$

Where:

c_{pou} = pressure coefficient outside
c_{pi} = pressure coefficient inside
ρ_{oi} = air density inside (neutral zone)
z_o = height of neutral zone above ground
z = height of observation point above ground
g = earth (rotational) acceleration (9,81 m/s^2)
T = temperature (exterior/interior) in K

Figure 76 is a schematic of wind-induced pressure distribution upon the built envelope of an oval building form. The inward-pointing red lines on the building fabric indicate positive pressure; the outward-pointing blue lines indicate negative pressure. As the schematic shows, both the positive and the negative pressures increase towards the top due to the wind profile (accelerated wind velocity at increased height).

The figure also shows that, in the upper region (assumed in the example to be 70 m high), there exists a maximum negative pressure of -40 Pa and a maximum positive pressure of +30 Pa. Similar values can be reached by buoyancy within a building (Figure 77). Because of the difference in interior and exterior temperature, a pressure differential of 80 Pa is created within the building, whereby the pressure on the exterior skin in the lower region affects the interior (from the outside in) while, in the upper regions, a pressure gradient forms (in theory) from the inside to the outside. Since buildings are generally air-permeable, these are theoretical observations resulting in a value unlikely to be reproduced in practice. Nevertheless, these pressure differences indicate ventilation due to infiltration from the lower region (from the outside in) to the upper region (from the inside out).

Figure 78 illustrates the combined influences of wind and buoyancy and the distribution of pressure differentials on the built envelope with average wind velocity (wind and buoyancy overlap, operation in winter). Buoyancy increases the negative pressure on the side walls of buildings, along, so to speak, the lee-side, while, at the windward side, the outward directed flow is reversed; in other words, there is infiltration from the outside in. The inner versus outer pressure distribution, seen in Figure 78, can be lowered by creating roof openings through stairways or interior shafts, resulting in the pressure distribution shown in Figure 79. A comparison of Figures 78 and 79 reveals that the forces exerted upon the interior of the building are greater than the negative pressure coefficients exerted upon the outside.

In summer, the temperature differences between inside and outside are very small: the impact of buoyancy so evident in winter is then no longer measurable. Rather, the warming of the façade surface through direct solar insolation results in localized buoyancy outside façades or inside double-leaf façades.

Figure 80 illustrates the same pressure distributions as Figure 76. Here, the inner pressure is almost equal to the surrounding pressure, so that the wind-induced pressure becomes the primary force acting upon the building. An atypical wind profile results when a large opening is created in the roof area and when the outer wind velocities are low (Figure 81). In the areas where the pressure is usually negative, we can now detect a slight positive pressure (a small positive pressure forms on the lee-side, exerted from the outside in). The previous example was of a relatively free-standing building fabric. However, if the fabric is surrounded by a densely built environment, considerable limitations and changes in the flow and pressure coefficients may result.

Figures 76–81
Pressure distribution on building envelope for wind and buoyancy

— Pressure
— Suction

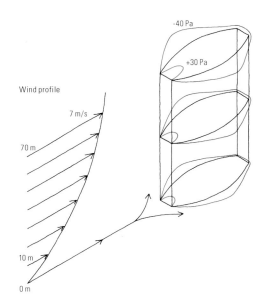

Wind profile

7 m/s

70 m

10 m

0 m

-40 Pa

+30 Pa

Figure 76
Wind-induced pressure
distribution on envelope
(schematic example)

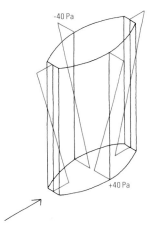

-40 Pa

+40 Pa

Figure 77
Pressure differences created
in winter through internal and
external temperature differences (schematic example)

$T_{ou} = 0°C$
$T_i = 20°C$

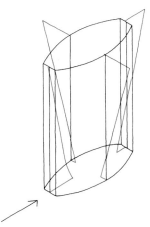

Figure 78
Distribution of pressure
differences on envelope
(winter) for average wind
and buoyancy

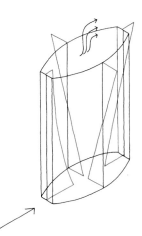

Figure 79
Reduction of internal pressure
through dominating roof openings (winter)

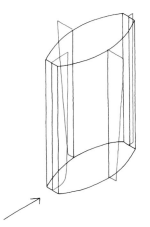

Figure 80
Wind-induced pressure
distribution (internal and
surrounding pressure)
in summer

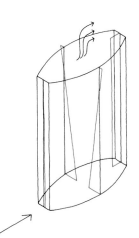

Figure 81
Internal pressure created by
roof openings (summer)

Distances between buildings and their impact on flow are shown, in simplified form, in Figure 82. A common urban development is schematized in Figure 83, revealing the very indifferent distribution of pressure on the building fabric with strongly defined negative pressure areas and a minimal negative pressure range. Options for natural ventilation are very limited in this arrangement. When the shape of the roof is modified (Figure 84), areas of both positive and negative pressure may form which, in turn, improve natural ventilation of the building.

Figure 85 is a schematic of the same building during a windstill period and the pressure differences caused by buoyancy, assuming a 5 K difference between interior and exterior temperatures. Due to buoyancy, additional flow is created near the building from the exterior toward the interior with simultaneous downward flow (negative pressure formation) in the roof area. These schematics show how modifications in the building mass or the built envelope may impact the infiltration and ventilation of a building, i.e. how the building fabric itself greatly influences natural ventilation when openings are used. These findings should be made use of to create a building design where natural ventilation is always possible and to avoid imposing limitations both inside and outside the building.

Figure 82
Basic flow variations for different building arrangements

Case 1
Isolated roughness
$S_c > 2.4\,H$
Oncoming wind settles on the ground in open space between buildings.

Case 2
Flow over buildings and mixing
$1.4\,H < S_c < 2.4\,H$
Between buildings there is an exchange of air between the recirculation area and oncoming wind.

Case 3
Flow over buildings with limited exchange
$S_c \leq 1.4\,H$

S_c: distance between buildings
H: height of buildings

The relative pressure difference above the built envelope, indexed to case 1, is approximately:

'1' for case 1
'1/3' for case 2
nearly '0' for case 3

Best results (good ventilation of space between buildings, case 1) are achieved when the distance between buildings is triple the height of the buildings.

Case 1

Case 2

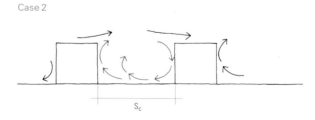

Case 3

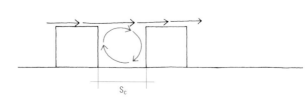

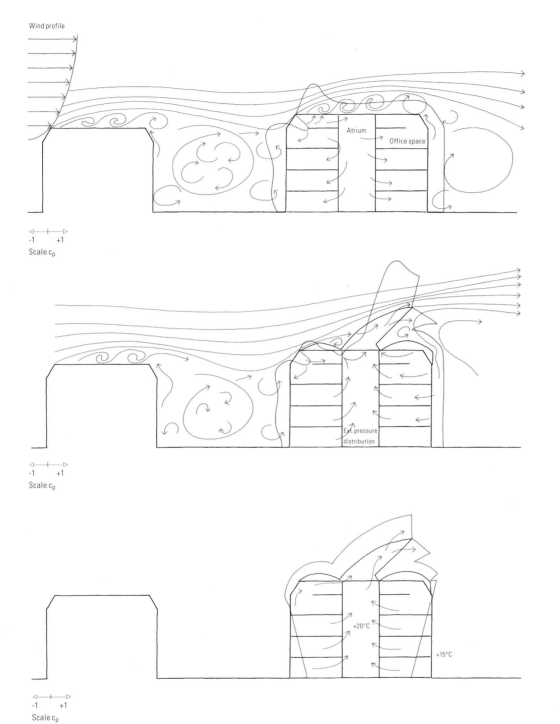

Wind profile

Atrium

Office space

-1 +1
Scale c_p

Figure 83
Neutral pressure distribution on
built envelope:
Limited possibility for natural
ventilation

Ext. pressure
distribution

-1 +1
Scale c_p

Figure 84
Deliberate utilization of prevailing winds to create defined
pressure differences:
The built form influences the
pressure differences to support
the buoyancy effect, naturally
ventilating the atrium.

+20°C

+15°C

-1 +1
Scale c_p

Figure 85
Pressure difference caused by
buoyancy ($\Delta T = 5K$):
The pressure differences
create natural ventilation.

Wind Tunnel Simulation

The atmospheric boundary-layer wind tunnel is an instrument for realistically predicting wind-induced flow conditions. Since wind is simulated in all its previously described complexity, this type of tunnel is structurally very different from wind tunnels commonly used for experiments in the fields of transportation or flight aerodynamics and from aeronautic wind tunnels, which are of limited use for studying building aerophysics.

Figure 86 is a schematic showing the principle of the atmospheric boundary-layer wind tunnel. The actual test section, through which air is forced with the aid of adjustable fans, is preceded by a longer approach section. In it, supported by additional components such as cyclone generators or variable ground roughness, a boundary layer forms which is sufficiently true to local conditions. The ceiling contour is also adjustable and prevents the formation of pressure gradients which might affect the measured results. The model to be tested and its surrounding built environment are placed on a turntable, which allows different wind directions to be studied. Visualization with smoke helps produce a qualitative impression of flow relationships. The smoke is introduced into the flow in a resonance-free manner and made visible by appropriate lighting procedures in light section beams (Figure 87, page 80). The conclusions drawn from these experiments can be integrated into the design and can, furthermore, lead to deliberate use of continued quantitative measurement methods. The pressure differentials on the envelope of a building are measured at drill holes in the envelope and are usually conducted to pressure sensors via pipes and mechanical scanners for the calculation of mean values. When these values are indexed to the dynamic pressure, dimensionless pressure coefficients result, which can be entered into the simulation program as boundary conditions.

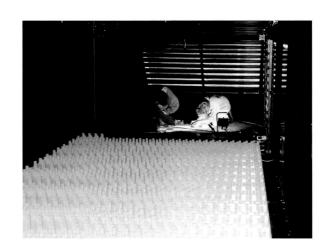

Figure 86
Atmospheric boundary layer
wind tunnel
Schematic

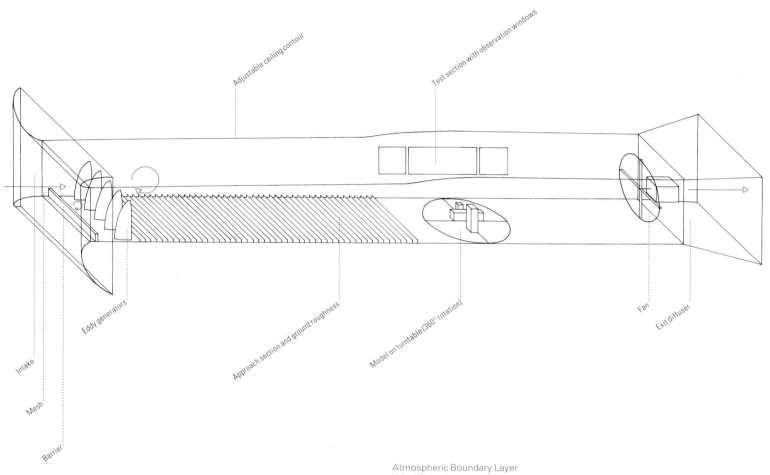

Adjustable ceiling contour

Test section with observation windows

Eddy generators

Intake

Mesh

Barrier

Approach section and ground roughness

Model on turntable (360° rotation)

Fan

Exit diffuser

Atmospheric Boundary Layer Wind Tunnel

The function of an atmospheric boundary layer wind tunnel is to simulate to scale the wind-induced flow mechanics and conditions near buildings. The simulation reproduces the distribution of velocity and the gustiness of wind, as they occur in the bottom 300 meters of a neutrally striated atmospheric boundary layer flow.

To accurately reproduce the conditions existing in the original objects, eddy generators, placed in front of the model, are programmed to recreate the height dependence of turbulence and wind velocity typical at the site under study.

The schematic shows the applied principles. The long approach section is necessary to achieve steady state in the developing boundary layer. The floor of the approach section has the same degree of roughness and unevenness as found in the environment surrounding the object on which the model is based.

The preparation and set up is different in this type of simulation than in aeronautic wind tunnels used for airplane and automotive engineering. The uniform oncoming flow, low in turbulence, achieved in those tunnels, makes them generally unsuited to application for studies in building aerodynamics.

Figure 87.1
Atmospheric boundary layer
wind tunnel
View of test section

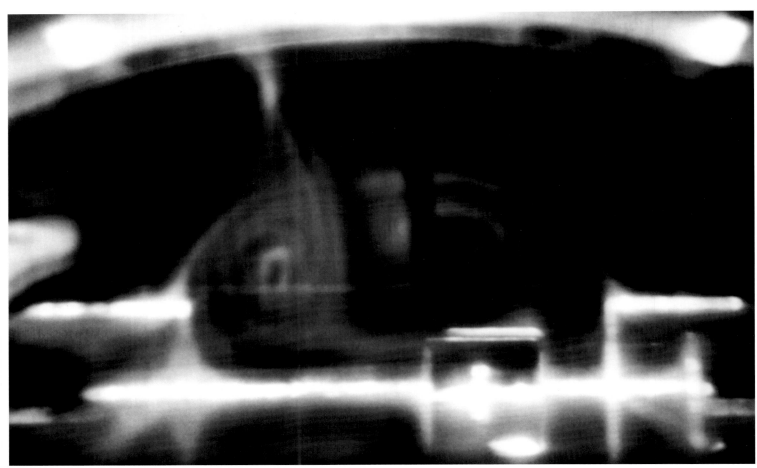

Figure 87.2
Wind-induced air movement
in atrium made visible in wind
tunnel experiment. (GfA,
Gesellschaft für Aerophysik,
München-Zürich)

To record local dynamic wind effects, miniature pressure scanners are installed directly on the model. This makes it possible to take true readings of the local spectral distribution in the pressure fluctuation. To simulate exhaust air and emissions and to evaluate the emissions at façades, tracer-gas procedures are used in wind tunnels. The tracer gas assumes the role of the noxious gas and the noxious-gas concentration in the exhaust air. Local tracing and analysis of the air at various points on the building envelope yield results from which the critical concentration field in various wind situations can be derived for each critically predictable noxious or emission source. An iterative process is used to determine the optimal position for air openings, chimneys, and additional air-exhaust openings with regard to air hygiene.

Furthermore, the pressure coefficients serve as a basis to predict flow relationships and ventilation behaviour throughout the building. To this end, the position as well as the size of negative or positive pressure coefficients are used, as shown in Figures 83 to 85.

Model experiments to scale are usually attempted on façade elements only to determine impermeability (airtightness) with regard to infiltration and precipitation. The same applies to predictions of thermally caused ventilation relationships in double-leaf façades. Model experiments on a 1:1 scale are usually realized by constructing true prototypes of a façade section, several storeys high with two or more window elements.

The tests are generally carried out by reproducing natural weather conditions. Oncoming wind is simulated by airplane motors and rain by sprinkling the relevant window elements. However, the relationships and conclusions thus arrived at are merely a rough approximation of normal weather conditions. The wind tunnel in Nantes (France) is unique in Europe. It covers an area of 22 m x 13 m and is 7.5 m high. In it, all weather conditions can be simulated realistically (gusts up to hurricane force; showers with various drop diameters; hail; snow; temperatures ranging from -15°C to +50°C; and solar insolation up to 1 kW/m^2). While wind tunnels of this kind are of great interest to research and development, they are also very expensive. The 1:1 scale wind tunnel will therefore surely remain the exception.

On the following pages, several examples are presented: buildings, some existing, some planned, which are deep-plan buildings or skyscrapers (the greatest challenge for natural ventilation) and which can all be naturally ventilated. These examples illustrate how wind flow can be integrated into the effort of meeting ecological requirements.

5.1
Deep-Plan Buildings

The new office building of Tchibo Holding AG, in Hamburg (architects: Bürgin Nissen Wentzlaff, Basel), is a prime example of natural ventilation in a deep-plan building. This project's aim was to naturally ventilate the building for as much of the year as possible. Figure 88.1 shows an elevation and Figure 88.2 a floor plan, indicating the outer zones which can be naturally ventilated. To make natural ventilation possible for this building, a glass-covered central court was designed, whose roof construction was in part developed in the streamflow laboratory. Finally, Figure 88.3 shows a cross-section of the building, including the office areas and the inner light well. The air current created by wind entering from the west and the formation of turbulent boundary layers with positive and negative pressures are clearly indicated in this figure.

Standard calculations are inadequate for designing a building of this kind to specification. A model of the building must be tested and analysed in a wind tunnel, especially since emissions from surrounding buildings act upon the naturally ventilated building. Models of the new and the existing building are shown in Figure 88.4 during a flow ex-periment in the wind tunnel; the old building contains a commercial kitchen emanating odorous air.

To study the aeration of an office building in detail, it is sometimes necessary to conduct large-scale model experiments, as in Figure 88.5. In this model trial (laboratory ROM, Hamburg), positive and negative pressures in the façade area are simulated to determine cross-ventilation and, above all, to ensure that the cross-ventilation is draught-free throughout the room depth. This yields the necessary design parameters illustrated in Figure 88.6, representing the interplay of the oncoming or main wind velocity, the window opening, the main wind direction, and the air change in the building.

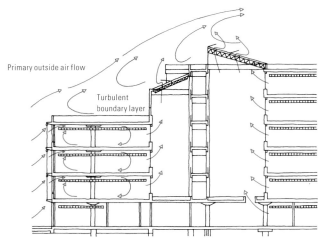

Figure 88.3
Schematic of natural air flow
in building

Figure 88.1
Tchibo Holding AG, Hamburg,
administrative building CN 2
(Architects: Bürgin Nissen
Wentzlaff, Basel)

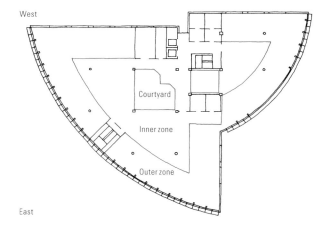

Figure 88.2
Floor plan with zones requiring
ventilation

Figure 88.4
Model study in wind tunnel
(emissions from neighbouring
buildings)

Figure 88.5
Model study of detail in
laboratory

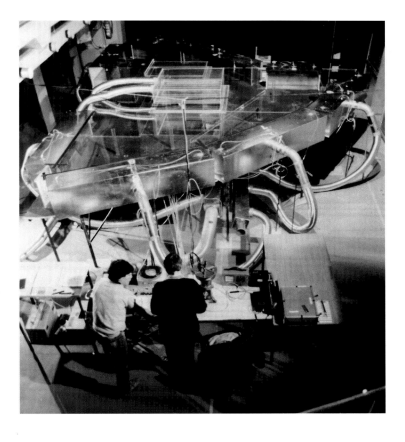

Figure 88.6
Diagram for natural ventilation
of the office building

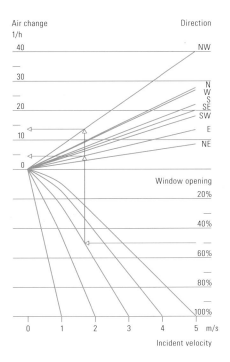

Air change
1/h

Direction

40 — NW

30

20

N
W
S
SE
SW
E
NE

10

0

Window opening

20%

40%

60%

80%

100%

0   1   2   3   4   5   m/s

Incident velocity

Figure 88.7 represents a section of the façade with shading and ventilation in this area. We can clearly see the upper and lower opening elements, allowing natural ventilation under many different weather conditions (strong oncoming winds, calm, thermal air change during calm, etc.). When oncoming winds are strong, the outer air flow is conducted into the rooms above the baffled ceiling, where it can spread (by tangential movement) to sufficiently fill and flow through the entire space.

The light-well, with its simply designed roof construction (Figure 88.8), serves to distribute the ventilation effect. The roof elements are openable, acting like spoilers and achieving a very high negative pressure coefficient which, in turn, extracts air from the surrounding office areas.

The entire ventilation system is controlled via panels (Figures 88.9 and 88.10), which also indicate when windows should be kept closed because high external temperatures require mechanical air-conditioning to prevent room temperatures from exceeding, for example, +28°C. The Tchibo AG office building is a high storage capacity building with supporting ventilation and cooling as well as largely natural lighting and ventilation. Thus, on the one hand, it meets today's requirements for natural ventilation, and, on the other hand, it provides reasonable maximum room temperatures for comfortable conditions during the summer months. Designs of this kind are usually only possible if client and architect are truly committed to implementing the requirements for an ecological building.

Figure 88.7
Façade close-up

Figure 88.8
View of detail in atrium with ceiling contour for natural ventilation

Figure 88.9
Control panel for mechanical/natural ventilation

Figure 88.10
Regulating variables

Conditions for:
○ Natural ventilation
□ Exhaust air
△ Air conditioning

1) additional variable T_{room}

Operating hours for natural ventilation 7 a.m. to 7 p.m.

Season	$t_{outside}$ in °C 1)	Wind pressure	Recommendation
Transitional season	+5° to +22°C	adequate too low too high	○ ○□ △
Summer	> +22°C		△
Winter	< +5°C		△
Night cooling	2 a.m. $t_r > t_{ou}$ (> +5°C)	adequate too low too high	○ ○□ △

5.2
Deep-Plan Low-Rise Buildings

Deep-plan low-rise buildings, such as supermarkets, sports halls, exhibition and fair halls, or similar structures, have special requirements for natural ventilation. In the development of buildings with extreme ground plan dimensions (depths far greater than 100 m), wind tunnel studies are essential, since the requirements for natural ventilation result in special building and, particularly, roof structures to create surface air extract. Buoyancy is a very important consideration here, as are, naturally, wind and the formation of negative pressure coefficients near the roof. From this it follows that additional air in the lower areas of large rooms should be conducted into the rooms at minimal velocities to favour and support thermal floor to ceiling cross-ventilation. How this kind of problem can be solved is shown in the following three examples (Figures 89), which were tested during a workshop at the ETH, Zurich, with engineering and architecture students.

to Figure 89
Klaus Daniels in conversation with students participating in the workshop

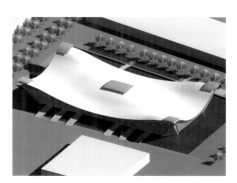

Figure 89.1
Model for a large hall built to ecological specifications (B.Eng. Ilg, GfA / ETH Zurich / CAD consultation by architecture student Summerauer, ETH Zürich)

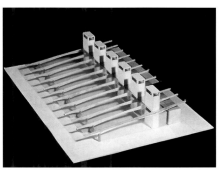

Figure 89.2 (to series 92)
Model photograph of the hall designed by group 1 in the workshop

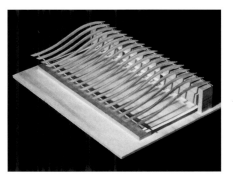

Figure 89.3 (to series 93)
Model photograph of the hall designed by group 2 in the workshop

Figure 90 (left) shows a hall model of 25,000 m^2 which is to be naturally ventilated. For financial reasons the fabric is usually rectangular in form. The pressure coefficients range from +0.6 to -2.0 and, depending on the angle of approach (wind direction), have a tendency to taper off sharply above the roof. In other words, near the roof surface air exhaustion is very uneven when certain light well or roof elements are opened.

Figure 90 (middle) shows the same building fabric with a vaulted roof structure. One can see that the negative pressure coefficients are more evenly distributed and are located at a greater height. Figure 90 (right) once again shows the same hall, but with a completely different roof shape achieving a relatively even distribution of negative pressure coefficients. We can, therefore, assume that evenly distributed roof openings and openings at corner and centre areas function almost equally well as exhausts.

When fresh air is brought into such a hall space from below, along the floor there is usually an even floor to ceiling cross-flow, supported by buoyancy (Figure 91). The above-mentioned requirements result in a building structure with a distinctive roof shape (see Figure 89.1), with air openings at the corners and in the middle of the hall, sheltered by covers to allow natural ventilation even when it rains.

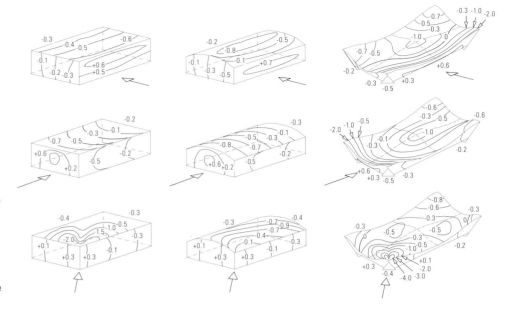

Figure 90
Distribution of pressure coefficients for different building forms

Figure 91
Schematic representation of air flow

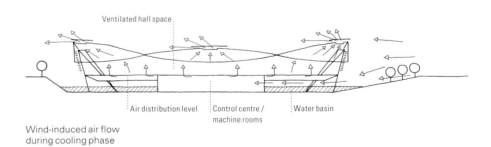

Ventilated hall space

Air distribution level   Control centre / machine rooms   Water basin

Wind-induced air flow during cooling phase

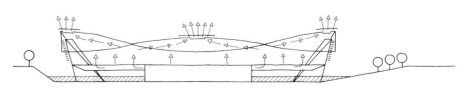

Air flow caused by buoyancy

To demonstrate that other building structures can produce the same results, during a workshop lasting several days student groups at the ETH, Zurich, and the engineering school of Luzern studied the hall as a large event and exhibition space. The Figure 92 series (Group 1) shows a hall structure with typical shape and fabric, which accommodates technical installations and exhaust-air outlets to provide consistent ventilation of the hall space under various conditions (natural ventilation, mechanical ventilation). The student sketches present several ideas for developing an ecologically oriented hall in which the widest possible use is made of natural resources. Electricity and natural gas are the only primary sources of energy, so as to attain the highest degree of environmental sustainability.

In contrast to Group 1, Group 2 based its roof shape on a very different design. This group focused on creating surface exhaust across the entire roof area with a quasi-double roof (solar deflector). This was achieved by conducting the primary air flow in between the two roof surfaces, which has the effect of inducing room air into the primary air flow. Intake air is circulated along the floor area, the buoyancy helping to cross-ventilate the building. The Figure 93 series illustrates the incidence of draught under various aspects.

All three designs show how architecturally different approaches may lead to the same result: ecological building does not restrict architecture. On the contrary, integrating ecological aspects can actually give rise to a new architectural language.

Workshop consultants:
ETH Zurich:
Prof. K. Daniels
Dr. Dan Nguyen dai
B. Eng. L. Ilg
B. Eng. B. Strickler
School of Engineering Luzern:
Prof. U. Pfammatter
Prof. M. Trawnika
Ch. Fierz
I. Zemp
Façade consultation:
B. Eng. A. Compagno

Model site plan
for Figure series 92

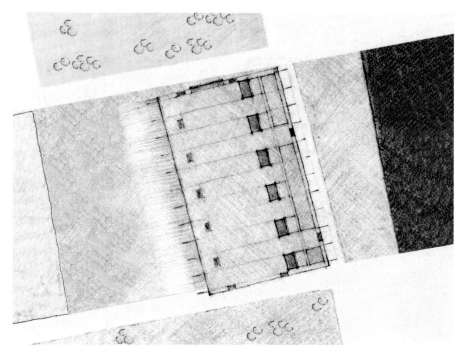

Model site plan
for Figure series 93

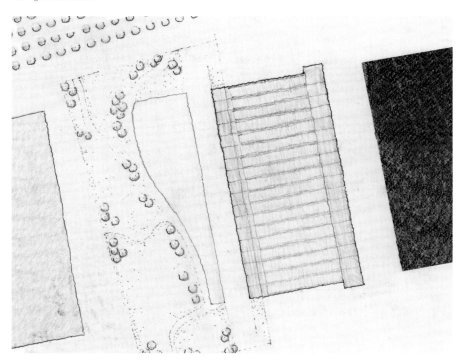

Figure series 92

Students in group 1:

René Herger
Simon Hess
Phil Indermühle
Paula Koch
Melinda Koopman
Gianreto Laager
Thomas Lehmann
Stefan Maag
Roger Oehrli
Serge Siegrist
Daniel Zemp

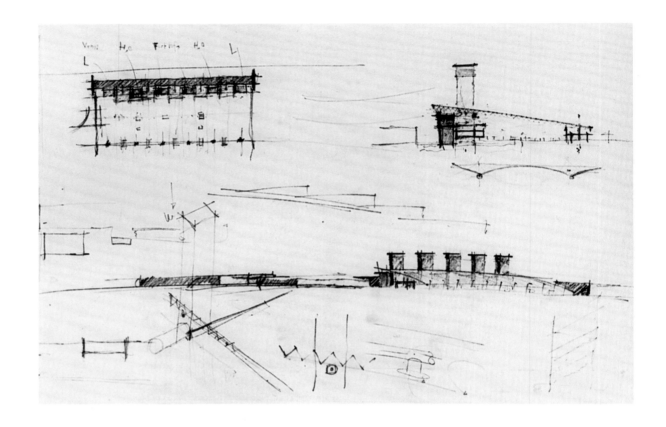

Figure series 93

Students in group 2:

Isab. Anderhalden
Michael Bucher
Florian Felder
Patrick Renold
H.U. Rechsteiner
Rahel Schmid
Matthias Sulzer
Michael Wetter
M. Winterhalder
Patrick Zimmerli
Heinz Zurkirchen
Sebastian Zwissig

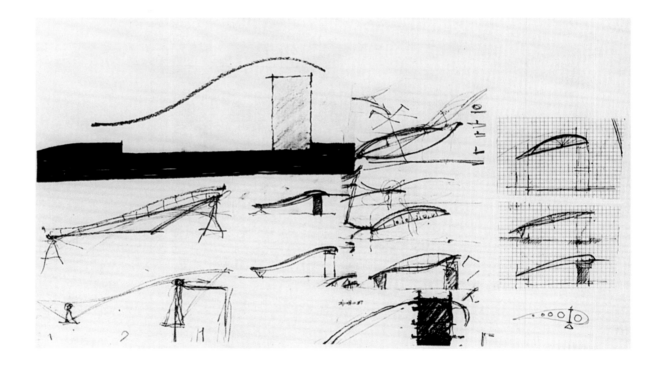

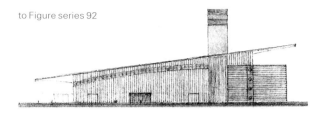

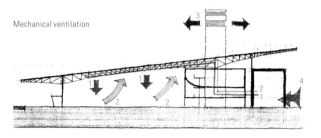

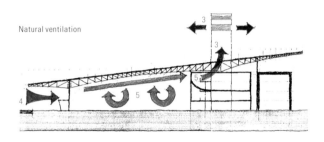

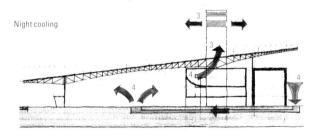

to Figure series 92

Mechanical ventilation

Natural ventilation

Night cooling

1 Supply air
2 Extract air
3 Exhaust air
4 Fresh air
5 Mixed air

to Figure series 93

1 Natural ventilation
2 Mechanical ventilation

Air flow in room:
3 Warm air flow by radiation
4 Warm air flow by convection

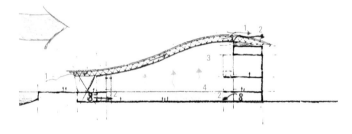

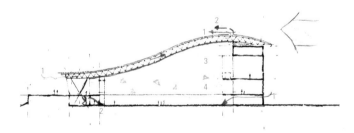

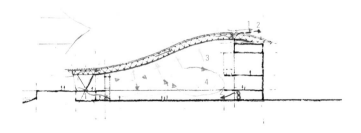

5.3
Skyscrapers

A close look at skyscrapers, e.g. in New York or Chicago (Figure 94), reveals that the newer, as well as the older, tall buildings are often equipped with openable windows. This author has long pleaded with developers to construct their skyscrapers in future so that, in the event of an energy crisis, they can be naturally ventilated (with heating by perimeter systems) and users be given the option of opening small window units for natural ventilation.

In general, it is important to note that when skyscrapers are naturally ventilated, precautions should be taken to counter high wind pressures and to ensure that pressure and suction forces on large window surfaces do not prevent people from opening the window units. The need for naturally ventilated skyscrapers and consideration of the ecological aspects have inspired several new designs in recent years. Some of these are currently under construction and will be presented on the following pages. The illustrations represent the draft or design phase of each project; modifications are still possible or may already have been made during the building phase, resulting in some discrepancy between draft-stage planning and the final building.

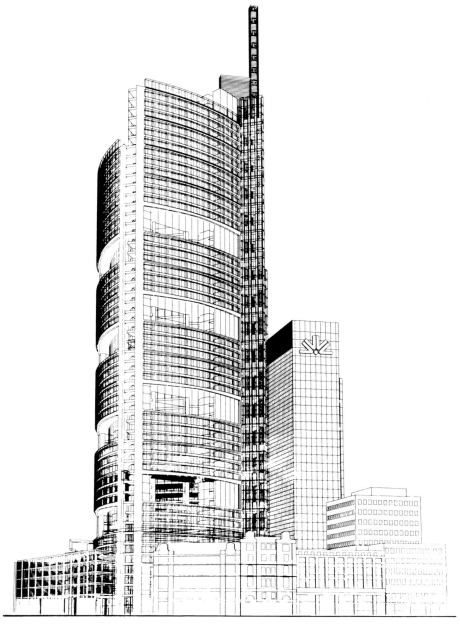

Figure 95.2
Typical floor plan
(initial design phase)

Figure 95.1
Building in the urban environment
(initial design phase)

The Commerzbank Building, Frankfurt

In the skyscraper designed by Sir Norman Foster and Partners, London, for the Commerzbank, Frankfurt, the planned three-storey winter gardens spiralling around the building, became four-storey while the double-leaf façade became single-leaf. Another fundamental change was to integrate the elevator areas in the service cores, which had previously been annexed in the 'fish tail'. However, the basic idea remains unchanged.

Figures 95 and 96 show the plan of the building site and the building in its urban setting. Here, we see a typical floor of the building, the integrated winter garden, and the courtyard behind it, as well as a cross-section of the building with the winter gardens staggered over three storeys (concept design). These provide natural ventilation for the adjacent office areas by erecting an initial barrier against high wind pressures and/or the influx of excessive amounts of fresh air. The winter gardens furnish all the usual advantages associated with them: heat gain, improved microclimate, reduction of external temperatures in the winter garden by evaporative cooling, etc.

Figure 94
The Chrysler Building in New York is an 'old', naturally ventilated skyscraper. View from Cloud Club

Figure 96
Commerzbank headquarters, Frankfurt
Site plan
(Architects: Sir Norman Foster and Partners, London)

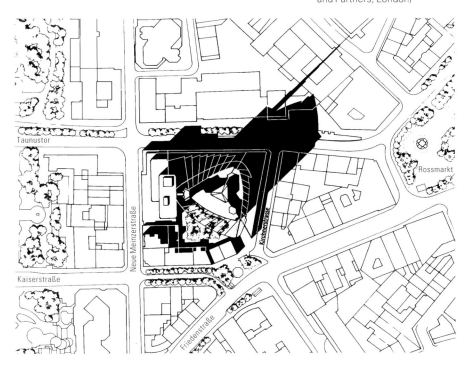

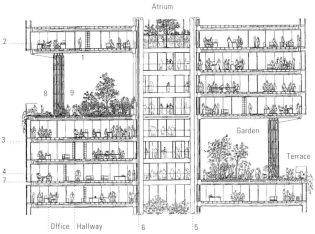

Figure 95.3
Cross section of building with winter gardens (draft)
Cross section and detail

1 pre-stressed concrete ceiling with integrated air ducts
2 adjustable sun protection
3 single glazing
4 double-glazed, floor to ceiling sliding doors
5 atrium glazing, floor to ceiling sliding doors
6 glazed ballustrade
7 girders
8 double glazing with openable windows (top and bottom)
9 'Vierendeel' (quadrilateral) girder

The design furthermore envisions a double-leaf façade for those office areas directly on the perimeter, to reduce suction and pressure forces in this area and to enable the installation of windows openable towards the work space. The passive measures in the façade area include elements which minimize the heating as well as the cooling requirements of the building. Of course, appropriate shading and heat and glare protection play an important role.

Heating requirements can be minimized by outfitting the entire building with insulating glazing with a thermal transmittance coefficient (u-value) of approx. 1.4–1.6 W/m^{2}K. In addition, the plan envisioned a protective outer skin or envelope, reducing the convective heat flow towards the outside during the day or which can be closed during the night in winter (dampers) to form a static air cushion as insulation. The winter gardens further contribute to the passive heat gain.

Cooling requirements (insolation and convective heat gain) can be minimized by using infrared-reflecting sealed double panes with inert gas filling for the winter gardens as well as a curtain wall for the perimeter office areas. This design makes these external shading measures feasible, because corresponding shades or blinds are installed behind the glass panes or can be set up in the winter gardens. The design also envisions the implementation of a ventilated, high thermal mass ceiling which can be used to cool the building over night (night air changes approx. 3–4ac/h, untreated fresh air).

By design, this building is ventilated naturally through either buoyancy or oncoming winds, so that its windward and lee orientation suffice for ventilation. During intensive solar radiation and activated external shading, the initial reduction of incident heat energy through the external glass envelope is followed by a second, massive reduction of heat radiation through the solar shading.

Thermal lift (or stack effect) develops (Figure 97.1), which thoroughly ventilates the façade cavity, causing the outside air entering from behind the shading to create an air flow which, in turn, provides a secondary circulation through the rooms. The air flow through the façade enters the rooms through opened window elements, is warmed, and exits again.

During direct solar radiation and calm days (approx. 3 % of the year), natural ventilation caused by buoyancy is clearly measurable, since the temperature increases per storey by approx. 1.5–3 K (for direct solar radiation) or by 1 K per floor on overcast days. Natural ventilation through buoyancy on calm days proves ineffective only when external temperatures are significantly higher than internal temperatures.

Figure 97.2 represents natural ventilation under the influence of wind and shows that only one-third of the building faces the windward side while two-thirds face the lee-side. Given Frankfurt's average wind velocity of approx. 4 m/s and measurable differences between the upper and lower building sections, it is safe to assume that the dynamic pressures, and/or suction forces, will naturally ventilate the building the whole year round when corresponding window elements are opened.

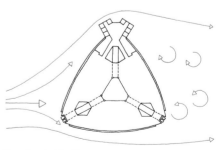

Oncoming wind direction

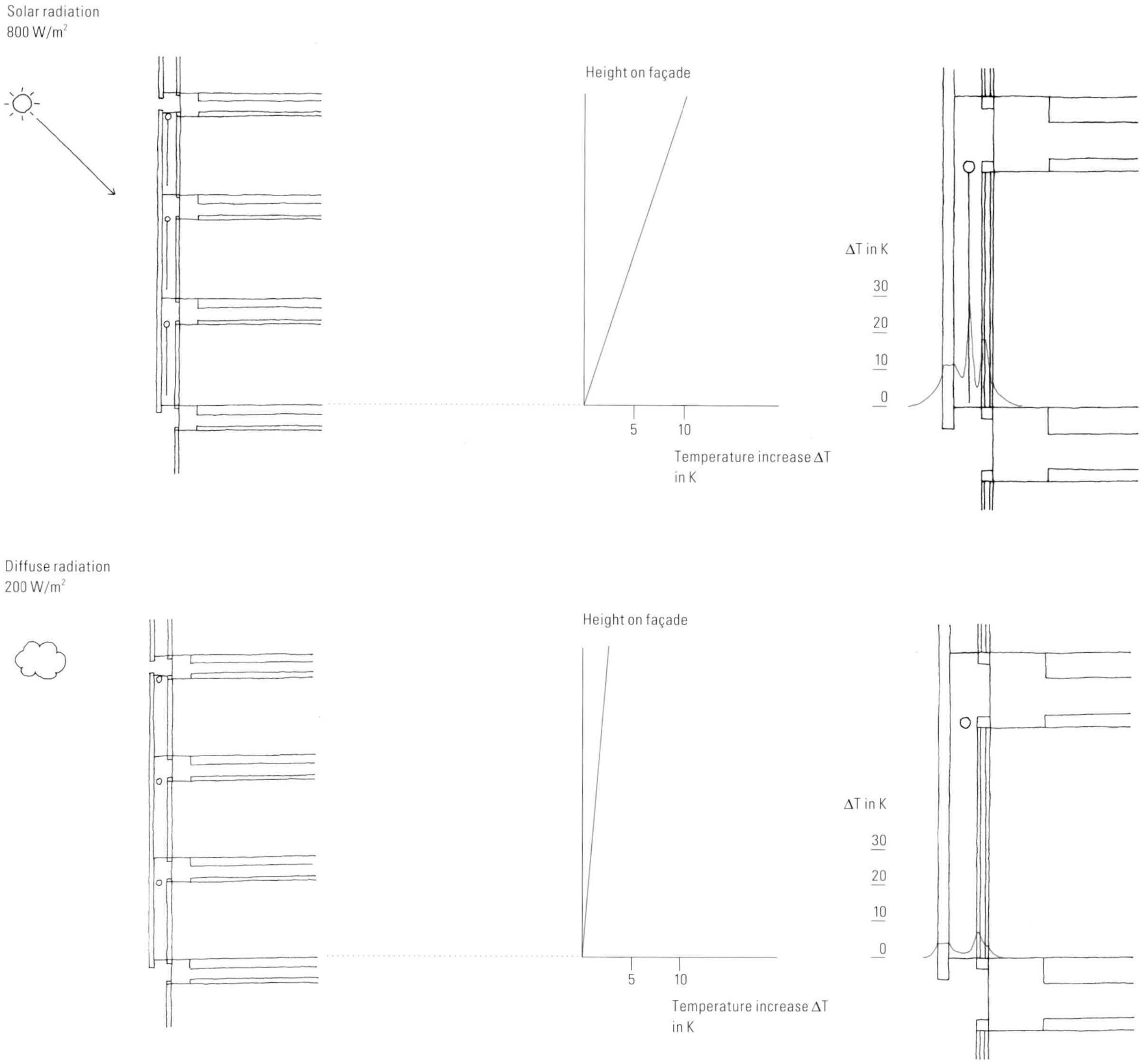

Solar radiation
800 W/m²

Height on façade

ΔT in K

30
20
10
0

5   10

Temperature increase ΔT
in K

Figure 97.1
Natural ventilation in high-rise
through thermal buoyancy

Temperature increase in
ventilated façade for sunny and
overcast skies

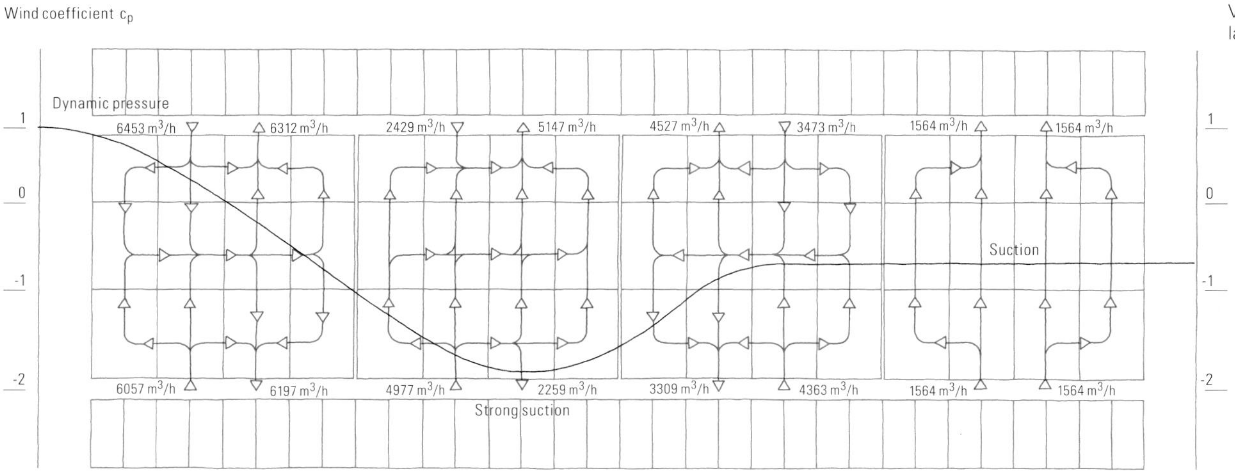

Diffuse radiation
200 W/m²

Height on façade

ΔT in K

30
20
10
0

5   10

Temperature increase ΔT
in K

Figure 97.2
Natural ventilation in high-rise
for windy conditions

Volume flow in cavities of ventilated façade, façade layout

Wind coefficient c_p

Dynamic pressure

1

0

-1

-2

6453 m³/h ▽   △ 6312 m³/h   2429 m³/h ▽   △ 5147 m³/h   4527 m³/h △   ▽ 3473 m³/h   1564 m³/h △   △ 1564 m³/h

Suction

6057 m³/h △   ▽ 6197 m³/h   4977 m³/h △   ▽ 2259 m³/h   3309 m³/h ▽   △ 4363 m³/h   1564 m³/h △   △ 1564 m³/h

Strong suction

1

0

-1

-2

93

In winter, all perimeter office areas can be assumed sufficiently, naturally ventilated, although it must be noted that a mechanical ventilation would save energy and provide for hygienic air conditions while regaining heat energy. The natural ventilation of the 'inner' (adjacent to the winter garden) offices and the building cross ventilation is better than in the perimeter offices due to the location of the winter gardens. They act as thermal buffer zones, in which direct or diffuse radiated heat energy helps to heat the entire building. During transitional seasons, i.e. when external temperatures range from approx. +5°C to +15°C, the same principles apply as during winter operation, although during this period mechanical ventilation is unnecessary because of the generally comfortable ambient temperatures.

The opening of windows (tilt-turn type) is feasible when main winds are moderate. These openings have been shown to generate air changes of 4–6 ac/h in a room. When main wind velocities are high and external temperatures fall below 15°C, windows should be kept closed, and a secondary means of ventilation or heating (possibly also humidification) resorted to. Floor to ceiling ventilation is best at this point, to create hygienic air flow through the rooms. Of course, each occupant in any room can manually activate the airconditioning and heating system and open windows temporarily (fresh air surge) to return to a natural ventilation.

Figure 98.1 depicts room temperatures during the transitional season (blue). The left half of the building shows daytime temperatures with natural ventilation only and the previous night's cooling, the right half temperatures after the building has been ventilated during the night, taking the storage effect of the ceilings into account. When calms occur in summer, the building must once again be ventilated and cooled by additional means, since, otherwise, the rooms will overheat. During this period, the winter gardens are opened wide to admit warm outside air at temperatures of approx. +32°C and to cool the air by approx. 0.5 to 1 K with the help of the dense internal foliage and evaporative cooling. The naturally cooled outside air moves through the courtyard into the central shaft area and continues onward to the next winter garden, where it exits from the building.

The red numbers in Figure 98.1 represent hot, summer room temperatures over the course of a typical day. At night, in anticipation of a hot summer day, the storage masses of the building are cooled with external air, whereby chilled ceilings (enthalpy regulation) absorb and release heat energy. Equipping rooms with chilled ceilings across approx. 50 % of the total ceiling area ensures sufficient storage capacity to maintain cool room temperatures on the following day from approx. 21°C (8 a.m.) to 28.5°C (6 p.m.) without resorting to airconditioning.

The building has been fitted with ventilation systems to maintain hygienic air levels. These systems conduct additional air into the rooms through a double floor to eliminate contaminants and odours. The extent of mechanical ventilation, and for cooling, used during the day can be decided by each occupant, simply by pushing a button or opening a window.

The frequency of natural ventilation (Figure 98.2 top) at this location during one year, taken as a reference point, reached 70 %. Only on 9 % of the days did high outside temperatures so elevate room temperatures that it was necessary, and indeed advisable, to use airconditioning. For 21 % of the total number of days, to achieve heat recovery, it seemed advisable not to rely exclusively on natural ventilation.

Nevertheless, natural ventilation is possible during this period. The aforementioned study yields the following percentages for natural ventilation of the building indexed to the total hours of operation (Figure 98.2 bottom):

– ventilation with cooled air, approx. 15 %,
– ventilation with untreated outside air 12 %,
– cooling by natural ventilation approx. 73 %.

Figure 98.3 compares the energy requirement for a naturally ventilated room with that for the same space conventionally (or mechanically) airconditioned.

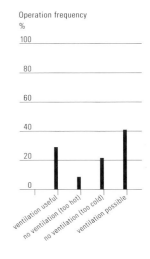

Operation frequency
%

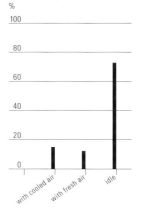

Operation frequency
%

Figure 98.2
Percentages of requirement for:
window ventilation during the day (above)
night cooling (below)

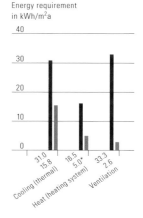

Energy requirement
in kWh/m²a

Figure 98.3
Energy requirements in standard room

■ conventional air conditioning system
■ natural concept
* heating subsequent to fresh air surge

Figure 98.1
Temperature simulations
(24 hours) in offices
External and room temperatures
over the course of one day
left column day, right column night

Summer (September 1st)
Transitional season (May 10th)

In conclusion, Figure 99 illustrates the current state of the planned building. The ground plan of the 50-storey skyscraper is triangular, with rounded corners and gently curved side walls. The 4-storey-high winter gardens are arranged spirally staggered over the building height. Altogether, there are nine winter gardens planted according to their orientation and providing adjacent offices with natural ventilation and lighting as well as views of the city. The glass wall enclosing the winter gardens is fitted with openable units to ensure fresh air intake.

The interior zones are mechanically ventilated with the minimum air-change rates required for hygiene, while a perimeter heating installation and chilled ceilings regulate room temperatures. The interior façade is composed of heat-insulating tilt-turn windows, with an integrated exhaust damper (small pivot-hung windows) and single glazing near the parapet. The exterior façade (double skin façade) consists of single and multiple glazing, to comply with radar requirements. Fresh air can enter the lower area of each ceiling through the ventilated façade cavity and can exit through louvres near the pivot-hung window.

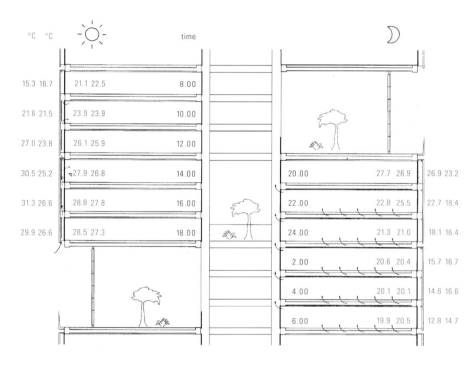

°C °C   time

15.3 16.7	21.1 22.5	8.00
21.6 21.5	23.9 23.9	10.00
27.0 23.8	26.1 25.9	12.00
30.5 25.2	27.9 26.8	14.00
31.3 26.6	28.8 27.8	16.00
29.9 26.6	28.5 27.3	18.00

20.00	27.7 26.9	26.9 23.2
22.00	22.8 25.5	22.7 18.4
24.00	21.3 21.0	18.1 16.4
2.00	20.6 20.4	15.7 16.7
4.00	20.1 20.1	14.6 16.7
6.00	19.9 20.5	12.8 14.7

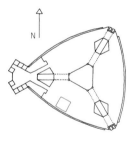

N

Floor plan location of office studied

Figure 99
View of Commerzbank head-quarters (model) in urban environment and typical floor plan

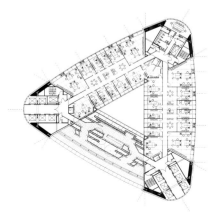

Skyscraper Project, Frankfurt

Another project developed to design stage is the skyscraper shown in Figure 100 (architects: Prof. Schweger & Partners; Building Climatology, Aerophysics, Building Services HL-Technik AG). This 52-storey skyscraper (200 m high), planned as a naturally ventilated building, consists of a square and a cylindrical tower; both building sections are linked by a transitional zone with elevator cores and traffic areas. The usable spaces within the building extend to the exterior walls; there are no internal zones, as can be seen in the ground plan (see Figure 104.1). Hence, office areas are naturally ventilated directly from the outside in without any larger buffer zones, conservatories, or similar constructional elements.

The original plan proposed one of three window options (single pane, double pane). It had to be determined which façade would best fulfill the task of natural ventilation with optimum shading and glare protection at minimum cost. The façade options in question are shown in Figure 101. Essential criteria for further deliberations are:

- frequency of wind velocity at site (Figure 102),
- average wind velocities at site,
- wind direction distribution at site,
- number of calms per year at site.

The excerpt from wind statistics for Frankfurt (Figure 103) shows that the main wind directions are south-west and north-east; furthermore, judging from the average wind velocity, it is clear that the highest wind velocities are from the west. Frankfurt experiences calms during 3.4 % of the year, with the notable exception of July and September, which attain frequencies of 5.7 % and 5.3 %, respectively.

The pressure coefficients at the building circumference are especially important, since they establish the pressure distribution on the (outer) envelope, depending upon wind speed and the direction of oncoming wind. Pressure and suction conditions on the outer envelope create air flow toward and away from the building, as well as cross ventilation from the pressure side of the building toward the suction side (windward-leeward-situation).

Figure 100
Classic high-rise, designed for natural ventilation
(Architects: Prof. Schweger & Partners, Hamburg; Climatology, and Building Services Design: HL-Technik AG, Munich; Aerophysics: Kessler + Luch, Gießen)

Figure 101
Façade options

Option 1
Triple pane system
with solar protection
Box window

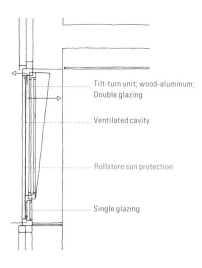

Tilt-turn unit; wood-aluminum;
Double glazing

Ventilated cavity

Rollstore sun protection

Single glazing

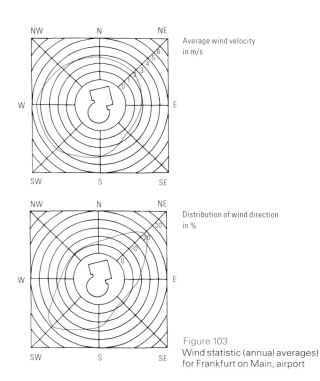

Wind velocity
in m/s

Figure 102
Annual frequencies of wind
velocities in Frankfurt on Main

Option 2
Single-leaf façade
Sun protection glass
Heat insulation glass

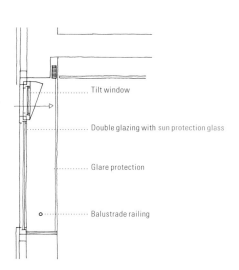

Tilt window

Double glazing with sun protection glass

Glare protection

Balustrade railing

Average wind velocity
in m/s

Distribution of wind direction
in %

Figure 103
Wind statistic (annual averages)
for Frankfurt on Main, airport

Option 3
Double-leaf façade with
stack ventilation
(Twinface, Alco Façade
Systems)

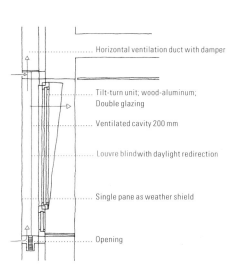

Horizontal ventilation duct with damper

Tilt-turn unit; wood-aluminum;
Double glazing

Ventilated cavity 200 mm

Louvre blind with daylight redirection

Single pane as weather shield

Opening

Figure 104.1
Distribution of pressure
coefficients on perimeter
South-west wind

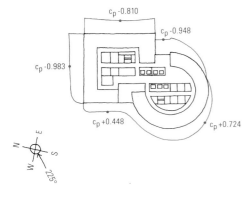

Figure 104.2
Pressure distribution on high-
rise (cylindrical ground plan)
South-west wind

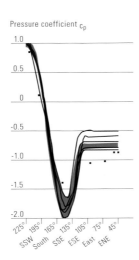

Figure 105.1
Distribution of pressure
coefficients on periphery
North-east wind

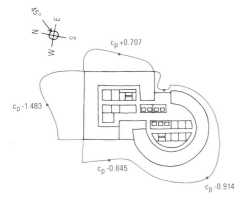

Figure 105.2
Pressure distribution on
high-rise (square ground plan)
North-east wind

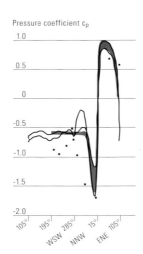

■ recorded values in flow
experiment (Kessler + Luch)
— documented reference
values
— pressure
— suction

Pressure Coefficients on the Façade (Mathematical Verification)

Figures 104.1 and 104.2 show the building sub-
jected to a main wind coming from the south-
west. Positive and negative pressure coefficients
are marked at the exterior of the building, describ-
ing the pressure distribution across the entire
building surface. The pressure coefficients for
main wind from south-south-west (225°), relative
to the cylindrical section of the skyscraper (Figure
104.2), exhibit noticeable differences. The first
computer simulation of the curves also includes
measurements from the wind tunnel study conducted in the laboratory of Keßler + Luch GmbH,
to be described hereafter. They show that, even in
an initial approximation, a computer simulation
gives useful hints on the distribution of pressure
coefficients.

Figure 105.1 describes the distribution of pressure
coefficients while the main wind is coming from
the north-east (45°). A comparison of Figure 105.1
and Figure 104.1 clearly indicates that the square
tower results in a less advantageous air flow than
the cylindrical tower. Figure 105.2, in turn, shows
the distribution of the pressure coefficients, relative to the square ground plan of the skyscraper,
with a comparison of the calculated values to
the wind tunnel experiment. The dimensionless
pressure coefficient c_p is generally used to
simplify the evaluation and comparison of such
experiments. Figure 106 illustrates the local wind
pressure coefficients of a square tower with its
windward and lee sides and its side walls, as well
as an elevation of the skyscraper.

Simulation with Buoyancy and Main Wind Directed at a Double-Leaf Façade with Shaft Ventilation

For the double-leaf (Twinface) façade (Figure 101,
option 3), a continuous shaft is planned in every
second axis from the second to the fifty-first floor,
to ventilate the 'box windows' next to the shaft
by stack effect. To achieve the desired thermo-
syphon effect from the box window into the shaft,
a density differential between the air in the shaft
(warmed or heated air) and the surrounding air is
necessary. The stack effect is, however, considerably influenced by the friction resistances inside
the shaft, as well as by the oncoming wind from
the outside (see Figure 202, page 157).

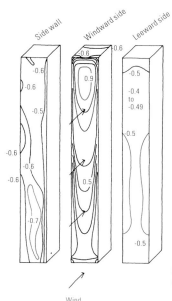

Figure 106
Distribution of pressure coefficients on square tower

Wind

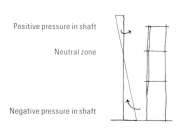

Positive pressure in shaft

Neutral zone

Negative pressure in shaft

Figure 107
Positive and negative pressure created by stack ventilation in façade

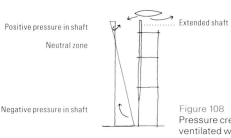

Positive pressure in shaft

Neutral zone

Extended shaft

Negative pressure in shaft

Figure 108
Pressure created in stack ventilated with high extended shaft and convex disc

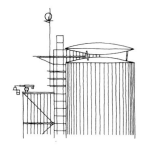

Figure 109
Roof line of cylindrical tower

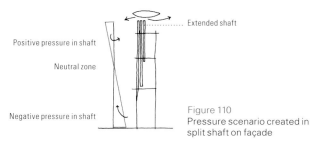

Positive pressure in shaft

Neutral zone

Extended shaft

Negative pressure in shaft

Figure 110
Pressure scenario created in split shaft on façade

Natural ventilation by buoyancy results in a neutral zone near the middle elevation of the façade, independent of the temperature difference between the air in the shaft and the outside air. In this scenario, fresh air enters the shaft in the lower region of the façade and exits again in the upper region. This may conduct exhaust air to the upper floors, an undesirable effect for the occupants on those floors. Figure 107 outlines the situation. To move the neutral zone as close as possible to the roof line of the building, it is necessary to extend the shaft and at the same time to achieve a high negative pressure near the chimney mouth, which would then exhaust the shaft. Figure 108 illustrates the working principle, Figure 109 a roof line in the form of a convex disc (similar to a 'Venturius'). To improve flow conditions with the help of the stack effect, an attempt was also made to divide the entire ventilation shaft into three sections, each creating a neutral zone near the roof (Figure 110).

The effect of this type of shaft ventilation is shown in the schematics in Figures 111 for buoyancy, dynamic pressure, and suction. The schematics list the relevant storey (second to fifty-first floor), together with air volumes, in m^3/h, outside the window and inside the shaft. Depending upon outside influences (buoyancy, pressure, suction), very different volumes of air are exhausted from the building. The flow resistances between windows and exhaust shaft were adjusted in order to equalize the suction in the ventilation shaft.

Another simulation reproduced the conditions during strong winds, in particular, the predicted average pressures. Figure 112 lists the positive and negative pressures in pascals (Pa), where 1.000 Pa is approximately equivalent to a weight of 100 kg/m^2. A comparison of positive and negative pressure areas in the upper floors shows that pressure differentials of approx. 170 to 200 kg/m^2 occur in the lateral faces between box windows and shaft. The difficulties caused by these pressures can be easily imagined; and it becomes evident that a shaft ventilation corresponding to option 3 would be a most unsuitable choice for skyscrapers and should only be used for buildings with a maximum of 8–10 floors.

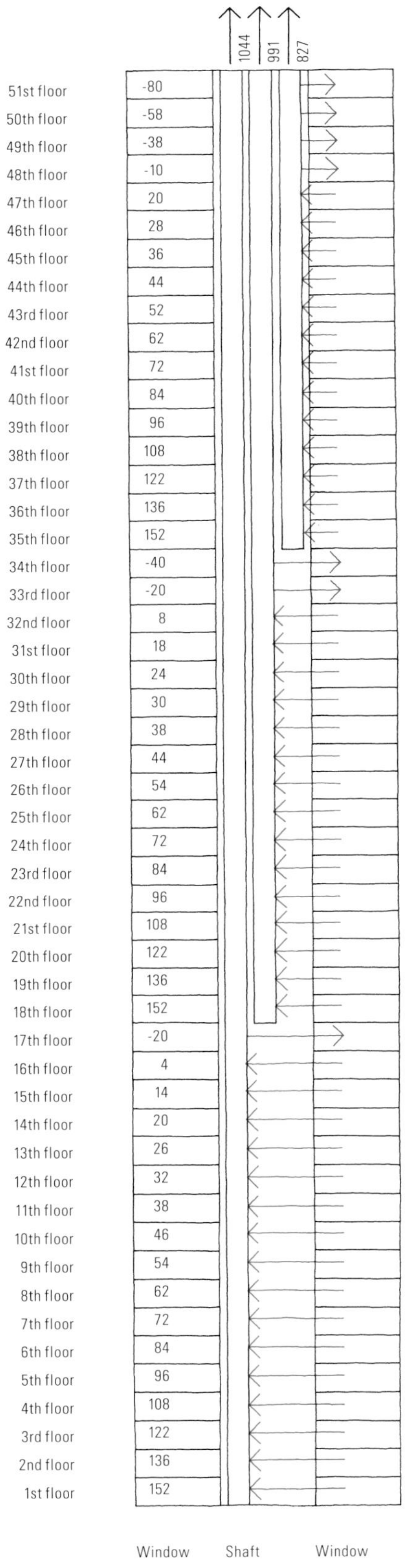

Figure 111.1
Schematic of shaft ventilation in façade; natural ventilation by thermal buoyancy ($\Delta T = 10$ K)

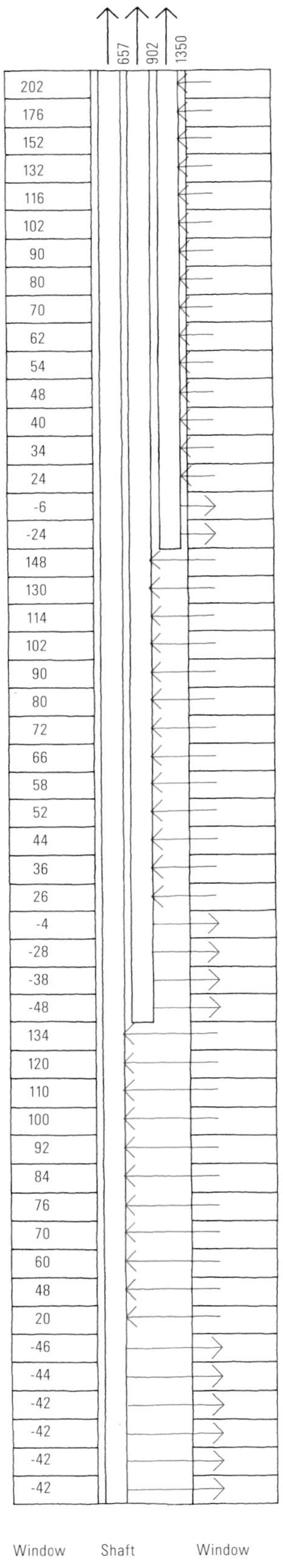

Figure 111.2
Schematic of shaft ventilation in façade; natural ventilation by wind ($w_m = 12$ km/h) Dynamic pressure ($c_p = +11.0$)

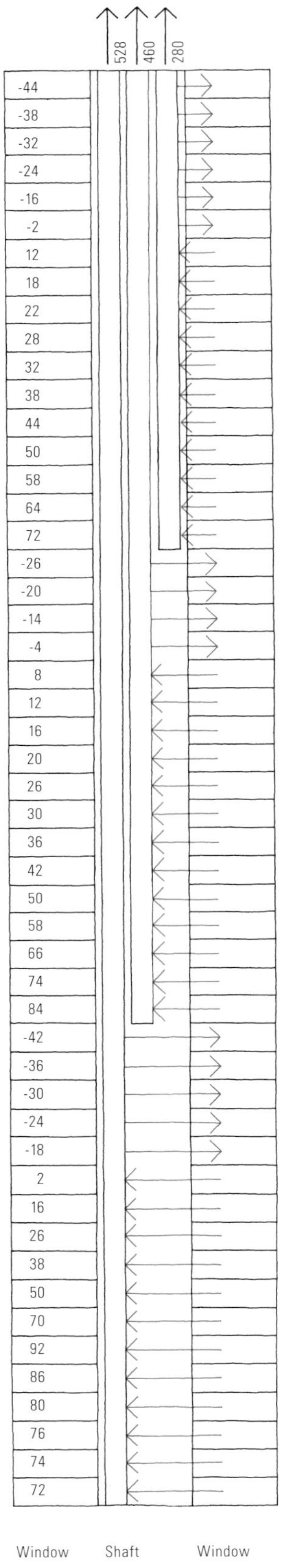

Figure 111.3
Schematic of shaft ventilation in façade; natural ventilation by wind ($w_m = 12$ km/h) Strong suction ($c_p = -2.0$)

Figure 112
Adjusted flow resistances Positive and negative pressures in shaft ventilation in façade

Figure 111.1 shaft top values: 1044, 991, 827
Figure 111.2 shaft top values: 657, 902, 1350
Figure 111.3 shaft top values: 528, 460, 280

Floor	111.1 Window	111.2 Window	111.3 Window	112 Window	112 Shaft	112 Window
51st floor	-80	202	-44	699	-1041	699
50th floor	-58	176	-38	690	-1018	690
49th floor	-38	152	-32	680	-997	680
48th floor	-10	132	-24	670	-976	670
47th floor	20	116	-16	661	-956	661
46th floor	28	102	-2	651	-937	651
45th floor	36	90	12	641	-919	641
44th floor	44	80	18	631	-902	631
43rd floor	52	70	22	621	-886	621
42nd floor	62	62	28	611	-870	611
41st floor	72	54	32	600	-855	600
40th floor	84	48	38	590	-841	590
39th floor	96	40	44	579	-828	579
38th floor	108	34	50	569	-815	569
37th floor	122	24	58	558	-803	558
36th floor	136	-6	64	547	-792	547
35th floor	152	-24	72	536	-781	536
34th floor	-40	148	-26	524	-7771	524
33rd floor	-20	130	-20	513	-762	513
32nd floor	8	114	-14	501	-753	501
31st floor	18	102	-4	489	-744	489
30th floor	24	90	8	477	-736	477
29th floor	30	80	12	465	-729	465
28th floor	38	72	16	453	-722	453
27th floor	44	66	20	440	-715	440
26th floor	54	58	26	427	-709	427
25th floor	62	52	30	414	-704	414
24th floor	72	44	36	400	-699	400
23rd floor	84	36	42	386	-694	386
22nd floor	96	26	50	372	-689	372
21st floor	108	-4	58	358	-685	358
20th floor	122	-28	66	343	-681	343
19th floor	136	-38	74	328	-678	328
18th floor	152	-48	84	312	-675	312
17th floor	-20	134	-42	295	-672	295
16th floor	4	120	-36	278	-669	278
15th floor	14	110	-30	261	-667	261
14th floor	20	100	-24	242	-665	242
13th floor	26	92	-18	222	-663	222
12th floor	32	84	2	201	-662	201
11th floor	38	76	16	179	-660	179
10th floor	46	70	26	155	-659	155
9th floor	54	60	38	127	-658	127
8th floor	62	48	50	95	-657	95
7th floor	72	20	70	53	-657	53
6th floor	84	-46	92	0	-656	0
5th floor	96	-44	86	0	-656	0
4th floor	108	-42	80	0	-655	0
3rd floor	122	-42	76	0	-655	0
2nd floor	136	-42	74	0	-655	0
1st floor	152	-42	72	0	-655	0

Column labels (each figure): Window · Shaft · Window

Buoyancy on Façades

During calms, a lift or buoyancy boundary layer results from thermals at the façade, depending upon the temperature difference between building and outside air, the principle of which is shown in Figure 113. The temperature difference between building and outside air is considerably affected by the incident radiation and the absorption coefficient of the building envelope. Assuming a maximum temperature difference of 20 K between building and outside air, the boundary layer in the upper floors can be expected to reach a velocity of 20 km/h. On hot windless summer days, the temperature differences may be significantly greater than 20 K; differences of up to 50 K have been recorded on existing skyscrapers, so that even the buoyancy velocity and the thermals may exceed the values indicated here.

Relevant relationships are given in Figures 114 and 115. Figure 114 illustrates the maximum air velocity in the boundary layer, Figure 115 the air movement along the façade, induced by buoyancy, depending upon the building height and the temperature difference between boundary layer and exterior space.

It is interesting to observe that even smaller skyscrapers, when they heat up, circulate large amounts of air, contributing to the ventilation of the urban space.

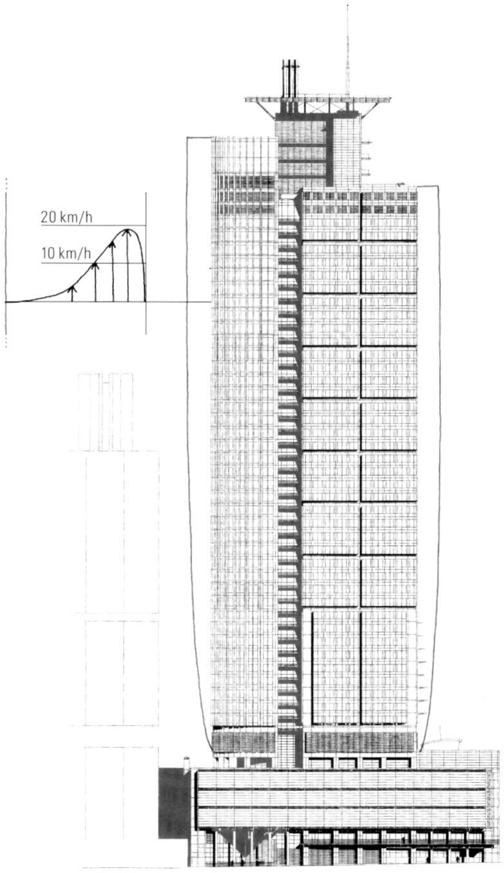

Figure 113
Thermal buoyancy on façade with 20 K temperature difference
Velocity profiles in boundary layer

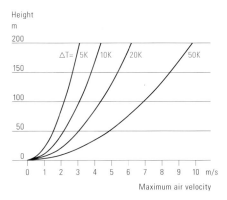

Figure 114
Maximum air velocity in boundary layer due to thermal buoyancy on façade

To Figure series 111
The numbers in the schematic represent the total volume of air in m³/h flowing into the shaft from the window units and the total volume of air exiting from the shaft respectively. The blue arrows mark façade units and hence offices where the air flow from the shaft is directed toward the office, red arrows mark air flow directed toward the shaft.

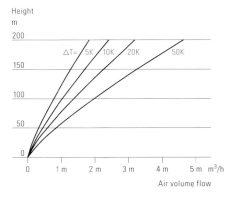

Figure 115
Air volume flow in boundary layer due to thermal buoyancy on façade

Air Exchange in Office Areas with Varying Façade Designs

In laboratory experiments, the air-change rate in a standard office was examined relative to windward or lee-side exposure and the window-opening angle of a box window and a single-leaf façade respectively. The result is shown in Figure 116. An average oncoming wind velocity of 3.4 m/s was assumed. As the data show, a box window with a peripheral joint of 18 mm on the lee side results in air-change rates which are too low, since these should be at least 2–2.5 ac/h in an office. Hence, to achieve acceptable rates, the joint should be enlarged to approx. 35 mm. In addition, Figure 117 depicts a situation in which the box windows are completely opened for natural ventilation and the pivot-hung windows are opened to 45°. The average wind velocity is assumed to be 3.4 m/s; the main oncoming wind direction is south-west (windward side). As is evident from the figure, a 45° opening of the pivot-hung windows results in very high air-change rates on the windward as well as on the lee-side, which means that this angle is generally unrealistic. At the same time, the box window should be designed as a tilt-turn window for more versatility. Figure 117 also shows that the average wind velocities common in the Frankfurt area are very conducive to natural ventilation, i.e. there is sufficient air change to extract contaminants and heat.

Depending upon design, type of construction, façade structure, etc., twin façades may vary in depth, up to a depth allowing access. For this reason, further experiments were undertaken to establish the difference in air change for these varying depths in box windows. Figure 118 illustrates such air-change rates in a standard office with various depths of box windows under the same criteria as those used for Figure 117.

If box windows are to be fitted with horizontal and vertical or only horizontal or only vertical joints, then further differences in ventilation emerge. These are shown in Figure 119 for oncoming winds and buoyancy respectively. The diagrams are helpful for roughly calculating the intake volume of air at the box window for each criterion.

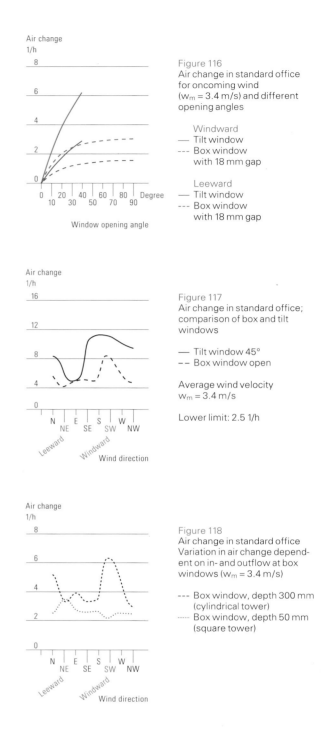

Figure 116
Air change in standard office for oncoming wind (w_m = 3.4 m/s) and different opening angles

Windward
— Tilt window
--- Box window with 18 mm gap

Leeward
— Tilt window
--- Box window with 18 mm gap

Figure 117
Air change in standard office; comparison of box and tilt windows

— Tilt window 45°
–– Box window open

Average wind velocity w_m = 3.4 m/s

Lower limit: 2.5 1/h

Figure 118
Air change in standard office Variation in air change dependent on in- and outflow at box windows (w_m = 3.4 m/s)

--- Box window, depth 300 mm (cylindrical tower)
...... Box window, depth 50 mm (square tower)

Figure 119
Box window ventilation during oncoming wind and thermal buoyancy respectively

Box window with 300 mm depth and 35 mm gap

III vertical louvres
III horizontal louvres

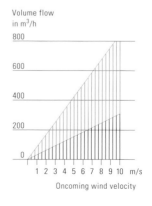

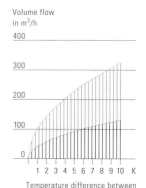

Flow Conditions in the Building

Cross-ventilation, and hence flow conditions, in a building depend not only on closed or opened windows but also on whether air movement through the building is possible. Figures 120 and 121 show flow conditions under various assumptions.

When windows are opened, the flow resistances near the façade are diminished, outside pressures become dominant, and the inner resistance (inner doors) takes on greater importance. It is assumed that all office and hallway doors (dividers) are tightly sealed (gap or joint ventilation coefficient $a_F = 3.0 \ m^3/m \ Pa^{2/3}$). When doors are opened in an office, the volume flows from the offices across the hall areas to the leeward façades. The cross ventilation is relatively intensive as a result, and air velocities of 0.2 to 0.3 m/s are quite possible near open doors.

When office doors leading to the corridors are closed, air flow is only just perceptible (Figure 120.2). The conditions are similar when office doors are closed but corridor doors are opened (Figure 120.3). The schematics in Figures 121.1 to 121.3 show that oncoming wind from the north-east produces similar results.

Open windows during high wind velocities (storms) cause such a strong cross-ventilation that pressure differences at closed office doors reach levels of between 200 and 600 Pa, making them impossible to open. Hence, it is important that windows be kept shut when air velocities outside exceed 10 m/s, to avoid complications in the operation of the building.

Open windows and average wind velocities (up to approx. 5 m/s) create conditions in which office doors should mostly be kept closed, since open doors cause intensive cross-ventilation, which can no longer be regulated by ventilation and air-conditioning systems. Keeping office doors closed during average wind velocities will result in low differential pressures and a problem-free environment. Closed fire doors on one floor can increase the internal resistance enough to improve cross-ventilation. Therefore, interior doors should also be located so as to optimize the air dynamics in the building.

South-west wind
Average wind velocity:
4.3 m/s

North-east wind
Average wind velocity:
2.7 m/s

Figure 120.1
Flow conditions in building with opened office doors

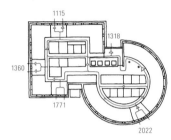

Figure 121.1
Flow conditions in building with opened office doors

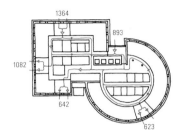

Figure 120.2
Flow conditions in building with closed office doors

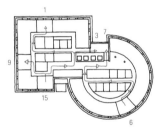

Figure 121.2
Flow conditions in building with closed office doors

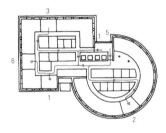

Figure 120.3
Flow conditions in building with closed office doors/opened corridor doors

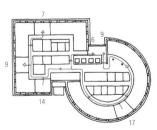

Figure 121.3
Flow conditions in building with closed office doors/opened corridor doors

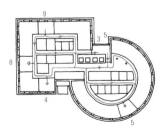

Numbers
indicate volume flow in m³/h

Numbers
indicate volume flow in m³/h

Wind Tunnel Studies with Varying Scale Models

To back up theoretic calculations and deliberations, tasks of this complexity should be tested
in a wind tunnel on models scaled from 1:300 to
1:100. The model scale is determined by the size
of the urban area to be studied (built environment)
and the size which can be accommodated in the
wind tunnel used.

In urban situations, as in Frankfurt, a large number of skyscrapers will considerably influence one
another, to almost incalculable effect. Figures 122
and 123 show a section of the site plan and the
location of the building studied within this environment (scale 1:100).

In Figures 124 through 127 various air currents are
made visible by smoke along and around the
skyscraper, as well as at the roof line. Figures 128
illustrate, in schematic form, typical air currents
and descending draughts on the buildings and air
movement in the streets, based on conclusions
drawn during wind tunnel studies. As these
sketches show, velocity increases noticeably
between individual skyscrapers and neighbouring
building fabrics, and strong turbulences occur
on the leeward side of the buildings. At the same
time, ascending or descending currents are observable on the façades, depending upon where
the stagnation point is, as are strongly turbulent
boundary layer currents near the top of the skyscraper combined with descending air movement
on the windward side. In naturally ventilated
buildings, fresh air supply for occupied areas and
knowledge about whether and how emissions
affect opened office spaces are vital issues; the
streamlines observed in the air movements
around the building are especially important for
deciding the correct placement of exhaust
air openings, chimneys or stacks, and cooling
towers.

Pressure Coefficients on Façades for Varying Air
Currents Around Buildings

Pressure coefficients on buildings should be
studied thoroughly. To this end, a number of
measurement probes are placed on and around
the model. Figure 129 shows several such probes
on the building (model) and a graphic representation of the pressure coefficients. The coeffi-

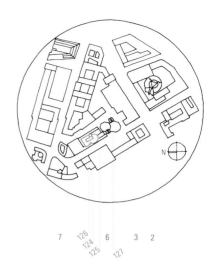

Figure 122
Turntable and model set up

1 Bank, height 275 m
2 Bank, height 110 m
3 Centre, height 102 m
4 Bank H1, height 125 m
5 High-rise H2, height 200 m
6 Built periphery,
  height 37 m
7 Insurance I, height 37 m
8 Tower, height 90 m

Figure series 124 – 127
Air flow images (smoke) in wind
tunnel

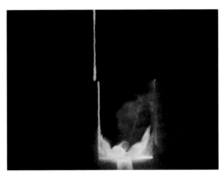

Figure 124
Air flow in street area

Figure 125
Descending air flow below
stagnation point

Figure 126
Air flow image at roof line with
leeward eddy

Figure 127
Accelerated flow between two
high-rises

Figure 123
Model and urban environment
(neighbouring buildings)

cients are clearly identifiable for oncoming wind from the south-west, and thus the pressure profile across the height of the south-west façade on the round and the square tower, as is their distribution on the façade at a height of 93 m with defined windward/leeward orientation.

Aside from the measurements recorded on the building itself, readings must also be taken at the street level, to evaluate the influences or dynamics created by a dense skyscraper environment on the surrounding microclimate.

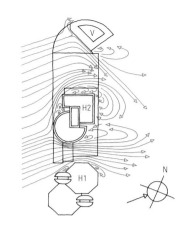

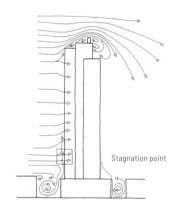

Figure 128
Typical air-flow pattern, floor plan and elevation, south-west wind

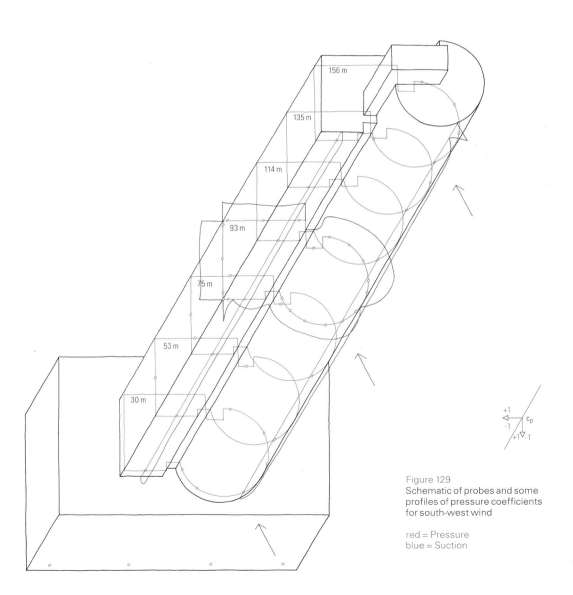

Figure 129
Schematic of probes and some profiles of pressure coefficients for south-west wind

red = Pressure
blue = Suction

Air Movement in Street Areas

To record air movement at street level, additional probes have to be placed on the model, which also record influences by roof areas of surrounding, lower buildings. Figures 130 and 131 again show a measurement grid, Figure 132 the percentages of wind velocity in the street area relative to the oncoming wind velocity w_0. As this figure demonstrates, air velocities in the street area are approximately 20–40 % of the oncoming velocity.

The air movement between neighbouring buildings displays different characteristics, although in this case, too, there are no noticeable velocity increases when an average velocity of approx. 3.3 m/s is assumed. These are approx. 20–40 % (Figure 133). Figure 134 furthermore illustrates a separate study of velocity fluctuations in the street area. This study proves that velocity fluctuations (wind gusts) are relatively low and are only approx. 0.3–0.4 m/s for an oncoming velocity of 3.3 m/s.

Figure 130
Location of probes
Wind velocities
(pos. 1–6 probe at 1.80 m)

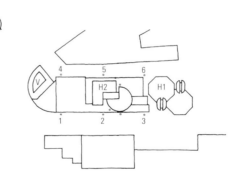

Figure 131
Location of probes
Wind velocities

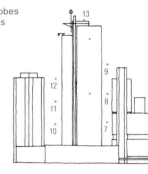

Figure 134
Fluctuating wind velocities
in street area
Probe No. 2
Pedestrian zone
South-west wind
$w_0 = 3.3$ m/s

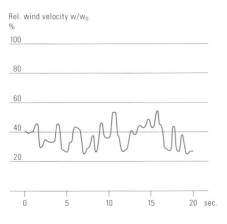

Figure 132
Wind velocities
Street areas
(locations as in Figure 130)
$w_0 = 3.3$ m/s

■ Wind SW
■ Wind NE
■ Wind S

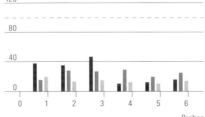

Figure 133
Wind velocities between
buildings
H2 - H1, H2 - V
$w_0 = 3.3$ m/s

■ Wind SW
■ Wind NE

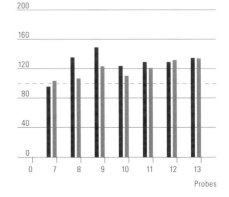

Degree of Contamination at Fresh Air Intakes

The degree of contamination describes the concentration of a contaminant across the dispersion area. When the average gas concentration at a measuring point is related to the specific emission factor, the result represents the dilution factor of the contaminant. The emission factor results from the source type and volume as well as its location.

Put simply, it is a question of determining whether air exhausted, above a roof, for instance from canteens, kitchens, restaurants, exhaust fumes etc., reaches intake locations, i.e. air-intake vents, on the building and in pedestrian areas as well as on façades with openable windows.

To prevent influx at openable windows, air-intake vents, etc., attempts must be made to expel the exhaust fumes as high as possible into the boundary layer region or above it. If necessary, the exit velocity of relevant gases must be so increased that contaminated exhaust air cannot settle onto the building. The diagram in Figure 135 serves as an initial assessment of the effective emission height h. It illustrates the interaction between exit areas, the relationship of exit velocity to mean wind velocity, and the resulting height difference between exhaust opening and emission height. Here, the height of the boundary layer stream is very dependent upon the influences of the built environment, the wind velocity, and the air flow on the building. The boundary layer stream may reach heights of several metres, resulting in an effective emission height of 5–10 m.

Natural Ventilation for Offices in Tall Buildings

The air change in office areas (see Figure 116, page 102) is usually reproduced in detail in model experiments, where Plexiglas models of varying scale are used. Figure 136 shows a floor of the cylindrical tower in Plexiglas and a section of the façade with box windows (Prof. Dr. R. Detzer, Kessler + Luch).

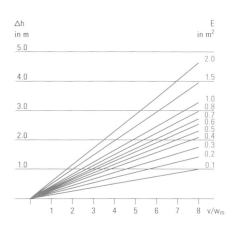

Figure 136
Plexiglas model rooms
for detail studies

E   = emission area
v   = emission velocity
w_m = mean wind velocity
h   = effective emission height

Figure 135
Diagram for calculation of
effective emission height h

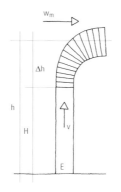

Figures 137 and 138 show model façades on a scale of 1:20 for the variation using a double-leaf (box windows) or single-leaf (opening light) façade. The air movement in the room is made visible by smoke (Figure 139). This figure also shows the typical eddy movement near the ceiling when air is drawn into the room from the outside, whereby it is important that the air can spread tangentially near the ceiling without hindrance or draught.

With an oncoming air velocity of 3.4 m/s, the various air changes on the model are quantified. To determine air change, the room is filled with an indicator gas, the measured dilution of which, over time, provides an index for the air-change rate. Figure 140 plots the air-change rates induced by oncoming air from the south-west for a box window and a tilted fanlight. It is evident from the comparison that when tilting light windows are used, air flow through the room is more intense, the interior window unit on the box window being tilted 20° and the fanlight in the single-leaf façade 45°. The graph in Figure 140 proves that an opening of 45° is usually not necessary: a 15° angle is sufficient to achieve the desired air-change rates of approx. 2–3 ac/h.

When the above mentioned opening angles are used with box windows (300 mm deep, 35 mm wide, 20° opening), the annual frequency distribution of air change is as shown in Figure 141. The graph shows that, for 130 days of the year, the desired air change is not reached, so that during these days secondary ventilation must be used to create comfortable and hygienic room conditions. When opening lights are used (45° opening), the 2.5 ac/h air change is not achieved on only 20 days of the year. Thus, it may be assumed that an opening light is generally better suited to ventilate rooms naturally than a box window unit and/or a double-leaf façade.

To help evaluate all these interactions, Figure 142 shows a range of comfort, delineating, in the lower region, a comfort limit (according to DIN 1946/2) for differences between inside and outside temperatures and, in the upper region, an average oncoming air velocity of 3.1 m/s. This graph indicates that the greater the difference is between inside and outside temperatures, the smaller the air-change values should be, i.e. window units should be restrained, to prevent uncomfortable conditions in the room.

Figure 137
Model of double-leaf façade
(scale 1:20)
Box window
Measurements in mm

Figure 138
Model of single-leaf façade
(scale 1:20)
Tilt window
Measurements in mm

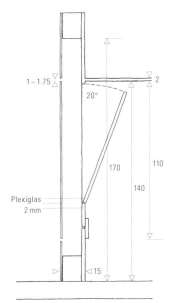

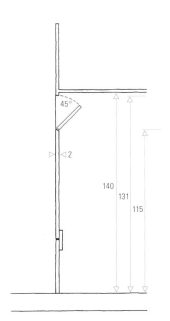

Figure 139
Smoke is used to give a picture
of air flow.

The windward and lee-side influences upon a box window are the subject of Figure 143. It shows that rooms on the windward side with a 30 mm wide joint have an air-change rate of approx. 5.3 ac/h, while lee-side rooms have only 3 ac/h. Since all these rooms, observed over the course of one year, may at one point or another be on the lee-side, the corresponding lee-side curve must be used as a design guide.

When the depth of the box window is decreased, for instance from 300 mm to 50 mm, then the lee-side exhibits the least dynamic air movement; in other words, the air-change values in this case are too low. To achieve satisfactory air-change rates in natural ventilation, care should therefore be taken to select sufficient cavity widths (>200 mm) for box windows in double-leaf façades and thermal-insulation glazing.

A final point to be considered for natural ventilation is smoke management. Should a fire break out, windward oncoming air flow in the room can be observed to cause the smoke to seep through the cracks whereupon it dissipates quickly and spreads along the façade, to left and right, much diluted. It is so diluted that only small amounts, which may on occasion flow into the rooms, are observable at neighbouring windows. On the lee-side, most of the smoke emitted flows directly into the surrounding air, minimizing any backflow of smoke on the façade caused by unstable, local, vertical and horizontal eddy formations along the façade. Since the eddies' movements are irregular, it is unlikely that the rooms will suffer more than slight contamination. Thus, in case of fire, any significant effect from smoke ventilation on adjacent rooms may be discounted.

When oncoming outside air moves parallel to the building surfaces, a plume of smoke forms on the building surface and drifts away only when it reaches the lee-side. However, smoke and fresh air are meanwhile so mixed that the smoke is much diluted and causes little damage.

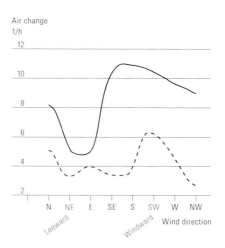

Figure 140
Air change in office dependent on wind direction

— Single-leaf façade,
Fanlight 45°
-- Box window 300 mm

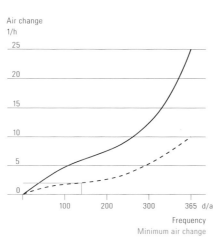

Figure 141
Annual frequency of air changes

— Tilt windows
-- Box windows 300 mm,
Gap width 35 mm

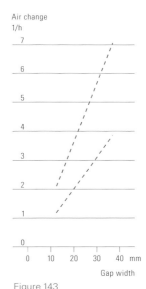

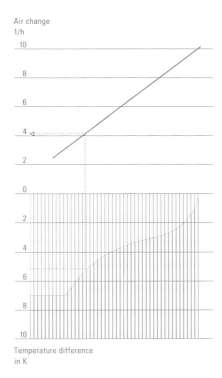

Figure 143
Air change dependent on wind direction and gap width (Twinface) box window depth 300 mm, $w_m = 3.4$ m/s

-- Windward ($c_p = 0.6$)
-- Leeward ($c_p = -0.8$)

Figure 142
Comfort zone

— average oncoming velocity 3.1 m/s
III comfortable
III uncomfortable
— boundary of comfort zone (DIN 1946/2)

Figure 145
Skyscraper in Essen
(Architects: Ingenhoven,
Overdiek + Partners, Düsseldorf)

Figure 144
Cylindrical skyscraper in urban
setting

RWE AG Main Office Building, Essen

The planned site of this skyscraper is a larger development project in Essen, Germany. In this project, too, it was a question of single- or double-leaf façade. The project is the design of architects Ingenhoven, Overdiek and Partners, Düsseldorf, who have chosen an aerodynamically favourable form (cylinder), the main features of which will be discussed here. Figure 144 shows the site location within the built environment, Figure 145 the skyscraper at night.

General

The skyscraper shown in the architects' model photograph is a 31-storey cylindrical tower with a double-leaf façade. This double-leaf façade is intended to provide good natural ventilation for perimeter office areas (Figure 146). The space inside the façade is supplied with outside air through a meandering arrangement of intake and exhaust louvres.

When the windows are opened, pressures from oncoming wind on the outer envelope are carried forward into the interior of the building and can create an intense cross-ventilation, depending upon interior resistance – especially doors – with such effects as:

– excessive force needed to open doors,
– draughts in offices and corridors,
– 'whistling' at cracks.

These limits define the extent to which natural ventilation is possible.

Natural ventilation may be restricted or influenced by such constructional parameters as:

– façade layout,
– ventilation slits or louvres,
– air-tightness of windows and doors,
– design of doors (revolving doors, opening and closing mechanisms).

In the study of these factors, cross-ventilation was investigated during natural ventilation. To limit the effect of wind in the building, a comparative study was made of a design for equalizing wind pressures inside a circular double-leaf façade, as it related to the wind pressures and to the development of summer temperatures inside a façade with standard box windows, respectively.

Figure 146
Cross-section of skyscraper
detail

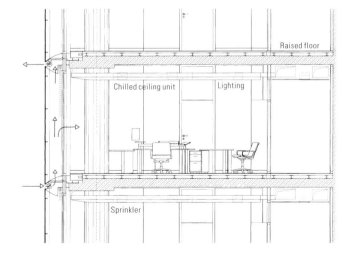

Wind Conditions

The wind conditions prevailing in Essen are described in Figure 147. They are comparatively moderate, with maximum wind velocities below 17 m/s (approx. 130 hours of operating time above 10 m/s and approx. 230 hours above 8 m/s). Winds are predominantly from the south, the south-west, and the west (a total of 60 % relative frequency throughout the year). The mean wind velocity (from DIN 4710) is 4.0 m/s. These wind velocities are measured at the local weather station.

Taking into account different wind profiles near the skyscraper and the meteorological conditions, it has been found that, at a height of 110 m, the wind velocities exceed by approx. 20 % the values measured at the weather station and, in the middle region (height approx. 60 m), wind velocities (average) increase by approx. 5 %. The latter value was used to simulate the cross-ventilation.

Building Aerodynamics

For the simulation, wind-pressure coefficients were determined in a wind tunnel study. Figure 148 shows the qualitative course of pressure distribution on the exterior for four different wind directions. The negative pressure peak for a cylinder, created by cross-winds, typically differs by approx. 80–90° from the stagnation point. The annexed elevator shaft causes a deviation from the pressure distribution observed on a perfectly round cylinder. The oncoming winds from the north-east to the south-west especially, do not bring about a defined suction peak near the elevator shaft.

The characteristic pressure coefficients for cylinders, measured in a wind tunnel, range from +1.0 to -2.3. The marked differences in pressure are likely to cause intensive cross-ventilation.

Façades

The double-leaf façade is intended to maintain floor by floor separation with the help of horizontally arranged dividers. The outer skin is fitted with one lower and one upper ventilation louvre per grid line. To prevent exhaust-air influx into the lower floors, the exhaust louvre is diagonal in relation to the intake louvre. With regard to the lateral dividers, the following variations were studied:

– box windows,
– perimeter double-leaf façade with two sectors.

– Box Windows
Vertical dividers in the façade seal the individual axes from one another and dampen the sound carried within the façade cavity, in effect creating a box window (Figure 149).

– Perimeter Double-Leaf Façade
When a vertical divider is not used, the façade is only divided into separate sectors (north-east and south-west skin) by the two elevator shafts. Within these two sectors, the air taken in through the façade can flow in the direction of the perimeter of the building.

Figure 147
Wind statistic for Essen
(annual mean values)

— TRY data
region 3 accord. to averaged
values from DIN 4710
(Met. stations Essen-Mühl-
heim and Essen-Bredeney)

— DIN 4710
(Met. station Essen-
Bredeney)

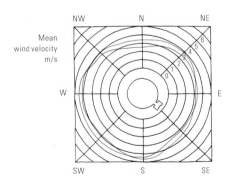

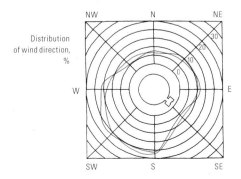

Figure 148
Qualitative Pressure
distribution on built envelope
for oncoming wind

Wind pressures
(approx.) during
north-east wind

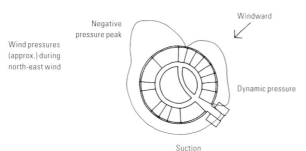

Wind pressures
(approx.) during
east-west wind

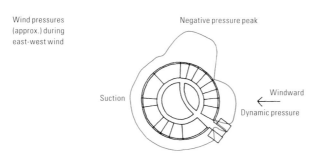

Wind pressures
(approx.) during
south-west wind

Wind pressures
(approx.) during
west-east wind

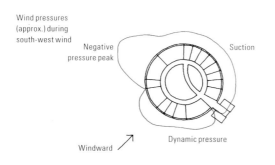

Figure 149
Sketch of façade structure
(box window variation)

Reduction of Wind Pressures

Without vertical dividers, the wind pressure can be partially reduced through free air movement in the direction of the building circumference in the double façade cavity. The pressures inside the perimeter façade are essentially defined by the relation of the flow resistances for the ventilation louvres and by the façade cross-ventilation (depending upon the distance between the double-leaf façade and the constructional components inside the façade).

The following diagram (Figure 150) depicts the range of pressure on the outer skin and in the façade cavity, as a result of the flow resistance for steady state conditions. These results are sufficiently exact for the evaluation of natural ventilation. For other purposes (structure, façade stresses etc.), such external conditions as wind coefficients, flow resistance at the site, gustiness of wind, etc., would also have to be evaluated. It is clear that the wind pressure differences acting in the cavity, circumferential across two sectors, can be reduced by 50 % during easterly wind in comparison with results given for the box window variation.

Figure 150
Typical pressure distribution on standard floor during east wind
Façade structure

— external
— façade perimeter
-- box window

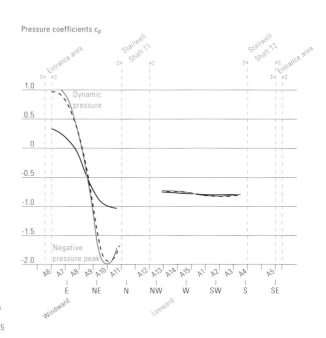

Natural Cross-Ventilation

The final simulation reproduces natural cross-ventilation, based on the pressure coefficients resulting from the wind-tunnel experiment. Since the wind coefficients are temporal mean values, the resulting calculation was a quasi steady state cross-ventilation. The intensity or degree of cross-ventilation and potentially increased door-opening forces are dependent on:

– the situation in which windows and office doors are opened,
– the wind direction,
– the wind velocity.

At this point, it is appropriate to mention that the wind pressure fluctuation, not considered in the wind coefficients, creates, despite the small ventilation slits, an additional one-way air change between office and surrounding area, which is combined with the cross-ventilation within the building. Since an additional one-way air change is also created by differences in temperature between office and surroundings, the following results should be regarded as an evaluation of draught in the building.

To simulate cross-ventilation, observations were made of the following opening situations for easterly wind at an average velocity of 4 m/s:

– in each office: one open sliding window,
– in two windward offices (opening to the north-east façade) and in one office located at the negative pressure peak (on the north-east envelope): one sliding window each,
– in one windward office (facing the north-east façade): one sliding window; in the negative pressure area (facing the south-west façade) three offices have opened windows.

It is assumed that the opened gap of the sliding windows is 15 cm and that office doors are completely open for this simulation.

The following diagrams (Figures 151) compare the air-change behaviour in the opening situations under observation for the perimeter façade (double-leaf) and the box window variation.

Offices with open sliding windows are identified in the diagrams as:

blue = intake air
red = extract air

Open and closed office doors are marked in the floor plan. The numbers represent hourly air-change rates due to natural cross-ventilation.

– Box Windows
When all sliding windows are opened (Figure 151.1 left), the air-change rate in a biaxial office space is up to 39 ac/h; in larger offices, this rate decreases proportionately. Offices near the dynamic pressure and at the negative pressure peak are most strongly cross-ventilated. Offices at the south-west envelope are less strongly cross-ventilated because the operative pressure differences taper off.

When sliding windows are opened in windward offices and in the office at the negative pressure peak (Figure 151.2 left), the air-change rates are predictably high (46 ac/h), since these are the areas where the maximum wind pressure differential has its greatest impact.

For the third opening configuration (Figure 151.3 left), the peak value is lower, 25 ac/h, since the pressure difference between the maximum at the north-east envelope and the negative pressure area in the south-west envelope is not as defined as in the windward tract.

– Perimeter Double-Leaf Façade
In contrast to the box-type windows, when windows are opened on all sides in this configuration (Figure 151.1 right), the air-change rates (max. 49 h^{-1}) are higher in both building envelopes since the intake and exit air respectively, of an office can enter/leave through several louvres whereas, for box-type windows, this is possible only through the opening louvre within the grid line, because of the divider.

When only some sliding windows are opened to the inner façade (Figure 151.2 right), the air-change rates are higher than observed for all-round opened sliding windows (max. 68 ac/h), since the outer air can flow more strongly across all air louvres of a façade segment towards the windows.

When office windows are opened in opposite envelopes (Figure 151.3 right), the room ventilation is almost double that observed when box windows are used. The air-change rates are less, despite the opposite envelopes, because a complete pressure balance is not achieved inside the north-east envelope and high pressure differences remain. The intensive air exchange between the two sectors can be counteracted by closing office doors.

Influence of Window Opening

Occupants can, at any time, lessen the opened gap of the sliding door to manipulate the cross-ventilation in the room and to adjust it to their comfort level. It has been observed that a reduction of the air change from 68 ac/h to 9 ac/h is possible when the gap is reduced from 15 cm to 1.5 cm for the perimeter façade with two sectors, and from 46 ac/h to 13 ac/h for box-type windows. The reduction is stronger in the case of the perimeter façade, because of the pressure balance created by the façade cavity.

Door-Opening Forces

When office doors are kept closed, cross-ventilation is very limited. However, the wind pressures on the outer envelope of the building also affect the offices, exerting pressure on the office doors and hence increasing door-opening forces.

Opening Situation

In the study of the interaction between higher door-opening forces and increased oncoming winds, it was assumed that office doors were kept closed and that the main wind was easterly at a speed of 8 m/s. This situation is schematized in the Figures 152 (page 116). In one situation, the effects were studied in a windward office (north-east envelope) and in three offices on the south-west envelope. The door of the windward office was kept open (Figure 152.3) to dampen the total pressure difference between the two building envelopes at a lee-side office door. This situation represents a critical case with regard to door-opening forces. (Doors not otherwise marked in the diagram are closed.)

Box window   Perimeter façade

Figure 151.1
Air change for average wind velocity
(w_m = 4 m/s)

Air flow parameters:
– oncoming direction: east
– all sliding windows open (gap 15 cm)
– all office doors open

Numbers:
air change 1/h

–ı– opened office door
–·– closed office door
— fresh air
— exhaust air

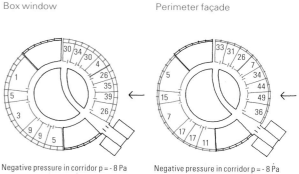

Negative pressure in corridor p = - 8 Pa   Negative pressure in corridor p = - 8 Pa

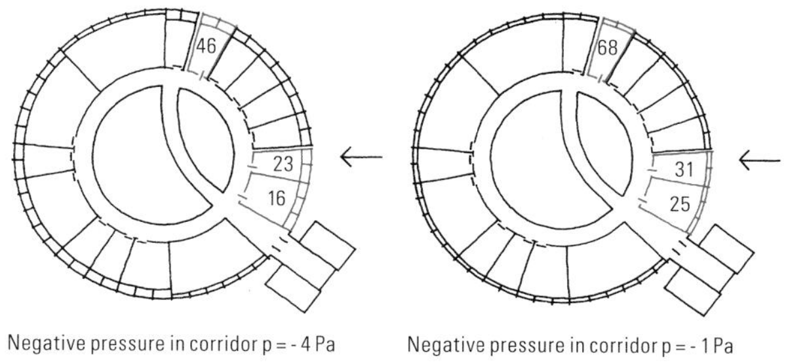

Figure 151.2
Air change for average wind velocity
(w_m = 4 m/s)

Air flow parameters:
– oncoming direction: east
– two leeside windows open as well as one sliding windows at negative pressure peak (gap 15 cm)
– 3 office doors open

Numbers:
air change 1/h

–ı– opened office door
–·– closed office door
— fresh air
— exhaust air

Negative pressure in corridor p = - 4 Pa   Negative pressure in corridor p = - 1 Pa

Figure 151.3
Air change for average wind velocity
(w_m = 4 m/s)

Air flow parameters:
– oncoming direction: east
– one windward and three leeward side windows open (gap 15 cm)
– four office doors open

Numbers:
air change 1/h

–ı– opened office door
–·– closed office door
— fresh air
— exhaust air

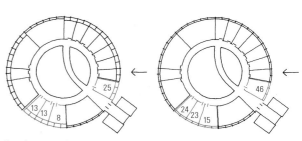

Negative pressure in corridor p = - 7 Pa   Negative pressure in corridor p = - 7 Pa

Evaluation of Door-Opening Forces

The following criteria were used to evaluate the forces acting upon doors:

– Door-opening forces should not exceed 40 N (corresponds to 4 kg) for continued operation.
– Intermittent door-opening forces up to 60 N are tolerable.
– The top limit for openability is a force of 100 N.

A force of 100 N can, according to ergonomical investigations, be opened easily by all persons of small body size. On a door with a surface area of $2\,m^2$, a width of 1 m, and opening to one side only, opening forces of 40, 60 or 100 N correspond to a pressure difference of 40, 60 or 100 Pa, respectively.

Furthermore, the evaluation was based on the assumption that no door closers would be used. When doors are equipped with closers, the opening forces would be exponentially increased by the door-closing force, whenever the operative directions of pressure force and door closers coincide.

– Box Window
Test results for the box-type window (Figure 152 left) were predictably poor. The flow resistance at the air slits is similar to that of the office door joints and can therefore only partially relieve the force acting upon the office doors. For winds of 8 m/s, the door pressure differences are up to 86 Pa, i.e. 86 N (Figure 152.2).

– Perimeter Double-Leaf Façade
For the scenarios studied, the resulting door-opening force was 43 N. The peak value is therefore only half that established for the box-type window. The opening situation with two windward side offices and one office near the negative pressure peak at the north-east envelope clarifies the pressure decrease within one sector of the perimeter façade, with a reduction of the door-opening force for box-type windows from 86 N to 39 N. The situation becomes more critical when windows in offices on both opposite sectors are open. Remarkably enough, the double-leaf façade with two perimeter sectors yields better results than does the box-type window configuration. This can be understood as a result of the simultaneous effect of the dynamic pressure and the negative pressure peak on a built envelope, so that the inner pressures in both envelopes are nearly identical. The remaining door-opening forces of 43 N could be even further reduced by closing individual office doors.

Box window   Perimeter façade

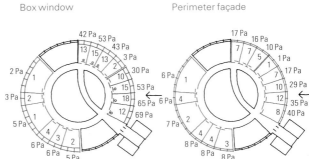

Negative pressure in corridor p = - 29 Pa   Negative pressure in corridor p = - 26 Pa

Figure 152.1
Door-opening forces and air changes for high wind velocity (w_m = 8 m/s)

Air flow parameters:
– oncoming direction: east
– all sliding windows open (gap 15 cm)
– all office doors open

Numbers:
air change 1/h
door-opening forces in Pa

–ı– opened office door
–ᴧ– closed office door
○ pressure difference at door > 40 Pa
— fresh air
— exhaust air

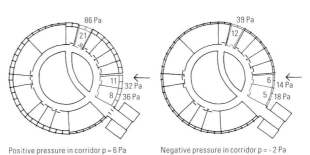

Positive pressure in corridor p = 6 Pa   Negative pressure in corridor p = - 2 Pa

Figure 152.2
Door-opening forces and air changes for high wind velocity (w_m = 8 m/s)

Air flow parameters:
– oncoming direction: east
– two leeside windows open as well as one sliding windows at negative pressure peak (gap 15 cm)
– all office doors closed

Numbers:
air change 1/h
door-opening forces in Pa

–ı– opened office door
–ᴧ– closed office door
○ pressure difference at door > 40 Pa
— fresh air
— exhaust air

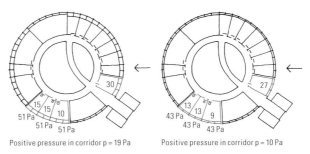

Positive pressure in corridor p = 19 Pa   Positive pressure in corridor p = 10 Pa

Figure 152.3
Door-opening forces and air changes for high wind velocity (w_m = 8 m/s)

Air flow parameters:
– oncoming direction: east
– one windward and three leeward side windows open (gap 15 cm)
– leeward office door open

Numbers:
air change 1/h
door-opening forces in Pa

–ı– opened office door
–ᴧ– closed office door
○ pressure difference at door > 40 Pa
— fresh air
— exhaust air

Operating Restrictions in Natural Ventilation

On the basis of meteorological wind data during the test reference year and an annual simulation, predictions can be made on how frequently natural ventilation may be restricted because of increased door-opening forces or draughts in a typical year (Figure 153). It is difficult to predict in detail how natural ventilation can be utilized; hence, two representative scenarios were chosen to indicate possible limitations. In one scenario, windows and office doors can be opened in the observed office space and in all other offices (15 cm opening, Scenario 1); and, in the other, doors and windows can be opened only in the office space observed and in one other office (mean value, Scenario 2). The results of this simulation must be interpreted with great caution since they assume that these doors or windows would be open all year round. The values therefore indicate only possibilities of potential excesses. Of course, when the air-change rate is too high, each occupant can lessen the window gap and recreate comfortable conditions.

Door-Opening Forces in Office Rooms

Figure 153.1 illustrates the frequency of increased door-opening forces for office rooms; in neither scenario, however, have door closers been taken into consideration. The results exhibit certain differences for both variations of façade design, i.e. for the door-opening forces and for the air-change rates. These differences, however, are not excessive and thus give a fair representation of typical values. For box-type windows, door-opening forces above 60 N may occur, in extreme cases, in Office 6 for approx. 9.5 % (234 h) of the total operating period (Figure 153.1 top). For the perimeter façade, this occurs only approx. 3 % (74 h) of the time in Office 1. Door-opening forces above 100 N should be avoided completely. All the same, they are likely to occur for box-type windows, for 3.5 % of the total operating period and for the perimeter façade for only 0.5 %. In both cases, the highest values are to be found on the south-west envelope. For the perimeter façade, the conditions could be improved by closing individual corridor doors.

The perimeter façade is clearly preferable with regard to door-opening forces. In the box-type window solution, care must be taken that windows remain closed on the upper floors during wind velocities above 8–9 m/s, to avoid excessive values.

Air-Change Rates in Offices

Figure 153.2 indicates the frequency of air-change rates higher than 25 ac/h caused by natural cross-ventilation. Local room flow velocities above 0.15 m/s, combined with air-change rates higher than 25, may be perceived as uncomfortable. The 220 ac/h air-change rate (air velocity of approx. 1.40 m/s near doors) represents a level of air movement strong enough to blow sheets of paper off a table.

In general, office air-change rates are slightly lower for the box-type window variation than for the perimeter façade scenario. Office air-change rates above 25 h^{-1} can occur with the box-type window for approx. 50 % of the total operating period (58 % for perimeter façade). Air-change rates above 200 are practically impossible in both scenarios. These observations apply to a standard floor plan with individual offices. For plan offices, the perimeter façade yields better results.

Summer Temperatures Inside the Façade

The fluctuation of summer temperatures inside the double-leaf façade is important in relation to window ventilation and the transfer heat rate of the offices. In the simulation, an automatic shading device was installed which closes when the solar incidence reaches 250 W/m^2.

Façade Ventilation and Temperature Development in the Course of a Day

Figures 154.1 and 154.2 show the temperature curves inside the façade for a sunny day in July with a maximum temperature of 32°C. The first diagram shows the conditions on a windstill day, the second those during average oncoming wind from the north-east and the south-west.

During calms, the temperature conditions in the box-type window and the perimeter façade are comparable. In the north-east envelope, the temperature peaks at 36°C; in the south-west envelope, at 42°C. Inside the perimeter façade, the maximum temperatures are somewhat offset in the direction of the perimeter.

It's a completely different picture for average wind velocities. The intensive cross-flow on the perimeter façade significantly decreases temperatures. In the north-east envelope, temperatures for both façade variations peak at 32°C; in the south-west envelope, they range from 36.0 to 39.5°C (box-type window) and 33.5 to 37.5°C (perimeter façade).

Box windows

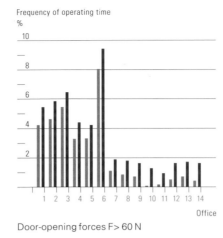

Door-opening forces F> 60 N

Perimeter façade

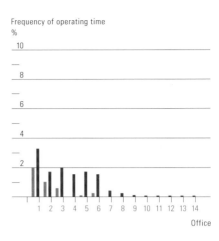

Figure 153.1
Frequencies of comfort loss (F> 60 N) and reduced operation through door-opening forces (F> 100 N) for natural ventilation by wind

■ Scenario 1
■ Scenario 2

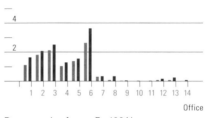

Door-opening forces F> 100 N

Figure 153.2
Frequencies of comfort loss through excessive air changes (AC > 25) for natural ventilation by wind

■ Scenario 1
■ Scenario 2

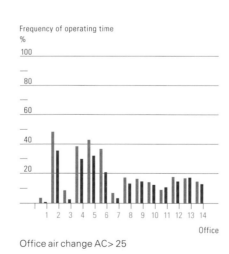

Office air change AC> 25

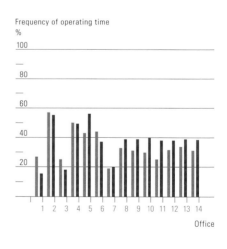

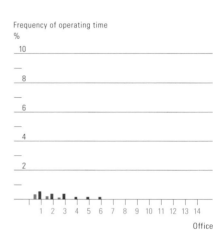

Numbers assigned to offices

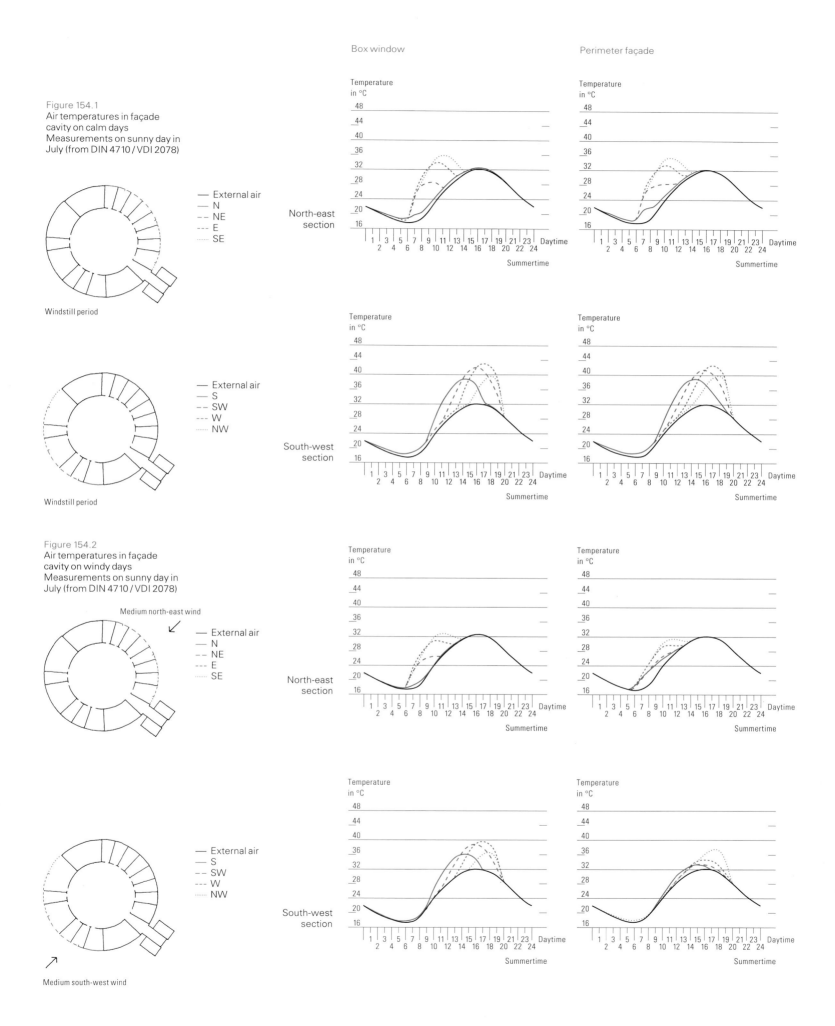

Box window

Perimeter façade

Figure 154.1
Air temperatures in façade
cavity on calm days
Measurements on sunny day in
July (from DIN 4710 / VDI 2078)

Windstill period

— External air
— N
-- NE
--- E
···· SE

North-east
section

Temperature
in °C

Temperature
in °C

Windstill period

— External air
— S
-- SW
--- W
···· NW

South-west
section

Figure 154.2
Air temperatures in façade
cavity on windy days
Measurements on sunny day in
July (from DIN 4710 / VDI 2078)

Medium north-east wind

— External air
— N
-- NE
--- E
···· SE

North-east
section

Medium south-west wind

— External air
— S
-- SW
--- W
···· NW

South-west
section

Box window

Perimeter façade

Figure 155.1
Natural façade ventilation
Air flow volumes
Windstill periods on sunny day
in July

■ Lower ventilation louvre
■ Upper ventilation louvre

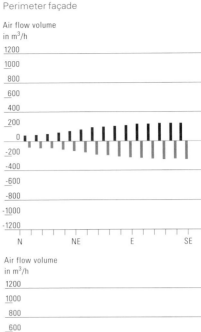

Air flow volume
in m³/h

10 a.m.
North-east section

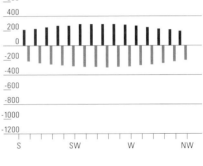

4 p.m.
South-west section

Figure 155.2
Natural façade ventilation
Air flow volumes
Average north-east and south-
west wind respectively on
sunny day in July

■ Lower ventilation louvre
■ Upper ventilation louvre

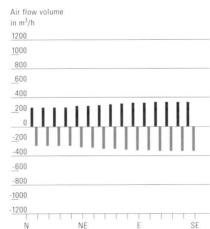

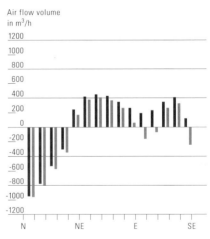

10 a.m.
North-east section

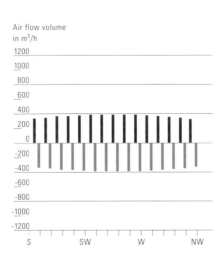

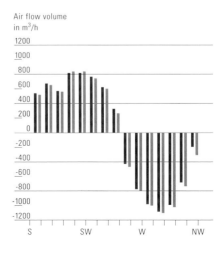

4 p.m.
South-west section

Figures 155.1 and 155.2 illustrate the varying cross-ventilation of both façades. During calms, both variations exhibit almost identical thermal ventilation, where intake air flows through the lower slit and exit air through the upper slit. For oncoming wind, the outside air, in the case of the perimeter façade, flows into the building on the windward side and exits the building on the lee-side. The more intensive cross-ventilation for the perimeter façade has a positive effect on natural ventilation so that some odour may be transported in the direction of the perimeter.

Increased Temperatures in the Course of a Year

The last figure of this experimental sequence (Figure 156) indicates the frequency of increased temperatures within the two façade variations. There are noticeable advantages for the perimeter façade. In the north-east section, depending upon orientation, temperatures rise above 30°C for 3 to 40 hours for box-type windows and 3 to 30 hours for perimeter façades, and temperatures rise above 26°C for 50 to 150 hours for box-type windows and 50 to 130 hours for perimeter façades.

In the south-west section, the differences are even more evident. Temperatures above 30°C can be expected for 10 to 70 hours for box-type windows and 10 to 40 hours for perimeter façades, and temperatures above 26°C for 85 to 180 hours for box-type windows and 85 to 125 hours for perimeter façades during the operating period.

As these observations show with regard to sky-scrapers and low building forms, the natural ventilation of buildings, being very complex, requires expert consultation if a building is to be designed which fulfills its function all year round. Architecture, building climatology and aerophysics merge with each other and must be considered in their totality. Making first estimates during a competition thus requires a great deal of experience.

Box window

Perimeter façade

Figure 156
Frequencies of annual façade temperatures in test reference year (TRY region 3)

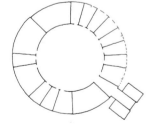

— External air
— N
-- NE
--- E
···· SE

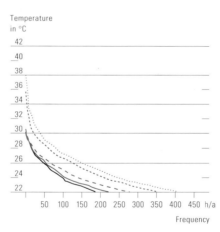

North-east section

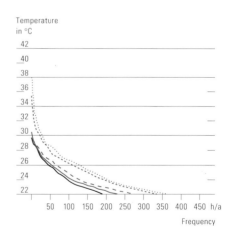

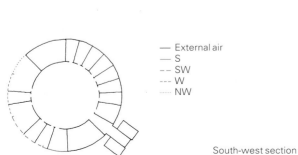

— External air
— S
-- SW
--- W
···· NW

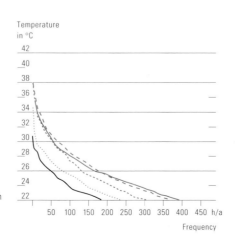

South-west section

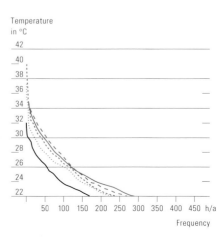

6

Practical experience of storage behaviour in buildings has sufficed for more than 2,000 years to create a comfortable environment with the help of climate and cooling systems. High storage buildings not only improve thermal comfort, they also considerably reduce energy requirements.

6.
Thermal Storage in Building Mass

Another important consideration in the planning of ecological buildings is the thermal capacity of such projects and, as indicated in the previous discussion, the correctness of façade design and surface.

Thermal storage in a building may be decisive for the reduction of cooling loads (heat gain in building) and the reduction of temperature increases. Heat gain in buildings is evident when the heat load is a result of solar incidence or when room temperatures change. In these cases the momentary loads are so changed by the storing elements that the heat gain time function changes into a cooling load time function. For calculating cooling loads, thermal storage may be approached in several ways (storage factors in the room, storage factors in external walls).

The room, as a unit, absorbs radiant heat at the interior surrounding walls, through windows (diffuse and direct solar incidence), (artificial) lighting, occupants, machines, etc., all of which have an effect. How far radiant heat penetrates walls or building storage components depends on the wall layout and the duration of the radiation, thus causing an increase in surface temperatures. The surfaces are in a constant state of reciprocal radiation exchange. Depending upon air and surface temperatures, a convective heat transfer is effected from the surfaces to the air and vice versa. For variable room temperatures, a rise in temperature triggers a reduction in the cooling load due to thermal storage. A fall in room temperature triggers an increase in the cooling load due to heat release. Of particular interest here is the heat backflow, i.e. convective heat transfer and heat absorption occurring at the same wall. The consequences of thermal storage processes for fixed load conditions are demonstrated by the diurnal curve of the cooling load factors, which describe fluctuation in the cooling load indexed to dampening and time delay. These correlations are made use of in corresponding basic calculations for the establishment of momentary cooling loads, multiplying the maximum values with the storage factors.

6.1
Storage Factors, Storage Behaviour

The room types relevant to thermal storage capacity are shown in Table 4. These are distinguished as follows:

- XL   very low thermal mass
- L   low thermal mass
- M   medium thermal mass
- S   high thermal mass

Rooms can be thus classified by following these guidelines:

- XL   total mass less than
       200 kg/m^2 floor

- L/M total mass
       200 – 600 kg/m^2 floor space
       L: thermal mass is covered
       (e.g. wall-to-wall carpeting, insulation
       below floor screed, suspended
       ceilings, etc.)
       M: thermal mass is partially free (stone
       floors, plastered concrete ceilings)

- S   total mass greater than
       600 kg/m^2 floor space

In this classification, it may be assumed that all rooms share the same geometry and heat insulation but vary in wall designs and layouts. During manual calculation, the room types are matched with corresponding cooling load factors (storage factors). However, care must be taken to base the storage calculation on the different operating times of air-conditioning systems, to ensure that the cooling loads are for the most part applicable to buildings where air-conditioning is used. Hence, calculation should begin with a qualitative comparison of the room to be studied with the room types in the table and the room should be identified as belonging to one of them.

Table 4

Room types and indication of
thermal storage capacity
according to VDI 2078

λ = Heat conductivity
ρ = Density
c = Specific heat capacity

Model room with following
parameters:

Window 7.0 m²
U = 2.1 W/m²K
Double glazing

Exterior wall 3.5 m²
U = 0.59 W/m²K

Average U-value of exterior wall
and windows:
U_A = 1.6 W/m²K

Room type XL "extra light"

Construction	Structure	Thickness [m]	$\lambda\ [\mathrm{W/m \cdot K}]$	$\rho\ [\mathrm{kg/m^3}]$	$c\ [\mathrm{J/kg \cdot K}]$
Ceiling and floor	Carpet	0.0045	0.072	–	–
	Underfelt	0.005	0.047	78	880
	Reinforced concrete	0.1	2.035	2100	920
	Air cushion	–	R=0.13 m²K/W	–	–
	Mineral wool mat	0.02	0.047	30	840
	Floor slab	0.02	0.05	35	1680
Interior walls	Sheet metal	0.001	58.0	7800	480
	Silan mat	0.078	0.047	60	840
	Sheet metal	0.001	58.0	7800	480
Interior door	Plywood	0.04	0.14	500	2520
Exterior wall	Corten steel	0.0015	58.0	7800	480
	Insulation	0.071	0.047	60	1680
	Sheet metal	0.001	58.0	7800	480

Room type L "light"

Construction	Structure	Thickness [m]	$\lambda\ [\mathrm{W/m \cdot K}]$	$\rho\ [\mathrm{kg/m^3}]$	$c\ [\mathrm{J/kg \cdot K}]$
Ceiling and floor	Plaster	0.03	1.4	2200	1050
	Rock wool	0.02	0.047	75	840
	Concrete	0.12	2.035	2100	920
	Air cavity	–	R=0.13 m²K/W	–	–
	Rock wool	0.02	0.047	75	840
	Metal ceiling	0.001	58.0	7800	480
Interior walls	Foam mortar	0.12	0.4	1200	1050
Interior door	Plywood	0.04	0.14	500	2520
Exterior wall	Slate boarding	0.01	0.14	500	2520
	Insulation	0.064	0.047	75	840
	Slate boarding	0.01	0.14	500	2520

Room type M "medium"

Construction	Structure	Thickness [m]	$\lambda\ [\mathrm{W/m \cdot K}]$	$\rho\ [\mathrm{kg/m^3}]$	$c\ [\mathrm{J/kg \cdot K}]$
Ceiling and floor	Concrete	0.12	2.035	2100	920
	Air cavity	–	R=0.13 m²K/W	–	–
	Rock wool	0.02	0.047	75	840
	Metal ceiling	0.001	58.0	7800	480
Interior walls	Foam mortar	0.12	0.4	1200	1050
Interior door	Plywood	0.04	0.14	500	2520
Exterior wall	Concrete	0.1	2.035	2100	920
	Insulation	0.06	0.047	75	840
	Air cavity	–	R=0.13 m²K/W	–	–
	Façade panel	0.025	0.45	1300	1050

Room type H "high"

Construction	Structure	Thickness [m]	$\lambda\ [\mathrm{W/m \cdot K}]$	$\rho\ [\mathrm{kg/m^3}]$	$c\ [\mathrm{J/kg \cdot K}]$
Ceiling and floor	PVC layer	0.002	0.21	1300	1470
	Plaster	0.045	1.4	2200	1050
	Rock wool	0.012	0.06	50	840
	Concrete	0.15	2.035	2400	1050
Interior walls	Hollow block	0.24	0.56	1300	1050
Interior door	Birch, solid	0.04	0.14	700	2520
Exterior wall	Concrete	0.1	2.035	2100	920
	Insulation	0.06	0.047	75	840
	Façade panel	0.025	0.45	1300	1050

The following comparative study demonstrates the effects of storage behaviour in a test room facing south. The room and its constructional layout (Option 1–6) are schematized in Figure 157

Essential differences in the room layout [for each option] are as follows:

Option 1
light to medium storage capacity room with full-height window glazing

Option 2
light to medium storage capacity room with parapet element (approx. 70 cm high)

Option 3
medium storage capacity room with parapet element as in Option 2 but without suspended ceiling

Option 4
high storage capacity room with parapet element, without suspended ceiling and with limited storage capacity floor

Option 5
high storage capacity room with parapet element and masonry partitions

Option 6
medium storage capacity room with parapet elements and demountable partitions (metal).

The curves in Figure 158 indicate room temperatures after five days of clear weather in summer for a room facing south. As the temperature chart shows, the storage factor in the external walls (Option 2) causes a temperature drop of approx. 1.2 K (maximum value) compared to full glazing (Option 1). This is an effect of not only the external wall's storage capacity but also, and especially, the reduction of solar incidence through the decreased glass surface. A comparison of Options 2 and 3 is of greater interest. A suspended ceiling is not used (in Option 3) and the room temperature drops by a further 1 K (approx. maximum value) compared to Option 2; this difference is entirely due to the increased storage capacity.

Figure 157
Room types with different surrounding structures

Dimensions:
Orientation:	South
Floor space:	21.0 m²
Occupants:	2
Room height:	2.90 m
Lighting:	158 W
Ceiling suspension:	0.15 m
Machines:	315 W
Balustrade height:	0.70 m

 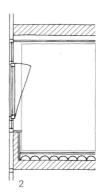 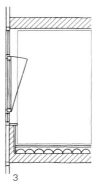  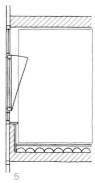 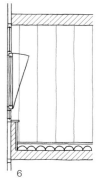

Option	1	2	3	4	5	6
Window	U = 2.0 W/m²K g = 62 %	U = 2.0 W/m²K g = 62 %	U = 2.0 W/m²K g = 62 %	U = 2.0 W/m²K g = 62 %	U = 2.0 W/m²K g = 62 %	U = 2.0 W/m²K g = 62 %
Sun protection	external/g = 0.20	external/g = 0.20	external/g = 0.20	external/g = 0.20	external/g = 0.20	external/g = 0.20
Balustrade	without	with	with	with	with	with
Susp. ceiling	with	with	without	without	without	without
Floor	Hollow floor	Hollow floor	Hollow floor	Floating screed	Hollow floor	Hollow floor
Side partitions	Drywall	Drywall	Drywall	Drywall	Brickwork	Metal single-plank wall
Rear partition	Drywall	Drywall	Drywall	Drywall	Brickwork	Metal single-plank wall
Exterior wall	Louvre 0.6 cm Insulation 8.0 cm	Louvre 0.6 cm Insulation 8.0 cm Concrete 12.0 cm Plaster 1.5 cm	Louvre 0.6 cm Insulation 8.0 cm Concrete 12.0 cm Plaster 1.5 cm	Louvre 0.6 cm Insulation 8.0 cm Concrete 12.0 cm Plaster 1.5 cm	Louvre 0.6 cm Insulation 8.0 cm Concrete 12.0 cm Plaster 1.5 cm	Louvre 0.6 cm Insulation 8.0 cm Concrete 12.0 cm Plaster 1.5 cm
Ceiling/ Floor	Suspension 2.0 cm Air 13.0 cm Concrete 25.0 cm Hollow floor 15.0 cm Carpet 0.5 cm	Suspension 2.0 cm Air 13.0 cm Concrete 25.0 cm Hollow floor 15.0 cm Carpet 0.5 cm	Concrete 25.0 cm Hollow floor 15.0 cm Carpet 0.5 cm	Concrete 25.0 cm Insulation 3.0 cm Plaster 8.0 cm Carpet 0.5 cm	Concrete 25.0 cm Hollow floor 15.0 cm Carpet 0.5 cm	Concrete 25.0 cm Hollow floor 15.0 cm Carpet 0.5 cm
Side partitions	Drywall 1.5 cm Insulation 7.0 cm Drywall 1.5 cm	Drywall 1.5 cm Insulation 7.0 cm Drywall 1.5 cm	Drywall 1.5 cm Insulation 7.0 cm Drywall 1.5 cm	Drywall 1.5 cm Insulation 7.0 cm Drywall 1.5 cm	Plaster 1.5 cm Brickwork 11.5 cm Plaster 1.5 cm	Metal single-plank wall 0.1 cm Insulation 9.8 cm Metal single-plank wall 0.1 cm
Rear partition	Drywall 1.5 cm Insulation 7.0 cm Drywall 1.5 cm	Drywall 1.5 cm Insulation 7.0 cm Drywall 1.5 cm	Drywall 1.5 cm Insulation 7.0 cm Drywall 1.5 cm	Drywall 1.5 cm Insulation 7.0 cm Drywall 1.5 cm	Plaster 1.5 cm Brickwork 11.5 cm Plaster 1.5 cm	Metal single-plank wall 0.1 cm Insulation 9.8 cm Metal single-plank wall 0.1 cm

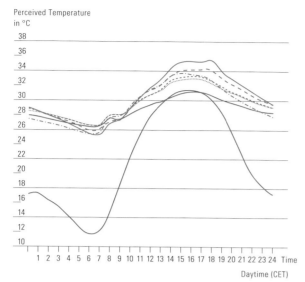

Perceived Temperature
in °C

Daytime (CET)

— Fresh air
— Option 1
– – Option 2
– – – Option 3
······ Option 4
— Option 5
– ·· – Option 6

Figure 158
Room temperatures following five day good weather period in summer Weather data from TRY (TRY region 8)

The room temperatures are indicated as perceived temperatures (from DIN 1946/Part 2), under consideration of building component and surface temperatures.

The difference between Options 3 and 4 is approx. 0.2 K, because the wall-to-wall carpeted floor almost cancels out the increased storage capacity of the floor compared to the hollow floor. A significant improvement could be achieved only if stone flooring were used instead of carpet. Option 5 shows the greatest difference, compared to all previously mentioned layouts, due to the extremely high storage capacity of the masonry partitions. The temperature is lowered by approx. 2 K to 3 K compared to the other room options (with the exception of Option 1).

In Option 6, the overall behaviour is similar to that in Option 3, but slightly poorer since the metal frame walls with insulation have an even lower storage performance rating than the drywalls in Option 2.

Judging from how the curves in Figure 158 relate, it is apparent that the temperature decrease due to storage for a room facing south reaches full effect only from 4:00 p.m. to 6:00 p.m., i.e. 4 hours after the maximum sun radiation into the room (external shading). For rooms facing east, therefore, the greatest reduction of the cooling load, and hence of the room temperatures, was observed between 12:00 a.m. [noon] and 2:00 p.m.; for rooms facing west, between 10:00 p.m. and 12:00 p.m. [midnight].

I Fresh air
I Option 1
I Option 2
I Option 3
I Option 4
I Option 5
I Option 6

Figure 159
Temperature statistic of room temperatures from May to September Weather data from TRY (TRY region 8)

Number of hours with temperature greater than indicated temperature from 7 a.m. to 6 p.m. (daily)

Figure 159 gives temperature statistics for the summer months of May through September for this room and the layout options described above.

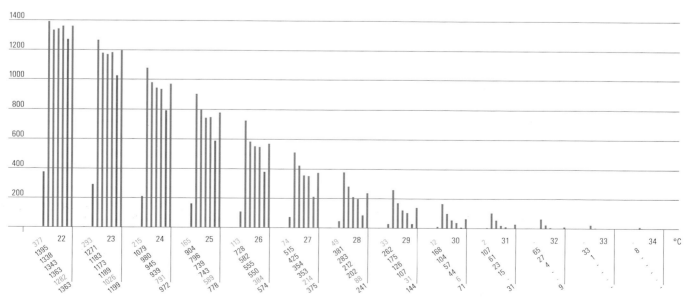

Frequency, number of hours
(h)

Frequencies
(h)

Because the room in Option 5 has the greatest storage capacity, its temperatures do not exceed 30°C, i.e. the temperatures in this room reach a maximum of 29°C without ventilation and cooling on approx. 20 days of the year. All other options, with the exception of Option 1, exhibit similar behaviour with regard to the predicted number of days when room temperatures range from approx. 22°C to 30°C. Option 1 shows the poorest performance with regard to recorded temperatures, although here, as was noted, the increase of incident heat due to the large window surface plays an important part.

The storage capacity of a room can be significantly improved by ventilating the space with outside air during the night. Figure 160 represents the temperature behaviour in two test rooms (Options 2 and 5) with and without night cooling. In the case of night cooling, a 3 ac/h air-change standard rate is assumed during average wind velocities and with slightly opened windows. A comparison of the curves, with and without night cooling, for Options 2 and 5 reveals that, in a light to medium storage capacity room, the temperature is reduced by approx. 2 K to 6 K, while, in Option 5, it is expected to be reduced by approx. 3 K to 4 K. It is important to note that the temperature level in Option 5 is approx 4 K less than that in Option 2. The increased storage capacity seems to have an effect, especially during the operating hours of the building in question. Finally, these curves and their comparative values demonstrate that night cooling in a building is equally as important as the increased storage capacity.

Therefore, the best way to reduce energy consumption and the investment cost in ventilation and air-conditioning systems is to design a room with not only high storage capacity but also efficient night cooling, to improve the storage behaviour.

Figure 160
Room temperatures
following five day good
weather period in summer
Comparison with / without
night ventilation
Weather data from TRY
(TRY region 8)

— Fresh air
– – Option 2 (without NV)
— Option 2 (with NV)
– – Option 5 (without NV)
— Option 5 (with NV)

NV = night ventilation
(air change 3.0 1/h
from 5 p.m. to 8 a.m.)

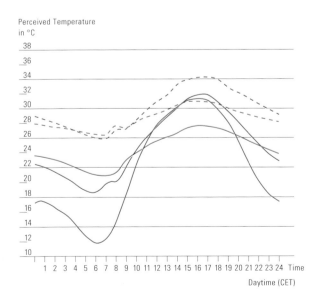

6.2
Buildings with Medium Storage Capacity

Buildings with medium storage capacity can be defined in several ways: either they have high storage capacity in their constructional layout and function without additional ventilation measures or else they have medium storage capacity and are ventilated day and (especially) night.

The office building of HL-Technik AG, Munich (architect: Dr. R. Hammann, Munich) is an example of a high storage capacity building without integrated active cooling or mechanical ventilation. Figures 161.1 and 161.2 show the floor plan of the building, shielded from the surrounding street noise by a solid wall and opening onto a park-like setting, as well as the building with its concrete structural components and the rotated glass cube with large windows for adequate natural lighting in all rooms. Although, in its construction, the building is of high storage capacity, it is light and transparent in appearance due to the large areas of glass. Each second window unit can be opened for adequate cross-ventilation. Figure 161.3 provides a view into the lobby interior with its massive concrete structural components and, to improve the storage capacity, stone paved floors. Since the building is neither actively cooled nor actively mechanically ventilated or aired, its storage capacity was increased as much as possible in the fashion previously described. Doing so prevents room temperatures in summer from exceeding outside temperatures.

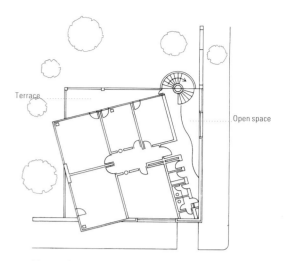

Figure 161.1
Example of high storage capacity building: office building of HL-Technik AG, Munich
(Architect: Dr. R. Hammann, Munich)
Floor plan 3rd floor

Figure 161.2
West elevation

Figure 161.3
View of atrium
(with stone floors, masoned walls and plastered ceilings)

Figure 162.1 shows an office building in Frankfurt (Triton House) used by a large German bank. This building has medium to high storage capacity and is equipped with air-conditioning (for peak summer operation). Unique to this building is the ceiling thickness of 25 cm, greater than the standard 22 cm, to increase the storage mass. To avoid limiting storage, suspended ceilings have been omitted (Figure 162.2). For illumination, cove lights provide indirect lighting (Figure 162.3) and, together with the velour carpeting, the acoustic absorption required in each room. In summer, the building is also mechanically ventilated every night, at an approx. 3 ac/h air-change rate, to allow for the storage of greater heat masses during the 24-hour period. The partitions are of a lightweight construction. This case is roughly similar to Option 3 of the previous scenarios for temperature behaviour (see Figure 157 ff).

Figure 162.1
Triton House in Frankfurt
(Architect's team:
Nägele, Hofmann, Tiedemann, Frankfurt
and Kiemle, Kreidt + Partners, Düsseldorf;
Building services design:
HL-Technik AG, Frankfurt)

Figure 162.2
Schematic of ventilation in action

Summer operation with cooling

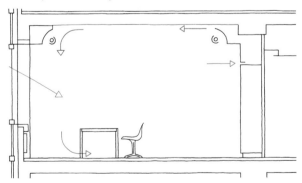

Winter operation with lighting

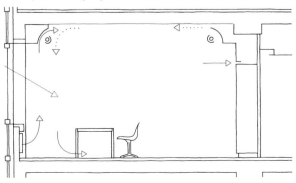

Figure 162.3
View of interior: closet partition with cove lights and integrated slat vents (tangential flow)

6.3
Buildings with High Storage Capacity

Finally, here are two examples of buildings with high storage capacity.

The Figures 163 series shows the European Investment Bank complex in Luxembourg (1980). The aim was to design an office building with high storage capacity and night cooling and thus be operable without air-conditioning systems, the room temperature in summer not exceeding 28°C. Figure 163.1 provides an aerial view of the building as well as a typical ground plan with individual room designs and the office areas across two axes open to all sides. Figure 163.2 shows a cross-section of one floor of the 2-grid office with the ventilation installations in the ceiling. As can be seen, the ceilings are hollow. Some sections (upper ceiling) were constructed with in-situ concrete, others with pre-cast units. Fresh air is conducted through the hollow spaces in the concrete ceilings during the night (Figure 163.3) whenever the outside temperature is less than the room temperature (Figure 163.4). A mechanical ventilation system ensures night cooling; it is manually set for conditions expected on the following day (outside temperature, clear or overcast, season). A central building management system cools the variously oriented concrete masses (loading sensor) to the degree determined by a corresponding computer program. This building has been in operation for more than 14 years and it has been established that when the shading components are used correctly, room temperatures do not exceed 27°C, in this resembling Option 5 (Figure 160) with night cooling.

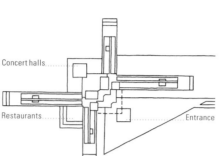

Figure 163.1
European Investment Bank in Luxembourg
Aerial view and floor plan
(Architect: Sir Denys Lasdun & Partners, London;
Building services design: HL-Technik AG, Munich)

Concert halls

Restaurants

Entrance

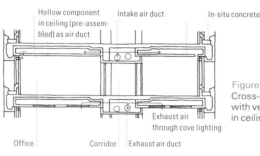

Hollow component in ceiling (pre-assembled) as air duct

Intake air duct

In-situ concrete

Exhaust air through cove lighting

Office

Corridor

Exhaust air duct

Figure 163.2
Cross-section of office floor with ventilation installations in ceiling

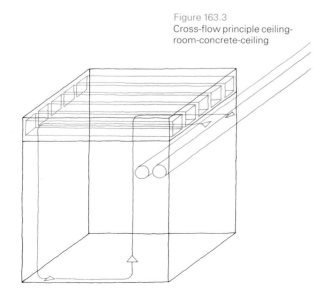

Figure 163.3
Cross-flow principle ceiling-room-concrete-ceiling

Figure 163.4
Room temperatures dependent on outside temperatures
(sunny day)

Operation of night cooling:
6 a.m.–7 p.m.

— Outside temperature

||| Range of room temperatures

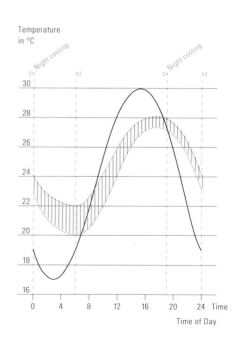

Temperature in °C

Night cooling

Night cooling

Time of Day

Another example of a high storage capacity building design is the Außenwerbungskontor Koblenz (AWK; an advertising agency), which was built approx. 12 years ago, the work of architect Prof. H. Struhk, Braunschweig, in collaboration with HL-Technik AG. Figure 164.1 is an external view of the building. Like the European Investment Bank in Luxembourg, it is situated in a green field site, an environment lending itself to natural ventilation.

Figure 164.2 shows a cross-section, Figure 164.3 a floor plan of AWK. As is evident from the ground plan, this building follows an essentially open plan approach, in which all areas cannot be naturally ventilated. At the same time, the client's wish to keep room temperatures in summer from exceeding 28–30°C, with minimal technical effort, had to be fulfilled.

To maintain relevant storage masses within the building, the architect used wall panels and open concrete coffered ceilings instead of pillars, which act as storing masses. Figure 164.4 is a view of the interior in which the extent of surfaces and masses capable of storage can easily be seen. Extract ducts were used for natural and supplementary ventilation. These ducts can extract air out of the building during low oncoming winds and thus force a recirculated flow of outside air across the window surfaces. A supply air diffuser (Figure 164.5) blows fresh air with a single air change into the central foyer in peak summer. The intake air is dehumidified and cooled before entering the building. This treated air enters the building with minimal positive pressure and moves across the building towards the lee-side sections of the block, where it exits and flows down the façades.

Figure 164.1
AWK Außenwerbungskontor, Koblenz
External view
(Architects: Kersten, Martinoff, Struhk, Braunschweig: Building services design: HL-Technik AG, Munich)

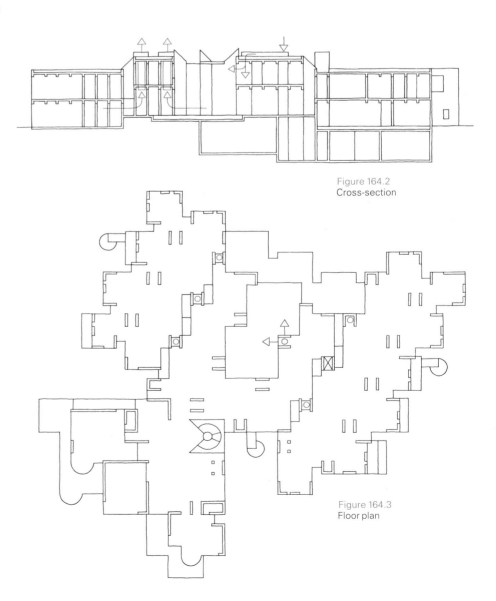

Figure 164.2
Cross-section

Figure 164.3
Floor plan

Figure 164.4
Room detail with
thermal masses
(ceiling and wall panels)

Figure 164.5
Central intake air louvre
in atrium

Figure 164.6 shows the room conditions (different temperature curves) during fair weather periods in May, June, July and August 1983. As the curves indicate, for only a single hour of the year did room temperature approach 30°C. Evidently, the high storage capacity masses serve to lessen the widely fluctuating outside air temperature, thus keeping room temperature well below that outside.

Figure 165 once again gives an overview of how specific building materials are able to store heat energy. The graph illustrates that higher density and greater specific weight in a building material are directly linked to greater storage capacity; this storage, however, usually only occurs up to a depth of approx. 10–15 cm (one-sided).

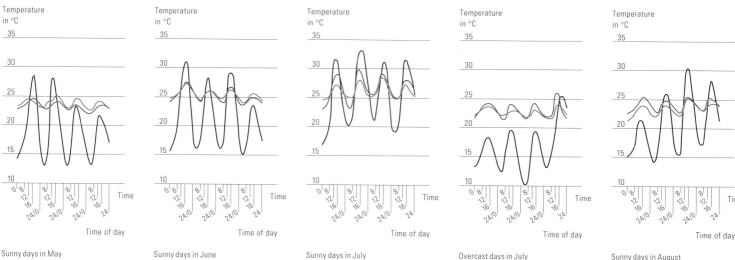

Sunny days in May

Sunny days in June

Sunny days in July

Overcast days in July

Sunny days in August

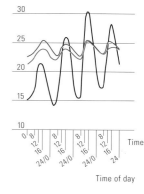

Figure 164.6
Room temperatures in peak
summer (1983), dependent on
outside temperatures

— External temperature curve
— Room temperature curve
  South-facing rooms
— Room temperature curve
  North-facing rooms

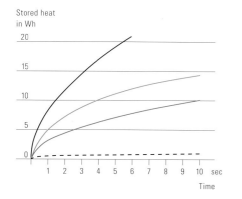

Figure 165
Thermal storage for
different building materials
(surface = 1 m²/ΔT = 10 K)

— Granite
— Concrete
— Brick
-- Mineral (or slag) wool

Buildings of Tomorrow: Examples and Ideas

7

Whereas, until the Middle Ages, the exterior walls of buildings were primarily weather shields, with the additional function of keeping the interior areas warm, the 20th century has put new demands on built envelope surfaces.

Façades used as envelope surfaces are not only architecturally challenging, they are also charged with a good number of functions for which appropriate solutions must be found. Daylight incidence, heat gain, and heat loss play as important a role as the correct form of outside air intake, pressure distribution of windward and leeward locations, and, finally, a targeted energy conservation based on the corresponding environmental options.

7.
Façades –
from Weather Protection to Polyvalent Walls

7.1
Technical Data – the First Step

In any study of glass façades on buildings, certain principal factors will be found to influence light and heat incidence, heat emission and colour-reproduction qualities. For climate and light experts working intensively with façades, these factors give important hints for an initial evaluation. The principal factors are:

Light Transmission Factor τ

The light transmission factor τ is the percentage of daylight which penetrates a glass or window pane from the outside. The light transmission value is indicated in the wavelength of visible light ranging from 380 to 780 nm (nanometres), related to the light sensitivity of the human eye.

Total Solar Energy Transmission g-value/ b-factor

The total solar energy transmission (g-value) is taken in the wavelength range of 320–2500 nm. It is the sum of direct energy transmission and secondary heat transmission to the inside (radiation and convection). The shading co-efficient b describes the percentage of energy permeating a double pane (80 %). Therefore, the shading coefficient b = g/0.80. Previously, b was related to a single pane (3 mm) and thus b = g/0.87. Many data collections today are still based on this definition (Table 5).

Thermal Transmittance (U-value)

The thermal transmittance U, e.g. of an insulating glass pane, indicates how much energy is lost through the pane surface. The smaller the value, the less heat is lost. The U-value of conventional insulating glass panes depends essentially upon the distance between the panes and the medium contained in it (air or inert gas). The U-value can also be improved by superimposed noble metal layers.

Product	Appearance (external)	Light transmission factor τ in %	Total solar energy transmission g-value in %	Shading coefficient b-factor	Comments
Standard clear glass	normal transparent				
single		90	83–87	1.00	
double 6/12/6		84	78	0.89	
triple per 12 mm air		74	70	0.81	
Calorex	"neutral" mirror effect (enhanced)				Metal oxide coating
single IRO		58	62	0.72	
double IRO		53	48	0.55	
IRA 1 single		42	50	0.57	
IRA 1 double		38	42	0.48	
IRA 1 + IR 2, double		33	29	0.34	
Parsol					Mass-tinted, values dependent on thickness, 2nd pane clear glass
Parsol bronze 6 + 6 mm		44	64	0.59	
Parsol grey 6 + 6 mm		47	47	0.56	
Parsol green 6 + 6 mm		64	49	0.56	
Infrastop					Superimposed gold or silver coating, with or without interference layer, only double pane, internal pane is clear
Auresin 66/44	blue mirror	66	44	0.50	
Auresin 50/36		50	36	0.41	
Auresin 39/28		39	28	0.32	
Bronze 36/26	bronze appears	36	26	0.30	
Gold 40/26	as light gold-tinted mirror	40	26	0.30	
Gold 30/23	dark gold tone	30	23	0.26	
Silver 36/33		36	33	0.38	
Silver 22/22	silver	22	22	0.25	
Metallic		50	47	0.54	
Parelio	slight bronze tint				Metal oxide coating on clear glass or Parsol, 2nd pane clear glass
Parelio 24 6 + 6 mm		57	56	0.59	
Parelio 50 6 + 6 mm		42	51	0.64	
Parelio 24 green 6 + 6 mm		46	33	0.38	
Parelio 50 green 6 + 6 mm		35	29	0.33	
Parelio 24 grey 6 + 6 mm		27	37	0.43	
Parelio 24 bronze 6 + 6 mm		30	36	0.41	
Thermolux standard		63	52	0.60	
Thermolux Insulating glass		53	46	0.52	

Table 5
Data for sun protection glass for near vertical radiation incidence

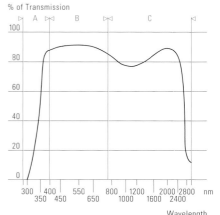

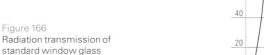

Figure 166
Radiation transmission of standard window glass

A Range of ultraviolet radiation
B Visible light
C Infrared range (thermal radiation)

Diminution Factor

The diminution factor of a shading element (from DIN 4108) measures the percentage of incident radiant energy which passes through a shading element and thus contributes to the warming of an interior space.

Other Factors

Other factors in the evaluation of (window) panes measure:

– the light reflected towards the outside, in %
– the general colour reproduction values (colour reproduction index R_a from DIN 6169),
– the UV-permeability in the wavelength range 280–380 nm, in %,
– selectivity factor S, representing the relationship of light transmission to total solar energy transmission, etc.

Table 5, opposite, cites data for brands of glass with sun protection (old definition); Figure 166 supplements this with the radiation transmission of standard window glass.

For large glass surfaces and high temperature differences, there is an increased risk of condensation and hence corrosion near the frame. In winter, large glass walls in rooms or halls have the additional problem that, as the room air cools, cold air dumping occurs at the glass surfaces, which must then be counteracted by upward-flowing warm air currents. Another way of avoiding cold air currents is to increase surface temperatures sufficiently. The temperature difference between room air and inner glass surface should not exceed 4–5 K. To avoid excessive cooling of the inner surfaces, convectors (warm water, electric) or warm air currents can be used.

Figure 167 provides a diagram for determining condensation points on window panes dependent upon the U-value, the relative humidity in the room and the inside and outside temperatures. This diagram is an essential tool for correctly designing relevant (window) pane surfaces.

Figure 168.1 shows the physical context for determining the total solar energy transmission g-value. In Figure 168.2, the graph illustrates typical ranges of transmission, absorption, and reflection on a specific glass pane (Calorex A1), used as an example, and thus indicates the percentages of incident daylight which permeate the room.

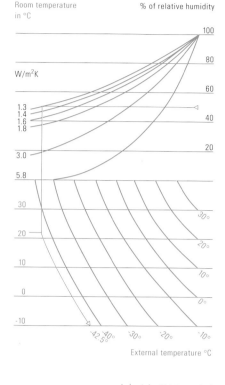

Figure 167
Dewpoint diagram with example

The dewpoint diagram serves to calculate the temperature necessary for condensation to form on the inside of a window pane (= dew point).
Shown example: pane iplus neutral
U = 1.3 W/m²K,
Room temperature +22°C, relative humidity 50 %

Result:
Condensation on the iplus neutral pane forms only at a temperature of -42.5°C

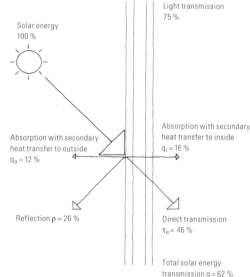

Figure 168.1
Total solar energy transmission of iplus neutral R
Distribution of incident energy
(g-value from DIN 67507)

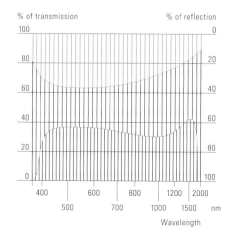

Figure 168.2
Schematic of transmission, absorption and reflection on pane (Calorex A1)

III Reflection
IIII Absorption
IIIII Transmission

137

Figure 169.1
Shading Options

Room dimensions:
Orientation: South
Floor space: 21.0 m²
Occupants: 2
Room height: 2.90 m
Lighting: 158 W
Ceiling suspension: 0.15 m
Machines: 315 W
Balustrade height: 0.70 m

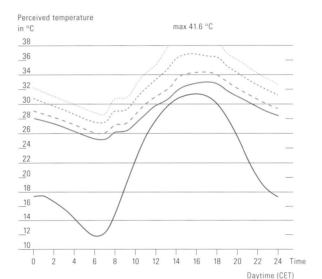

Option	2a	2b	2c	2d
Window	U = 2.0 W/m²K	U = 2.0 W/m²K	U = 2.0 W/m²K	U = 2.0 W/m²K
	g = 62 %	g = 62 %	g = 62 %	g = 62 %
Shading	external/g = 0.12	external/g = 0.20	external/g = 0.35	internal/g = 0.60
Balustrade	with	with	with	with
Suspend. ceiling	with	with	with	with
Floor	Hollow floor	Hollow floor	Hollow floor	Hollow floor
Side partitions	Plaster	Plaster	Plaster	Plaster
Rear partition	Plaster	Plaster	Plaster	Plaster

Figure 169.2
Room temperatures following
a fiveday fair weather period
in summer

Weather data from test
reference year (TRY region 8)

—— Fresh air
—— Option 2a (g = 0.12)
– – Option 2b (g = 0.20)
--- Option 2c (g = 0.35)
······ Option 2d (g = 0.60)

Room temperatures are indicated as operative (perceived)
temperatures (from DIN 1946/
Part 2), i.e. including building
component and surface temperatures.

Figure 170
Temperature statistic for
observed room options from
May to September

Weather data from test
reference year (TRY region 8)

❙ Fresh air
❙ Option 2a (g = 0.12)
❙ Option 2b (g = 0.20)
❙ Option 2c (g = 0.35)
❙ Option 2d (g = 0.60)

Number of hours with
temperatures higher than
indicated between 7 a.m.
and 6 p.m. (daily).

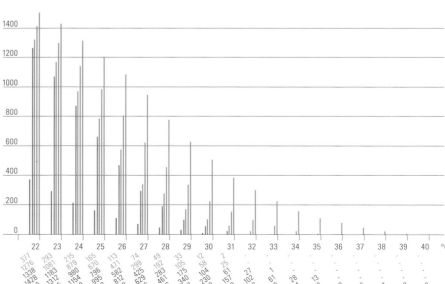

7.2
Effect of Shading on Room Temperature

Like Figure 157 (Room Option 2), the following is a study of the combined effect of the total shading coefficient of a sun protection element and insulating glazing upon a room's cooling loads and temperature. Figure 169.1 shows the room (Option 2) fitted with various types of shading. The options are as follows:

– Option 2a   external louvre
– Option 2b   closed external louvre
              (highly reflecting)
– Option 2c   open awning
– Option 2d   indoor shading and glare protection

Figure 169.2 shows the curves representing predictable room temperatures on a warm summer day in a southward-facing room of medium storage capacity based on the varying total solar energy transmission coefficients. As can be seen, the differences between the most effective shading (lowest total solar energy transmission) and the least effective shading (indoor vertical blinds or curtains) are considerable. The maximum temperature difference resulting from these shading types may reach almost 10 K, causing a significant change in the thermal comfort perceived in a room. Furthermore, it should be noted that ventilation and air-conditioning systems are sized according to a "peak" temperature during a fair weather period, which may result in higher or lower technical investment costs.

Displaying temperature statistics for the period May to September, Figure 170 clarifies the effects of the several shading options. This graph emphasizes how poor shading may push room temperatures up to approx. 39°C, while good shading limits temperatures to 30°C.

Hence, the utmost care should be taken in selecting and designing shading elements; furthermore, some thought should be given to additional measures for indoor shading (e.g. in skyscrapers) to improve the overall environment, as in Option 2d. An investment in good shading is usually more than offset by cost-savings on technical systems.

The combination of shading, cooling load and temperature behaviour is, however, but one aspect in defining and designing the means for shading a room. Another, equally important aspect is the incidence of daylight in the corresponding rooms.

7.3
Daylight Incidence and
Total Solar Energy Transmission

To minimize external cooling loads, it is essential that the incident radiation on window and roof surfaces be considerably reduced to minimize additional energy. At the same time, daylight should penetrate into the room as much as possible to minimize usage of artificial lighting.

Unwanted energy absorption in well insulated office buildings may occur with outside temperatures as moderate as +5°C, since the indoor heat sources are likely to provide sufficient heat to the building during the day. The graphs in Figures 171.1/2 (pages 140 and 141) serve as a general introduction to the topic by depicting the incidence of radiation (direct and diffuse) on the southward-facing façades and roof areas. Figure 172 shows the cumulative frequency of radiation on roof surfaces and indicates which portion of the energy can generally be directly utilized, e.g. in office buildings (passive solar gain), assuming that a building must be heated to, say, +10°C. The annual time line of radiation illustrates the dilemma presented by large solar gains in well insulated buildings. Only a small portion of the radiation is actually beneficial for heating the building, most of it being, instead, a potential source of discomfort.

Figure 172
Cumulative frequency of
radiation on roof surfaces

|||| Direct energy potential
|||| Low energy potential
|||| Barely useable
     energy potential

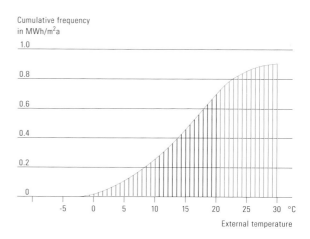

Cumulative frequency
in MWh/m²a

External temperature

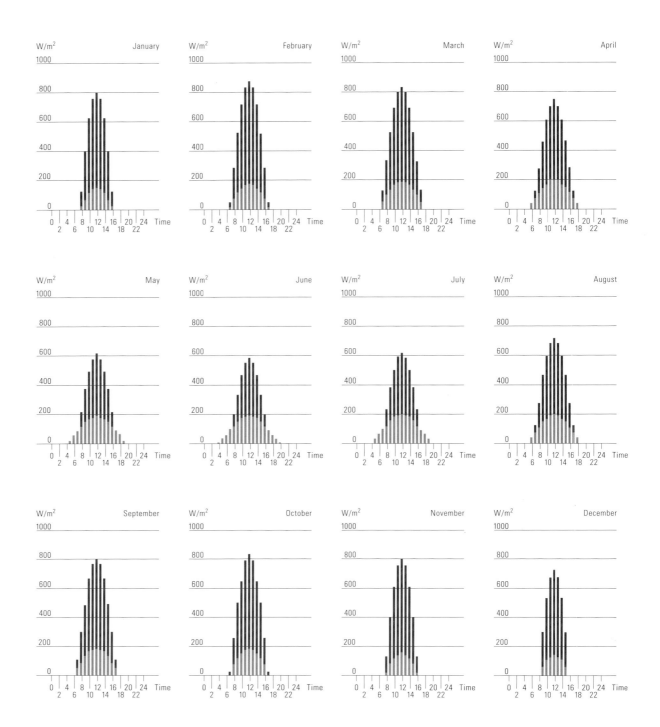

Figure 171.1
Incident radiation (vertical)
on south façade during 24 hour
period

■ Direct radiation
■ Diffuse radiation

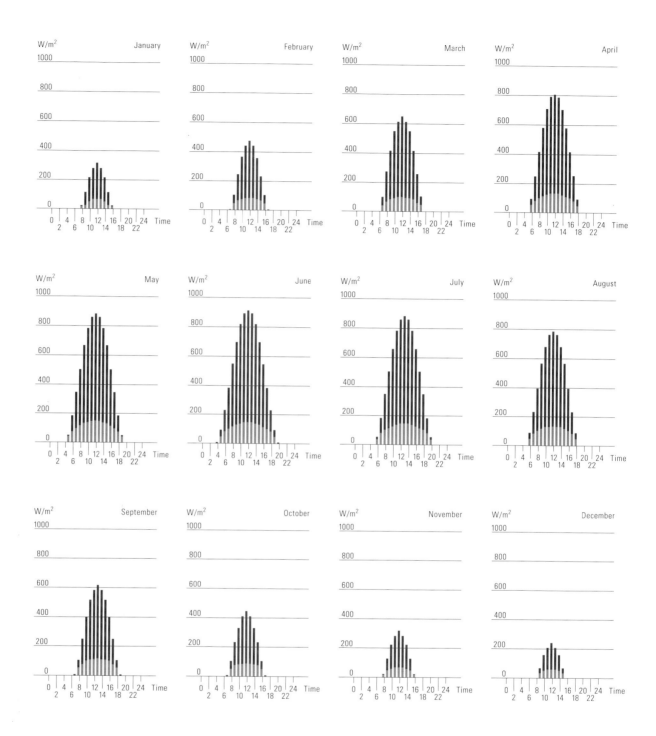

Figure 171.2
Incident radiation on roof
during 24hour period

■ Direct radiation
▪ Diffuse radiation

The total solar energy transmission is very important for minimizing the incident heat energy from direct or diffuse radiation. This coefficient should be as low as possible, combined with maximum light transmission. Figures 173.1–173.2 show the values for these factors for several examples of neutral and reflective glazing for single-leaf façades and window options for single- and double-leaf façades respectively. Optimal window combinations exist for each case.

Different solutions for internal and external sun protection result in different total solar energy transmission coefficients, shown in Figure 174. These can be improved by removing heat absorbed in a room (secondary heat output/convective heat flow) to prevent undue cooling loads in the room.

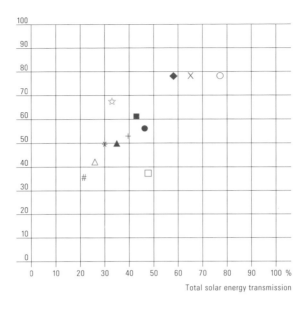

Light transmission
in %

Total solar energy transmission

Figure 173.1
Selectivity of neutral and reflecting glazing
(single-leaf façade)

○ Insulating glazing
× Thermal glazing
◆ Thermal glazing
■ Luxguard Natural
☆ Ipasol Natura
▲ Climasol Neutral
□ Parsol grey
● Antelio Silber
+ Ipasol Silber
* Infrastop Silber (50/30)
△ Luxguard Silber
Infrastop Silber (37/22)

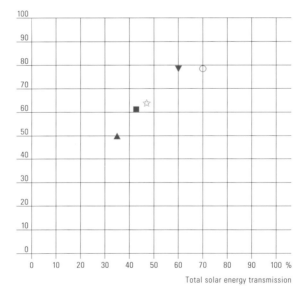

Light transmission
in %

Total solar energy transmission

Figure 173.2
Selectivity of different window combinations

Double-leaf façade
○ Box window
   Insulating glazing/
   Single glazing

☆ Box window
   Single glazing/
   Thermal glazing

Single-leaf façades
▼ Thermal glazing
■ Luxguard Natural
▲ Climasol Neutral

Figure 174
Total solar energy transmission coefficients for different shading options in a single-leaf façade

1 DIN 4108
2 Ferrari Soltis 86,
   silk tinted (external)
   alu (internal)
3 Agero G-1907
4 MHZ Hachtel No. 400
5 Hüppe No. 10
   silver/black
6 Siemens prisms
   injected

Total solar energy transmission coefficient g with (heat) extraction in %

Total solar energy transmission coefficient g without (heat) extraction in %

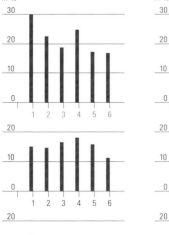

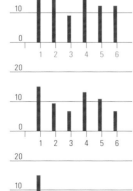

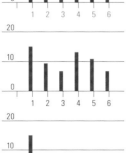

Total

Secondary heat output

Radiation transmission

7.4
Increasing Daylight Incidence with Light-Deflecting Elements

Shading elements frequently double as glare protection. This is not, however, the best solution, since, even on overcast days, glare protection must be used for PC workstations, to adjust the light densities near windows to the required ambient glare intensity. Glare protection is provided not only by blinds and awnings but also by daylight-deflecting systems, which are intended to achieve satisfactory daylight incidence in combination with sufficient glare protection.

Light-Deflection with Holographic Diffractive Films

Holographic diffractive films (HDS), also called grid or zone panels, are holographically manufactured. They are used to bend incident light in a predefined direction. The grids are singular in that they bend each wavelength of light at a different angle. The result is a distribution of light somewhat like a rainbow. Red light is redirected the most, blue light the least (Figure 175.1)

To understand the principle of diffraction, each light wave may be imagined broken down into spherical waves (Huygens' principle), (Figure 175.2). When some of the spherical waves forming the oncoming wave front pass through a gap, the remaining spherical waves form a typical interference pattern at the aperture. The interference pattern depends on the size, shape and distance of the diffracting medium and the wavelength.

Holographic diffractive films are usually manufactured by photographic means. A distinction is made between grids created by dual-beam laser interference and those which, after computing, are created by exposure to light-sensitive material. Computer-generated holograms are currently only capable of small bending angles, because of the diffraction limitations of optomechanical plotters. Complex bending patterns require a correspondingly greater computing effort. Especially large-scale HDSs are, therefore, created mainly with laser interferometry.

For hologram manufacture by interferometry, lasers must serve as the source of mono-chromatic, coherent light. The light beam originating from the laser is split into two beams. Each beam, after appropriate shaping via such optical elements as lenses or diffraction discs, overlaps the other, and thus they create an interference pattern on the (light-) sensitive material. After the latter has been developed, this pattern then constitutes the bending grid (HDS). One of the beams, named the reference beam, represents, in a subsequent application, the incident light to be redirected, while the second beam represents the redirected light source. The processed film is placed between two panes of glass and thus protected against mechanical damage and environmental influences. This technique makes nearly all light shapes possible, as is particularly apparent in display holograms, which contain very complex structures.

The efficiency (in bending) of a hologram (HDS) depends upon several factors. In so-called 'thick' holograms, efficiency is considerably influenced by incident angle and wavelength (Figure 175.3). For certain angles, the ratio of redirected radiance to total incidence may be zero, i.e. there is no diffraction. When these elements are used, care must be taken to avoid glare within the building's interior for incident radiation in the 0° range. For 'thin' holograms, which have in principle a lower efficiency coefficient, efficiency nevertheless remains constant in the large angle range and depends only slightly upon wavelength.

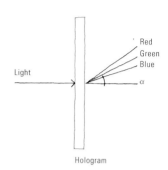

Figure 175.1
Effect of diffraction grating or hologram on direction of visible light (400–780 nm)

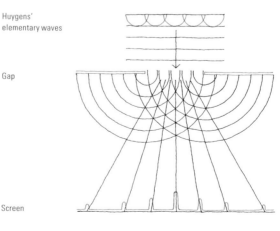

Huygens' elementary waves

Gap

Screen

Interference pattern

Figure 175.2
Diffraction at gap

When light of one wavelength (e.g. 650 nm = red) passes through a gap, the wave spreads from the edge of the gap in spherical waves. A typical interference pattern is seen on a screen at some distance from the gap.

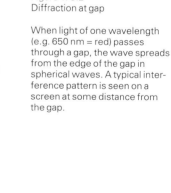

Figure 175.3
Directional characteristic of HDS for vertical incident angle (all wavelengths)

Direction of incident light

For the 1993 Stuttgart International Garden Exhibition, HHS Architects + Planner BDA (Hegger, Hegger-Luhnen and Schleiff, Kassel) designed a residential complex (Figure 176.1) in which innovative techniques in solar energy utilization were applied and tested. HDS systems were developed by the Institute for Light and Construction Technology at the Polytechnic University of Cologne (Prof. Dr. Gutjahr, Prof. Dr. Müller). This research project was supported by the Federal Ministry for Research and Technology, the contractor and the participating companies and planners (FlagSol, Gartner & Co., Arnold Glassworks) as well as by Solar Ltd.

The architect Prof. Manfred Hegger writes about the project: (Quote)
"The goal of the project was to turn the concept of a south façade with optimum solar and light technology into a reality. The sun heats and lights the rooms. Superfluous solar energy, which could lead to glare, is captured via transparent shading units with holograms and transformed into electricity.

Climatic conditions in the region of Stuttgart are, as throughout Germany, characterized by a discrepancy in both summer and winter, between existing radiant solar energy and that needed for lighting and heating purposes.

This fact calls for an 'intelligent' façade, i.e. a building envelope which can be adjusted or adapted to changing climatic conditions. To do justice to this task, several façade units were integrated into the above-mentioned row of residences. The wintergarden area, rotated by 16° south-east, was fitted with glass cladding in a mullion and transom frame with an inclination from the horizontal of 50° and towards the east of 4°. Different shading units (some fixed, some mobile) improve the building climatic conditions and energy balance. They permit, even in their shading position, a mostly unimpeded view of the outside (Figure 176.2) and enable natural lighting (Figure 176.3) as well as optimum utilization of solar energy for heating, cooling and the generation of solar electricity.

Figure 176.2
Interior of façade

Figure 176.3
Interior of façade

Figure 176.1
Main elevation of building

This building designed for the
Stuttgart International Garden
Exhibition demonstrates the use of
photovoltaics and holography
(Architect: Prof. M. Hegger, Kassel)

The top row of slanted glass façade units is equipped with PV modules made from a compound combining insulating glass with integrated polycrystalline solar cells. They provide seasonal shading (like that provided by a roof overhang) for the recessed living areas, depending upon the sunpath (Figure 177). The PV modules have a transparency of 35 % and satisfy, with an energy yield of 1300 kWh per year ($\eta = 11.5$ %), approx. two-thirds of the buildings' annual electricity requirement.

The lower part of the façade is equipped, over a surface of approx. 30 m² per building, with shading louvres, which follow the course of the solar azimuth. These shading louvres are fitted with holographic grids which focus the incident light onto a silkscreen strip 11 mm behind them, whence it is again reflected and thus kept out of the room (Figure 178). In one of the three buildings, the silkscreen strips are mounted with solar cells which photovoltaically transform the incident and concentrated solar light and, like the PV modules, feed it into the building network. The surface ratio of HDS to solar cell and PV module is 1:1. For this reason, an ideal concentration effect of factor 2 would be expected for the radiation strength (or force) on the solar cells. Because of the holograms' bending coefficient, a concentration effect of close to 1.9:1 is obtained for the visible spectrum. Combined with the sensitivity of the solar cells, this increases electrical energy by a factor of 1.3.

The directional selectivity of the diffraction, which has the positive side-effect of concentrating and diffracting only direct insolation and not diffuse radiation, necessitates a secondary system. The transmission of approx. 50 % diffuse radiation means that even in the 'shading' position no artificial lighting is required as a light source."
(End of quote.)

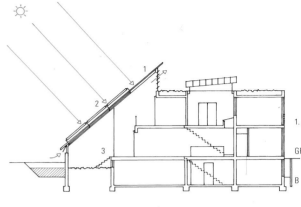

Figure 177
Schematic of façade function for high solar altitude and shading position (top) and low solar altitude and open position (bottom)

1 Solar cells
2 Adjustable glass elements with holograms and solar cells
3 Winter garden

Summer

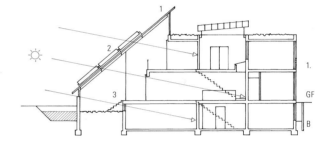

Winter

Figure 178
Cross-section of holographic-photovoltaic element

The broken lines indicate the shape of a lense which diffracts the light in the same manner as the hologram.

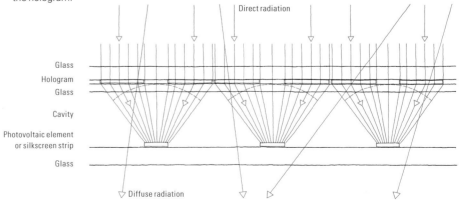

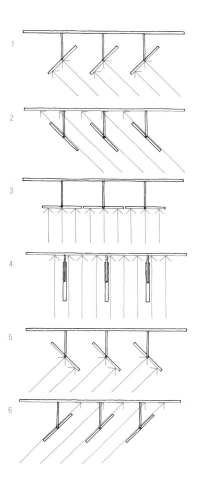

The movement of glass panels fitted with the HDS for optimal shading with constant daylight incidence is achieved by a system of levers controlled in response to outside temperature, radiation strength, interior temperature and sun-path (shading/open positions) (Figure 179).

First measurements taken in this complex during the Stuttgart Exhibition yielded an absolute transmission coefficient of 6 % for the visible portion of direct radiation and of 45 % for the diffuse radiation. The reduction factor z of a corresponding HDS as shading unit is approx. 0.2 to 0.3.

Whether and how much holographic optical elements succeed in the long term remains to be seen. It will most probably depend upon the economic feasibility of their manufacture.

Figure 179
Various positions of the photo-voltaic elements at different daytimes and for different requirements

1 9 a.m.
PV utilization,
shading requirement,
diffuse radiation lights rooms

2 9 a.m.
PV not utilized,
utilization of incident light,
passive utilization of solar energy

3 12 noon
PV utilization,
shading requirement,
diffuse radiation lights rooms,
overheating prevented on south façade

4 12 noon
PV not utilized,
utilization of incident light,
passive utilization of solar energy,
unimpeded visual contact to outside

5 3 p.m.
PV utilization,
shading requirement,
diffuse radiation lights rooms

6 3 p.m.
PV not utilized,
utilization of incident light,
passive utilization of solar energy

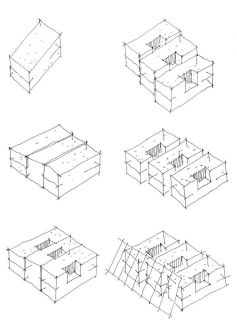

Daylight Refraction with Mirrors and Prisms

Daylight refraction not only reduces the number of hours artificial lighting must be used and hence running costs, it also creates a visual environment more acceptable to the occupants, since human visual perception is adapted to daylight. The seasonal and annual fluctuations in daylight necessitate the use of artificial lighting during certain periods (at night, during storms, etc.). Lighting systems should, therefore, be designed to complement natural light when necessary and to create a good lighting environment in the room.

These are the essential criteria for additional architectural measures for the improvement of daytime lighting:

- sufficient amount of daylight,
- improved range of brightness,
- improved optical perception (light density ratios),
- improved contact with the outside and, at the same time, active shading,
- improved shading,
- improved energy balance.

When rooms are lit from the side, the amount of daylight and its penetration into a room are defined by the geometry of the side-opening and the type of window and its components. Figure 180 shows a typical daylight situation in a room lit from the side. With each change in the room angle (reduction of room angle in room depth) there is a progressive drop in brightness. The distribution of brightness is such that near the window there is a lot of daylight, but farther back in the room it drops off rapidly. Assuming a luminance requirement of approx 500 lx at the workstation, up to a depth of 1–1.5 m the requirement would only be met in this type of room.

The uneven distribution of brightness may easily interfere with adaptation in the brain of an occupant exposed to it. The resulting effort to adapt is of the same order as mental effort and hence leads to a reduction in performance, e.g. during concentrated office work.

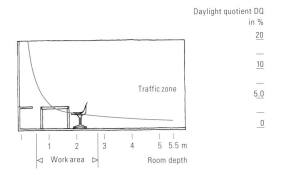

Figure 180
Typical office room
(l = 5.5 m, w = 4 m, h = 3 m)
Work area with sufficient daylight. A daylight quotient of 100 % corresponds to a luminance of 10^4 lx.

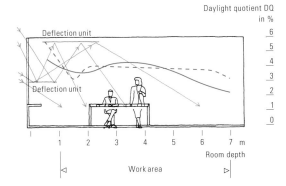

Figure 181
Comparison of deflection of daylight by daylight reflectors in the room, mirror reflectors at the window, with deflection surface consisting of a matte aluminum mirror or other wide-angle deflecting materials (dull-finish lacquer). The quotients indicated in this diagram are achieved according to the quality of the system and its settings.

– – Aluminum,
reflective, matte
—— Dull-finish lacquer, white

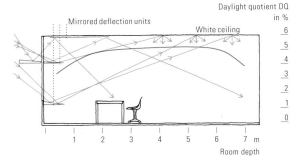

Figure 182
The daylight deflection units, exterior and interior, receive a greater zenithal fraction. The utilization of the balustrade with the help of an aluminum reflective finish directs more light into the depth of the room. Arrangements of this kind increase the daylight quotient and help direct daylight further into the room.

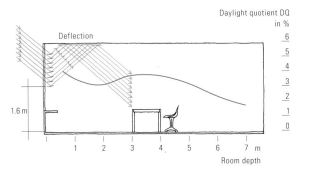

Figure 183
Daylight redirection with interior mirrored deflection slats

Approximate course of daylight quotient

To improve the situation, the daylight must be 'redistributed'. This redistribution can be achieved by various techniques, such as:

– interior mirrored deflection units (Figure 181),
– exterior and interior mirrored deflection units (Figure 182),
– interior mirrored deflection slats (Figure 183),
– daylight redirection via glass prisms (Figure 184 – 185).

Figure 184 shows daylight redirection via a prismatic panel, Figure 185 various locations of the panel under different ambient conditions (ceiling structures). As Figure 186 shows, the daylight quotient is increased considerably. A definite improvement can be seen to result from the redistribution of daylight for each variation. The criteria for shading and light permeability are satisfied in the good to excellent range:

Total solar energy transmission = 0.1–0.15
Light transmission = 0.7–0.9

(All values supplied by Lichtplanung Christian Bartenbach)

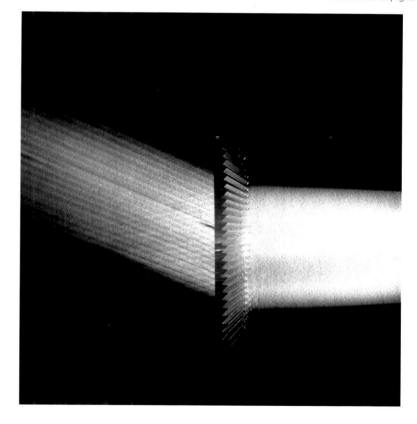

Figure 184
Prism technology makes it possible to redirect and redistribute daylight.

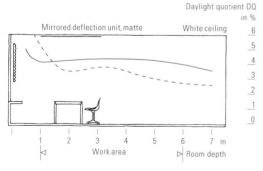

Figure 186
DQ curve for different systems

—— for Figure 185.1
– – for Figure 185.2/3

Figure 185.1
Redirection of light by prismatic panels, whereby only a fraction of the light is bounced off the ceiling.
Good light utilization, however, insufficient light diffraction makes this option practical only for rooms of maximum depths from 5–6 m.
No glare protection.

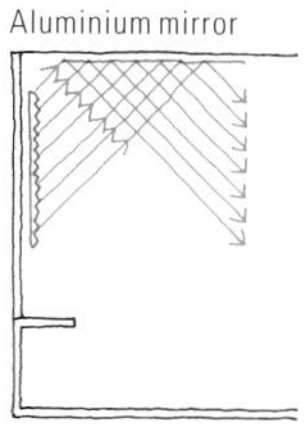

Figure 185.2
Light diffraction via ceiling system. Optimum light redirection without glare, well suited to light redirection for rooms with greater depths (up to 8 m). Special ceiling design required.

Figure 185.3
Illustrates exterior prismatic panel, set at an angle. No advantages to option shown in 185.2. The increased light diffraction is reduced again due to accumulated dirt on exterior panel and decreased surface.

The quality and precision of the system are determined by the manufacturing and in installation. The total solar energy transmission for indoor prism elements rises from approx. 0.15 to 0.25 and thus still corresponds to very good conventional indoor shading. The following presents several installation examples, their technical data and their advantages and disadvantages (Figures 187.1–187.5).

To diffuse direct sunlight in a situation with lighting from above (skylights, glass roofs) and to aim the diffuse daylight into the room, the Siemens and Christian Bartenbach companies have developed a grid system of specially formed obverse and transverse slats (Figure 188). It can be integrated into skylight panes set at different angles. When installed, the obverse slats run from east to west, and the opening of the grid faces west. The direct radiation from the south is reflected through the geometrical form of the obverse slats. The room is not excessively heated by this process, since the reflection is approx. 80 %. The intense zenith and north light is allowed into the room without any hindrance. The plastic shading grid, plated with high-grade aluminum, in the insulation glass composite (Figure 189) is an optical element and correspondingly sensitive. Its installation in insulating glass units protects it from such environmental influences as dust or humidity. Figure 190 illustrates the installation situation and the technical data as well as positive and negative aspects of the system.

Besides Siemens AG, which markets a number of daylight-deflecting units based on developments by Prof. Christian Bartenbach, Okalux Kapillarglas (capillary glass products) has designed a similar system under the trademark Okasolar. The product is available in several models (in various profiles), corresponding to the Okasolar glazing's direction and angle, and depending upon the technical lighting requirements. The Okasolar system varies the transmission of radiation according to the sunpath, so that the particular design of the model reflects to a great extent the incident sun- and daylight (Figure 191, page 152).

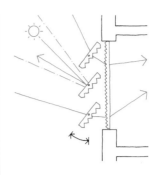

Figure 187.1
Daylight system for vertical windows

Adjustable prismatic panels on exterior with diffracting prisms/louvres integrated into the window

Manufacturer:
  Siemens AG
Effect:
– Redirection of direct solar radiation
Technical parameters:
– Total solar transmission factor: 0.1
– Thermal transmittance: 1.8–1.9 W/m²K
– Light transmission: 20 %
Advantages:
– Light is directed into depth of room
Disadvantages:
– High installation and maintenance effort
– Customized, metallic ceiling system required
– View to outside restricted by diffraction system
– Very technical in appearance

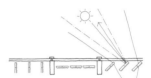

Figure 187.2
Daylight system for vertical windows

Vertical, rotating prismatic louvres

Manufacturer:
  Siemens AG
Effect:
– Redirection of direct solar radiation by adjusting louvres to solar path
Technical parameters:
– Total solar transmission factor: 0.18
– Thermal transmittance: 1.7 W/m²K
– Light transmission: 73 %
Advantages:
– Openable sun protection/shading
Disadvantages:
– Colour separation of light
– Complicated mechanics required
– High maintenance

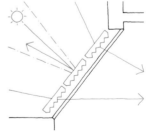

Figure 187.3
Daylight system for skylights

Solar shading prism in laminated glass panels

Manufacturer:
  Siemens AG
Effect:
– Redirection of direct solar radiation with good transmission for diffuse daylight
Technical parameters:
– Total solar transmission factor: 0.13–0.15
– Thermal transmittance: 1.65–2.15 W/m²K
– Light transmission: 35 %
Advantages:
– No maintenance shading
– Installation same as for standard window
Disadvantages:
– Restricted visual contact to outside (blurred view of sky)
– Depending on orientation, slanted installation required

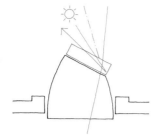

Manufacturer:
  Siemens AG
Effect:
– Redirection of direct solar radiation
– North light (incident daylight)
Advantages:
– Excellent light redirection
Disadvantages:
– No visual contact to outside
– High construction effort
– Very large roof cowl

Figure 187.4
Daylight system for skylights/
fanlights
(Custom solution: Naturhisto-
risches Museum Stuttgart)

Funnel shaped skylight

Manufacturer:
  Siemens AG
Effect:
– Redirection of direct solar radiation
   through slanted aluminium window
– Daylight redirection through shape
   of skylight shaft
Advantages:
– Excellent light diffraction
– Good shading
– Easily combined with artificial
   lighting
Disadvantages:
– Complicated construction

Figure 187.5
Daylight system for skylights
(Customized solution:
Kunstmuseum Bern)

Skylight system with light
diffraction

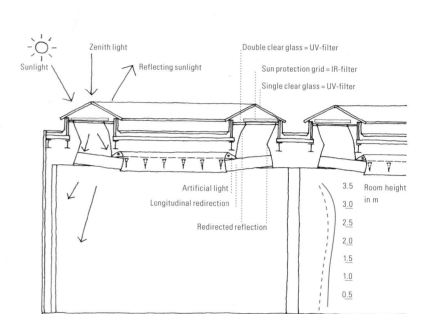

Cross-section diagram,
Kunstmuseum Bern, with
daylight quotient curve

— at center of wall
–– along edge of wall

Manufacturer:
  Siemens AG
Effect:
– Redirection of direct solar radiation
Technical parameters:
– Total solar transmission factor: 0.2
– Light transmission, direct: 5 % – 65 %
– Light transmission, diffuse: 5 % – 22 %
– Shading factor: 0.75 – 0.20
Advantages:
– No maintenance required
– Installation same as for standard
   window
– Relatively inexpensive
Disadvantages:
– No visual contact to outside
– View to outside only on north side

Figure 190
Daylight system for skylights

Solar shading grids in laminated
glass panels

Figure 188
Functional principle

Figure 189
Detail

1 Butyl
2 Thiokol
3 Molecular sieve
4 Aluminum, insulating
   glass segment
5 Plastic support

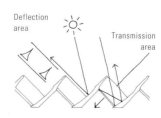

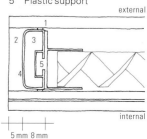

The point at which the Okasolar system begins to close (high reflection) and open, respectively, is assessed by daylight- and sunpath-dependent calculations which determine how the particular model is designed. The system is usually installed so as to allow the greatest amount of light and energy to penetrate the building in winter, thus achieving passive solar utilization. In summer, only diffuse radiation, as direct radiation is mostly reflected by the Okasolar system, is permitted to enter the building. Figure 192 gives an overview of the technical data and the advantages and disadvantages of the system solution. Figure 193 shows the same system technology installed in vertical glass units. The company Okalux also markets a light-diffracting insulating glass with capillary panel (similar to a TIM element), shown in Figure 194. Here, too, the technical data and positive and negative effects are listed.

In conclusion, one can say that all light-deflecting elements must be integrated into the architecture so as not to appear as foreign objects. In each case, a study is necessary to determine whether it is worth the investment and whether the advantages of the system in question justify the considerable cost increase (in initial investment). The costs per square meter of this type of system solution range from 600 to 3000 DM and more.

Figure 192
Daylight system for skylights

Shading louvres in laminated glass

Manufacturer:
  Okalux GmbH
Effect:
– Redirection of direct
  solar radiation

Technical parameters:
– Total solar transmission factor:
  0.18 – 0.65
– Thermal transmittance:
  2.5 – 1.6 W/m²K
– Light transmission, direct: 5 % – 64 %
– Light transmission, diffuse: 4 % – 22 %
– Shading factor: 0.77 – 0.21
Advantages:
– Maintenance-free
– Installation same as for standard
  window
– Inexpensive shading solution
Disadvantages:
– Redirection limited
– Reduced visual contact to outside

Figure 193
Daylight system for vertical/
slanted windows

Shading louvres in laminated
glass 'Okasolar'

Manufacturer:
  Okalux GmbH
Effect:
– Redirection of direct solar
  radiation by diffraction

Technical parameters:
– Total solar transmission factor:
  0.20 – 0.65
– Thermal transmittance:
  2.5 – 1.6 W/m²K
– Light transmission, direct: 5 % – 60 %
– Light transmission, diffuse: 35 %
– Shading factor: 0.77 – 0.24
Advantages:
– Maintenance-free
– Installation same as for standard
  window
– Inexpensive shading system
Disadvantages:
– Redirection limited
– Reduced visual contact to outside
– Good visual contact to outside and
  shading when sun is low in the sky
  are mutually exclusive

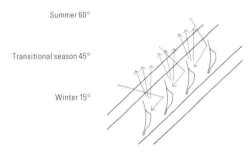

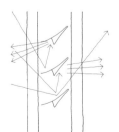

Figure 191
Principle of system technology
for vertical and slanted installation of OKASOLAR units,
respectively

Figure 194
Daylight system for skylights

Light-diffracting insulating
glass 'Okalux' (see schematic,
right)

Manufacturer:
  Okalux GmbH
Effect:
– Redirection of direct solar
  radiation
– Diffraction of natural light
  into room

Technical parameters:
– Total solar transmission factor:
  0.30 – 0.40
– Thermal transmittance:
  3.36 – 1.14 W/m²K
– Light transmission: ≤ 76 % adjustable
– Shading factor 0.5 – 0.3
Advantages:
– Relatively good shading
– Even light distribution through
  diffuse reflection
– Installation same as for standard
  window
Disadvantages:
– No visual contact to outside
– High light density near window

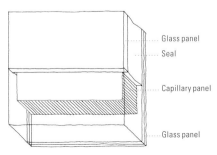

Glass panel

Seal

Capillary panel

Glass panel

7.5
The Use of Double-Leaf Façades

The use of double-leaf façades is currently in fashion and is normally justified by an apparent early return on the initial high investment. This is generally, in simple terms, a misconception. Double-leaf façades cost, per square metre, anywhere from 800 to 3000 DM more than well insulated and finished single-leaf façades, while the energy savings often amount to only approx. 1.5 to 2 % of the extra investment. Hence, in the case of double-leaf façades, it is worth considering whether they should be marketed solely on the basis of energy savings or whether other essential aspects argue for their use. These may be factors like sound protection or reduction of high wind pressures on skyscraper façades. The classical building forms of double-leaf façades are:

– box type windows,
– ventilated windows,
– second skin façade.

Temperature Curves in Double-Leaf, Ventilated Façades

Assuming that fresh air enters a building through the cavity between a double-leaf façade, it is very important, especially during transition periods and when individual occupants want natural ventilation, that no extreme temperature increase occurs in the cavity between the window panes, because the heated outside air would then overload the room temperature. The Figure 195 series compares the temperatures in this transition space for different types of shading (reflection quotient). In this example, fresh air enters into the window-pane configuration at a temperature of 25°C and is already heated in the boundary layer region of the outer pane. On its path through the cavity between panes, the temperature rises further. The rise in temperature in this space due to reflection and especially due to light absorption may vary greatly and reach maximum temperatures of 70°C. Such extreme temperatures, however, have very little effect on the room when the interior glazing is sealed, but they do become uncomfortable when the inner glass unit is opened and outside air enters the room at high temperatures.

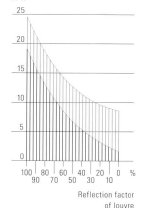

Figure 196
Total solar transmission factors indexed to decreasing reflection factors
(Double-leaf façade with standard insulating glass)

III Secondary thermal
     transmittance to inside
III Radiation transmission

Toral solar transmission factor g
in %

Reflection factor
of louvre

Furthermore, temperature differences are very noticeable when air is exhausted exclusively by stack effect during calms instead of by natural ventilation during oncoming winds. The lowest temperatures between window surfaces occur when the cavity blind is of a high-reflecting nature as is the case with the Hüppe No. 10 louvre.

Once the louvre is installed, its reflection quotient changes because of age and pollution. This should be studied in its effect on the total energy coefficient of permeability. Figure 196 presents a calculation of the change in total solar energy transmission per changing reflection quotient. When the reflection quotient diminishes (pollution), the total solar energy transmission does too, because there is less radiation transmission, which is usually positive in terms of heat for the adjoining rooms. On the other hand, the light quality may suffer.

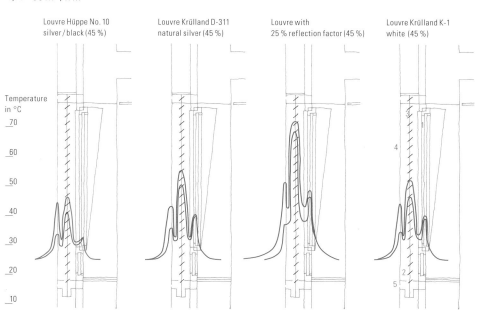

Figure 195
Temperatures in double-leaf, ventilated façades

Outside temperature:
$T_{ou} = 25°C$
Incident radiation:
$\dot{q}_r = 800 \, W/m^2$
Ventilation:
$\dot{V}/A = 50 \, m^3/h \, m^2$

— Temperatures for
  wind-induced ventilation
— Temperatures for venti-
  lation due to buoyancy
  (windstill periods)

1 Top-hung windows/
   alu double glazing
2 Ventilated cavity
3 Blind
4 Single pane as
   weather protection wall
5 Air intake

Temperature
in °C

Louvre Hüppe No. 10
silver / black (45 %)

Louvre Krülland D-311
natural silver (45 %)

Louvre with
25 % reflection factor (45 %)

Louvre Krülland K-1
white (45 %)

Energy Balance in Double-Leaf, Ventilated Façades

The energy balance with regard to the radiation transmission quotient (τ_e), the secondary heat transfer (q_i) and the total solar energy transmission is shown in Figure 197. As the comparison of different shading measures in the double-leaf, ventilated façade proves, the total solar energy transmission varies considerably for different types of shading.

The previously described prismatic louvres exhibit a radiation transmission factor of 8 %, compared to the façades presented in this section, and a secondary heat transfer of approx. 4 %, resulting in a total solar energy transmission of approx. 12 %. This value represents a happy medium and is somewhat less than that for the diffuse reflecting slats. However, it is far from the excellent values of the highly reflective louvre with silver-plated surface and matte underside.

While the surface of the louvre is most important, the angle at which it is placed has an influence as well and changes the total solar energy transmission. Figure 198.1 shows an example of two different louvres and how the total solar energy transmission changes, depending upon their angle. Hence, the correct form of angle control (computer-aided) is key to the optimization of a façade, since direct radiation of office areas should be avoided for lengthy periods of the year while maintaining high daylight utilization (radiation transmission). Depending upon the season and the time of day, the angle control of the louvres achieves optimal daylight incidence in combination with minimal heat gain. 'Intelligent façades' operate with automated angle control regulated by incident radiation and outside air temperature. During periods of unwanted outside thermal gain, the louvres are positioned at a steeper angle than during periods when passive solar gain reduces the energy costs for heating the room.

Angle control is thus clearly an important factor with regard to total solar energy transmission. Another is the type of glazing used between the indoor space and the air cavity separating it from the outside.

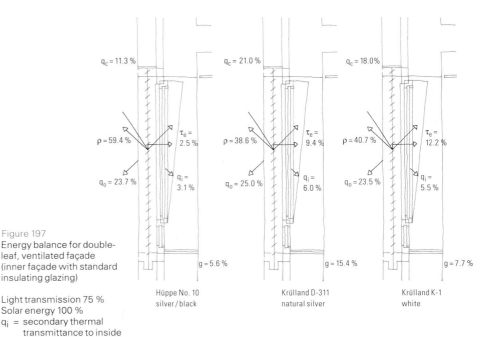

Figure 197
Energy balance for double-leaf, ventilated façade (inner façade with standard insulating glazing)

Light transmission 75 %
Solar energy 100 %
q_i = secondary thermal transmittance to inside
q_o = secondary thermal transmittance to outside
q_c = thermal transmittance to outside by convection
ρ = reflection
τ_e = direct transmission
g = total solar transmission factor

Hüppe No. 10 silver/black

Krülland D-311 natural silver

Krülland K-1 white

Figure 198.1
Total solar transmission factors for double-leaf, ventilated façades depending on angle of louvres

‖‖ Secondary thermal transmittance to inside
∥∥ Radiation transmission

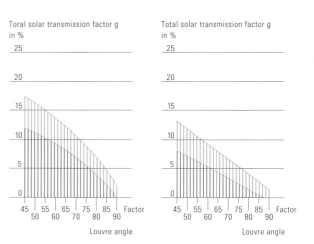

Louvre K-1 white (Krülland)/ standard insulating glazing

Louvre white/medium grey/ standard insulating glazing

If the inner insulating glass has heat-protection qualities, then the total energy coefficient of permeability decreases for the complete shading system. Figure 198.2 compares two types of glazing with a difference in total energy coefficient of permeability of approx. 15 % (box-type window with standard insulating glass g = 0.6/box-type window with heat-insulating glass g = 0.45).

The overall window combination can be optimized by maximizing the efficiency of individual panes and of the shading system, which will vary from case to case. This cannot be done by assuming steady state conditions. Rather, seasonal changes must be taken into account if shading is to be created which is effective and compatible with the overall measures taken, thus achieving heat gains from the outside which are as high or low as requirements demand.

Cost-Comparison of Active Technical Measures in Single- and Double-Leaf Façades

For the purpose of this comparison, an office building is discussed in which maximum room temperature in summer is 28°C and which is, therefore, equipped with air-conditioning (2ac/h) to maintain hygienic air quality. As the cooling loads are not adequately compensated by this 2 ac/h, the difference will be covered by a chilled ceiling.

The specific investment costs of building services are listed in Figure 199 (page 156) and clearly demonstrate the advantages of double-pane window variations, especially box-type windows with heat-protective glass and high-efficiency shading. In this case, the total investment costs are approx. 750 DM/m² net lettable areas (NLA), in contrast to the single-leaf façade with heat-protective glass and indoor shading, where costs approach 900 DM/m² NLA.

In this comparison, it is significant that due to lower specific cooling loads in solutions with double-pane façades, only approx. 50 % of the ceiling surfaces need to be fitted with cooling elements, which, in turn, results in a higher ratio of building component cooling. For single-leaf façade variations, the chilled ceilings must be installed as suspended ceilings across nearly the entire (ceiling) surface, which strongly limits the storage capacity. Façade costs themselves were not taken into account; of course, these are much higher for double-leaf façades than for single-leaf façades.

The specific energy costs of different façade options are listed in Figure 200. Here, too, the box-type options are clearly frontrunners with regard to energy consumption and costs and even for operating costs, since solutions using box-type windows require less extensive systems, resulting in lower maintenance and repair costs than those required for single-leaf façades. Once again, the additional costs for cleaning double-leaf façades have not been taken into account; these tend to tip the balance in favour of single-leaf façades. For the energy cost calculation, the following specific prices were used:

heat energy	80.–	DM/MWh,
electric energy	300.–	DM/MWh,
cooling energy	120.–	DM/MWh,
water	4.50 DM/m³.	

Figure 198.2
Total solar transmission factors for double-leaf, ventilated façades with different louvres and glazing systems

1 DIN 4108
2 Ferrari Soltis 86 silk toned (external)/alu (internal)
3 Krülland K-14
4 Krülland D-311
5 Krülland K-1
6 white/medium grey

Total solar transmission factor g in %

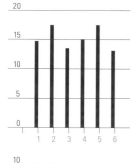
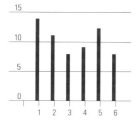
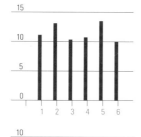

Total

Secondary thermal transmittance

Radiation transmission

Different louvres (45° position)/ standard insulating glazing

Different louvres (45° position)/ thermal insulating glazing

The costs for maintenance and operation per year total approx. 3 %, the costs for installation approx. 2 % of the investment costs for the building services systems.

The comparison of the annual total costs (Figure 201) for each façade variation shows that the costs for systems are lowest when box-type windows are used, assuming an amortization rate of 10 %, a utilization period of 20 years and an annuity of 11.75 %. The total costs for single-leaf façades are clearly higher. However, as before, additional costs arising from the initial investment and the cleaning for double-leaf façades were not taken into account. All things considered, the use of double-leaf façades is clearly favourable for the building services installation; however, the meaning of double-leaf should not be restricted to two envelopes with a slight separation. On the contrary, many other structures might be developed which display double-leaf characteristics.

Once more, it should be clearly stated that although double-leaf façades are favourable for building services, they are more expensive than single-leaf façades because of their additional cleaning costs and much higher investment costs. Whether or not double-leaf façades will have a future depends on the ingenuity of the architect and the industry, since the client will always insist on a value for money solution. At the outset, we listed arguments in favour of double-leaf façades, especially when noise emissions are to be dampened and high wind pressures reduced for tall buildings with natural ventilation, so that year-round draught-free operation is guaranteed. In conclusion, here are further examples of double-leaf façades in recent installations.

1 Box window
   Insulating glazing
2 Box window
   Thermal insulating glazing
3 Thermal Insulating glazing
4 Luxguard Natural
5 Climasol Neutral

Figure 199
Specific investment costs of building services for different façades

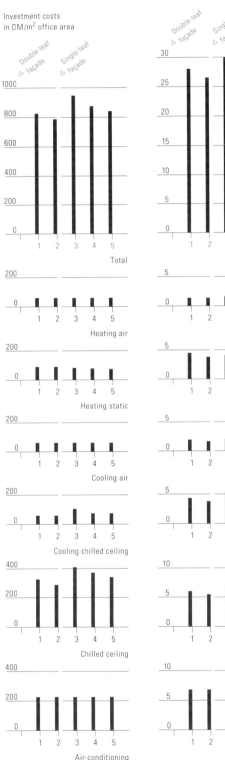

Figure 200
Specific energy costs of building services for different façades

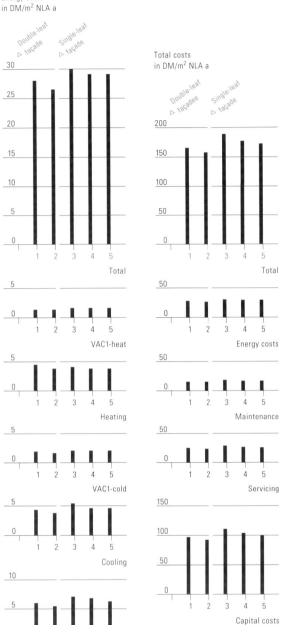

Figure 201
Specific annual total costs of building services for different façades

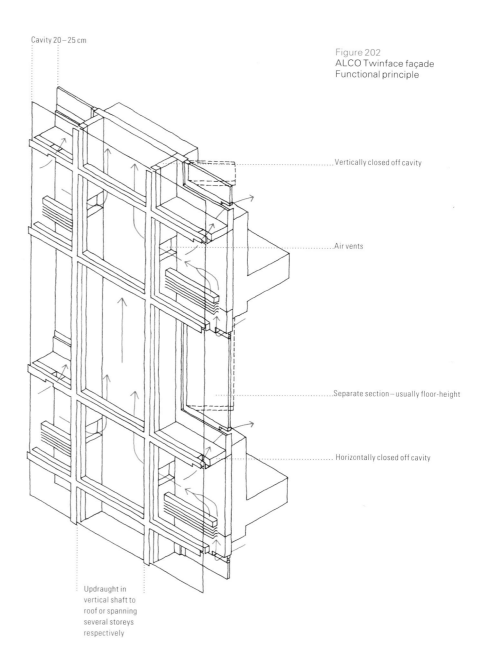

Figure 202
ALCO Twinface façade
Functional principle

Cavity 20–25 cm

Vertically closed off cavity

Air vents

Separate section – usually floor-height

Horizontally closed off cavity

Updraught in
vertical shaft to
roof or spanning
several storeys
respectively

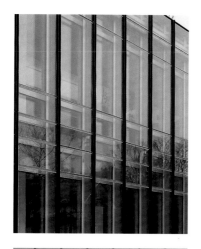

Figure 203
Research and construction
facility of Rudolph GmbH,
Mahlow/Berlin
Architect: M.Kock, Berlin

Figure 204
Administrative building
Frankfurt
Architects: P. Scheele and
J. Zimmer, Dortmund

Alco Systems GmbH in Münster, Germany, has
developed a patented system solution called
Twinface Façades, especially well-suited to buildings less than ten storeys high and utilizing the
stack ventilation shown in Figure 202 in its original
form. Figure 203 shows a Twinface Façade
installed on the research and construction building
of Rudolph GmbH, Mahlow/Berlin, Figure 204
a trapezoidal, angled Twinface Façade for the
administrative centre in Frankfurt.

The façade for Milton Court, an office building in London (architects: Lasdun, Softley and Associates), was developed by the Gartner company in Gundelfingen (Germany) (Figure 205). This example is a good illustration of the recently popular lightweight construction using a second skin. An early precursor of this second-skin façade is the Steiff machine hall, from the year 1903 (Figure 206).

The characteristics of modern second-skin façades, with their exterior glass fronts and an inner, conventional fabric envelope, can be seen in Figure 207. For the air movement between the two façades, the temperature rise from floor to floor must be closely monitored, since it would obviously not make sense for a double-leaf façade to have moderate temperatures near the ground but excessively high temperatures in the upper areas of the building at the inner façade (stack effect).

Bild 205
Milton Court, London
Architects: Lasdun and
Softley Ass., London

Figure 206
Steiff machine hall
with second-skin façade,
dating back to 1903

Diagram of a second-skin façade

1 External glass skin
2 Internal façade
3 Cavity
4 Quasi external sun
   protection
5 Oncoming fresh air flow
6 Openable interior window
7 Fresh air vent (bottom)
8 Air exhaust (top)

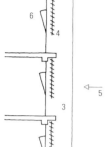

A façade created by architects Herzog + de Meuron in Basle together with Schmidlin AG (Façade Planning) is shown in Figures 208.1 and 208.2. The structural design of the double-leaf façade is shown in Figure 209. It has three different service bands for light bending, for ventilation and viewing, and for generating solar power (photovoltaic, not yet installed), respectively. The façade is controlled by various factors. Direct factors are the sunpath, the external temperature and the time of day. Other factors are oncoming wind direction and rain. The chief objective of this project was, on the one hand, to make optimal use of sunlight and daylight and, on the other, to create, as the architect wished, a façade responsive to seasonal changes. Both requirements are met by having the individual glass bands move in response to light and heat (computer-controlled movement), so that the facade opens partially (in transition seasons and summer) or closes (in winter) to effect passive solar utilization. Sectioning the façade helps improve the daylight quotient in the room while diminishing the light density. Thus, less artificial light is needed and (visual) adaptation near computer workstations can proceed unimpeded.

As mentioned, photovoltaic elements are not yet installed. Hence, this façade yields, at present, only minimum energy savings compared to its considerable initial investment costs.

Figure 208.1
View of façade of SUVA building, Basle
Architects: Herzog + de Meuron, Basle

Figure 208.2
Diagram of banding with moveable top-hung windows

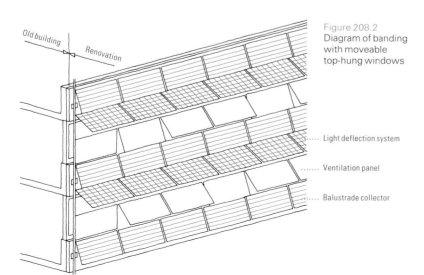

Old building
Renovation

Light deflection system
Ventilation panel
Balustrade collector

Figure 209
Cross-section of façade, detail

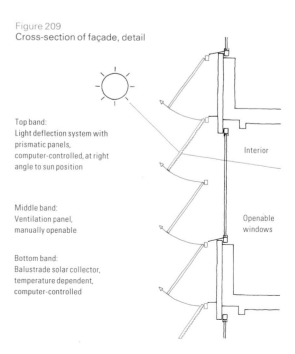

Top band:
Light deflection system with prismatic panels, computer-controlled, at right angle to sun position

Middle band:
Ventilation panel, manually openable

Bottom band:
Balustrade solar collector, temperature dependent, computer-controlled

Interior

Openable windows

7.6
The Concept of Polyvalent Walls

Façades are not 'intelligent' but can be designed
in an intelligent fashion to meet all future users'
requirements while utilizing environmental resources in harmony with user needs. Figure 210
shows the structure of a glass installation suitable
for a polyvalent wall, according to Mike Davis
(Richard Rogers Partnership, London). This polyvalent wall should be so designed that it will,
depending upon user specification and season,
function as shading or heat insulation, reflect heat
energy outside the building or bring heat energy
into the building, and open and close itself automatically. Thus far, the manufacturing industry
has been unable to transform M. Davis' ideas into
reality and so it is up to us, the planners, to recreate a polyvalent wall with conventional means.
Figure 211 is a flow chart showing how a polyvalent wall operates and illustrating the requirements an 'intelligent' façade needs to fulfill in
order to heat, ventilate, light and cool a building
with as little technological help and energy
consumption as possible.

Figure 210
Proposal for polyvalent wall
by Mike Davis (Richard Rogers
Partnership)

1   Silica weather skin and
    deposition substrate
2   Sensor and control logic
    layer, external
3   Photoelectric grid
4   Thermal sheet radiator /
    selective absorber
5   Electro-reflective deposition
6   Micro-pore gas flow layers
7   Electro-reflective deposition
8   Sensor and control logic
    layer, internal
9   Silica deposition substrate
    and inner skin

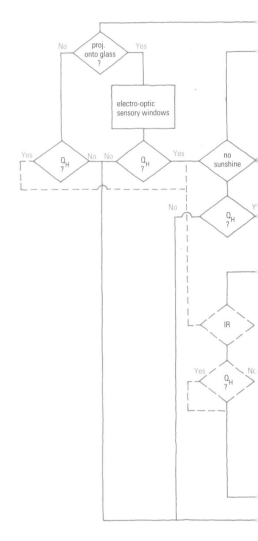

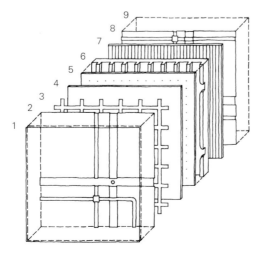

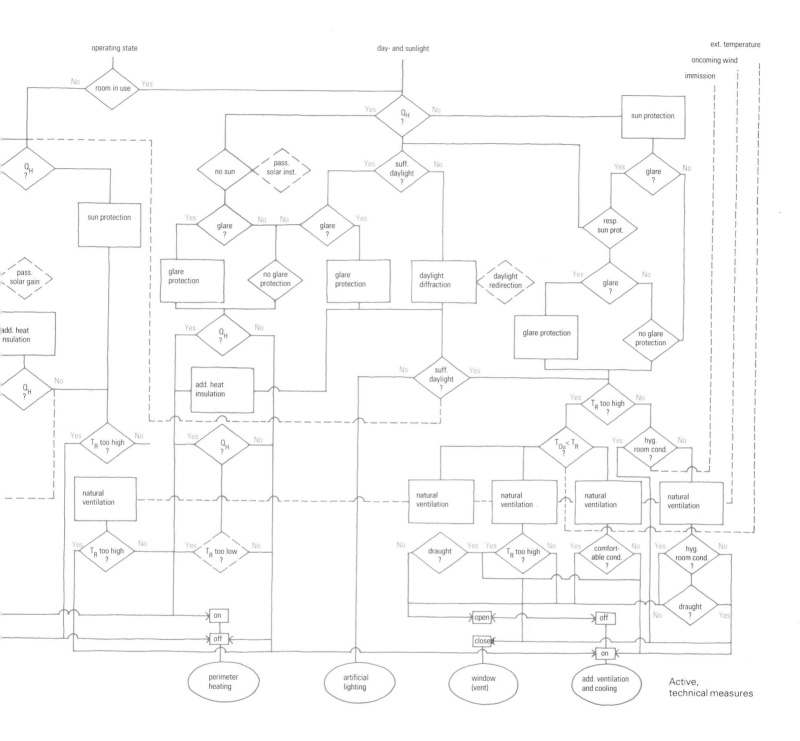

Figure 211
Diagram for operation of polyvalent wall systems and active,
technical building services

Q_H Heat requirement
T_R Room temperature
T_{Ou} External temperature
IR   Infra-red reflective area

Buildings of Tomorrow: Examples and Ideas

Buildings of Tomorrow: Examples and Ideas

8

9

Not only are atria and buffer zones interesting
spatial design features, they also help save
energy and passively utilize solar energy because
of the advantageous volume/surface ratio. The
technical design of atria is based on function. Any
design solutions must reflect these requirements.

Could the microclimate be considerably improved
by internal foliage? Could plants improve hygienic
conditions by eliminating contaminants because
of their microorganisms? This is a wide field,
worth exploring further.

8.
Rooms under Glass
Optimized Building Services for Different
Requirements

In pursuit of improved infrastructures for urban areas, designs with atria, malls and light wells are enjoying a revival. The architecture of the late 70s and early 80s rediscovered the special features of rooms under glass and their versatility as meeting places, lobbies, climate buffers, modifiers of the microclimate, noise protectors, etc. Depending upon the specific requirements, different solutions present themselves for servicing these projects. Yet glass-covered 'sun' rooms should cost no more than ordinary or closed rooms and should, furthermore, contribute to savings in energy and operation costs. Whether and to what extent such solutions are economically viable and how much technical effort is to be expended on the construction of such rooms is a matter for intelligent planning. Certainly, as is the case with double-leaf façades, the cost-benefit ratio remains in question and atria are usually not feasible from an energy perspective alone, unless they combine special utility with spatial quality.

In principle, atria should be naturally ventilated, or ventilated exclusively by the air movement originating from adjacent office areas, keeping the technical effort for building systems at a minimum. Temperature dynamics on large glass surfaces are especially important and must be considered, since they can be catalysts for large, thermally caused, air movements and currents.

Atria intended as rest or work areas must be designed to ensure that cold surfaces do not create cold-air circulation with noticeable draught effects and that perceived temperatures lie within a

comfortable range. In winter, differences between room temperature (temperature in atrium) and glass surface temperature may exceed 4 K, causing draughts whose velocity creates cold air streams in the direction of the floor. Draught is only preventable when the temperature difference falls below 4 K. Temperature control of the glass surfaces (horizontal and vertical) can be direct or indirect. Direct control is possible with:

– frame heating with electrical resistance,
– frame heating with water circulation,
– heating of glass surfaces with warm air flow.

Figure 212 shows a model study of various temperature differences between glass surfaces and interior space, in which air streams in the room have been made visible by strips. When the difference between room temperature and glass surface temperature is 10 K (instant exposure), intensive air movement becomes visible throughout the atrium, in which air velocities may reach 1.5 m/s near the ground (ascending thermals in the border area, descending thermals in the centre of the hall space). When the temperature difference is less pronounced, e.g. 7 K, the thermally caused air movement slows down considerably, reaching comfortable levels only when the difference falls below 4 K.

Another essential detail in halls is shading. There are many different solutions, as examples on the following pages will demonstrate. It is important that thermal behaviour and stratification within the space be closely studied (building climate studies) in the planning and design of halls. Besides shading, storage capacity and surface colours play an important role. When the surrounding areas of a hall are designed appropriately, shading may become superfluous and it may only be necessary to install sun or glare protection on the inner façade along the margins of the space (e.g. office areas, commercial areas, etc.). Depending on room space and user requirements, there are various options for decreasing heat incidence in summer, in which thermal ventilation (stack effect) should always be given special attention.

Interior glass surface temperature
10 K below room temperature

Interior glass surface temperature
7 K below room temperature

Interior glass surface temperature
4 K below room temperature

Figure 212
Cold air circulation caused
by excessively cold roof areas
(instant exposure shot) in
atrium (left)

8.1
The Central Lobby

Figure 213 shows the central lobby of the
New Leipzig Fair building (designed by
von Gerkan, Marg + Partners).

Figure 214 shows an entrance area of the
exhibition hall (250 m long, 80 m wide, 35 m high)
and the chief construction features. The vaulted
glass hall has a skin of tempered safety-glass
panes supported by a tubular steel grid. Figure 215
provides a view into the interior, flooded with daylight. The calculations were based on the following
options:

– float glass VSG (laminated safety glass) 20 mm,
total solar energy transmission 73 %,
light transmission 84 %,

– white glass VSG (laminated safety glass) 20 mm
with silkscreen pattern (Type B),
total solar energy transmission 52–67 %,
light transmission 62 %.

Figure 215
Interior of hall during
construction phase

Figure 213
Model photo of glass hall of the
New Leipzig Fair buildings.

Figure 214
Entrance hall under construction
showing arched load-bearing
structure with suspended glass
panels.

Many calculations and studies were carried out to illustrate the temperature behaviour in mid-summer and throughout the year, as well as the effects of cooling floors with water and roof surfaces with a layer of water (as additional sun protection). Excerpts are presented here.

The exposed framework of the glass hall reduces the incident insolation by approx. 30 %. The distribution of radiation absorption is illustrated in Figure 216 for both glazing variations. In the comparison of clear and tinted glazing, it can be seen that the tinting has a shading effect and also redistributes the absorbed radiation from the ground to the roof. The same is true of energy distribution for both glazing variations (Figure 217.1). When clear instead of tinted glass is used in single glazing, there is an increased storage (capacity) in the building mass and simultaneously a decrease in the release of heat to the outside. The perceived (or operative) temperature in the hall (Figure 217.2) is decreased by approx. 1 K with tinted glazing, compared to clear glazing; this applies to daily and yearly readings.

The floor treatment uses natural rock and floor screed with good storage capacity. To decrease the room and perceived temperatures, a floor-cooling system can be integrated (pipe diameter 25 mm, pipe spacing 300 mm, installation depth 100 mm, cooling water temperature approx. 18°C). As an alternative, the temperature behaviour and energy flow for water-sprinkled glass roof surfaces were studied. Figures 218.1 and 218.2 show the corresponding energy flows as well as the air and building component temperatures for each active, additional (or secondary) technical measure.

Figure 216
Distribution of radiation absorption in July

Fair weather period from DIN 4710 / VDI 2078

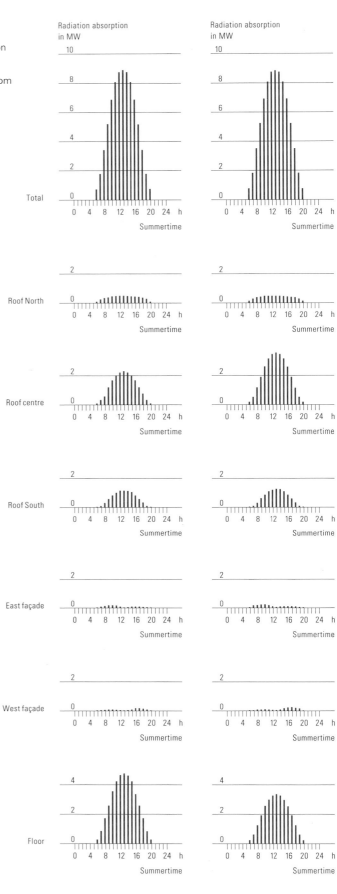

Clear single glazing

Energy distribution
in MW

Tinted single glazing

Energy distribution
in MW

Tinted glazing
with floor cooling

Energy distribution
in MW

Tinted glazing
with 50 % sprinkling

Energy distribution
in MW

Figure 217.1 (left)
Energy distribution for natural
ventilation for different glazing
types

Figure 218.1 (right)
Energy distribution for natural
ventilation for different cooling
systems

all values for fair weather period
from DIN 4710 / VDI 2078

Total

Storage

Ventilation

Heat transfer to outside

Evaporation

Clear single glazing

Temperature
in °C

Tinted single glazing

Temperature
in °C

Tinted glazing
with floor cooling

Temperature
in °C

Tinted glazing
with 50 % sprinkling

Temperature
in °C

Figure 217.2 (left)
Temperatures for natural
ventilation and different
glazing types

Figure 218.2 (right)
Temperatures for natural
ventilation and different
cooling systems

— Exterior air
— Flooring
– – Interior air
······ Roof
— Perceived temperature

167

An important criterion for the most appropriate choice of technology (glazing, flooring and sprinkling options) is the annual temperatures curve (frequencies). Figures 219 to 221 illustrate the air temperatures, as well as the perceived temperatures, for different glazing options, floor construction and sprinkled roof areas. In this comparison, the tinted glazing, in combination with sprinkled or moistened glass areas, yields the most favourable values, and the perceived temperature is approx. 4 K less than the worst scenario. The evaporative performance (cooling performance) is approx. 3 MW, corresponding to an evaporated volume of water of approx. 5 m³/h. To evenly moisten the glass roof, a somewhat greater amount of water than necessary must be sprayed. Hence, the dimensioning of corresponding pipelines should be based on a max. volume of 25 m³/h.

Temperatures near floor

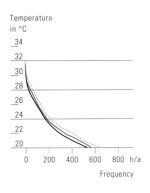

Perceived temperature

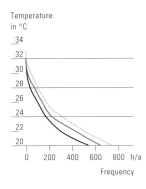

Figure 219
Annual perceived temperatures for different glazing types

Frequencies between 9 a.m. and 7 p.m. accord. to TRY

—— Exterior air
······ Clear single glazing
—— Tinted single glazing

Temperatures near floor

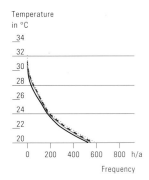

Perceived temperature

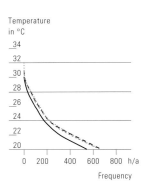

Figure 220
Annual temperatures for different flooring types

Frequencies between 9 a.m. and 7 p.m. accord. to TRY

—— Exterior air
······ Insulated flooring
– – Solid flooring
—— Floor cooling

Temperatures near floor

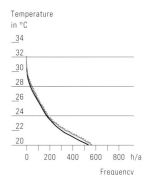

Perceived temperature

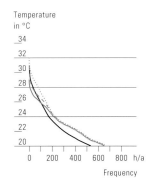

Figure 221
Annual temperatures for different intensities of sprinkled exterior skin

Frequencies between 9 a.m. and 7 p.m. accord. to TRY

—— Exterior air
······ 0 % sprinkled roof area
– – 20 % sprinkled roof area
—— 50 % sprinkled roof area

Figure 222.1 shows a cross-section of the hall with the sprinkled roof areas and the fan-lights arranged centrally for natural ventilation via buoyancy and cross-wind. Figures 222.2 and 222.3 illustrate details of the sprinkling system. The sprayed water can be taken either directly from the drinking water or, even better, from rain-water cisterns, which would be preferable in the long term and certainly more ecologically friendly.

Wind tunnel studies were undertaken to determine natural ventilation and smoke exhaust in case of fire. Two images from the studies are shown in Figure 223 and 224. The domed roof shape results in high negative pressure coefficients in the top roof chamber, which promote ventilation of the air volume in the hall. When the lower glass areas are opened, natural ventilation is excellent.

Figure 222.3
Water distribution on ancillary trusses

1   Pipeline DN 25, 2fold
    sprinkling and cleaning
2   Pipeline DN 15 for nozzle
3   Nozzle
4   Main truss
5   Ancillary truss
6   Glass panels

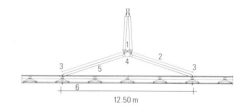

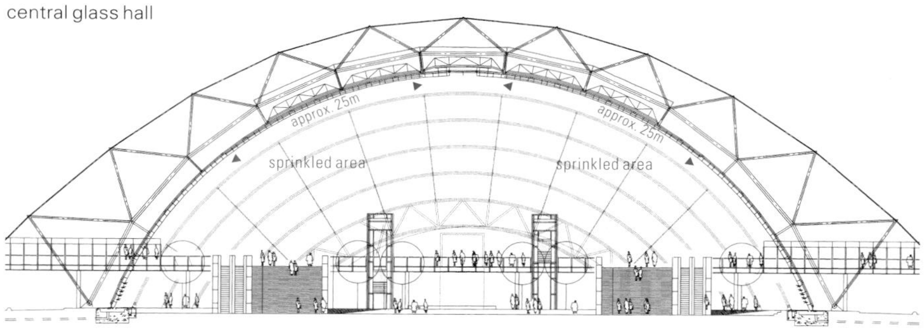

Figure 222.1
Cross-section of
central glass hall

Figure 223
Wind tunnel study
Oncoming winds,
light section

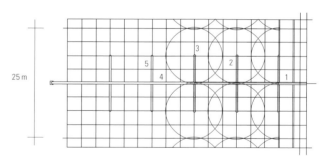

Figure 222.2
View of glass surface with
dynamic trajectory image of nozzle
(radius 6.4 m)

Sprayed water volume:
9.2 l/min (5.2 l/min for 180° nozzles)

1–5 as in Fig. 222.3

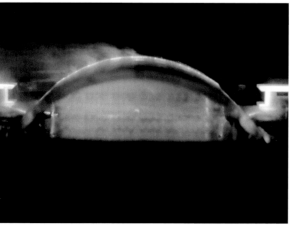

Figure 224
Wind tunnel study
Oncoming winds,
light section

8.2
Utility and Traffic Zones under Glass

The persistent question of heat gain via atrium and hall construction, especially during periods when additional heat is required, was once more raised for the Galleria Opfikon project (Zurich). Thermal behaviour and temperature stratification were studied as well as the dynamics in the hall in case of fire. Some of the relevant studies are presented here.

Figure 225 shows the Galleria Opfikon/Zurich project, developed and designed by Spaltenstein Real Estate AG and the architects' group D. Gerber & X. Nauer, Burckhardt + Partners AG, B.E. Honegger and W. Glaus.

The house within a house is so flexibly designed with regard to building services that only the basic structure is defined, leaving it open to modifications and subsequent use for expansion into rental units. The client formulated the following goals for his own project:

– top level of communication,
– material and non-material ecological values,
– partly civic space – partly social space,
– transparency as a symbol of openness,
– an 'intelligent' house.

The atrium is the focal point of the building, as can be seen in Figure 226. It serves not only as a central access and traffic zone but also for various special applications, with a restaurant area, concert and theatre performances, fashion and art shows. Thus, the central atrium is a multipurpose space and highly important for the building as a whole. Figure 227 is a view into the atrium and the high glass front on the east elevation.

Figure 225
Galleria Opfikon, main elevation
(Spaltenstein Real Estate AG,
Architects' team
D. Gerber & X. Nauer,
Burckhardt + Partners AG,
B.E. Honegger and W. Glaus)

Figure 226
Floor plan

Figure 227
View into atrium

Passive Solar Gain in Atria

Figure 228 (Option 1) depicts the fluctuations in heat requirements for offices and utility spaces adjacent to the courtyard, without taking the atrium into consideration. The graphs show typical requirements, peaking at approx. 50 MWh in January and reaching a low of approx. 5 MWh in July. The heat transfer coefficients in this study were 0.35 W/m² K for the walls and 1.8 W/m² K for the windows.

To support summertime cooling in the atrium, the heat transfer coefficients in Option 2.1 (Figure 228) were increased to 2.8 W/m²K near the inner windows, located between offices and atrium. The heat transfer coefficients for the glass roof and the vertical glass enclosures were 3.1 W/m²K. It is evident that the heat requirements are similar for comparable offices during winter months; there is also an additional heat requirement for the atrium itself. In the summer months May through September, the heat requirement is almost nil, proof of the noticeable heat gain through radiation.

The heat transfer coefficients for Option 2.2 (Figure 228) were defined as follows: U-value approx. 2.8 W/m²K for interior windows and 1.8 W/m²K for the glass roof and large vertical glass surfaces. A comparison of Options 1 and 2.2 shows that the heat requirement is cut nearly in half for office spaces and that a definite heat gain in the months April through September suffices to compensate for heat losses. As a rough guideline, atria generally cut in half the heat requirement of areas adjacent to them.

The diagram shown in Figure 229 is based on empirical data (HL-Technik AG). The two graphics depict air-change rates dependent on outside air velocity for oncoming winds on the long and short sides of the atrium. They help to estimate the probable air-change rates in the atrium for different outside air velocities.

Figure 228
Heat requirements in offices (perimeter heating) for different options

Option 1
Offices adjacent to courtyard, atrium not taken into consideration

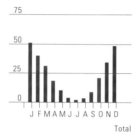

Figure 229
Air-change rates dependent on outside air velocity

Option 2.1
Offices adjacent to courtyard, atrium with double insulated glazing

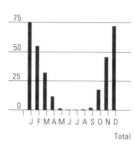
Total

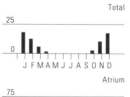
Atrium

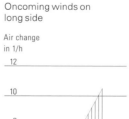

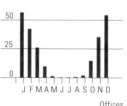
Offices

Oncoming winds on long side

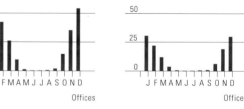
Oncoming wind speed

Option 2.2
Offices adjacent to courtyard, atrium with double thermal glazing

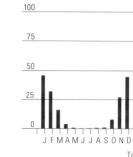
Total

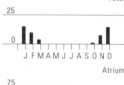
Atrium

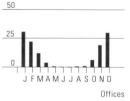
Offices

Oncoming winds on short side

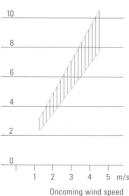

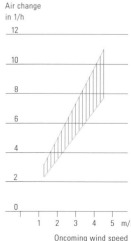
Oncoming wind speed

Figure 230 shows the temperatures near the atrium ground (utility) level for periodic and for constant natural ventilation and various air-change rates. As expected, relatively small air-change rates (1 ac/h) and an estimated operation time (opening time of atrium roof) cause the highest room temperatures near ground level (approx. 40°C). This can be counteracted by ventilating naturally and constantly (in summer, all roof surfaces remain open to allow for buoyancy, which decreases the temperatures considerably. When outside air velocities are small, approx. 1.5 to 2 m/s, air-change rates are usually 3 ac/h, so that the atrium space never overheats, as confirmed during subsequent operation. To ensure a steady temperature in summer, the horizontal glass surfaces in the Galleria project are equipped with simple awnings, used during periods of intense radiation.

Figure 231 shows an initial estimate of temperature stratification in the atrium space for minimal air change and limited natural ventilation. This diagram depicts conditions with the least favourable parameters assumed (lowest air-change rate, least number of hours for natural ventilation). Figure 232 shows the frequency of high temperatures, under the same assumptions as in Figure 230. When air-change rates are lower and combined with less natural ventilation time, a long period of high temperatures results (approx. 320 h/a above 30°C). For the actual air-change rates (> 3 ac/h) and optimum utilization of natural

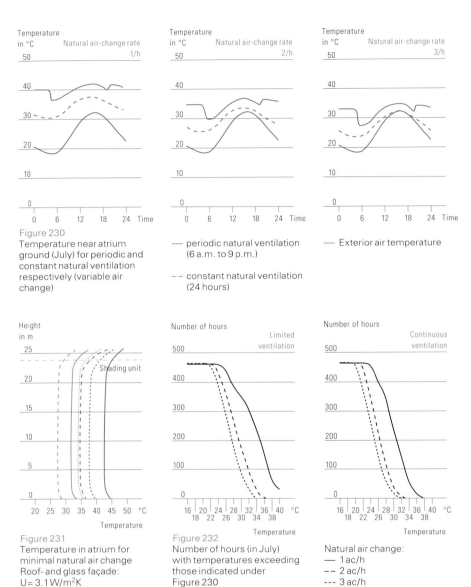

Figure 230
Temperature near atrium ground (July) for periodic and constant natural ventilation respectively (variable air change)

— periodic natural ventilation (6 a.m. to 9 p.m.)

– – constant natural ventilation (24 hours)

— Exterior air temperature

Figure 231
Temperature in atrium for minimal natural air change
Roof- and glass façade:
$U = 3.1\,W/m^2K$

– – April
...... June
- - - August

– – May
— July
— September

Figure 232
Number of hours (in July) with temperatures exceeding those indicated under Figure 230

Natural air change:
— 1 ac/h
– – 2 ac/h
- - - 3 ac/h

Table 6
Functional processes of naturally ventilated courtyard or atrium spaces

Integrated façade heating:	Flow temperature approx. 40 to 45 °C Return temperature approx. 30 to 35 °C (compensated) (temperature at interior glass pane = f (room temperature of courtyard [atrium])) ΔT surfaces/room = max. 4 K (applies also to air heating)
Roof louvres:	approx. 10 % of 'horizontal' glass surface (ventilation/cooling/smoke exhaust)
Lower louvre:	approx. 5 to 7 % of 'horizontal' glass surface (ventilation/cooling/smoke exhaust)
Sun protection:	Active only on sunny days
	(All louvres are 'operator controlled' – linear control function)

Outside air velocity in m/s	Functional units	Outside air temperature in °C					In case of fire
		< +/-0	< +/-0 to 5	+5 to +15	+15 to +20	> +20	
< 1.0	Integrated façade heating	on	on	—	off	off	on
	Roof vents	closed	closed	min. open	open	open	open
	Lower louvres	closed	closed	min. open	open	open	open
	Shading unit	open	open	closed	closed	closed	open
1.0 to 2.0	Integrated façade heating	on	on	—	off	off	on
	Roof vents	closed	closed	min. open	open	open	open
	Lower louvres	closed	closed	closed	min. open	min. open	open
	Shading unit	open	open	closed	closed	closed	open
2.0 to 5.0	Integrated façade heating	on	on	—	off	off	on
	Roof vents	closed	closed	min. open	open	min. open	open
	Lower louvres	closed	closed	closed	closed	closed	open
	Shading unit	open	open	closed	closed	closed	open
> 5.0	Integrated façade heating	on	on	—	off	off	on
	Roof vents	closed	closed	min. open	min. open	min. open	open
	Lower louvres	closed	closed	closed	closed	closed	open
	Shading unit	open	open	closed	closed	closed	open

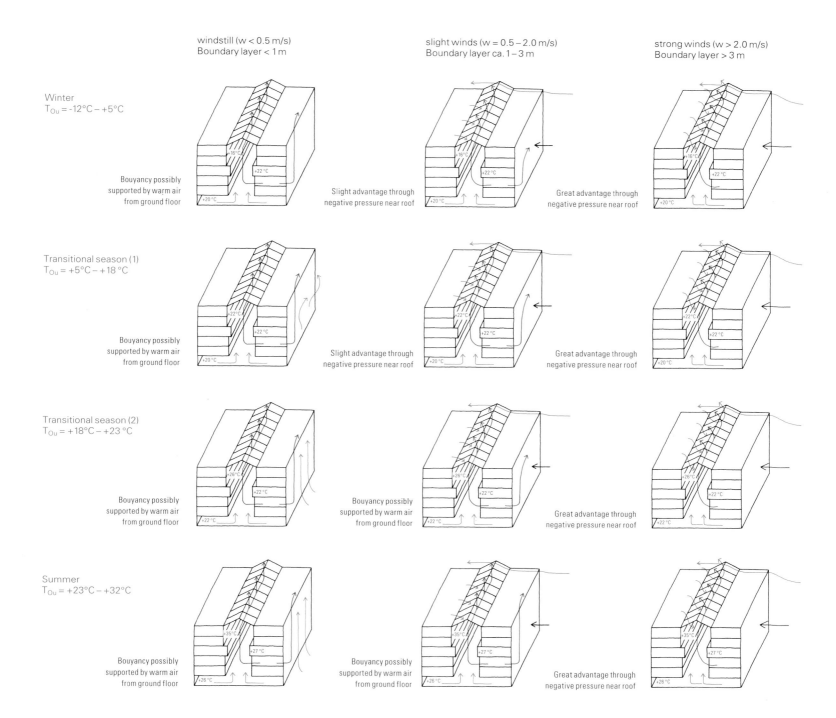

windstill (w < 0.5 m/s)
Boundary layer < 1 m

slight winds (w = 0.5 – 2.0 m/s)
Boundary layer ca. 1 – 3 m

strong winds (w > 2.0 m/s)
Boundary layer > 3 m

Winter
T_{Ou} = -12°C – +5°C

Bouyancy possibly supported by warm air from ground floor

Slight advantage through negative pressure near roof

Great advantage through negative pressure near roof

Transitional season (1)
T_{Ou} = +5°C – +18 °C

Bouyancy possibly supported by warm air from ground floor

Slight advantage through negative pressure near roof

Great advantage through negative pressure near roof

Transitional season (2)
T_{Ou} = +18°C – +23 °C

Bouyancy possibly supported by warm air from ground floor

Bouyancy possibly supported by warm air from ground floor

Great advantage through negative pressure near roof

Summer
T_{Ou} = +23°C – +32°C

Bouyancy possibly supported by warm air from ground floor

Bouyancy possibly supported by warm air from ground floor

Great advantage through negative pressure near roof

Figure 233
Different types of smoke gas exhaust

Smoke gases rise in atrium through buoyancy. Ventilation through roof. Roof areas are open.

ventilation, high temperatures above 30°C occur for only approx. 20 hours per annum. The conclusion to be drawn from these measurements is that atria should be naturally ventilated as much as possible during the summer months without the aid of air-conditioning and mechanical ventilation systems, to create comfortable environment and room temperatures. Table 6 lists additional functional processes of naturally ventilated courtyard or atrium spaces, depending on outside air velocity and outside temperature.

Not only does opening horizontal and vertical glass surfaces in atria influence the temperature behaviour, it is also important with regard to smoke extract and smoke ventilation in case of fire. Figure 233 depicts natural smoke gas exhaust through opened vertical or horizontal glass surfaces during the different seasons and for different oncoming wind directions.

8.3
Atria as Noise Buffer Zones

Zurich Insurance's new office building is located at a high traffic zone in Hamburg (architects: von Gerkan, Marg + Partners) (comb-shaped building). The complex incorporates two large atria, around which the offices are grouped. The atria are buffers for noise insulation. Figure 234 is a view of the front of the building, Figure 235 a view of the atrium and Figure 236 a view along a hall-way, through and past an office area into the atrium.

The basic concept was to ventilate all offices naturally. Future occupants of the building could then retrofit air-conditioning and ventilation for individual areas within the building. Therefore, empirical data were needed to determine the probable air-change rates between the atria and the adjacent office spaces.

Based on mean, annual wind velocities (Figure 237) and the distribution of wind directions, two empirical studies were conducted whose results are shown in Figure 238. With minimal oncoming air velocities of 1.5 – 4.5 m/s, the air-change rates fluctuate from 3 to 12 ac/h, depending upon whether wind is directed at the long or the side walls of the atrium. The air-change rates for the office areas are then approx. 2 to 5 ac/h when windows are opened (pivot or rotating position). Air-change rates in the offices are measured, on the one hand, for the unheated atrium (air change resulting from buoyancy) and, on the other hand, for air movement in the atrium itself (primary air flow), which may create secondary air movements in the adjacent offices (air induction).

Figure 235 (top)
View of atrium

Figure 236
Hallway leading to atrium

Figure 234
Zurich Insurance, Hamburg
(Architects: von Gerkan,
Marg + Partners)

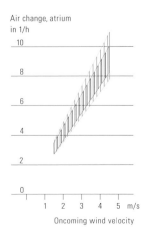

Air change, atrium
in 1/h

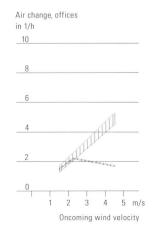

Air change, offices
in 1/h

Oncoming wind velocity

Oncoming wind velocity

Figure 238
Air-change rates in atrium
and adjacent offices

|||| Wind directed at side walls
|||| Wind directed at long walls

Figure 237
Wind statistics at Hamburg
site

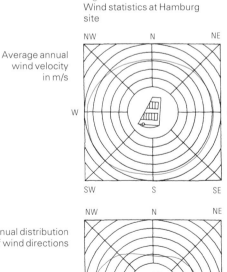

Average annual
wind velocity
in m/s

Average annual distribution
of wind directions

8.4
The Atrium as Office Space

The design for the administrative offices of the Badenwerke Karlsruhe (architects Auer + Weber) settled, in the planning phase, an interesting question. The discussion focused on whether to erect a conventional building with one diagonal wing on this corner lot or to place the entire building underneath a glass skin, i.e. to construct a double-leaf façade on the sides facing the road and to close the building with a five-storey-high glass enclosure on the courtyard side. The atrium was to be naturally ventilated in summer and in the transitional season (atrium open) and remain closed in winter, to utilize solar energy for heating the entire building. Figure 239 shows the design model, Figure 240 an elevation where the desired double-leaf façade is visible (partial transparency). The ground floor (Figure 241) illustrates the extent of the plan, above all the utilization there, between the two building angles, of the atrium, which on the upper floors is closed off diagonally by vertical building components.

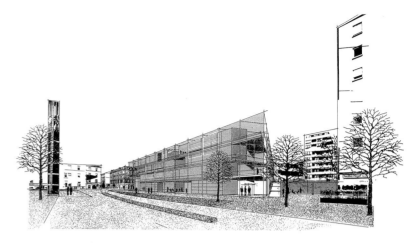

Figure 240
Elevation of building with planned, double-leaf façade

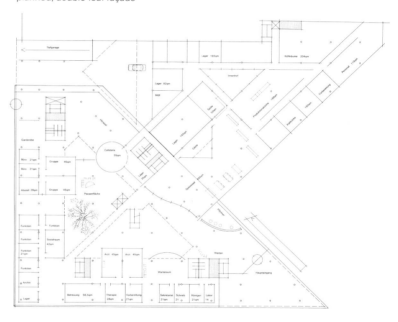

Figure 241
Floor plan of ground floor

Figure 239
Design model of administrative building Badenwerke AG, Karlsruhe
(Architects: Auer + Weber, Munich)

Figure 242 lists the options under discussion. The conventional solution (Option 1) has a well insulated outer skin and external sun shades, as well as a glass covering over the ground floor and, above it, a naturally ventilated courtyard. In Option 2, the entire building, as shown, is covered in a second skin and the glass roof is now located in the area of the five-storey sector of the building (atrium). The values listed below make clear which specific energy and operating cost savings result from Option 2. The parameters for the areas to be covered are:

Option 1– Single Façade

Exterior Walls
– U-value   0.35 W/m²K
Windows
– U-value   2.0 W/m²K
– τ-factor   0.79
– g-value (no shading)   0.67
– b-factor:
  (no shading)   0.77
  (with shading)   0.3

The cooling system to maintain a max. room temperature of 28°C in summer must have an air-change rate of 5 ac/h.

Option 2– House under Glass

Glass-Roof Atrium
Heat-insulated glazing
– U-value   2.0 W/m²K
– τ-factor   0.79
– g-value (no shading)   0.67
– b-factor   0.77

Inner façade to atrium
Single glazing (room height)
Awnings (between inner façade and atrium)
– U-value   5.0 W/m²K
– τ-factor   0.88
– g-value (no shading)   0.87
– b-factor:
  (no shading)   1.0
  (with shading)   0.3

Double-leaf outer façade
Outer pane = single glazing
Inner pane = heat-insulated glazing
Shading = as for inner façade

Total τ-factor = 0.79 · 0.88 = 0.70
      g-value = 0.67 · 0.87 = 0.58

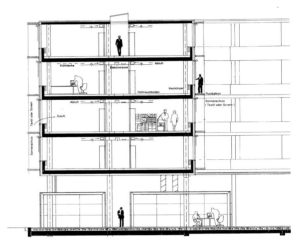

Figure 242
Façade options

Option 1
Conventional solution
(glass cover above first floor)

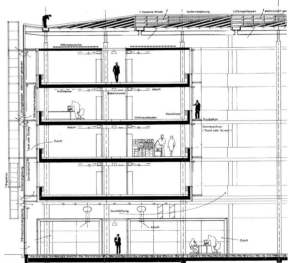

Option 2
House under glass
(double-leaf façade and
five-storey atrium)

Figure 243 lists the specific energy costs for both variations. The costs are divided into different energy consumption factors (pumps, lighting, humidification, cooling, heating and air movement). Figure 244 shows the energy costs, including expenses for maintenance and repair of technical installations. Finally, Figure 245 shows the specific total costs/m² of lettable area per annum and indicates total savings in Option 2, compared to Option 1, of approx. 40 DM/m² per annum. When this amount is added to the higher initial investment costs for a double-leaf façade and the large glass roof of approx. 500 to 600 DM/m², a sufficient amortization rate may still be achieved, especially when rising energy costs are factored into the equation.

Here, as with double-leaf façades, it should be remarked that particular atria and double-leaf solutions must always be designed and executed as economically as possible, to develop and create an ecologically efficient building.

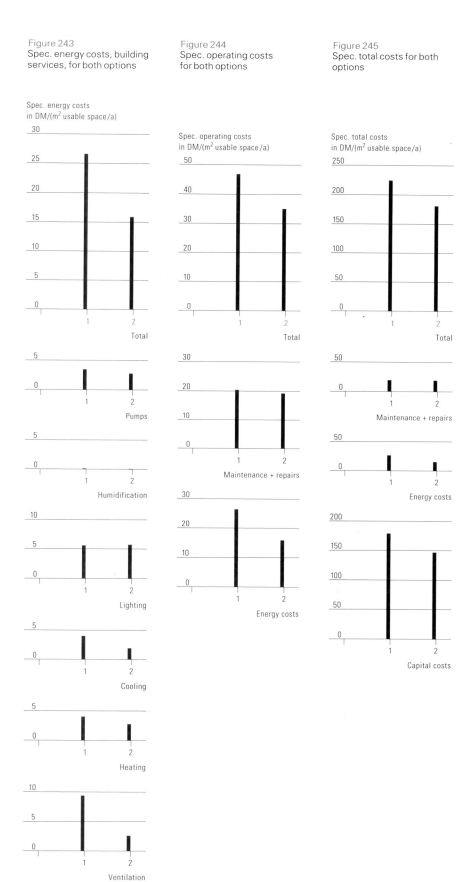

Figure 243
Spec. energy costs, building services, for both options

Figure 244
Spec. operating costs for both options

Figure 245
Spec. total costs for both options

8.5
Atria as Thermal Towers

Buildings with high-ceilinged atria and shafts are
particularly well suited to natural ventilation by
buoyancy, moving air volumes through the building and thus extracting heat energy as well as
contaminants and odours.

Figure 246 shows, in principle, the interactions
between the ascending current (in theory) and the
dynamic draught and friction losses counteract-
ing the buoyancy. Figure 247 illustrates the principle of buoyancy for inner heat gain in an atrium
and illustrates the basics of calculating volume
flows caused by buoyancy as well as intake and
exit velocities. Natural ventilation by buoyancy is
generally somewhat restricted by the formation
of positive and negative pressures from the
oncoming winds. Natural ventilation by buoyancy
alone can only occur during calms, if at all. Nevertheless, ventilation by buoyancy is especially
important for large glassed-in areas and plays a
role in atria, glass-covered halls, etc. Figure 248
shows a model design for a skyscraper. This skyscraper has an atrium which utilizes buoyancy
to naturally ventilate the building. The right side
of the building adjacent to the thermal tower
(offices) faces north and the offices to the left side
face south. The northward offices have a double-
leaf glass façade, to facilitate natural ventilation
and, at the same time, to insulate the offices from
excessive traffic noise.

In summer, fresh air is brought into the atrium
through the glass roof and is cooled by the surrounding concrete masses. The air sinks gradually
from the top to the ground, passing through
open areas towards the north façade (double-leaf
façade) where it rises again because of the heat
gained in the offices. Thus, on the north façade,
an upward directed flow develops which passes
by the offices. When the office windows to the
inside (towards the atrium) are open, fresh air can
enter through them from the double-leaf façade.

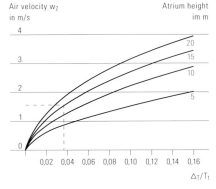

Figure 246
Ascending current in shafts

h   Shaft height (m)
γ   Density (kg/m³)
T   Temperature (°C)
b   Barometric pressure
     (in mm)
D_{dyn} Dynamic draught loss
D_F Friction loss

H_B = Buoyancy (in theory)

$$H_B = 273 \ h \ \left(\frac{\gamma_{IA}}{273 + T_{IA}} - \frac{\gamma_{OA}}{273 + T_{OA}}\right) \frac{b}{760}$$

Figure 247
Principle of buoyancy during
heat gain in room

Air velocity w_2
in m/s

Atrium height
im m

$$w_1 = \sqrt{\frac{s \cdot h \ \Delta_T / T_1}{1 + A_2^2 / A_1^2}} \ \ [m/s]$$

$$\dot{V} = \frac{\dot{Q}}{c_p \cdot \rho \cdot \Delta_T} \ \ [m^3/s]$$

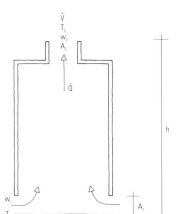
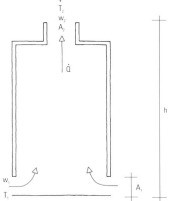

w_1 Intake velocity (m/s)
s   9.81 m/s²
h   Atrium height (m)
Δ_T Temperature
      difference between
      intake and exit (K)
T_1 Intake air temperature (K)
T_2 Exit air temperature (K)
A_1 Lower
      intake opening (m²)
A_2 Upper exit opening (m²)
w_2 Upper exit velocity (m/s)
$\dot{V}$ Thermally caused
      volume flow (m³/s)
$\dot{Q}$ Heat volume in room
      (kW)

In winter and in the transitional season, i.e. whenever the outside temperature is lower than the room temperature, fresh air enters through the north-facing double-leaf façade and flows from the top to the ground. To prevent excessive cooling of the double-leaf façade, the air brought in from the outside is heated to approx. +15°C with the help of a heat-recovery installation connected to the atrium. The outside air then flows through the double-leaf façade while gaining more heat from the offices (heat flow from inside out) and from diffuse radiation. As shown in the diagram, the outside temperature reaches approx. 20°C at the ground level of the atrium and rises because of suction (negative pressure co-efficients interacting with opened window units in the atrium) inside the thermal tower, whence it exits again after it has been cooled by the circulation heat-recovery installation. Hence, in winter there exists a roof-to-ground circulation near the north façade. Opened window units in the offices adjacent to the double-leaf façade can admit fresh air into the utility areas. Figure 249 shows the conditions in summer and in winter for the corresponding office rooms.

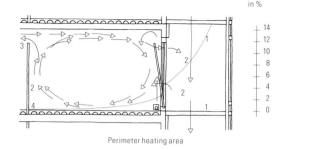

Daylight quotient in %

Perimeter heating area

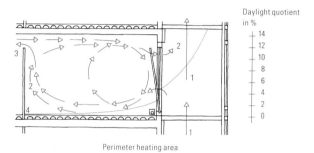

Daylight quotient in %

Perimeter heating area

Figure 249
Ventilation options with double-leaf façade

Above: Ventilation of office in winter/cool transitional season (external temperature -10°C to approx. +10°C)

1 Primary fresh air flow (approx. +12°C to +15°C)
2 Secondary fresh air flow
3 Mechanical ventilation (warm air flow when windows are closed)
4 Daylight quotients

Below: Ventilation of office in summer/warm transitional season (external temperature +22°C to +30°C)

1 Primary fresh air flow (approx. +26°C to +30°C)
2 Secondary fresh air flow
3 Mechanical ventilation (cold air flow when windows are closed)
4 Daylight quotients

Figure 248
Natural ventilation by buoyancy in high-rise design with atrium

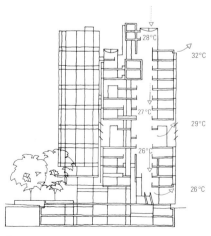

Summer
External temperature 27°C

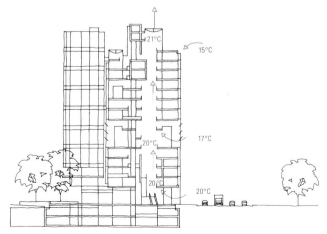

Winter and transitional season
External temperature 15°C

When natural ventilation by bouyancy or wind
pressure is not feasible, the building is mechanically ventilated and cooled or humidified by secondary systems. The supplementary air-conditioning system would need to be activated for
approx. 15 to 20 % of the total operating time for
this building, fulfilling the requirement of utilizing
natural resources for energy savings (Figure 250).

Figure 250
Design model of building
(Architect: Prof. J. Friedrich,
Hamburg) and schematic
of thermal tower, ground plan
and isometric drawing

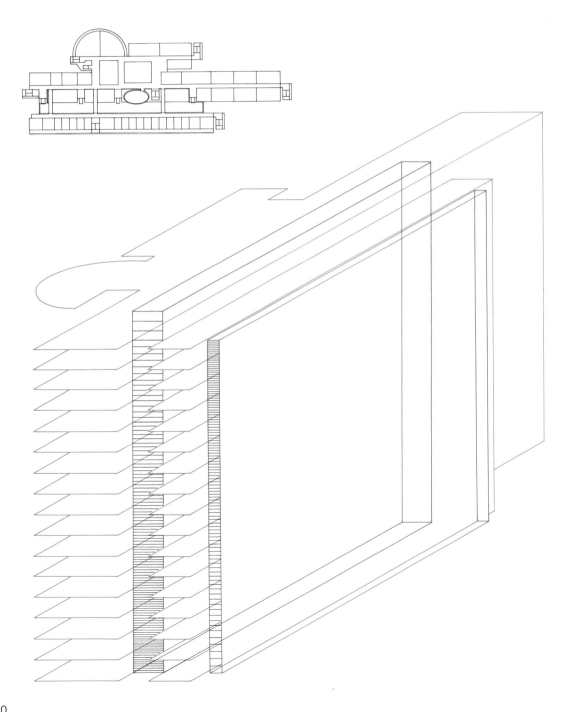

The De Montfort University building in Leicester (architects: Short Ford & Ass., London) is another example of the use of thermal towers. This building was the first in the UK to implement natural ventilation by buoyancy. The heat generated in the building by occupants and machines is extracted through the thermal towers. Mechanical ventilation can thus be mostly avoided and air-conditioning eliminated altogether.

Fundamental to this design are the clever room layout and the selection of materials. To reduce the cooling load, the designers minimized solar heat gain by using a compact built form: the building has high storage capacity (open ceilings) and is mostly naturally ventilated.

Maximum natural ventilation was achieved despite the diverse requirements for various spaces in the building relative to their use (lecture halls, machine rooms, laboratories, studios). Most rooms, such as laboratories, offices, and classrooms, can be ventilated directly with openable windows, while the remaining rooms such as machine rooms and lecture halls are ventilated by means of the thermo-syphon effect. The air heated by indoor heat sources rises and exits to the outside through the thermal towers; in doing so it moves cool outside air through low-lying intakes from the building.

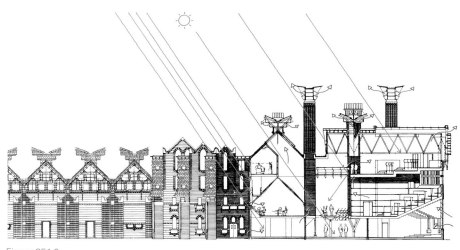

Figure 251.2
Concept of natural ventilation and lighting

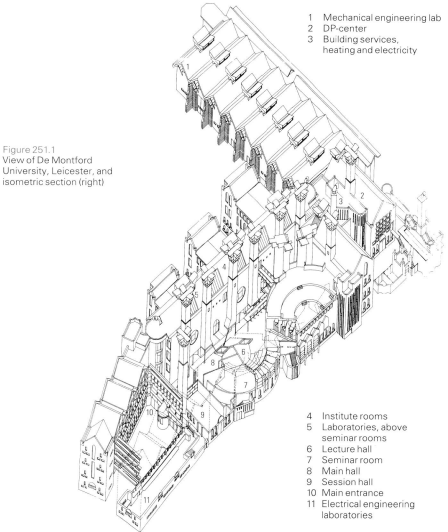

Figure 251.1
View of De Montford University, Leicester, and isometric section (right)

1 Mechanical engineering lab
2 DP-center
3 Building services, heating and electricity

4 Institute rooms
5 Laboratories, above seminar rooms
6 Lecture hall
7 Seminar room
8 Main hall
9 Session hall
10 Main entrance
11 Electrical engineering laboratories

8.6
Atria as Planted Winter Gardens

The DAK building (Health Insurance [Fund] for German Salaried Employees), Hamburg (architects: Pysall, Stahrenberg + Partners) was designed as a comb-like built form with integrated winter gardens. Like the Zurich Insurance building, this structure was intended to protect the office areas from excessive noise emissions while contributing to an improved microclimate in the building. Figure 252.1 is an aerial view of the building complex (model). Figures 252.2 and 252.3 show a ground plan and a cross-section of the winter gardens, respectively. The design posed particular difficulties for naturally ventilating the winter gardens, because the concave glass roofs between the solid structures of the building are nestled on the four-storey-high building sectors, i.e. are protected from oncoming winds. Wind-tunnel studies were therefore conducted early on, to determine the best position for roof openings as well as for openings in the lower area of the winter garden. Figures 253.1 and 253.2 show the section of a winter garden and the primary and secondary air flow in it and in the (adjacent) offices. Since the air movement through the winter garden is relatively low-velocity in nature, above all when the outside oncoming air moves horizontally across that particular winter garden, good secondary side ventilation was needed for the offices (for isothermal conditions). Instead of the usual tilt-turn windows, others with pivoting leafs had to be used to literally 'draw' air from the winter gardens into the offices.

Figure 252.1
DAK building , Hamburg
(Architects: Pysall, Stahrenberg
+ Partners, Braunschweig)
Model and view into winter
garden

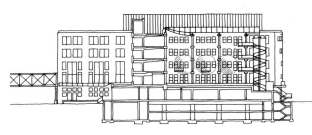

Figure 252.2
Cross-section of winter garden

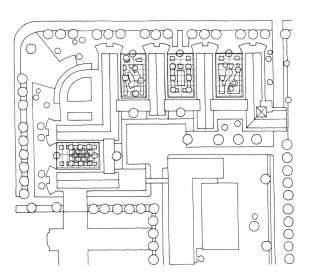

Figure 252.3
Bird's eye view of building
with integrated planted areas
(winter gardens)

When halls or atria have concave roofs, especially halls which, as in this example, are more or less enclosed (in the structure of the building), it is not uncommon for additional 'exhaust systems' to be required to achieve satisfactory ventilation. In each case it is strongly recommended that wind tunnel studies be conducted, to evaluate the overall solution and to avoid potential design errors.

The next step in this project was to use computer simulations to predict the mean air temperatures in the winter gardens, to determine the probable winter garden room temperatures, for different air-change rates (air change 1 ac/h / 5 ac/h) with and without vegetation. A single (1 ac/h) air-change rate in the winter garden is the absolute minimum value and quite unrealistic for this building at this location. Figure 254.1 plots the calculated temperature at various times of the day under a number of different assumptions. Any simulations of temperature curves in winter gardens executed to date are usually based on a temperature reduction by foliage of approx. 2–3 K. Often, however, this value is only realistic when buoyancy or natural ventilation by wind are sufficiently well developed.

South-west facing winter gardens

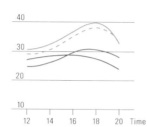

North-west facing winter gardens

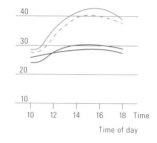

Figure 254.1
Computer simulation of average air temperatures in winter garden

Façade: clear glass
Roof: Elioterm neutral 50/38
    Internal sun protection

— Air change = 1/h
   without plants
–– Air change = 1/h
   with plants
— Air change = 5/h
   with plants
— External temperature

Figure 253.1
Air flow horizontally across winter garden (made visible by smoke – wind tunnel study, Kessler + Luch)

Figure 253.2
Diagram of natural ventilation of offices through winter garden

Structural measures for natural ventilation

1   Fresh air opening on face of building approx. 15 m² (net) for windstill periods (ventilation by buoyancy)
2   Exhaust/intake opening approx. 45 m² (gross)
3   Exhaust/intake opening approx. 40 m² (gross)
4   Pivoting window to exhaust natural air flow

Temperatures in winter garden are near +7°C for external winter temperatures of -12°C.

Figure 254.2
Criteria for plant selection
for winter gardens

| Temperature in °C | 5 | 6 | 7 | 8 | 9 | 10 | 11 | 12 | 13 | 14 | 15 | 16 | 17 | 18 | 19 | 20 | 21 | 22 | 23 | 24 | 25 | 26 | 27 | 28 | 29 | 30 | 31 |

General conditions
required by users

Room temperature ▷

Maximum temperature range ▷ air-conditioned

Local conditions
in winter gardens

Winter:

Max. low temperature ▷

Absolute lowest temperature ▷

Ideal daytime temperature
during sunshine ▷

Ideal nighttime temperature ▷

Summer:

Max. high temperature ▷

Absolute highest temperature ▷

Ideal daytime temperature
during sunshine ▷

Ideal nighttime temperature ▷ as low as possible

Figure 254.3
Planting design of a winter garden with control detail of man-
made pond (above) and view
of winter garden

Plants:
Trees
1 Kentia palm
2 Hemp palm

Large solitary shrubs
3 African hemp

Solitary shrubs
4 Aubuke

Ground cover
5 Green lily
6 Mondo grass
7 Creeping fig

Creepers
   Clerodendrum thomsoniae
   Cape or Madagascar
   jasmin

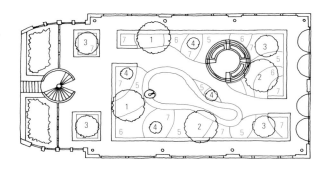

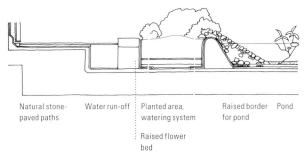

Natural stone-paved paths   Water run-off   Planted area, watering system   Raised border for pond   Pond

Raised flower bed

Landscape architect Hess, Norderstedt, developed a design using verdant foliage and plants to
improve the microclimate. The criteria outlined
in Figure 254.2 were the basis for the selection of
plants. The Figure 254.3 series depicts one planting design. The following remarks by the landscape architect further clarify the 'green design':

Quote
"For interior spaces with constant living room
temperature or for conservatories with pronounced differences between summer heat and
winter cold, there are many documented case
studies with indoor plants. This was not the case
for the DAK winter gardens, which have a relatively wide range of temperatures coincident with
an absence of winter 'downtime' and shade.
To ensure a good plant selection, the botanical
gardens in Hamburg prepared a consultant report.

According to their recommendations, only plants
of the subtropical rainforest type or comparable
indigenous zones were good choices. These are
plants
– which are used to deep shadow from
  tall trees,
– which have a wide temperature range and
  high tolerance to cold.

Examples of these plants are the
– Kentia palm (Howeia forsteriana),
– African hemp (Sparmannia africana),
– Silk oak (Grevillea robusta), now the
  principal plant in the courtyards.

– Bird-of-paradise (Strelitzia reginae),
– Flowering maple (Abutilon hybrids),
– Cape or Madagascar jasmin (Stephanotis
  floribunda) as flowering plants and

– Creeping fig (Ficus pumila),
– Ivy tree (Fatshedera lizei),
– Mondo grass or lilyturf (Ophiopogon jaburan)
  as groundcover.

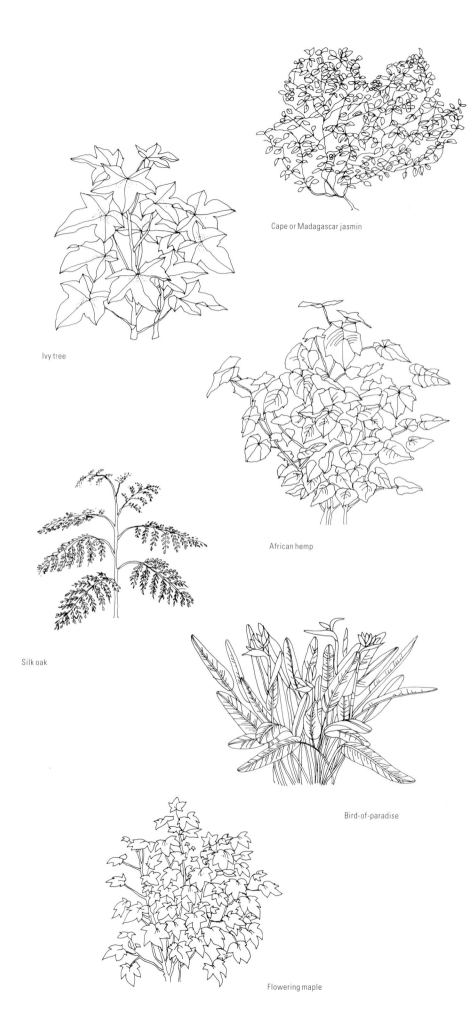

Cape or Madagascar jasmin

Ivy tree

African hemp

Silk oak

Bird-of-paradise

Flowering maple

While ground cover and flowering plants are usually available from local landscaping and gardening supplies, large plants (e.g. kentia palms and silk oak) are imported. In the US, South America and some areas of Africa, these plants reach impressive heights in optimal climate conditions. To transplant them from those conditions, after an arduous voyage, directly to their new location would surely kill them. They must be carefully adapted to the climate and light conditions of their new environment. This adaptation generally requires a minimum of 6 months; a full year of acclimatization is best. The goals set for this project have already furnished a description of the environment and conditions in which the plants are to thrive.

Regardless of how carefully plants are prepared for their future environment, their initial reaction to the transplantation is always shock, affecting growth. Especially large trees adapt with great difficulty. Planting in spring with subsequent good light conditions, as in the DAK building, greatly encourages the plants to take root. But even under these ideal conditions loss of foliage and blossoms and stunted growth cannot always be avoided. When this happens the stress on the plants can be lessened by increasing the humidity and by frequent sprinkling until they have developed a sufficient root system to draw moisture from the ground.

Yet, all the studies, expert reports and adaptation times cannot in themselves guarantee the plants' 'functioning'. In the DAK, however, there was only one type of plant which turned out to be unsuited. The otherwise indestructible tradescantia (Tradescantia cerinthoides) could not adapt to the combination of heat and shade in the summer months. It reacted with excessive growth and rotting and had to be replaced with green lilies (Chlorophytum comosum). These lilies have now replaced the tradescantia at the corresponding location as covering undergrowth."
(End of quote)

Until two or three years ago, there were hardly any accurate studies on temperature reduction with internal foliage, although this is obviously a very important topic. To learn more about improving the microclimate in closed hall spaces with internal foliage, the ETH Zurich (building services faculty) was assigned a research project. Some of the findings are presented in Section 9.

Figure 255
Office building and orangery,
Bavarian State Court, Munich
(Architect: D. Siegert, Munich)

8.7
Buildings under Glass

When atria in front of office rooms are narrowed
to a few metres, the result is, in effect, an orangery (or conservatory)-like structure. Figure 255
shows the west elevation of the new Bavarian
State Court building, a complex with two double
wings connected to the former Military Museum
(architect: D. Siegert, Munich).

To lighten the building mass facing the Hofgarten,
a public park in the center of Munich, and also
for security reasons, a glass-fronted orangery
was annexed to the complex. Figure 256 shows a
cross-section of the orangery with ventilation
openings, shading units in the upper area, and the
actual inner building with office and hall areas.

The orangery is mostly naturally ventilated and
is closed off in winter, to function as a heat buffer
for the office building (solar heat gain). In summer,
radiation is reduced with the aid of the louvred
shading system, to minimize heat gain in the
office areas. Additional awnings, adjustable by
each occupant, reduce the cooling loads in each
office and act, at the same time, as glare protection. On the second floor, some vertical, rotating
glass prism elements are used as shading units.

Figure 256
Shading units in orangery of
Bavarian State Court building
in Munich and view into the
orangery

Upper ventilation louvres

Louvred shading system
(adjustable)

Natural air flow

Ground floor

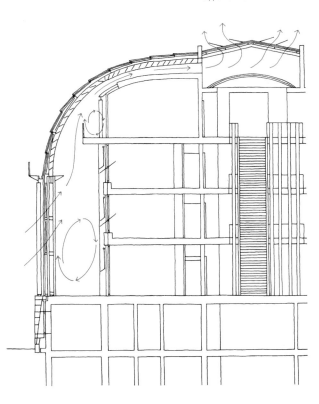

Figure 257
Model of State Court building
in wind tunnel
(Wind direction = 240° / scale
1:250)

The orangery so placed is, in fact, nothing less than a polyvalent wall model for a large variety of operational functions, enabling environmentally responsive operation throughout the year, reacting to heat influx as well as heat loss.

To obtain accurate data for planning, extensive model studies were conducted (Department of Fluidmechanics and Department A for Thermodynamics, Technical University Munich; HL-Technik AG). Figure 257 shows the model of the State Court in the wind tunnel, and Figure 258 the measured pressure distributions on various cross-section levels of the building for one of the many case studies.

Since the orangery is also, to some extent, a work and rest area and top-security rooms are located on the fourth floor, additional detail studies were conducted on a scale of 1:5 (Figure 259). These studies, on the one hand, verified certain methods of calculation and, on the other hand, determined the air-change rates resulting from the heat load generated by the orangery.

Figure 259
Model study of internal air movement in orangery
View of model without insulation and shading units. The exhaust cylinder of the extract fan is visible at the top of the image. The slanted roof is partially covered by the extract fan box (scale 1:5).

Figure 258
Pressure distribution
on State Court building
Wind direction: 240°

— Pressure
— Suction

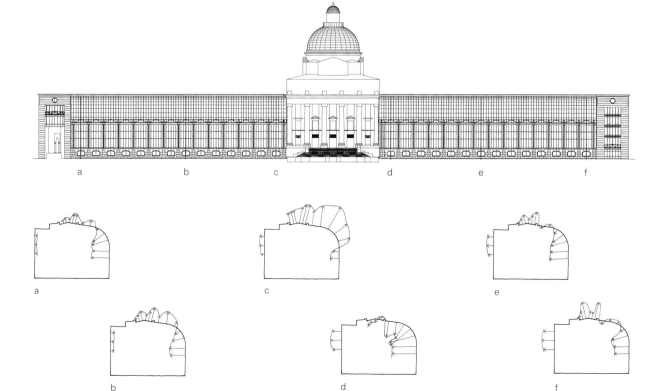

a   Shading unit
b   Small eddies below
    shading units
c   Lowgrade flow core
    in panoramic range
d   Position of back wall in
    standard cross-section
    of orangery building
e   Ventilation flow towards
    slanted roof area
    (standard cross-section)

Figure 261
Vertical section through
orangery, panoramic view
(diagram)

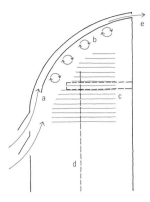

The graph of thermally caused air movements and air-change rates in Figure 260 may be very applicable to future design. Furthermore, computer-generated and model studies were conducted to determine air movements (Figure 261) and air temperatures (Figure 262) resulting during calms because of heat gain in the orangery. The data contained in the diagrams also help in drawing conclusions for other buildings, especially as far as temperature increase in double-leaf façades due to heat gain is concerned. Figures 263.1–263.2 show predictable air temperatures for various shading positions in the orangery and in the office areas without cooling. These are: external shading, shading units located on the inner façade (interior) and shading elements on the building (recessed).

Figure 264 provides a final evaluation of shading measures throughout the year and the resulting temperatures and number of hours for those temperatures. As the graph shows, outside shading has, predictably, the best results (e.g. 30°C, 100 h/a) and would thus be, in theory, the most recommendable. However, building technology and aesthetics argued for inner and recessed shading.

To obtain accurate findings in the planning of particular buildings, to minimize active, building services and to protect against legal action, design studies in building climate and aerophysics should and must be conducted. Their expense is amply justified and usually bears little relation to the planning fees.

Figure 260
Thermally caused air flow for
heat loads in orangery (during
windstill periods)

— Calculation
— Model experiment

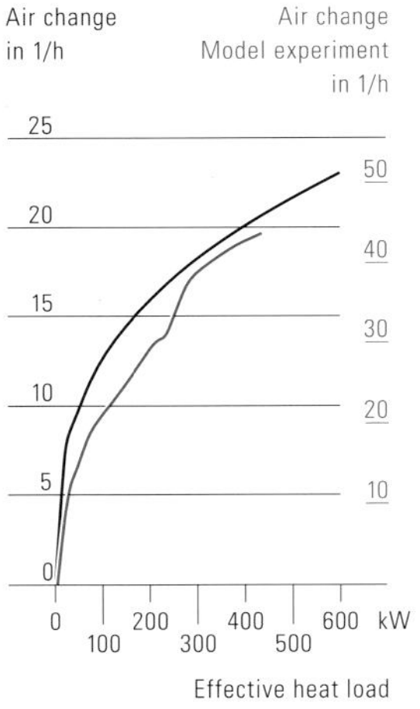

Figure 262
Air temperatures for different
heat loads in orangery
(during windstill periods)
External air temperature 32°C

Calculation:
— second floor
– – fifth floor
- - - exhaust exit

— Model experiment

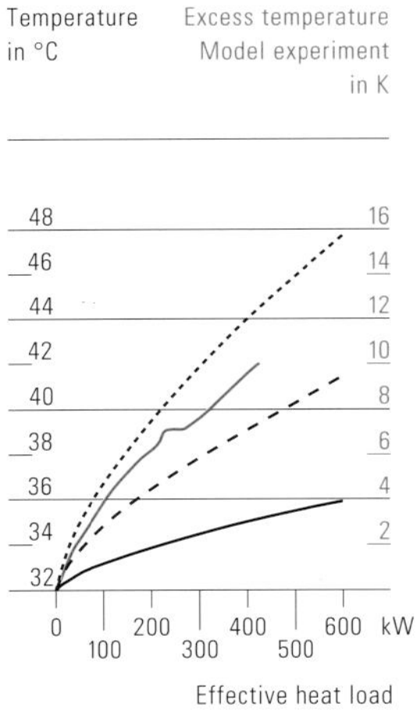

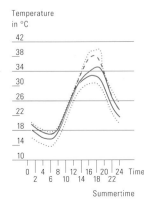

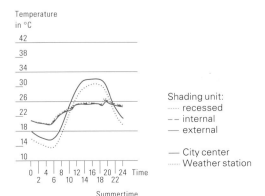

Figure 263.1
Air temperatures
in orangery
(warm summer day)

Figure 263.2
Air temperatures
in offices
(warm summer day)

Shading unit:
······ recessed
– –   internal
—   external

—   City center
······ Weather station

Figure 264
Annual frequencies of raised
temperatures in orangery
(quasi external space in front
of offices)

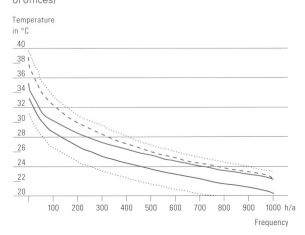

8.8
Multipurpose Hall

On the following pages, the Design Centre in Linz, Austria (design and planning: Herzog + Partners, Munich) is introduced in a category all its own. It is shown in Figures 265 to 271 (pages 190 and 191).

Quote:
"In 1988, the capital of Upper Austria, Linz, tendered a nationwide and anonymous architecture/engineering competition for the design of a Convention and Exhibition Centre and Hotel. International participants were encouraged to join in the competition. Our team (engineer K. Stepan) was awarded first prize.

The Design:
The open environment of the competition site had to be considered and integrated as an urban space. The west elevation had to be harmonized with the (neighbouring) ORF site (architect: Gustav Peichl). Trees, following the line of an old path and augmented by new plantings, set the stage for the convention centre. All building components are connected to the path. The main hall of the Design Centre (204 m x 80 m) is located on the east side of the property as a flat, low building. The hotel, a separate building, borders onto Frankfurt Street. The restaurant is situated between hotel and convention centre, as befits its function.

This layout creates, on the one hand, a large, open space facing the city, which can be used and designed in many ways for specific events, and, on the other hand, a long fair-ground in the courtyard, reserved for pedestrians and onto which all hall entrances open. Individual exhibits can be placed in this open-air setting. A landscaped green zone stretches between restaurant and fairground. The underground garages of hotel and convention centre are linked. All deliveries are made on the east side; large vehicles can approach the front of the building as well.

The conference and exhibition rooms are gathered under one roof in a large hall for maximum interior flexibility. The ground plan is parallel to the building axis. Conference hall and auditorium (650 and 1200 seats, respectively) share a foyer. The entrances are deliberately divided, to prevent audiences for separate but simultaneous events from mixing. Continuous hallways accessible across the length of the building permit the linking of all exhibition halls and the integration of the gallery. Even the secondary zones are arranged in linear fashion. The dividing walls are moveable. The system is open to modifications.

We were interested in giving a new interpretation of the 'crystal palace' idea in our approach to the design of the convention and exhibition hall. This building type, first created in the 19th century, was initially intended exclusively for exhibitions (e.g. in London 1851–1936) and for other social gatherings (e.g. in Munich 1854–1931) and is sometimes still used for these purposes (e.g. in Madrid).

One of its main characteristics was to recreate the daylight qualities available in the open air inside a building through glazing on all sides. In the historic forerunners, the large transparent envelopes were successful in protecting the interior from wind and the elements, but they had considerable weaknesses with regard to thermals: High heat-transfer coefficients resulted in a great loss of heating energy. Furthermore, the volume to be heated was enormous because of the great building height.

Improving these conditions and meeting modern comfort requirements called for three main adjustments to this particular case:

– The interior room height had to be reduced to the minimum necessary for exhibitions and fairs. Therefore, a maximum height of 12 m is available only in a few areas: hence the use of arched trusses to create a transverse section of the room with variable heights and to reduce the volume to be heated.

– Modern, coated, heat-insulating panes were necessary to drastically reduce the heat-transfer values of the glazing.

– Finally, the daylight had to be optimized. The goal was to achieve a very bright light quality and an 'active room environment', which draws the eye to the exhibits and to the interior. Any glare by direct sun was to be avoided, above all additional heat gain in summer time, when the hot-house effect is strongest. Appropriate measures had to be envisioned to deal with this problem.

In reference to the last problem, we developed, in collaboration with Christian Bartenbach and Assoc., a system of new light grids, which are integrated into the glass panels in a complex performance profile (cf. Figure 190). A fine-grade aluminium-plated retro-reflecting grid, only 16 mm high, is installed between the panes. This grid permits indirect light incidence through small 'light shafts', which are closely spaced, but keeps out direct solar incidence.

Figure 266
View into flat steel arch
construction extending freely
across 73 m

To make use of this shading system (distributed in Germany by Siemens, Daylight Technology, Traunreut), certain external and internal parameters are important: the altitude and azimuth angle of the sun in each season, the exposition and orientation of the building, the slope of the surface (which, for a cylinder for instance, changes constantly from the bottom to the roof ridge and leads to different reflection angles when the building axis shifts left and right from the ridge, as it overlaps with the incident angle). Of course, some additional effort is required for injection moulding dies for differing grid geometries.

Figure 265
Design Center Linz
View onto 204 m long
glass roof

The slats of the grid forming small light shafts must be bent in several locations to create the desired retroreflection of the direct radiation. For the glazed envelope in Linz, this also applies to each horizontal glass panel strip (2.70 m wide, parallel to the panels shaping the cylinder), which is given a different geometry for the grid. The geometry can be accurately defined by programs loaded on powerful computers.

The u-values and, above all, fire safety were greatly improved by the inlaid, mirroring grid. The glass encasement of the grid consists of thermally divided steel profiles.

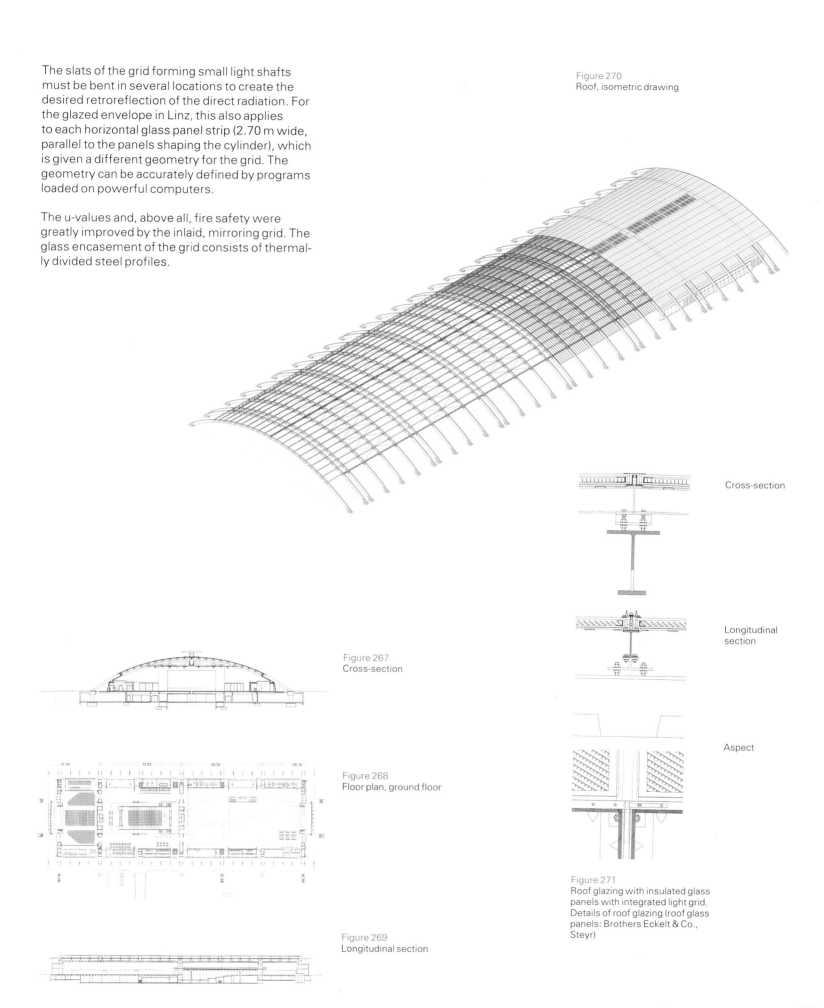

Figure 270
Roof, isometric drawing

Cross-section

Longitudinal section

Aspect

Figure 267
Cross-section

Figure 268
Floor plan, ground floor

Figure 269
Longitudinal section

Figure 271
Roof glazing with insulated glass panels with integrated light grid. Details of roof glazing (roof glass panels: Brothers Eckelt & Co., Steyr)

191

As the example shows, the structure and technical functionality of built envelopes – and hence their aesthetic effect– are highly changeable when directing functions for daylight and temperature are added to the traditional 'protection functions' of the envelope. Thus, new structures for the skin of the building greatly influence the architecture as well as the interior design and layout. Contemporary options in planning and manufacture make designs possible whose impact extends right into urban development, because the perfomance profile of the built envelope is very flexible and has, therefore, been tailored to the requirements created by the locality.

The supporting framework of the glass skin consists of a flat steel arch construction, extending freely across 73 m with truss distances of 7.20 and 2.40 m. In the transverse direction, secondary trusses are spaced 2.70 m apart. The horizontal forces from the tangential thrust are assumed by bracing cables installed between the supports. The longitudinal stiffening (or bracing) is created by bonds in the arched roof. The shape of the (roof) ridge promotes the effectiveness of natural ventilation. The steel supporting framework is a custom design developed by the architect in collaboration with the structural engineers Sailer + Stepan. All parts of the structure are exposed and define the interior ambience of the hall.

For several months, numerous model experiments on a 1:1 scale were carried out, to meet construction and structural requirements and to further study and fine-tune the aesthetic quality of the project.

This project is not focused on creating a simple convention centre but, rather, a building expected to meet the highest standards, for example for banquet events, when a festive mood must be enhanced by the differentiated, technically stringent and yet visually arresting steel structure. The personality of modern, filigrane steel construction should become visible, even to the layperson. For the Design Centre, we have created a custom solution in which the trusses are finished with box beam sections and the secondary trusses as welded fabricated sheet steel structures."
(End of quote)

Here are some additional comments on T. Herzog's statement in reference to thermals and natural ventilation. A study was conducted to calculate interior air temperatures resulting from continuous conferencing and fair exhibition over the course of a test year with ventilation by stack effect and the use of long throw-jet nozzles. Figure 272 shows the corresponding frequency distribution for the convention centre in Linz.

The design of the hall itself is further characterized by a very favourable pressure distribution on the built skin, which assists natural ventilation through wind and buoyancy. The designer has carried out a number of wind tunnel studies in collaboration with the Technical University Munich, to design fresh air openings in the lower region of the hall as well as, and especially, in the upper region (roof ridge). The result is a Venturi disc, typical of this building, protecting the exhaust air openings against rain while ensuring controlled air exhaust (Figure 273).

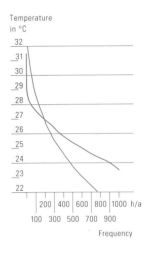

Figure 272
Distribution of frequencies of average air temperatures with fair hall in constant use

g = 0.11, ventilation by stack effect and long throw-jet nozzles

—— Temperature, interior
—— Temperature, exterior

Figure 273
Horizontal section of hall roof with Venturi disc

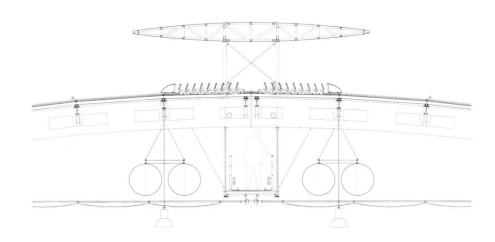

General Comments on the Theory

As many examples demonstrate, buildings in the shape of a reclining, flat cylindrical section are especially suited to natural ventilation. Usually, the physical properties of wind movement around the building and buoyancy are utilized within the hall. In Figure 274.1, the measurements of distributed pressure coefficients, taken on a model of the envelope of a long airplane hangar with a semi-circular cross-section, are shown for oncoming wind at slight angle to the cross-axis. The accelerated flow across the gently curved roof results in a well-defined negative pressure at the roof ridge without any additional measures. Together with the slight positive pressure on the windward-oriented transverse side, a driving force is created for cross-ventilation, which is in harmony with the natural ascending thermal of the warmer hall air when intake and exhaust-air openings are placed correctly.

Next, the findings of Figure 274.1 are related to a hall structure comparable to the Design Centre in Linz in Figure 274.2. In certain situations, it may become necessary to study the impact of neighbouring buildings on the flow conditions. Figure 274.3 shows that a tall, neighbouring building may change the pressure conditions, may even, in the example shown, reverse. Adjusting the dimensions of deflecting surfaces goes a long way to improve such a situation. Where any doubt or questions remain, wind-tunnel studies should be carried out in which the built environment and the wind flow are recreated to scale. Figure 274.4 depicts the return to a favourable flow situation, even under negative influences because of neighbouring buildings. The probable pressure distribution and frequency must be determined. With the help of insight gained from wind-tunnel studies, the optimum position and dimensions for the ventilation and smoke exhaust openings can be established.

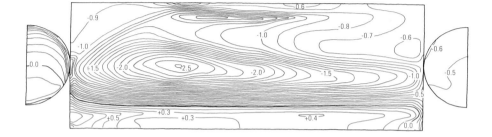

Figure 274.1
Pressure distribution on model of airplane hangar roof for oncoming wind at an angle to cross-axis

Figure 274.2 – 4
Negative influence of built environment on natural ventilation, despite advantageous pressure distribution on built skin.

Figure 274.2
Beneficial negative pressure around skylight on roof of free standing hall. Promotes air-change rates, harmonizes with natural ascending thermal

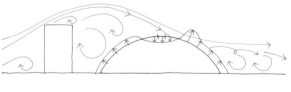

Figure 274.3
Reversal of conditions because of neighbouring buildings, wind-induced pressures counteract natural ascending thermal, poor air exchange

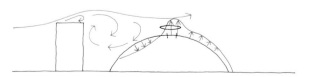

Figure 274.4
Return to favourable flow situation through modifications to built form

9.
Air Quality Improvement through Internal Foliage

In the context of ecological building, it would be ideal to achieve and maintain comfortable room temperatures and humidities and to remove contaminants through internal foliage alone, without having to resort to any technical or mechanical means. The extent to which this may be possible was studied at the ETH in Zurich with reference to previous research projects at NASA. The evaporation of the plants and, hence, evaporative cooling, as well as the production of oxygen and the elimination of contaminants played important roles.

B. Wolverton (NASA) carried out studies on the elimination of contaminants. Formaldehyde, benzol, and trichloroethylene were studied on different plants. Table 7 shows the rates of elimination, in per cent, for various plants after 24 hours. It is notable that the elimination is initially rapid but slows down after a period of two hours. At the Botanical Institute in Cologne, Dr. Weidner is currently studying how much plants or microorganisms purify the soil. It is as yet unclear whether the elimination process reaches a saturation point, i.e. whether it decreases considerably or even ceases altogether after several days, since all studies to date have been carried out on a 24-hour basis. Further, long-term studies are necessary to determine the actual behaviour.

As is evident from Table 7, certain plants are especially well suited to the elimination of contaminants. For instance, during a single day in an office, an ivy plant is able to eliminate 90 % of the benzol contained in and released through tobacco smoke, artificial fibres, dyes and plastics. True aloe, bananas, spider plants and philodendron are effective agents against formaldehyde, which may seep from insulating foam and particle board. Trichloroethylene from lacquers and glues are best eliminated with the help of chrysanthemums and gerbera.

It is certain that roots and the microbes symbiotic with root systems, and not the plants themselves, are largely responsible for eliminating contaminants.

As regards humidification, plants are better agents than electrically powered air humidifiers and even humidifiers combined with air-conditioning systems, because they do not provide a favourable breeding ground for bacteria. To determine the degree to which plants are able to create a healthy room climate, studies were carried out with five different plant types at the ETH in Zurich. The research team wanted to ascertain the amounts of water evaporated by plants for certain lighting strengths and temperatures as well as surrounding humidities. The plants included in the study were the ficus benjamina, hedera heliz, dizygotheca castor, dracoena dereménsis 'Warneckii', and philodendron imperial.

Table 7
Green filters:
Elimination of contaminants,
in per cent, after 24 hours

Plant	Formaldehyde	Benzol	Trichloroethylene
Banana	89	–	–
Bowstring hemp	–	53	13
Chrysanthemums	61	54	41
Dracoena dereménsis (Janet-Craig)	–	78	18
Dracoena dereménsis (Warneckii)	50	70	20
Dracoena dereménsis (massangeana)	70	–	13
Dracoena dereménsis (yellow-variegated)	–	79	13
True aloe	90	–	–
Ivy	–	90	11
Devil's ivy	67	73	9
Spathe flower	–	80	23
Creeping hairy spurge	67	–	–
Ficus benjamina	–	–	11
Gerbera	50	68	35
Green lily	86	81	
Chinese evergreen (Aglaonema)	–	48	–
Philodendron (domesticum)	86	–	–
Philodendron (oxycardium)	71	–	–
Philodendron (selloum)	76	–	–

Figure 275 shows the moisture released by the plants in the study, all of them suited to use in office and living areas, depending upon surrounding temperature and humidity as well as the illumination strength in lux. All the plants give off more moisture in relation to illumination strength, i.e. the brighter the room, the more moisture is released by the plants. Higher surrounding temperatures further encourage the moisture release. The influence of relative humidity in the environment, far from being decisive for how much moisture is released by the plants, is, in some circumstances, negligible. The volumes of moisture release indicated in the diagrams correspond to a water volume of g/m^2 leaf surface. To better appreciate the dimensions involved, imagine that approx. 1 m^2 of ivy leaf surface corresponds to approx. 5 % of the wall surfaces in an average office room. The evaporated volumes of water differ greatly from plant to plant. Peak values exist for the papyrus plant, which evaporates approx. 2000 g of water per day when the plant is approx. 1.5 m high.

When the water volumes evaporated by plants in summer are compared to the moisture released by one person during various activities, it is obvious that the humidity influence of plants is relatively low:

Moisture source	Moisture released		
person (light work)	approx. 50	–	60 g/h
person (hard work)	approx. 100	–	150 g/h
bath	approx. 600	–	800 g/h
shower	approx. 2000	–	3000 g/h
cooking	approx. 600	–	1500 g/h
potted plants	approx. 7	–	15 g/h
potted tree	approx. 10	–	30 g/h

Figure 275
Moisture released by plants, depending on surrounding temperature and humidity as well as the illumination strength in lux

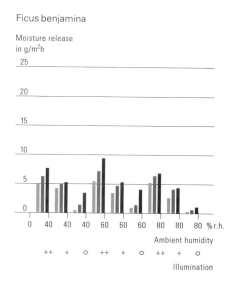

Ficus benjamina

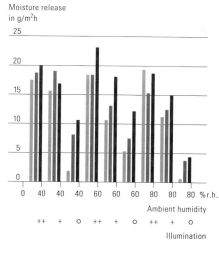

Hedera helix

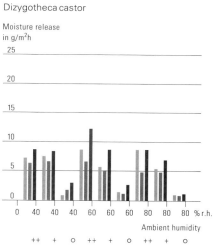

Dizygotheca castor

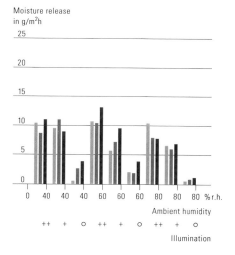

Dracoena dereménsis 'Warneckii'

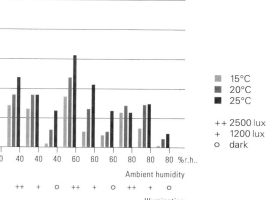

Philodendron imperial

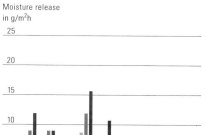

■ 15°C
■ 20°C
■ 25°C

++ 2500 lux
+ 1200 lux
o dark

195

To determine how plants influence room temperature by evaporative cooling, aside from the aforementioned (inherent) evaporative performance, relevant cooling effects were also measured. The following cases were studied:

– interior space, air change (T1)
  approx. 0.8 ac/h without plants,

– interior space, air change (T2)
  approx. 0.3 ac/h without plants,

– interior space, air change (T3)
  approx. 0.8 ac/h with plants,

  water evaporation
  day   72 g/h (7 a.m.– 7 p.m.)
  night   16 g/h (7 p.m.– 7 a.m.),

– interior space, air change (T4)
  approx. 0.3 ac/h with plants,
  planting and evaporative performance as in T3.

Note: 5 m² of ivy correspond to approx. 25 % of the wall surface or 12 m² of ficus benjamina.

— Outside condition

Conditions in room:
— AC = 0.8 ac/h
   without plants T1
-- AC = 0.3 ac/h
   without plants T2
— AC = 0.8 ac/h
   with plants T3
-- AC = 0.3 ac/h
   with plants T4

Figure 276
Room temperatures on warm summer day with and without plants
(AC = 0.3/0.8 ac/h)

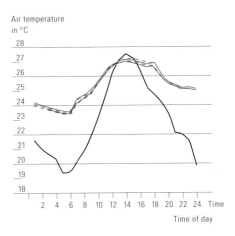

Figure 277
Room humidity on warm summer day with and without plants
(AC = 0.3/0.8 ac/h)

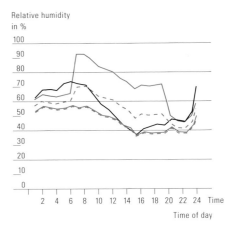

Figure 278
Room temperatures on cold winter day with and without plants
(AC = 0.3/0.8 ac/h)

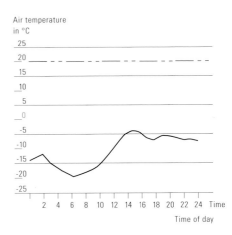

Figure 279
Room humidity for +20°C with and without plants
(AC = 0.3/0.8 ac/h)

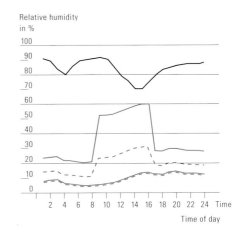

Figure 276 shows the measurements taken on a test-reference summer day in Zurich. The outside temperatures fluctuate between 19.5°C and 27.6°C. The room temperatures (T1, T2), with air-change rates of 0.8 or 0.3 ac/h without plants, reach a maximum of 27.3°C. For average internal foliage and again with assumed air-change rates of 0.8 ac/h (T3) or 0.3 ac/h (T4), room temperatures are approx. 0.3 K less.

The corresponding humidity fluctuations (Figure 277) are approx. 60 %. This moisture content is at a comfortable level. However, the curve T4 (air-change rate approx. 0.3 ac/h, average internal foliage) leads to a marked humidity increase of 90 % in the morning hours, which must be described as humid. Hence, rooms with intense internal foliage must also have sufficient air-change rates to improve the microclimate. This, however, reduces the impact of evaporative cooling.

In winter, the room temperature is kept at a constant +20°C (Figure 278), even though the outside temperature changes dramatically on a cold winter day. The indirect influence of the plants on the temperature is so slight as to be negligible. Figure 279 shows the relative air humidity for +20°C, again with or without plants for different assumed air-change rates. This graph makes clear that low air-change rates and average internal foliage can result in relative humidity of up to 60 % and that the air humidities of rooms without plants are noticeably different. The effect, in this respect, is, therefore, clearly positive.

In summary, plants can only create a definite decrease in temperature in summer when all surrounding surfaces, with the exception of windows, are intensely covered in internal foliage. Individual plants do not result in a noticeable change. Nevertheless, the use of plants in buildings should be given more attention in the future, since the overall effects are unquestionably positive, especially the psychological effect of verdant foliage on the occupants. However, it must be acknowledged that plants need an environment providing more than the minimum level for survival (i.e. the compensation point between photosynthesis and respiration). This can only be achieved by choosing the best plants and location and combining plants which have long life expectancies. Light being the source for photosynthesis, plants should especially be used in very bright, naturally lit areas, e.g. winter gardens, atria, large, open glassed-in office areas, etc. When lighting conditions are poor, the synthesis and breakdown of plants are equal (averaging to compensation point). When plants are forced to grow in an environment below the compensation point, they receive too little light, begin to fade after a while and eventually die altogether.

Active Measures
of Renewable Energy Usage

10

The course followed by price increases for energy in recent years clearly indicates the advantages of saving energy. Furthermore, for environmental reasons, we can no longer afford to waste energy, especially fossil fuels.

11

Utilizing solar energy will become increasingly important in the coming years. In approx. 20 to 30 years, solar energy will cover an estimated 20 % of the world energy requirement. As this is clearly to be the main focus of ecological building, the sooner measures needed to convert existing buildings are taken, the better.

10.
Cost Development – Water and Energy

Buildings of the future must face inevitable
challenges:

– environmental protection
– minimizing energy consumption
– extensive utilization of environmental energies
– technical systems only when necessary
– intelligent building and servicing concepts.

It is natural to ask: "Why?". Since, at the beginning, it was established that our energy resources
will suffice for a thousand years to come, one may
well wonder. Take a look, however, at the price
increases for energy (natural gas, oil, electricity)
and potable water and the answer becomes
obvious. Figures 280 and 281 prove how shaky
the ground is – especially the political one – on
which we stand. The rising trend of energy pricing
is frequently accompanied by a surtax, on which
consumers have no influence. Any day, we may
be faced with a massive rise in utility costs.

Figure 282 plots the development of costs for
electrical energy, with a marked tendency to rise,
again not a comforting picture. The image is
even more dramatic for potable water. Figure 283
shows the price without waste-water surtax.
These costs currently often double or triple potable water prices for the consumer. At several
locations in Germany, water and waste water already costs up to 12 DM/m^3, i.e. four times more
than in the graph. Without doubt, rising costs
alone offer the counter-argument to current positions and attitudes.

The same applies, of course, to the emissions
of contaminants and thus to environmental protection. We are all familiar with such topics as
the ozone hole, acid soil, forest depletion, dead
waters, etc. This is another urgent appeal for
action. Our future credo, like it or not, must be:
"Less is more".

The potential contribution of proactive building
technology to this issue is represented in Figure
284. The following chapter will focus on all those
areas, out of the total number of possible savings
due to alternative energy supply, which are most
relevant to the design of future buildings.

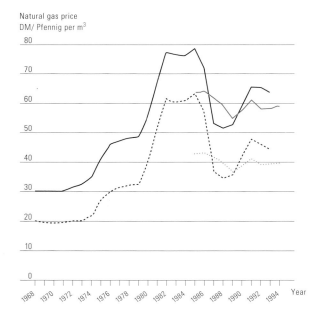

Natural gas price
DM/ Pfennig per m^3

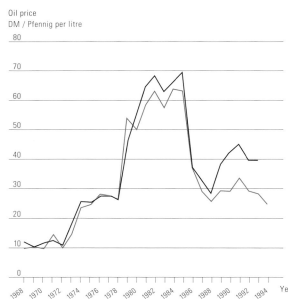

Oil price
DM / Pfennig per litre

Figure 280 (left)
Cost development for
natural gas in Germany
and in Switzerland

Germany
— Private households
--- Industry > 1 m kWh/a

Switzerland
— Private households
--- Industry > 1.3 m kWh/a

Figure 281
Cost development
for oil in Germany and
in Switzerland

— Germany
— Switzerland > 20000 kg

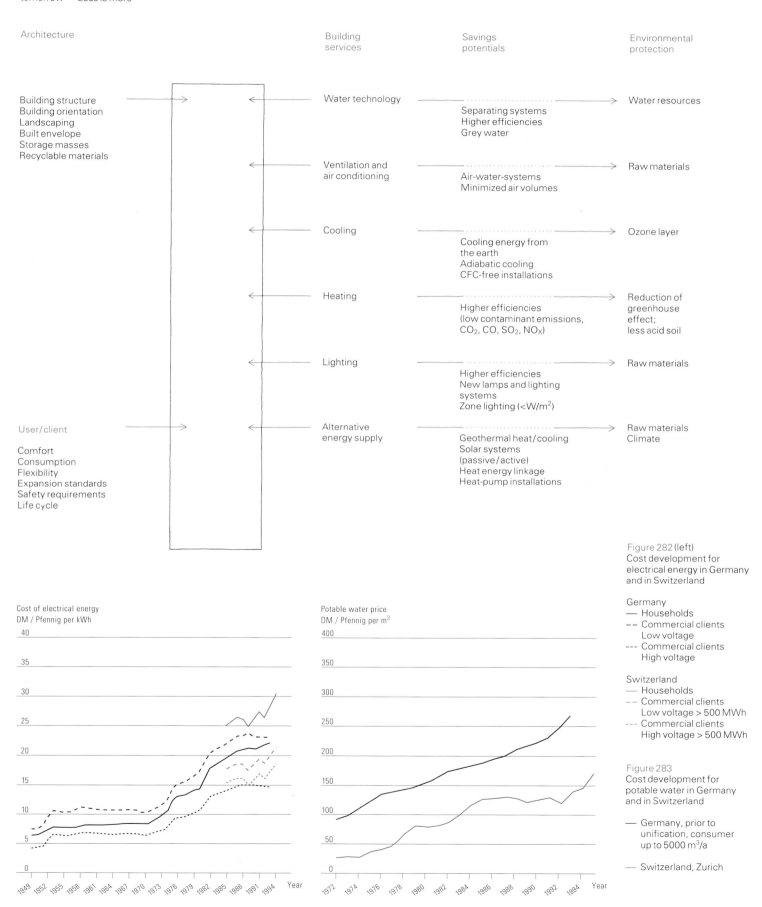

Figure 284
Motto for buildings of
tomorrow – "Less is more"

| Architecture | | Building services | Savings potentials | Environmental protection |

Architecture

Building structure
Building orientation
Landscaping
Built envelope
Storage masses
Recyclable materials

User/client

Comfort
Consumption
Flexibility
Expansion standards
Safety requirements
Life cycle

Building services

Water technology

Ventilation and
air conditioning

Cooling

Heating

Lighting

Alternative
energy supply

Savings potentials

Separating systems
Higher efficiencies
Grey water

Air-water-systems
Minimized air volumes

Cooling energy from
the earth
Adiabatic cooling
CFC-free installations

Higher efficiencies
(low contaminant emissions,
CO_2, CO, SO_2, NO_x)

Higher efficiencies
New lamps and lighting
systems
Zone lighting ($<W/m^2$)

Geothermal heat/cooling
Solar systems
(passive/active)
Heat energy linkage
Heat-pump installations

Environmental protection

Water resources

Raw materials

Ozone layer

Reduction of
greenhouse
effect;
less acid soil

Raw materials

Raw materials
Climate

Cost of electrical energy
DM / Pfennig per kWh

Potable water price
DM / Pfennig per m³

Figure 282 (left)
Cost development for
electrical energy in Germany
and in Switzerland

Germany
— Households
–– Commercial clients
  Low voltage
––– Commercial clients
  High voltage

Switzerland
— Households
–– Commercial clients
  Low voltage > 500 MWh
––– Commercial clients
  High voltage > 500 MWh

Figure 283
Cost development for
potable water in Germany
and in Switzerland

— Germany, prior to
  unification, consumer
  up to 5000 m³/a

— Switzerland, Zurich

11.
Solar Energy

In the search for new energy sources, many people have turned to the sun as a more or less inexhaustible energy source, especially following the energy crises of 1973 and 1978.

Solar energy has been utilized in the sunny regions of the Earth since ancient times for heating and, more recently, for cooking. Utlizing solar energy is, therefore, hardly a new idea. What is new, however, is that even countries with brief periods of sunshine are, with considerable effort, harnessing the sun's energy to supplement, if not replace conventional energy sources. Solar energy will remain a secondary energy source in Central and Northern Europe for some time and will supply only a portion of the necessary heat energy. There are two main reasons. First, the annual availability of solar energy is too low in the northern latitudes (Figures 285 and 286). And, second, the solar power is greatest when requirements (for heating) are non-existent.

Furthermore, the brief sunshine periods in Central and Northern Europe mean that high investment costs are disproportionate to subsequent energy savings, since approx. 70 % of the radiation occurs from April to September. The amortization calculations of solar systems yield much better results for Southern Europe, because the annual sum of radiation is noticeably higher than, for instance, in our latitudes (Marseille 1,860 kWh/m^{2}a, Zurich 1,160 kWh/m^{2}a, Hamburg 930 kWh/m^{2}a).

All the same, it is now time to give solar energy an equal chance since, in the long term, solar energy can help solve some of our problems.

11.1
Principles

The sun delivers approx. five thousand times more energy per year than is consumed worldwide. Atmospheric solar radiation is approx. 1,300 W/m^2, of which approx. 1,000 W/m^2 reaches the Earth's surface, in our latitudes, as global radiation when conditions are favourable. Global radiation consists of direct and diffuse radiation.

The direct radiation is that part of the sunlight which falls onto the Earth's surface without diffraction and which is the principal design parameter for solar technology.

The diffuse radiation is that part of the direct radiation which is dispersed, on its way through the atmosphere, by dusts, aerosols, etc. It reaches the Earth's surface from all directions and is noticeably weaker than the direct insolation (see the Figure 171 series, pp. 140–141). In addition to the global radiation, a radiation or insolation portion results from reflection at ground level, at built environment surfaces, etc.

In the dimensioning of solar installations (photothermal and photovoltaic systems), the total number of sunshine hours and the global radiation at the respective location are most important (Table 8).

Black surfaces absorb sunlight especially well and transform it into heat. This transformation of light into heat is a result of the tendency of black dyes to form long chains of atoms with weak bonds. They are disturbed to such a degree by incident, visible light in the form of light quanta (photons) that the individual atoms or atom groups in the molecule chain begin to vibrate: heat is created. The stronger the vibrations are through incident light, the higher is the resulting temperature. Black bodies with high temperatures, in turn, give off excessive heat as radiation. The radiation intensity is a function of the spectrum (wavelength) of the corresponding radiating agent which, in turn, depends on its temperature. Hence, for a photothermal transformation, the incident light-wave (range 0.4 μm to 0.7 μm (μm = 1/1000 mm) is transferred to the longwave heat radiation (infrared radiation > 2 μm).

To make thermal use of incident radiation energy, radiation transformers are installed. These may be blinds, heat-absorbing venetian blinds, heat-absorbing surfaces, or thermal collectors.

Figure 285
Average, annual sunshine
hours in Central and Northern
Europe

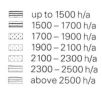

up to 1500 h/a
1500 – 1700 h/a
1700 – 1900 h/a
1900 – 2100 h/a
2100 – 2300 h/a
2300 – 2500 h/a
above 2500 h/a

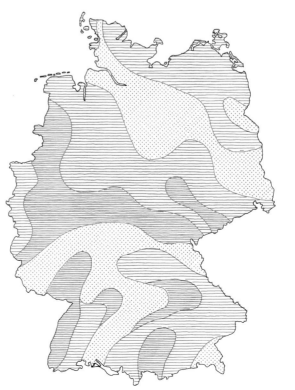

Figure 286
Average, annual sunshine
hours in Germany

1400 – 1500 h/a
1500 – 1600 h/a
1600 – 1700 h/a
1700 – 1800 h/a
1800 – 1900 h/a

203

Table 8
Average global radiation and insolation

Average global radiation in Germany

Postal (ZIP) code	City	Jan.	Feb.	March	April	May	June	July	Aug.	Sep.	Oct.	Nov.	Dec.	kWh / m²a
							Average global radiation per day (kWh/m²d). Reference: flat surface							
13000	Berlin	0.54	1.14	2.47	3.72	4.83	5.56	5.02	4.21	3.16	1.59	0.64	0.39	1015
22000	Hamburg	0.48	1.01	2.13	3.60	4.65	5.29	4.66	3.89	2.82	1.39	0.58	0.33	940
28000	Bremen	0.49	1.07	2.07	3.58	4.64	5.15	4.52	3.87	2.81	1.44	0.62	0.37	934
30000	Hannover	0.51	1.10	2.18	3.62	4.69	5.24	4.59	3.95	2.86	1.49	0.64	0.38	953
37073	Göttingen	0.56	1.18	2.32	3.58	4.57	5.09	4.49	3.80	2.84	1.55	0.68	0.43	947
38700	Braunlage	0.58	1.22	2.34	3.62	4.55	5.15	4.56	3.79	2.90	1.63	0.68	0.45	959
44137	Dortmund	0.53	1.16	2.28	3.73	4.67	4.71	4.33	3.79	2.85	1.53	0.72	0.43	937
45127	Essen	0.56	1.13	2.20	3.52	4.51	4.94	4.36	3.80	2.83	1.59	0.72	0.43	932
46399	Bocholt	0.56	1.15	2.32	4.01	4.93	5.15	4.61	3.90	2.86	1.46	0.72	0.42	978
48147	Münster	0.54	1.17	2.32	3.95	4.96	5.08	4.59	3.86	2.94	1.52	0.70	0.41	978
49074	Osnabrück	0.51	1.10	2.11	3.48	4.54	5.05	4.37	3.75	2.78	1.53	0.66	0.40	923
50679	Köln	0.62	1.26	2.42	3.91	4.73	4.95	4.58	4.10	3.04	1.78	0.79	0.51	996
52062	Aachen	0.63	1.26	2.43	3.92	4.74	4.96	4.59	4.11	3.05	1.79	0.79	0.52	1000
54290	Trier	0.63	1.29	2.47	3.76	4.77	5.08	4.91	4.07	3.04	1.65	0.74	0.49	1004
58507	Lüdenscheid	0.53	1.19	2.37	3.49	4.48	4.45	4.03	3.48	2.76	1.54	0.70	0.43	897
59995	Kahler Asten	0.59	1.25	2.36	3.65	4.72	4.80	4.43	3.68	2.87	1.60	0.69	0.43	947
60313	Frankfurt	0.63	1.29	2.56	3.86	4.92	5.29	5.04	4.26	3.15	1.67	0.72	0.48	1033
68167	Mannheim	0.69	1.37	2.72	4.04	5.11	5.37	5.34	4.48	3.34	1.81	0.78	0.54	1086
70173	Stuttgart	0.75	1.42	2.60	3.78	4.83	5.23	5.37	4.53	3.37	2.03	0.88	0.61	1080
72076	Tübingen	0.78	1.42	2.64	3.86	4.79	5.18	5.36	4.45	3.33	2.02	0.96	0.63	1079
76137	Karlsruhe	0.71	1.36	2.67	3.89	5.05	5.37	5.42	4.55	3.38	1.90	0.81	0.57	1088
79106	Freiburg	1.04	1.75	2.78	4.24	5.06	5.63	5.69	4.67	3.73	2.25	1.16	0.84	1160
80335	München	0.77	1.44	2.60	3.83	4.72	5.27	5.25	4.41	3.48	2.06	0.87	0.57	1076
87437	Kempten	0.91	1.58	2.80	3.79	4.06	4.90	5.13	4.47	3.43	2.19	1.04	0.76	1085
89075	Ulm	0.75	1.40	2.69	3.90	4.88	5.26	5.43	4.54	3.34	1.83	0.80	0.56	1080
93047	Regensburg	0.72	1.37	2.69	2.98	4.92	5.38	5.36	4.43	3.35	1.87	0.78	0.54	1088
97040	Würzburg	0.65	1.33	2.63	3.94	4.99	5.40	5.26	4.37	3.20	1.76	0.76	0.51	1062

Average global radiation in Austria

Postal (ZIP) code	City	Jan.	Feb.	March	April	May	June	July	Aug.	Sep.	Oct.	Nov.	Dec.	kWh / m²a
							Average global radiation per day (kWh/m²d). Reference: flat surface							
6800	Feldkirch	1.00	1.76	2.94	4.05	4.75	5.15	5.07	4.20	3.26	2.05	1.18	0.85	1106
6370	Hahnenkamm	1.27	1.97	3.06	3.84	4.20	4.70	4.72	4.32	3.51	2.30	1.54	1.10	1115
6460	Imst	1.06	1.88	2.89	3.78	4.41	4.73	4.76	3.97	3.11	2.04	1.26	0.90	1060
6020	Innsbruck	1.12	1.90	2.95	3.86	4.50	4.89	4.92	4.00	3.17	2.11	1.25	0.94	1085
5020	Salzburg	1.05	1.75	2.72	3.83	4.70	5.20	5.08	4.43	3.41	2.13	1.15	0.86	1110
	St. Michael	1.26	1.99	3.27	4.46	5.24	5.30	5.23	4.60	3.47	2.23	1.30	1.04	1201
5700	Zell am See	1.04	1.80	2.85	3.97	4.56	4.83	4.82	4.04	3.17	2.09	1.17	0.84	1073
4470	Enns	0.72	1.50	2.56	3.70	4.58	4.93	4.90	4.22	3.14	1.73	0.83	0.54	1017
4802	Feuerkogel	1.16	1.86	2.95	3.91	4.20	4.44	4.41	4.17	3.37	2.25	1.34	1.04	1069
1180	Hohe Warte	0.81	1.53	2.63	3.96	4.83	5.36	5.32	4.50	3.35	1.93	0.88	0.64	1090
8983	Bad Mitterndorf	1.14	1.77	2.92	3.90	4.89	5.07	4.95	4.44	3.40	2.29	1.28	0.93	1127
8010	Graz	1.05	1.80	2.93	3.98	4.84	5.34	5.38	4.74	3.53	2.22	1.15	0.85	1154
9020	Klagenfurt	1.08	1.91	2.98	4.07	4.76	5.32	5.40	4.58	3.29	1.94	1.03	0.78	1132
9500	Villach	0.90	1.99	3.13	4.06	4.83	5.40	5.49	4.89	3.63	2.33	1.23	0.99	1193

Average global radiation in Switzerland

Postal (ZIP) code	City	Jan.	Feb.	March	April	May	June	July	Aug.	Sep.	Oct.	Nov.	Dec.	kWh / m²a
							Average global radiation per day (kWh/m²d). Reference: flat surface							
1000	Lausanne	1.00	1.85	3.03	4.50	4.91	6.14	6.26	4.98	3.75	2.33	1.17	0.85	1244
1200	Genf	0.95	1.76	2.88	4.41	5.22	6.07	6.32	4.98	3.70	2.34	1.10	0.77	1303
1700	Fribourg	0.99	1.76	2.79	4.37	5.12	5.93	6.12	4.90	3.69	2.32	1.17	0.83	1120
1820	Montreux	0.98	1.72	2.93	4.39	4.90	5.73	5.95	4.74	3.59	2.31	1.14	0.90	1198
1920	Martigny	1.20	2.08	3.21	4.63	5.17	6.06	6.30	4.93	3.96	2.79	1.43	1.10	1307
1950	Sion	1.32	2.17	3.43	4.82	5.47	6.16	6.40	5.21	4.14	2.86	1.51	1.20	1363
2000	Neuchàtel	0.85	1.63	2.78	4.40	5.14	6.01	6.01	4.85	3.57	2.06	0.99	0.71	1189
2800	Delémont	0.92	1.64	2.63	4.12	4.98	5.37	5.50	4.34	3.37	2.09	1.06	0.72	1121
3000	Bern	0.99	1.77	2.78	4.23	4.97	5.79	5.89	4.73	3.65	2.68	1.12	0.83	1190
3920	Zermatt	1.58	2.50	4.05	5.43	6.06	6.57	6.69	5.46	4.43	3.19	1.79	1.47	1500
3962	Montana	1.52	2.39	3.71	5.24	5.95	6.49	6.79	5.36	4.31	3.07	1.69	1.37	1461
4102	Basel-Binningen	1.02	1.64	2.63	4.06	4.78	5.49	5.60	4.57	3.52	2.28	1.14	0.85	1147
4600	Olten	0.78	1.50	2.53	4.02	4.08	5.53	5.61	4.52	3.28	1.94	0.91	0.64	1100
6000	Luzern	0.84	1.56	2.59	3.99	4.80	5.28	5.46	4.37	3.23	2.03	1.03	0.68	1094
6390	Engelberg	1.22	2.10	3.20	4.41	5.23	5.44	5.56	4.53	3.65	2.75	1.40	1.14	1239
6460	Altdorf	1.05	1.85	3.13	4.32	5.16	5.66	5.67	4.64	3.86	2.55	1.17	0.83	1216
6600	Locarno	1.50	2.17	3.47	4.70	5.34	6.39	6.51	5.15	3.85	2.92	1.55	1.47	1343
6780	Ariolo	0.72	1.95	3.63	4.92	5.35	6.05	6.14	4.02	3.87	2.40	0.78	0.60	1244
6900	Lugano	1.33	2.00	3.20	4.43	5.04	6.05	6.28	5.03	3.65	2.70	1.42	1.31	1294
7000	Chur	1.30	2.07	3.20	4.42	4.08	5.51	5.56	4.73	3.94	2.78	1.38	1.09	1252
7050	Arosa	1.58	2.45	3.79	5.05	5.67	5.63	5.78	4.95	4.07	3.05	1.70	1.40	1376
7260	Davos	1.56	2.45	3.83	5.02	5.51	5.52	5.67	4.91	4.12	3.03	1.70	1.39	1363
7500	St. Moritz	1.35	2.44	3.90	5.15	5.73	5.87	6.02	4.94	4.00	3.01	1.55	1.22	1377
8000	Zürich	0.94	1.77	2.83	4.24	5.19	5.72	5.89	4.76	3.60	2.22	1.08	0.74	1190
8200	Schaffhausen	0.84	1.67	2.70	4.15	5.07	5.74	5.78	4.73	3.58	2.04	0.98	0.69	1158
8400	Winterthur	0.90	1.69	2.68	4.08	5.05	5.62	5.67	4.67	3.62	2.13	1.04	0.69	1089
9000	St. Gallen	0.96	1.71	2.81	4.20	5.11	5.60	5.76	4.61	3.56	2.16	1.10	0.75	1169

Average sunshine hours in Germany

Postal (ZIP) code	City	Jan.	Feb.	March	April	May	June	July	Aug.	Sep.	Oct.	Nov.	Dec.	h/a
13000	Berlin	49	70	139	172	218	248	229	204	182	114	48	35	1708
22000	Hamburg	47	61	116	169	210	233	205	185	158	98	46	32	1560
28000	Bremen	44	65	108	164	207	221	193	181	153	100	50	36	1519
30000	Hannover	42	64	114	164	208	225	196	184	154	103	49	34	1537
37073	Göttingen	45	68	120	157	196	211	186	169	147	103	47	37	1486
38700	Braunlage	50	75	123	161	195	216	191	169	153	113	49	42	1537
44137	Dortmund	38	65	117	168	203	186	175	168	147	100	55	37	1459
45127	Essen	42	61	110	152	191	201	177	168	145	106	53	36	1442
46399	Bocholt	46	67	122	191	223	216	195	177	150	92	57	37	1573
48147	Münster	43	70	123	187	226	212	194	175	160	102	56	36	1584
49074	Osnabrück	41	62	107	153	196	211	180	168	146	105	51	35	1455
50679	Köln	51	74	125	178	205	200	190	188	160	123	62	49	1605
52062	Aachen	51	74	125	178	205	200	190	188	160	123	62	49	1605
54290	Trier	42	70	123	162	203	205	209	181	153	101	44	33	1526
58507	Lüdenscheid	36	67	123	149	186	169	155	145	138	99	49	34	1350
59995	Kahler Asten	46	75	122	160	205	191	181	159	147	105	46	34	1471
60313	Frankfurt	44	71	132	170	215	220	219	196	164	105	43	34	1613
68167	Mannheim	51	79	142	181	227	224	239	211	177	116	48	41	1736
70173	Stuttgart	56	79	128	159	204	212	239	211	175	133	58	48	1702
72076	Tübingen	58	77	130	163	200	208	237	204	170	130	63	51	1691
76137	Karlsruhe	50	73	135	168	220	220	243	214	177	121	49	43	1715
79106	Freiburg	56	81	121	168	202	219	254	214	177	127	66	56	1741
80335	München	54	77	125	160	194	213	228	199	180	131	51	36	1648
87437	Kempten	77	89	138	155	185	188	218	202	173	142	76	70	1713
89075	Ulm	53	74	133	166	206	213	242	210	170	110	43	37	1657
93047	Regensburg	53	74	137	174	211	223	239	205	175	118	45	37	1691
97040	Würzburg	46	75	136	175	219	227	234	204	167	113	47	37	1680

Average sunshine hours in Austria

Postal (ZIP) code	City	Jan.	Feb.	March	April	May	June	July	Aug.	Sep.	Oct.	Nov.	Dec.	h/a
6800	Feldkirch	65	95	155	175	203	209	223	213	187	144	79	61	1809
6370	Hahnenkamm	100	113	155	159	179	195	212	204	186	160	107	98	1868
6460	Imst	71	100	134	132	150	157	172	170	156	136	89	67	1534
6020	Innsbruck	75	106	157	166	185	193	211	200	180	150	85	67	1775
5020	Salzburg	73	101	149	167	211	226	234	224	186	142	71	62	1846
5700	Zell am See	65	94	135	151	167	172	180	182	162	138	72	51	1569
4470	Enns	42	79	135	165	206	211	226	213	173	105	45	27	1627
4802	Feuerkogel	93	104	142	153	178	179	192	190	174	151	103	95	1754
1180	Hohe Warte	58	84	138	184	231	252	266	247	196	132	55	46	1889
8010	Graz	74	107	151	177	211	231	257	239	188	136	70	60	1901
9020	Klagenfurt	74	118	167	187	214	234	258	242	183	119	53	43	1892
9500	Villach	127	142	163	159	173	195	229	212	182	158	113	112	1962

Average sunshine hours in Switzerland

Postal (ZIP) code	City	Jan.	Feb.	March	April	May	June	July	Aug.	Sep.	Oct.	Nov.	Dec.	h/a
1000	Lausanne	54	89	138	177	198	233	276	221	182	135	71	52	1826
1200	Genf	50	85	135	182	204	232	285	225	183	125	65	41	1812
1700	Fribourg	50	74	110	157	174	201	247	199	169	124	66	45	1617
1820	Montreux	50	74	124	162	164	179	226	192	157	119	64	54	1565
1920	Martigny	56	87	128	175	178	194	239	199	177	135	76	54	1698
1950	Sion	100	117	163	201	215	227	279	227	201	179	114	103	2126
2000	Neuchâtel	35	70	119	172	193	222	254	208	167	107	49	32	1628
2800	Delémont	36	59	96	144	175	170	206	158	136	88	47	30	1345
3000	Bern	52	80	117	157	181	211	252	201	171	126	65	49	1662
3920	Zermatt	84	101	147	163	176	181	225	190	168	148	90	78	1751
3962	Montana	116	120	159	187	197	209	258	214	202	184	123	123	2092
4102	Basel-Binningen	62	75	113	155	175	193	234	192	165	129	73	58	1624
4600	Olten	24	53	101	144	170	188	226	183	145	92	37	20	1383
6000	Luzern	31	60	103	139	172	176	219	170	137	100	51	26	1384
6390	Engelberg	41	85	116	131	157	151	179	152	148	135	63	29	1387
6460	Altdorf	39	71	117	145	173	169	199	169	152	113	49	30	1426
6600	Locarno	119	126	182	204	202	235	278	232	192	189	120	138	2217
6780	Ariolo	109	72	162	171	164	185	219	187	175	122	137	98	1801
6900	Lugano	102	112	163	178	181	217	261	216	175	171	107	121	2004
7000	Chur	74	91	133	154	184	185	223	190	178	146	78	67	1703
7050	Arosa	97	98	140	148	174	160	201	180	174	156	95	98	1721
7260	Davos	90	97	138	157	172	161	202	182	171	145	92	93	1700
7500	St. Moritz	71	107	155	159	177	168	207	174	169	161	86	75	1709
8000	Zürich	45	80	120	153	191	199	242	198	168	120	62	34	1612
8200	Schaffhausen	27	63	97	133	173	189	221	181	152	88	39	25	1388
8400	Winterthur	22	57	100	139	179	191	226	188	158	97	39	15	1411
9000	St. Gallen	41	66	109	142	172	176	215	176	151	105	54	31	1438

Unlike the photothermic process, the photovoltaic (or photoelectric) process transforms energy from incoming light directly into electrical energy. Silicon solar cells are used to effect this transformation. The structure found in a monocrystalline silicon solar cell is a good illustration of the functional properties of photovoltaic elements (Figure 287).

A silicon atom has four free electrons. They can be shared with up to four adjacent atoms, which we might imagine arranged in a tetrahedon shape. In this arrangement, the silicon atom is fully bonded. When silicon is doped with a foreign atom, the interatomic-bond structure near the foreign atom, used for doping, is changed. For instance, if pentavalent Phosphorus is used, then a bond remains free, i.e. an electron remains free (n-silicon).

In a monocrystalline solar cell, two distinct and differently doped regions adjoin; the boundary is known as an n-p junction. The remaining free electrons from the n-doped region can shift to the adjacent p-doped region and bond with a hole there. This creates an electrically charged field between the two differently doped areas (diffusion potential), the so-called space charge region. The deficient electrons in the n-doped region cause it to be positively charged and, conversely, the excess electrons in the p-doped region cause it to be negatively charged.

When light (quanta) reaches the space charge region, the energy contained in it can be used to free an electron from its bond, thereby creating an electron-hole-pair (electron and defect electron). These two charges are separated in the electrical field of the space charge region. This means that there is a charge between these two differently doped regions. When contacts of the solar cell are linked to each other, the charge carrier pairs can be reunited and an electrical current can flow.

Silicon-based solar cells function according to this principle – charge separation through light – although, in various technical solutions, different semiconductor properties play a considerable role as well.

Figure 287
Monocrystalline, silicon solar cell, functional principle

The structure of the silicon atom can be visualised as a tetrahedon (diamond shape).
The four triangles ..... formed by atoms 1–4 shape the tetrahedon (triangular pyramid) in whose middle the atom (5) is bonded ⎯ in four directions.

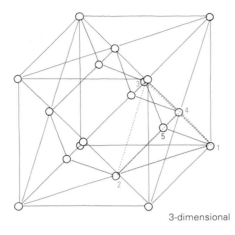

3-dimensional

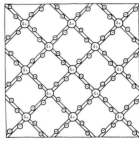

2-dimensional

Interatomic-bond structures of doped silicon

In the n-silicon the additional electron ⊖ remains 'free'.
At the doped atom (5+) an additional, fixed, positive charge remains. At the p-silicon a fixed, negative charge remains at the location of the doped atom (3+) following the release of the 'free' defect electron ⊕.

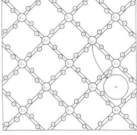

n-silicon

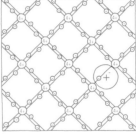

p-silicon

In a n-p junction an electrically charged field forms (diffusion potential) creating the space charge region. The resulting electric charge counteracts the diffusion.

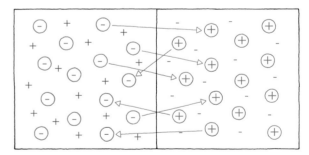

Light (quanta) can create electron-hole pairs in the space charge region, which can be reunited in an external current.

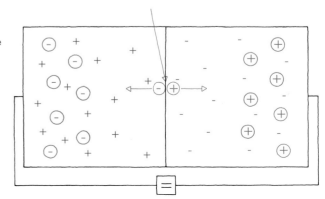

11.2
Window Collector Panels

Window collector panels are glazed box elements in which solar energy is transformed into heat and transmitted as heated air to a storage unit inside the building. Between collector (box element) and storage unit, the heated air is completely separate from the room air. Window collectors are south-oriented façade units where air is heated to 30–70°C by absorption when radiation is intense (Figure 288; see also Figure 195). The air heated in the box element is conducted to a storage unit through air pipes (fan-driven).

The south-facing window collector is generally equipped with interior and exterior high-insulating glazing, to avoid losing the thermal energy absorbed through the slats directly to the outside or to prevent too high a heat radiation toward the interior. When the thermal process is not wanted, the heat-absorbing slats are raised and insolation is used as direct (heat) gain. During the night the slats are lowered again and closed, to reduce heat loss from the interior toward the outside. In summer, it is advisable to install additional outside shading in the form of slats or awnings.

The storage unit can be placed horizontally in the basement. Natural stone is often the chosen storage mass in basement or cellar vaults, since its high density enables it to absorb a lot of heat energy. Horizontal storage has the great advantage of interfering least with the ground plan of a floor. Vertical storage units located in the centre of a building, on the other hand, facilitate the transport of the heated air to the south- and north-facing rooms and can heat several floors of a building simultaneously.

Window collectors (approx. 1/3 of the façade surface) can save up to 10 % of the heat energy, values similar to those generated by winter gardens. Window collectors are a typical solution for low single- or multi-family dwellings and are most commonly used where solar radiation is high during the day but temperatures plummet at night.

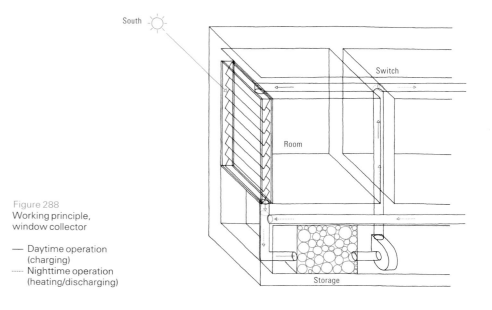

South

Switch

Room

Storage

Figure 288
Working principle,
window collector

—— Daytime operation
(charging)
······ Nighttime operation
(heating/discharging)

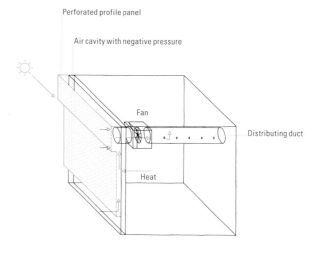

Perforated profile panel

Air cavity with negative pressure

Fan

Distributing duct

Heat

Figure 289
Working principle air collector
(winter days)

Heat is prevented from escaping through the walls and is captured in the rear ventilated cavity. The fans of the system create a slight negative pressure which draws fresh air through the perforation in the profile panels. The incoming air absorbs heat from the dividing wall and transfers the heat to the building.

11.3
Air Collector Panels

Air collector panels are a cost-efficient addition to warm-air heating systems when solar energy is used, e.g. in atria, where the intake air is directly heated by air collectors, during corresponding radiation, and then blown into the atria. Figure 289 depicts the working principle of the air collector, Figure 290 a panel profile in detail. The fabric of the hall or atrium itself stores energy.

The most important elements in the façade are perforated aluminium profile panels, whose dark coating can transform solar radiation into heat on sunny as well as overcast days. Fresh air flows through the holes in the perforation to the rear fan, where it is heated. In the upper area, the air is collected in a long chamber and supplied into the atrium or hall by one or several ventilators. Air collectors are, in efficiency, similar to window collectors and have the additional advantage, in summer, of reducing cooling loads as these façades have, in effect, a ventilated cavity.

11.4
Transparent Insulating Materials (TIM)

Incident solar radiation falls onto a black-painted absorber wall with transparent heat insulation. This wall, heated, transfers the heat to the rooms located behind it in a timed release, as determined by the wall's material and strength. To achieve a high efficiency coefficient, the wall material should have a density of at least 1,400 kg/m^3 (sand-lime brick, quarry stone, natural stone or concrete).

As in all systems which directly utilize solar energy, TIM's weak point is that the time of maximum heat gain does not correspond to the time of maximum heat loss. Figure 291 compares the heat requirement of a particular object and the heat gain through a TIM façade. From June to September, unless it is shaded or covered, a TIM façade generates a great amount of excess heat. Only on overcast days during that season are TIM elements in the south-oriented façade able to satisfy the entire convective heat requirement.

Figure 292.1 shows a TIM façade without water circulation (conventional system), Figure 292.2 a façade with water circulation through which, above all in the transitional season, heat energy from the south-oriented façades can be transported onto a plate heat exchanger, making heat energy available to other façade areas as well.

Figure 290
Air collector panel (Alcan)

Detail of profile panel: Air flows through the perforations and is heated in the cavity between aluminum panel and dividing wall.

Figure 291
Heat gain for non-regulated TIM wall (South façade, U-value 0.5 W/m^{2}K for 0.5 m^2 TIM wall per 1 m^2 façade)

■ Heat requirement
■ Heat gain through absorber

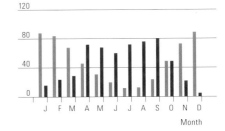

Heat flow
in W/m^2 façade surface

Figure 292.1
TIM façade
without water cycle
U-value 0.5 – 0.3 W/m^{2}K
(South façade)

Figure 292.2
TIM façade
with water cycle
U-value 0.5 – 0.3 W/m^{2}K
(South façade)

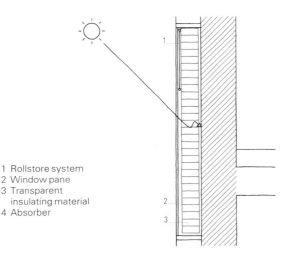

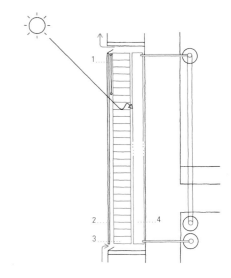

1 Rollstore system
2 Window pane
3 Transparent insulating material
4 Absorber

For a south-oriented façade, the energy gain per annum is a maximum of 100 kWh/m² (without water circulation) and 135 kWh/m² (with water circulation).

The costs for a TIM façade (approx. 900 to 1200 DM/m² of façade surface without water circulation; 1300 to 1600 DM/m² of façade surface with water circulation) bear no relation to the energy savings and, therefore, do not yield reasonable amortization rates. Consequently, when amortization alone is considered, a TIM façade is hardly recommendable, whereas, when global energy savings and environmental protection are considered, the positive effects obtained recommend installation.

1.5
Solar Absorber

Solar absorbers are simple absorber mats consisting of high-grade rubber with moulded-on distributing and collecting tubes, able to withstand cleaning, and temperature resistent from -50°C to +120°C. They are also permanently elastic and remain flexible in the cold. Solar absorbers (Figure 293) can be installed on roof surfaces and on the ground across large areas, creating warm water temperatures of up to 50°C. Generally used for the heating of swimming pools (Figure 294), the absorber mats' surface should be approx. equivalent to 50–80 % of the water surfaces to be heated. Of course, solar absorbers can also be used to heat household water. In this case, the usual circulation system between absorber mat and swimming pool must be replaced by a system which uses a storage tank.

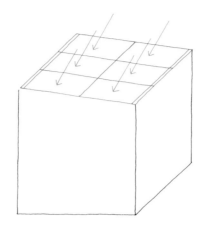

Solar absorbers can be used wherever there are open surfaces onto which sunshine falls.

Figure 294
Solar absorber for swimming pool
300 m² absorber surface

11.6
Flat Plate Collectors

In thermal solar collectors, the incident energy is transformed into heat and, thus, increases the temperature of the radiation absorber. The temperature can be regulated through the released heat with the help of a liquid thermal medium.

The losses encountered by solar collectors are

– optical losses (reflection),
– thermal losses (system dependent).

To keep such losses at a minimum, solar collectors are covered with high light-permeable glass (light transmission factor ≥ 92 %. The coating on the collector, which absorbs the solar radiation, is highly absorbent with low emission rates. The covering of a collector usually consists of 4 mm thick, pre-tensioned low-iron safety solar glass, with very low reflection properties.

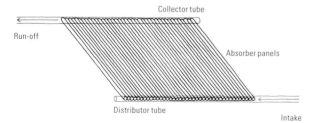

Figure 293
Structure of solar absorber

The heat energy gained by the collector is transported to a storage tank by water circulation. The entire system must be frost- and corrosion-proof. The system is controlled and regulated by measuring temperature differences. Figure 295 depicts temperatures and radiation intensities measured on a single day in a flat plate collector system. The relationship between radiation intensity and collector temperature is easily visible in the graph. Figure 296 shows a vacuum flat plate collector which, because of the vacuum, has a higher heat-insulating efficiency than flat plate collectors.

To derive the best possible efficiency coefficient from the solar system, the collectors must face south. Poorer efficiency coefficients, caused by any deviation from this ideal orientation, can sometimes be compensated for by installing larger collector surfaces. Figure 297 shows the reduction of the maximum efficiency coefficient for deviations from the azimuth angle of 180°. The optimum collector position, at a northern latitude of 50°, is approx. 45° and, hence, a lesser efficiency coefficient for the collector when other angles are used.

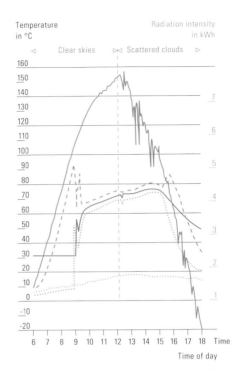

Figure 295
Energy curve of flat plate collector over the course of one day (measurements Bell + Grossett)

— Radiation intensity
-- Surface temperature of collectors
— Water temperature (exiting from collector)
.... Water temperature (entering collector)
.... Outside temperature

Figure 296
Vacuum flat plate collector
(Thermosolar)

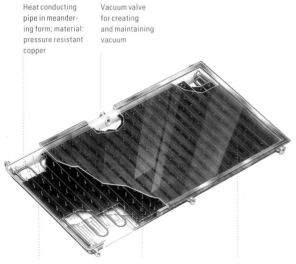

Heat conducting pipe in meandering form; material: pressure resistant copper

Vacuum valve for creating and maintaining vacuum

Absorber plate with galvanized, super selective special coating for maximum light-heat transformation with rapid heat transfer to heat conducting pipe

High temperature constant, elastic support units for power transfer of atmospheric pressure from glass panel to membrane bottom of container

Low reflecting, non-mirroring, high-transparent solar specialty glass panel made of thermally tempered, hardened white glass, hail proof by ISO standard

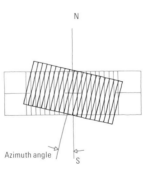

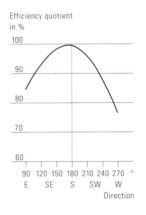

Efficiency quotient in %

Figure 297
Adjustment of collector installation in case of less than optimal placement

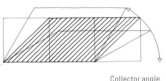

Collector angle

Efficiency quotient in %

Period of active use	Optimum angle
Jan. – Dec. (year round)	30 – 50°
April – Sept. (seasonal)	25 – 45°
May – August (seasonal)	20 – 40°
Sept. – April (heating period)	50 – 70°

210

11.7
Evacuated Tube Collectors

Evacuated tube collectors, like flat plate collectors, transform incident solar energy into heat. The solar radiation permeates the glass evacuated tube and falls onto the absorber surfaces inside the tube, where it is transformed into heat. The absorber surface's high-grade selective coating and the vacuum almost completely prevent heat loss to the surroundings. The heat energy collected on the absorber surface can be transferred to a heat tube, located on the underside of the absorber. During heat transfer, the liquid in the heat tube evaporates and arrives at the condenser as steam. In the condenser, the heat energy is then transferred to a water stream, condensing and returning it in the heat tube to evaporate once again, due to heat radiation. Figures 298 and 299 show a typical evacuated tube collector and the working principle. The same placement (azimuth angle/slant angle) as for flat plate collectors applies.

The efficiency coefficients of corresponding collectors are given in Figure 300. It shows that the vacuum tube collector has noticeably better efficiency coefficients than do flat plate collectors when temperature differences are high (mean collector temperature/outside space).

Collector installations are usually components integrated into a two-way heat-supply system. It should always be determined whether the return on investment will be satisfactory and, above all, whether the heat gained in summer will be high enough to supply energy to absorption chillers.

Figure 298
Evacuated tube collectors
(Stiebel-Eltron)

Figure 299
Principle of evacuated tube
collector

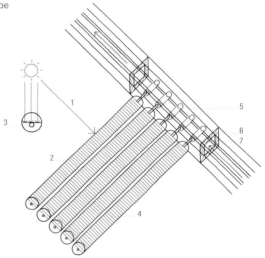

1   Heat radiation
2   Glass tube
3   Conducting tube
    with filling
4   Absorber, selectively
    coated
5   Condenser
6   Heat insulation
7   Heat exchanger tube

Figure 300
Efficiency quotient of flat plate
collector/vacuum flat plate
collector and evacuated tube
collector (Stiebel-Eltron)

– – Flat plate collector
— Vacuum flat plate collector
— Evacuated tube collector

ΔT = Temperature difference
between surroundings and
average collector temperature
(Flow/return)

Indoor measurement;
wind velocity 4 m/s and
radiation strength 730 and
750 W/m^2 respectively

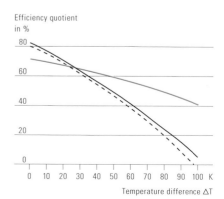

Efficiency quotient
in %

Temperature difference ΔT

Figure 301 shows a typical system installation
in which solar energy provides energy not only for
heating but also for a refrigerating system.
However, it is possible that, instead of the collector systems mentioned (flat plate principle), a
line-focused system will be installed to achieve
temperatures which are clearly above 100°C.
The schematized system solution has the definite
advantage that, in times of high radiation intensity, and thus high cooling loads, the heat energy
necessary for the absorption refrigerating system
is usually available, so that – in other words –
energy costs will be low. Another process for air
cooling via heat energy and heat created by solar
energy is the desorption process, i.e. cooling by
means of adsorptive dehumidification and adiabatic cooling. It is discussed again later on under
the topic of combined heat and power plants
(CHPs).

Figure 301
Solar energy heating and
cooling installation

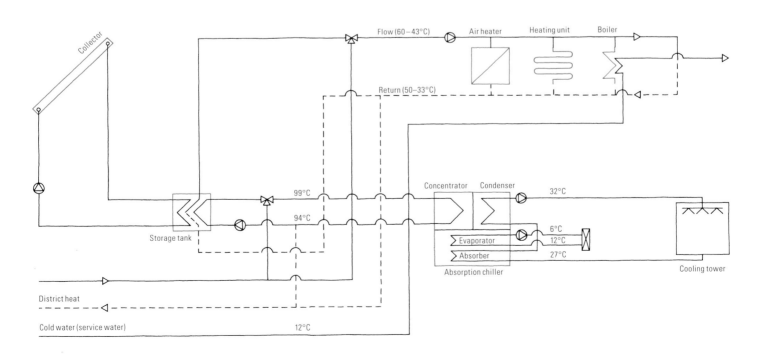

11.8
Photovoltaics

Photovoltaic elements contain different types of cells which have different efficiency coefficients. These are typically:

- monocrystalline silicon cells,
  efficiency coefficient 14 %,
  direct voltage approx. 0.48 V,
  direct current approx. 2.9 A.

- polycrystalline silicon cells,
  efficiency coefficient approx. 12 %,
  direct voltage approx. 0.46 V,
  direct current approx. 2.7 A.

- amorphous solar cells –
  silicon plated onto support substance
  (opaque module),
  efficiency coefficient 5 %,
  direct voltage approx. 63 V,
  direct current approx. 0.43 A.

- amorphous solar cells – semi-transparent,
  efficiency coefficient approx. 4 %,
  direct voltage approx. 63 V,
  direct current approx. 0.37 A.

Figures 302.1 and 302.2 show examples of a module's voltage characteristic for different incident solar energy, i.e. different module temperatures. The outer appearance of the solar cells is shown in Figure 303.1. The corresponding solar modules are usually embedded between two glass panes and supertransparent film to protect them from the elements (Figure 303.2).

Crystalline modules (monocrystalline and polycrystalline cells) have high efficiency coefficients, depending on the basic material, and offer many design options. However, they are much more expensive than amorphous modules, whose efficiency coefficients are approx. 5 %. Furthermore, the latter have the advantage of a considerably higher initial voltage, leading to simpler system designs. The use of photovoltaic elements (photovoltaic generators) makes sense only for those sections of a building which receive direct sunshine. This section of the building façades or roofs gives off the greatest amount of energy, so that even a small solar gain due to diffuse insolation with a very low efficiency coefficient is noticeable. Photovoltaic elements should utilize the direct and the diffuse radiation as much as possible. Hence, the active surfaces should face south-east or south-west.

Figure 303.1
Photovoltaic modules

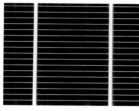

Monocrystalline solar cell

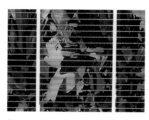

Polycrystalline solar cell

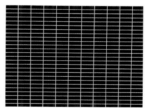

Semi-transparent amorphous solar cell

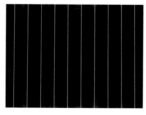

Opaque amorphous solar cell

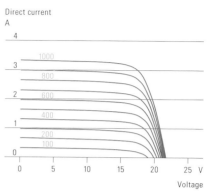

Figure 302.1
Voltage characteristics of monocrystalline photovoltaic module (Siemens SM 55) for different incident solar energy in W/m^2
Module temperature 25 °C

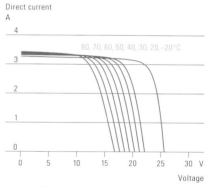

Figure 302.2
Voltage characteristics of monocrystalline photovoltaic module (Siemens SM 55) for different module temperatures
Incident solar energy 1000 W/m^2

Figure 303.2
Diagram of insulating glass in module

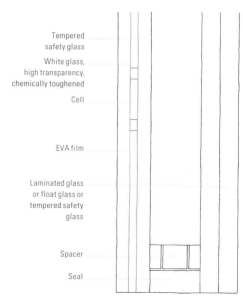

Tempered safety glass

White glass, high transparency, chemically toughened

Cell

EVA film

Laminated glass or float glass or tempered safety glass

Spacer

Seal

Figure 304 shows an example of a cold façade section with 'opaque' modules (System CW 80, Schüco International). The schematic in Figure 305 (page 215) illustrates how the electrically gained energy is collected and transported to the electrical energy units of a house via a transformer. Since photovoltaic systems generate electric power of approx. 1.0 – 1.5 W with full solar radiation (> 800 W/m²) and since approx. 100 kW/a of electrical energy can be gained per square metre, they are at this point not yet economically competitive (amortization periods too long).

To get a better return on investment, several research facilities are working on developing new building forms for photovoltaic elements. One technology showing promise is the so-called surface technology, in which five thin layers are superimposed onto a substrate, usually glass. These are the external contact layer (e.g. zinc or zinc oxide), a p-doped region, a highly resistant intermediate zone, an n-doped region and an inner contact layer made of aluminium or zinc oxide. Cells and conduits can be structured by silk-screening, laser etching (vaporization of the material with a pulsating laser beam) or photographic techniques. Surface technology is currently still plagued by certain problems with long-term stability and the translation of laboratory production into mass production. Only when these problems have been solved will it become apparent how far investment costs for photovoltaic systems can be reduced with these new modules, because the reduced efficiency coefficient of the thin-layer cells (< 6 %), compared to monocrystalline cells, must be compensated for as well.

Another futuristic technology in the area of photovoltaics has been developed in the past several years by Prof. M. Grätzel at the Technical University in Lausanne. This deals with photovoltaic elements based not on silicon but on the semiconductor titanium oxide (TiO), which allows them to imitate photosynthesis (Figure 306). The efficiency coefficients which have been created in the laboratory are in the range of 7 %, the same as amorphous solar cells. Low manufacturing costs, due to the simplicity of the process and approx. one-tenth those for silicon-based cells, make these cells especially interesting. However, time will tell whether they can be successfully marketed and whether this technology will prove itself in practice.

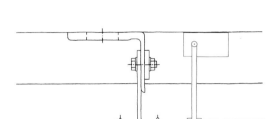

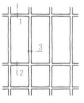

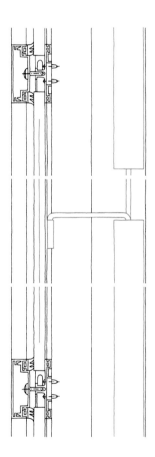

Figure 304
Façade sections, cold façade system CW 80 with 'opaque' amorphous modules (Schüco International)

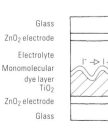
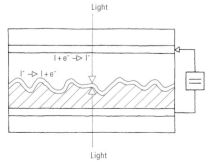

Glass
ZnO₂ electrode
Electrolyte
Monomolecular dye layer
TiO₂
ZnO₂ electrode
Glass

Light

$I + e^- \rightarrow I^-$
$I^- \rightarrow I + e^-$

Light

Figure 306
Diagram of Grätzel cell

When light falls onto the dye layer, the layer releases one electron to the TiO₂-layer. The electrons reach the upper electrode via the external current from which point they are transported once again to the dye layer by means of electrolytes.

Despite the sometimes excessive investment costs, it seems increasingly sensible and necessary to make greater use of photovoltaic systems in the future, both to advance technology and to protect the environment. Current investment costs of approx. 1500 DM/m² module surface generate a yearly savings of approx. 75 DM/m² module surface, resulting in an amortization rate of approx. 20 years. The use of photovoltaic systems and their integration into architecture can lead to highly innovative overall designs and thus also to special design characteristics and qualities.

Figure 307 shows a solar shed roof on the cantonal school in Solothurn, Switzerland, a solar shed roof on a new building of the municipal works in Halle, Westphalia (Systemlösung Flachglas Solartechnik GmbH) and the British pavilion in Seville, Spain.

Figure 307
Solar shed roof of cantonal school in Solothurn, Switzerland. Interior view of solar shed roof (4.0 kWp) of the municipal works in Halle, Westphalia and the British pavilion in Seville, Spain. (Architect: Grimshaw, London)

Figure 305
Wiring diagram of a photovoltaic installation

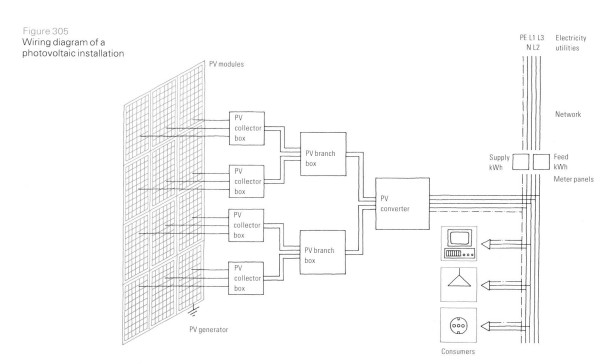

215

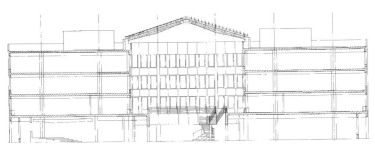

Figure 308.1
The Atrium of the new DEC
administrative building in
Geneva-Morgenes
(Architects: J.-F. Leccouturier,
L. Caduff, Geneva)

The Figure 308 series shows the atrium of the renovated DEC administrative building in Geneva-Morgenes. The light well (approx. 300 m²), previously open, was changed into an atrium, to save and gain energy, and was covered in a glass pyramid with free supported steel construction. Photovoltaic slats (Shadovoltaic, Solution AG, Härkingen, CH) function automatically as shading elements and, simultaneously, as energy source units (with the exception of those units facing north). The photovoltaic slats are screwed onto frames, which, in turn, are fixed onto a torque rod rotated by a steering lever drop arm. The three 'Shadovoltaic' sides of the pyramid are individually controlled and directed by a computer data program (solar gains approx. 16,000 kW/a).

Figure 308.5
Detail of Shadovoltaic
installation (15 kW)

Figure 308.4
Shadovoltaic units

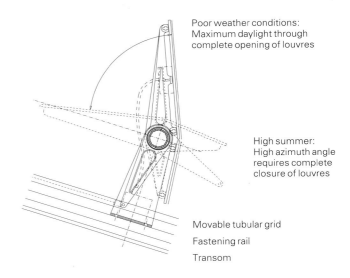

Poor weather conditions:
Maximum daylight through
complete opening of louvres

High summer:
High azimuth angle
requires complete
closure of louvres

Movable tubular grid

Fastening rail

Transom

Figure 308.2
Glimpses of sun are fine, but
not glare or undesired heat gain
caused by too much sun. The
DEC Shadovoltaic pyramid positioned for a high solar altitude.

Figure 308.3
Daylight for offices and an open
ambiance conducive to communication and interaction.

Figure 309.2
Typical Swiss weather – high fog, overcast skies:
The partially mirror-coated Shadovoltaic wings guide the zenith daylight against the mirrored ceiling; the façade remains in vertical position.

Figure 309.3
The fog lifts and the sun peaks through:
The Shadovoltaic wings shift to shading position, the façade begins to shift into an angled position. Both systems are responsive to the sunpath.

Figure 309.4
Bright sunshine:
Optimum shading and optimum photovoltaic performance. The façade is now in its maximum angled position.

Finally, there is R.P. Miloni's 'thinking space', intended to define and exemplify the technical interfaces common to a building or an exterior space (Figure 309 series). R.P. Miloni wanted to demonstrate light deflection, solar electric gain and shading in a suitable façade module, allocating investment costs to three areas, so to speak. A demonstration of this was put before the public at various trade fairs in 1993.

The technical data for the demonstration were:

Solar cells	SSI monocrystalline, 2.9A performance 216 Wp
PV slats	2 x 1,323 x 183 mm
	2 x 1,323 x 264 mm
	4 x 1,323 x 147 mm

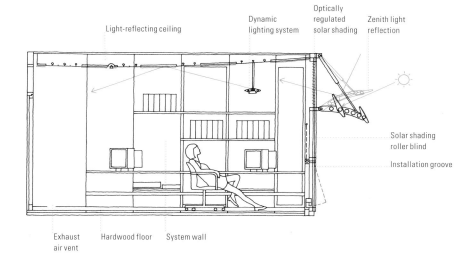

Light-reflecting ceiling Dynamic lighting system Optically regulated solar shading Zenith light reflection

Solar shading roller blind

Installation groove

Exhaust air vent   Hardwood floor   System wall

Figure 309.1
Thinking space in theory and practice as shown at Swissbau 93. Initiator: Reto P. Miloni, architect in Baden (Switzerland). In the thinking space light-intensive zenith light is redirected to the ceiling by means of reflectors. This reduces glare in the area while maintaining visual contact to the outside – creating in effect a 'monitor friendly window' and at the same time increasing daylight even in the recessed areas of the room.

Figure 309.5
Detail of façade
The single-axial sunpath-responsive Shadovoltaic system protects the middle window area especially well, while maintaining good visibility to the outside world from a sitting or standing position.

An essentially similar concept can be found in the Suva building in Basel, shown in Figures 208 and 209 (page 159) in section 7.5, if photovoltaic elements were added to the installation.

Unfortunately, it must be pointed out that many of the system solutions described are not yet cost-effective and that some architects will suggest certain solutions out of a sense of vanity rather than a real understanding and commitment to the matter at hand.

12

In regions with frequent winds, wind energy has exceptional importance. In urban centres, however, it can only be used to a limited extent and is thus of secondary importance in the planning of buildings.

13

Utilizing rainwater means not only utilizing grey water but also cooling building surfaces or building components. Evaporation effects near buildings can create improved conditions for natural ventilation.

14

The utilization of earth or soil heat and cold energy has thus far played only a minor role in energy generation. In the future, shallow and deep geothermal power will, next to solar energy, take a dominant position, since this is an energy source of universal, and almost unlimited, availability. While there are only some pilot installations in Germany for the utilization of soil heat, Switzerland has, to date, already installed 1,600 bore holes in combination with heat pumps. This is the main reason that CO_2 emissions in Switzerland are approx. 50 % less than in Germany.

12.
Wind Energy

Utilizing wind energy in building technology is primarily an issue of direct application (see Sections 4.1.1 and 5). Of course, there is also the conversion of wind energy into electrical energy by means of windmills.

Whereas their use in Central Europe is fairly limited, in California more than 16,300 wind-energy conversion systems (WECS), with rotor diameters of 10–35 m, were in operation by 1992. With an established performance of approx. 1,680 MW, California is currently a 'world champion' contender in the utilization of renewable energy sources.

In Mesopotamia, windmills were probably being used as early as 1700 B.C. for irrigation. The utilization of windmills is also documented in 7th century writings in Afghanistan. In Central Europe, the earliest windmills were in operation around the 12th century (England and France). The performance of the wind energy P is a result of:

$$P_{wind} = 1/2 \, \rho \, A \, v^3$$

Where:
ρ = air density
A = area through which wind flows
v^3 = oncoming (air) velocity (to power of 3)

In Central European latitudes, wind energy is used primarily to create and store electrical energy for public supply. In regions with favourable wind conditions, the alternative power generation, in parallel with the grid, has already reached or exceeded the threshold of economic viability. The installations provide power in the range of 0.5–4,200 kW. WECSs can be used independently of the public power grid as stand-alone systems, although this chiefly applies to countries or areas without adequate infrastructure (e.g. the developing countries, newly industrialized countries, non-electrified rural areas).

With such a great variety of applications putting many different demands on each wind-energy conversion system, technical solutions must accommodate the specific application.

Wind-energy conversion systems can be roughly categorized by rotor diameter:

– megawatt-stations, $\varnothing > 50$ m
– medium-performance stations, $\varnothing = 20 - 40$ m
– Danish-style stations, $\varnothing = 10 - 35$ m
– stand-alone stations, $\varnothing < 10$ m

Besides the compatibility of application and dimensioning, another decisive factor is the operating principle (operational design). The operational design includes parameters for output control – including measures for limiting the output – and security for the installation through power cut-off or blade-angle tilting. The operational design of most wind-energy conversion systems is electronically controlled and includes control mechanisms for the following:

– standstill ($w_m = 0$ m/s)
– non-regulated output ($w_m = 3.5 - 13.5$ m/s)
– strong wind operation ($w_m = 13.5 - 25$ m/s)
– storm setting ($w_m > 25$ m/s)

Wind data at the installation site, principal measurements of the wind-energy conversion system and installation-specific efficiency coefficients together determine the energy gained at a particular station. Selecting the generator size depends upon the requirements of the designer and the developer (e.g. strong-wind or weak-wind design). The main data of larger, medium, and small wind-energy conversion systems are approx. as follows:

Large wind-energy conversion systems:

Rotor $\varnothing$	approx. 110 m
Mast height	approx. 100 m
Performance	approx. 3,000 kW

Medium wind-energy conversion systems:

Rotor $\varnothing$	approx. 30 m
Mast height	approx. 35 m
Performance	approx. 300 kW

Small wind-energy conversion systems:

Rotor $\varnothing$	approx. 15 m
Mast height	approx. 23 m
Performance	approx. 55 kW

As the wind velocities and the measurements indicate, wind-energy conversion systems are not well suited for use in urban spaces or for direct application in building development. This section has served merely to introduce the topic; it will not be further discussed here.

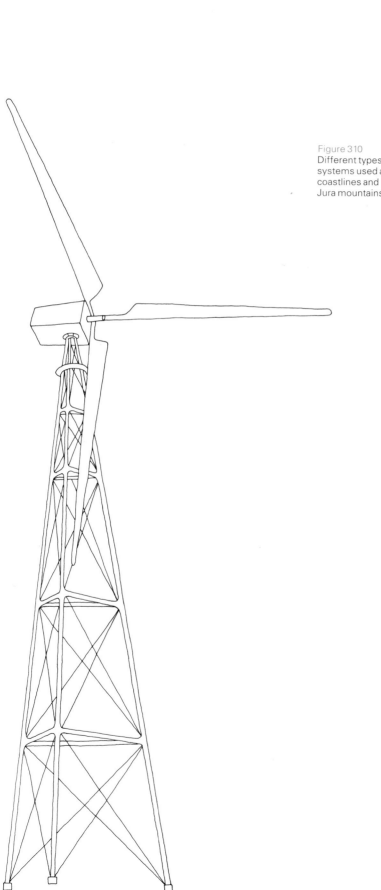

Figure 310
Different types of windmill
systems used along German
coastlines and in the Bavarian
Jura mountains.

13.
Rainwater

As was mentioned (in Section 4.1.3 Water), fresh water is one of our most precious resources, for which there is no substitute. Section 10 discussed the cost development for water in the last 10 years. A dramatic increase of water costs is inevitable in the near future and the utilization of rainwater will become a matter of course.

An analysis of the rain chart (Figure 27) to determine average annual precipitation in Germany clearly demonstrates that this is a zone with an abundant supply of rainwater. To conserve fresh water supplies in this region, rainwater is therefore a sensible choice for the use of natural resources.

On the other hand, both experts and the public are critical of rainwater utilization. The principal arguments against it are:

– the potential contamination of the rainwater cistern,
– the resulting risk of contaminating potable water in case of links between rainwater and potable water,
– possible links as a result of inexpert installation,
– low savings potential and high costs, especially for households,
– water shortage almost unkown (in Germany).

These criticisms will be considered in the following sections. Only in the future will the true energy savings potential become calculable. This should be verified carefully in each case. The comment that Germany does not have a water shortage is, of course, correct. Yet Germany does have a water quality problem, already felt by consumers in many areas in the form of high waste-water surtaxes. Rainwater utilization equals conservation of potable water supplies.

Figure 311
Diagram of rainwater treatment plant

13.1
Usage as Grey Water

Rainwater utilization should be restricted to run-off water from roofs, to ensure that no heavy contaminants flow into the rainwater cycle. Planted roofs considerably improve the results, since they are able to filter out heavy metals, soot and dusts. Rainwater is usually collected in a cistern, cleared of mud and exposed to UV radiation before it is gathered in the final holding tank. This is the actual water reservoir from which rainwater is fed to the consumer. The water in the holding tank is immediately filtered and treated in a dosing device until it has reached the necessary hardness. From there, the water is pumped to a distributor for individual consumers. Grey water is always conducted through a separate grey water system (local system) and must under no circumstances merge with the potable water system. Figure 311 shows a schematic of a rainwater treatment plant with grey water system. For a standard office building plan, rainwater can generally supply about 50–60 % of the necessary grey water needed for toilet flushing and urinals as well as watering landscaped areas near the building, which means that potable water must supply the remaining 40–50 %.

13.2
Usage for Cooling

Grey water can be used for cooling in a variety of ways, to be introduced and discussed in several examples. Among other applications, there is the cooling of the built envelope, indirect cooling of building components and evaporative cooling near buildings.

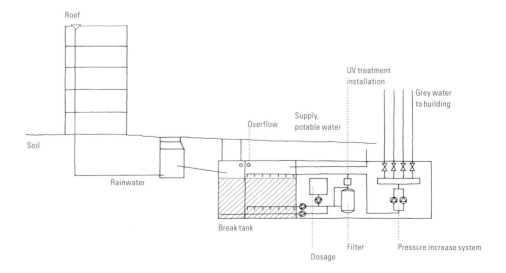

Roof

UV treatment installation

Grey water to building

Supply, potable water

Overflow

Soil

Rainwater

Break tank

Dosage

Filter

Pressure increase system

13.2.1
Built Envelope Cooling

Section 8 (Rooms under Glass) discussed the central entrance atrium for the New Leipzig Fair, where the built envelope is cooled with potable or rain water. A similar plan was developed in the competition for renovating the Reichstag in Berlin (by Calatrava Valls SA, Paris/Zurich/Valencia). Thanks to engineer E. Rabe (Federal Development Ministry Berlin I), HL-Technik was given access to old plans of the historical building (architect: P. Wallot, consulting engineer: David Grove). The Figure 312 series on the following pages shows the design and expansion stages from 1884 to 1994.

Figure 312.1
Blueprint of old Reichstag building, Berlin

Steam pipes and ventilation, basement

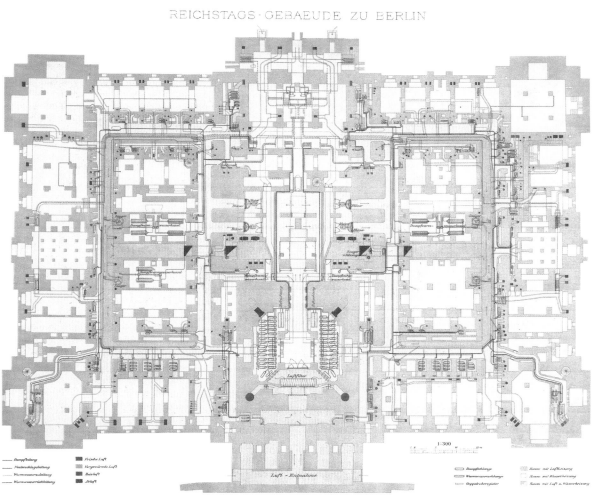

REICHSTAGS · GEBAEUDE ZU BERLIN

KELLERGESCHOSS: DAMPFLEITUNG UND LÜFTUNG.

The original central air-conditioning system for the Reichstag was very progressive and is worthy of consideration even today. Similar to a 'Hypocaust' system, building elements are used for energy storage. The keystone were the five supply and extract fans, installed below the plenary hall, which conducted air through masonry passageways, large enough to hold a person, to all areas of the Reichstag building, and from there directly or through separately controllable secondary heating chambers to the individual rooms and offices.

The warm- and cold-air shafts leading from the cellar passageways were similar to the type known today as a 'dual duct' system. The rooms were connected, as desired, to the cold-air riser, to the separately controllable warm-air riser, or both. This made fine-tuning the air supply in each room possible without losses through mixing. Modern folded steel ducts were not available then, which proved to be an advantage for summer cooling by means of the massive masonry walls.

For rooms in the perimeter zones having transmission heat requirements, there was a warmwater heating system which served as the principal heating system for the entire building. Hence, all building components were in place which provide rapid and individual control for every room. Because of the elaborate wood panelling and furnishing, the outside air was humidified after initial heating. This measure was supported by extensive use of plywood, to prevent cracking.

The dimensions of the original air-cooling and -heating system can be deduced from some (documented) measurements:

– 2 pre-heating chambers, 6.5 m wide and 7.5 m high,
– oncoming flow area for bag filters 48 m^2,
– diameter of the four large axial fans 2 m,
– pressure floor beneath plenary hall for ventilation from ground to ceiling (night cooling only) with a room height of 2.5 m.

Figure 312.2
Blueprint of old Reichstag building, Berlin

Condenser and hot water recycling system, basement

REICHSTAGS·GEBAEUDE ZU BERLIN

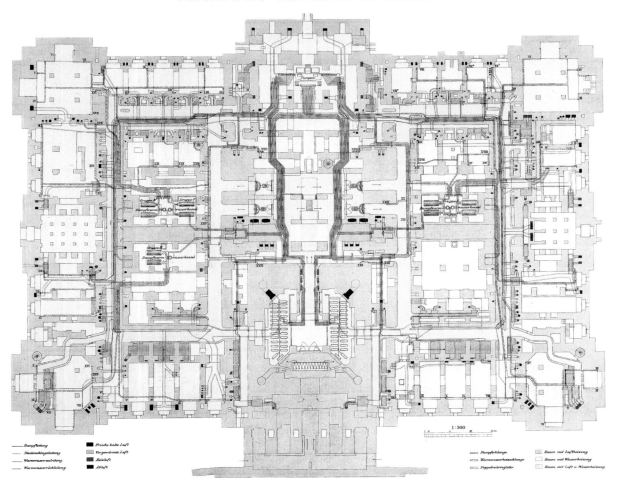

In another remarkable feature, fresh air intake was effected through two open corner towers on the west side and the air exhausted through two other corner towers on the east side, which prevented the mixing of fresh air and exhaust air under prevailing wind conditions (predominantly west winds). Linking the ventilation and heating system to the large storage masses of the building was a tremendous help in reducing energy costs. Another advantage was provided by the generous dimensions of the passageways which, because of the low air velocities in them and consequently small friction losses, kept electric power costs low. Air transport was also supported in winter by buoyancy from the supplementary heat chambers. Controlled air movement in the old meeting chamber, realized through a system separate from the main installation in the building, was another shining example of contemporary engineering skill and of collaboration between engineer and architect. When the meeting chamber was seated to capacity, fresh air was brought in from the top at approx. 18°C or in the condition imposed by summer temperatures in the building (storage effect) and extracted from underneath the chairs in the meeting chamber and the visitor's gallery. The empty meeting chamber could also be ventilated from below for exhausting contaminants and pre-cooling (night time cooling) by switching or reversing the airflow. The used air was exhausted through the large cupola above the glass ceiling by natural (non-mechanical) means to the outside and thus contributed to the cooling of the heated space below the glass cupola.

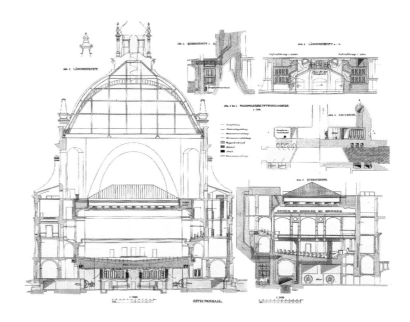

Figure 312.3
Blueprint of old Reichstag building, Berlin

Plenary, sections and warm water heating chamber, sections and ground plan

Figure 312.4
Blueprint of old Reichstag building, Berlin

Basement
Detail of ground plan and section

In contrast to modern practice, the machine rooms of the historic Reichstag were located not inside the building but in a separate machine house behind it. Steam and power lines were installed in a connecting tunnel. The machine house itself held eight boiler plants, producing not only low-pressure steam but also electrical energy, so that a combined heat and power system was already in place. All steam lines in the basement of the Reichstag building were directly connected to over one hundred air-heating chambers and also to steam transformers, producing warm water and heating water in what was tantamount to a gravity circulation heating system. A double return pipe could operate different heating cycles. In short, David Grove's design succeeded in compensating for the lack of automatic temperature control for heating and ventilation with a customized installation, thus creating a very efficient and economical system. Paul Wallot's positive attitude as an architect did much to facilitate the collaboration of architect and engineer. He had to integrate extensive masonry passageways and the entire basement or cellar area into his design to accommodate the engineer's technical requirements.

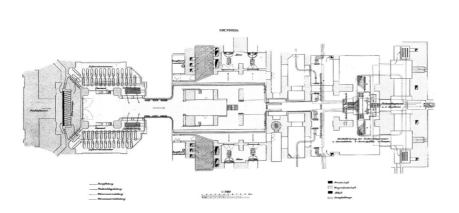

At the opening ceremonies of the Reichstag on December 1, 1894, Paul Wallot responded as follows when asked how the arts of architecture, painting and sculpture are related:

(Quote):
"Today some have spoken of three 'sister arts'. But in our time there is a fourth art which has joined these, the art of engineering. A steam engine, in my opinion, is the highest artistic achievement in that purpose and means are combined to perfection. In any harmonious collaboration of all the arts, I would include the art of engineering. I propose a toast to a melting together of all four arts, to their unity." (End of quote)

The 1993/94 competition entry by Dr. S. Calatrava (building climate and technical services design: HL-Technik AG, Munich), although not realized, was developed with a very similar approach to design philosophy, stipulated for the competition as ecological design. At the top of the list of requirements were:

– utilization of natural resources as much as possible,
– avoidance of contaminants,
– minimization of energy consumption,
– minimization of investment costs,
– easiest maintenance and operability.

Ecological design in this case included all possible passive measures for the reduction of heat consumption, the creation of solar heat gain in winter and the minimization of heat in summer. The building was to be responsive to the environment (sun, wind, temperatures, etc.), outside, in the envelope area, as well as inside, and to harmonize natural environmental conditions with user needs during different seasons.

Figure 312.5
Blueprint of old Reichstag building, Berlin

Branch diagram of steam/warm-water heating system

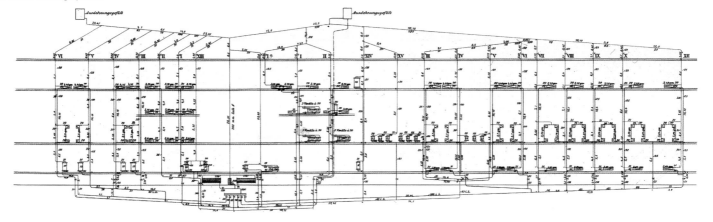

SCHEMATISCHE DARSTELLUNG DER GRUPPE I DER DAMPFWARMWASSERHEIZUNG.

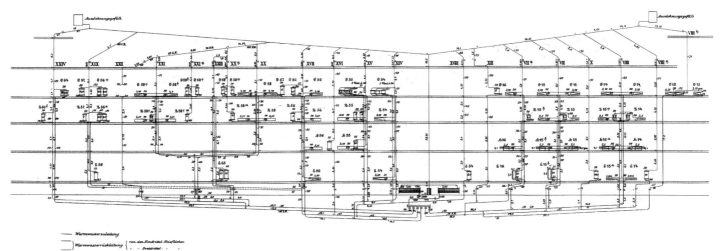

SCHEMATISCHE DARSTELLUNG DER GRUPPE II DER DAMPFWARMWASSERHEIZUNG.

The technical design focused on the utilization of wind energy for natural ventilation of the building fabric itself (Figures 313 and 314) as well as natural lighting and the utilization of the thermal masses (building masses for cooling).

Another important aspect to be researched was the proper construction of the glass surfaces in the hall and the cupola area (Figure 315). In the end, it was found that cooling the glass roof and the cupola with grey water presented the best solution, including cost-usage considerations.

Figure 315
Schematic of glazing variations

Insulating glazing with interior shading units

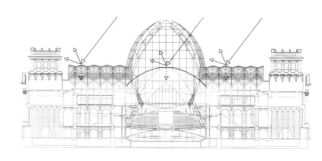

Sun protection glazing with photovoltaic units (semitransparent)

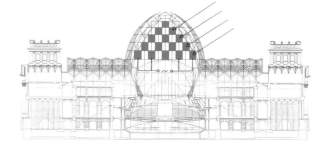

Figure 313
Wind statistics at Berlin-Tempelhof,
1969–1974

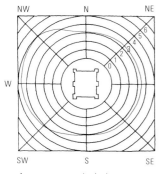

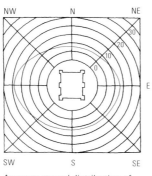

Average annual wind velocity in m/s

Average annual distribution of wind direction in %

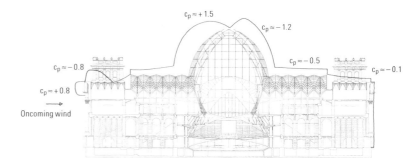

$c_p \approx +1.5$

$c_p \approx -1.2$

$c_p \approx -0.8$

$c_p \approx -0.5$

$c_p \approx -0.1$

$c_p \approx +0.8$

Oncoming wind

Oncoming wind

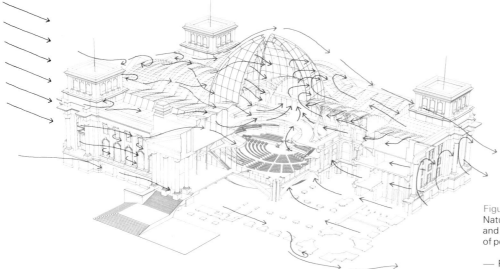

Bild 314.1
Example of pressure distribution on building for oncoming wind

$c_p = f(\rho/2 \cdot w_\infty^2)$

— Pressure
— Suction

Figure 314.2
Natural air movement around and through building as a result of positive or negative pressure

— Primary air movement
— Secondary air movement

Figures 316.1–316.2 plot the daily room temperatures in the upper area of the building with water sprinkling in summer and autumn. This solution is comparable to the 'built-envelope cooling at the British pavilion in Seville' shown in Figure 317. Figure 318 shows the schematic layout for using rainwater to reduce the building's cooling load by built-envelope cooling. The electrical energy requirements were minimized in this design by:

– reducing the cooling load through built-envelope cooling with water,
– reducing the operating hours for mechanical ventilation through mostly natural ventilation,
– minimizing the electrical energy requirements with optimal daylight lighting through the upper glass surfaces.

Figure 317
Example of 'external wall cooling' on British pavilion in Seville
(Architect: Grimshaw, London)

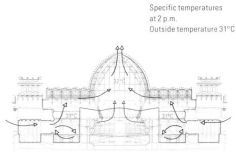

Figure 316.1
Daily measurements of room temperatures in upper section of building, insulating glazing with water sprinkling, during good weather period in summer

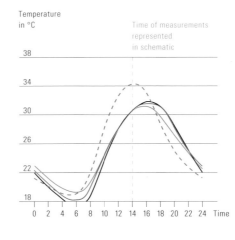

Temperature in °C

Time of measurements represented in schematic

Specific temperatures at 2 p.m.
Outside temperature 31°C

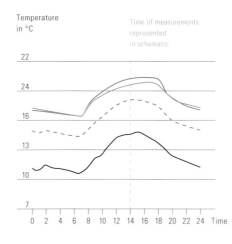

Figure 316.2
Daily measurements of room temperatures in upper section of building, insulating glazing with water sprinkling, autumn, transitional season

— Outside temperature
– – Roof temperature
— Air temperature in atrium
— Perceived temperature

Temperature in °C

Time of measurements represented in schematic

Specific temperatures at 2 p.m.
Outside temperature 15°C

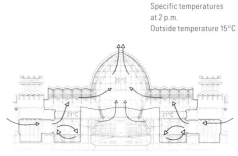

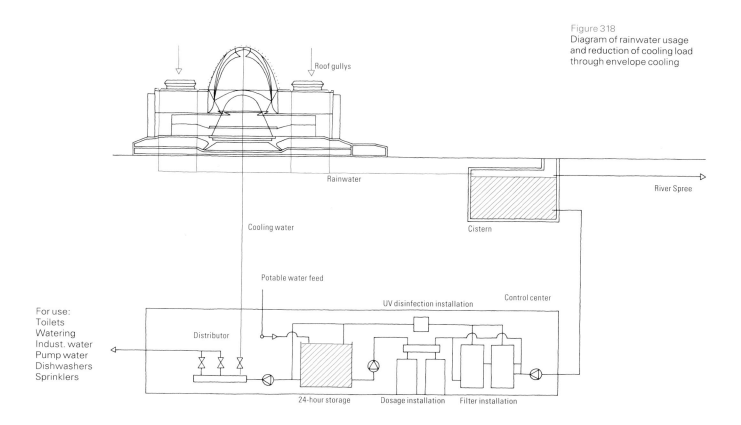

Roof gullys

Rainwater

River Spree

Cistern

Cooling water

Potable water feed

Control center

UV disinfection installation

For use:
Toilets
Watering
Indust. water
Pump water
Dishwashers
Sprinklers

Distributor

24-hour storage   Dosage installation   Filter installation

Figure 318
Diagram of rainwater usage
and reduction of cooling load
through envelope cooling

In conclusion, Figure 319 shows the daylight
quotient curve for a cross-section of the building.
The daylight quotients for many areas in the
building being well above 10 %, it can safely be
assumed that the daylight factor would have been
excellent. This project was an excellent example
for demonstrating how to utilize renewable energies and apply natural resources, above all by pro-
perly reactivating the existing built volumes.

Figure 319
Daylight quotients as seen
on cross-section of plenary
in %

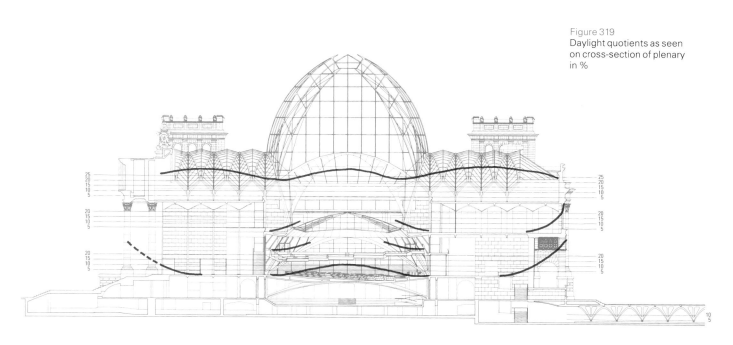

13.2.2
Cooling of Building Components

Figure 320 shows the model of an administrative building for the Nürnberger Beteiligungs AG in Nürnberg, Germany, which won first prize as competition design and is planned for construction in several stages.

The basic idea of the design by architects Dürschinger & Biefang is, on the one hand, a square corner lot (approx. 150 x 150 m) and, on the other, a generous open space at the centre. The placement of the high-rise at the intersection of access lanes is especially important for urban design. The block boundary is by no means a limitation. Rather, it sets the stage for a playful treatment of free forms and functions, to the east and to the south, as noise protection from a high-traffic road (Cherusker Street) and the subway respectively. By opening the block to the north side, the design responds to the existing terrain. It creates an interesting view and access situation into the open space at the centre, with its large connected waterscape, defining the experiential value of this open space and giving it a symbolic value for the new building. A cafeteria is planned for an 'island in the lake'.

The client wished for a mainly naturally ventilated building, whose peak cooling would limit maximum summer temperatures in all rooms to 27°C to 28°C. Because of the large water surface planned, one goal of this design was to appropriately utilize this body of water, to create synergy effects and to gain cooling energy by evaporation.

Figure 320
Building complex with man-made lake to promote evaporative cooling (Architects: Dürschinger & Biefang, Ammerndorf)

Figure 321 indicates the frequencies of air temperature prevailing at this location between 8 a.m. and 5 p.m. and the resulting lakewater temperatures before and after partial evaporation through fountains. Figure 322.1 shows the principal schematic of an office room with the basic technical data for the façade. Figure 322.2 illustrates the various possible layer structures of an indirect cooling system of building components (cooling by water) for a typical office.

The schematic illustrates how partial cooling ceiling units can be installed: suspended from the concrete ceiling, as cooling pipes superimposed on the ceiling, or as pipes integrated into the concrete of the ceiling. It is also conceivable, however, with reduced efficiency, that water pipe coils might be installed in a 'cooling screed'.

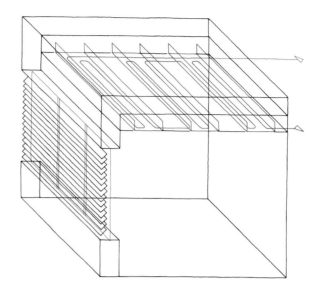

Figure 322.1
Natural ventilation with chilled ceilings (50 % of ceiling suface)

Shading
Diminution factor = 0.15

Insulating glazing
Thermal transmittance
U = 1.7 W/m²K
Light transmission factor
τ = 76 %
Total solar energy transmission
g = 54 %
Glass surface 65 % of total surface

Figure 322.2
Layer structures for indirect cooling system (cooling by water)

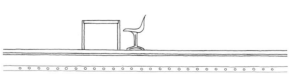

Partial ceiling units

Integrated chilled ceiling

Pipes integrated into concrete of ceiling

Insulating layer
Sound proofing

Water coils installed in 'cooling screed'

Figure 321
Annual air and water temperatures in atrium

— Surrounding air
–– Lake water
— Lake water with fountain

For a typical cooling load situation at a southwest-oriented façade, as in Figure 323, the load compensation (cooling) achieved by natural ventilation and cooling elements are illustrated. The graph in Figure 324 shows the air and building-component temperatures as well as the perceived temperature, based on a load compensation as in Figure 323.

The cooling loads were to be compensated by so dispersing and evaporating water from the lake as to ensure that the unevaporated water volumes would still cool the building. Figures 325.1 to 325.3 illustrate possible options. Figure 325.1 shows an example of indirect building-component cooling. Surface-type cooling coils on concrete ceilings, through which lake water is pumped, provide most of the cooling load compensation and create the temperatures shown in Figure 324.

Alternatively, the load can be compensated by additional air intake (air-change rate 2 ac/h, displacement ventilation) or through building-component cooling, wherein again all cooling units are supplied with lake water drawn near the fountain.

Figure 323
Cooling load and load compensation

Natural ventilation with chilled ceilings (50 %)

Required loads
in W/m²

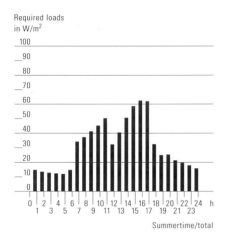

Summertime/total

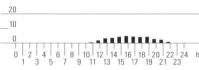

Heat transfer

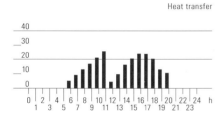

Solar radiation

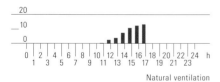

Natural ventilation

Interior loads

Persons

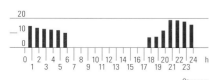

Storage

Load compensation
in W/m²

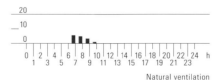

Summertime/total

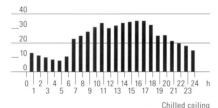

Chilled ceiling

Natural ventilation

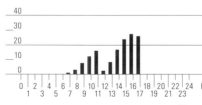

Heat transfer

Storage

Figure 324
Air and building-component temperatures

— Windows
······ Walls
— Floors/Ceilings
········ Room air
— Perceived temperature
— Outside temperature

Comfort zone according to
DIN 1946/2

Temperature
in °C

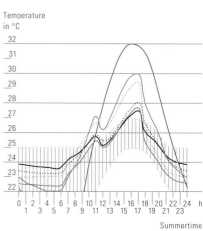

Summertime

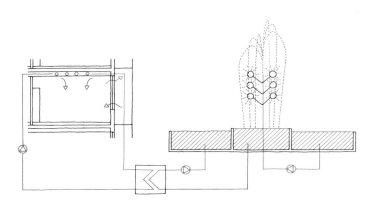

Figure 325.3 shows, as an alternative, the cooling of the building fabric through displacement ventilation using cold lake water. A water basin in front of the building (approx. 1–1.5 m deep) serves as cold-water reservoir. The fountains are so arranged that the sprayed water is collected in special water cups. Locating the fountains in the middle of the basin so intensifies evaporation that the lake-water temperature is reduced. The same effect occurs in summer with cooling towers. The water surfaces, in combination with the fountains, are, in fact, a combined system of storage and evaporative cooling – like a free-cooling cold storage. The simulation of the cooling effect of the water is based on meteorological data from the test reference year, including outside temperature, solar radiation, outside humidity and evaporation on the surface. The temperature curves shown in Figure 321 (page 231) with and without fountains were used for comparison with typical annual data, wherein the calculations for the fountains were based on five times the size of the water surface, from which the required number and placement of fountains were determined.

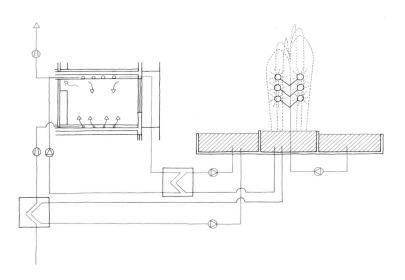

Adiabatic cooling of surface water with increased evaporation through fountains or similar installations has practical application for many projects and is also a factor when large glass surfaces require cooling, e.g. in the New Leipzig Fair project (Section 8.1).

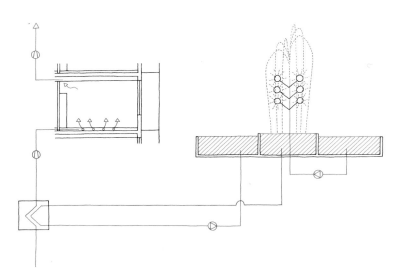

Figure 325.1
Natural ventilation with indirect cooling of building components
Schematic

Figure 325.2
Mechanical ventilation with fresh air and building-component cooling
Schematic

Bild 325.3
Mechanical ventilation with indirect fresh air cooling
Schematic

13.2.3
Evaporative Cooling near Buildings

To naturally ventilate a building in which high ambient temperatures in summer coincide with relative low humidities, the space near the building can be cooled instead of the building directly. Lowering the temperatures near buildings is made possible by adiabatic cooling, i.e. water evaporates onto or from a surface or is sprayed. Evaporation occurs when water with temperatures well below 100°C evaporates from the water surface or moistened surfaces. The evaporation increases in direct proportion to water and air temperatures as well as air velocities.

Evaporative cooling options are:

– evaporation at the water surface (still body of water),
– evaporation due to water dispersion,
– evaporation due to compressed-air water dispersion,
– evaporation at moistened surfaces.

For still or water surfaces in slight motion, the evaporative performance in summer is approx. $0.1-0.2$ kg/m^{2}h, from which evaporative heat losses ranging from approx. $65-135$ W/m^2 result. When the surface available for evaporation is increased by appropriate means of water dispersion, the interchange of heat and mass is greater than for a still surface. The evaporative heat losses can be several times greater than the values indicated for still water and the cooling effect is correspondingly higher.

Water sprayed by compressed air (Figure 326) further increases the cooling effect. Compressed air produces spray that is nearly dropless and evaporates very quickly in the outside air. With air pressures of $0.5-1.5$ bar, air velocities are approx. $300-500$ m/s. The water is sucked into the compressed air stream and then sprayed as an aerosol.

Air cooling by evaporation from moistened surfaces (Figure 327) (air-water countercurrent principle, similar to contact humidifier) also increases the evaporative, and hence the cooling, effect, in direct proportion to higher air and water temperatures and air velocities. The estimated resulting

Figure 326
Evaporative cooling
due to compressed-air water
dispersion
(French pavilion, Seville)

Figure 327
Evaporative cooling
due to moistened surfaces
near building
(Dutch pavilion, Seville)

relative humidity for moistened surfaces depends upon the surface itself, as well as upon the factors mentioned, and reaches a maximum of 60 %.

In the case of this particular project, the Nürnberger Beteiligungs AG, a cooling option (Figure 328) could also be developed in such a way as to act like a fabric wall behind a sound-deflecting glass wall which is sprinkled from top to bottom with water (cooling similar to contact humidifiers). The estimated air temperatures resulting from the evaporative cooling over the course of a year are shown in Figure 329, as is the temperature of the incoming ambient air. Good air flow and widespread dispersal of ultra-fine water jets across the fabric itself are essential for evaporation through a water-sprinkled fabric surface.

Figure 328 shows an additional evaporative cooling near the building by evaporation installations in the form of fountain-like structures. Outside air cooling, like that shown in Figure 330, is another option. In this out-side space cooling by evaporation, water is expelled in a fine spray through pipes in front of the building (handrails for balconies), to adiabatically cool the oncoming outside air. The limitations and efficiency of such a system depend largely upon the existing outside humidity and temperatures and are considerably reduced if the building is located at a site with generally high temperatures and high humidities. Adiabatic cooling, as in the example shown in Figure 331, creates, on the one hand, a decrease in temperature by approx. 5 K but, on the other hand, an increase in relative air humidity by approx. 40 % – 62 %. The relative humidity is still within the range of thermal comfort. High outside air humidities (storm conditions) massively limit evaporative cooling but also decrease the necessity for it, since the outside loads fall at the same time as outside temperatures.

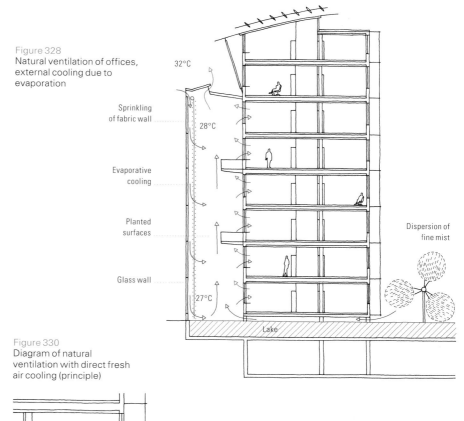

Figure 328
Natural ventilation of offices, external cooling due to evaporation

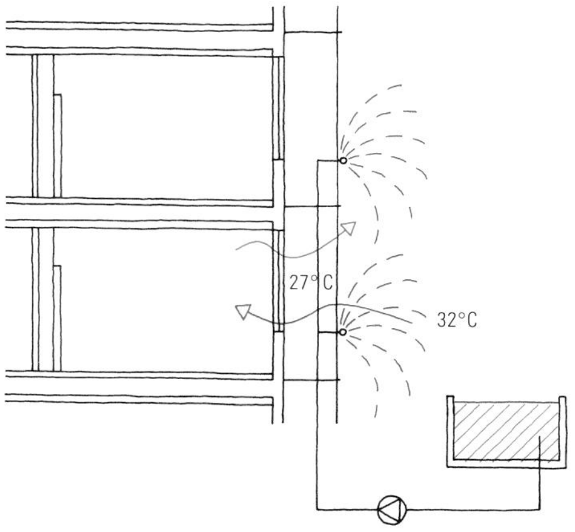

Sprinkling of fabric wall

Evaporative cooling

Planted surfaces

Glass wall

Dispersion of fine mist

Lake

Figure 330
Diagram of natural ventilation with direct fresh air cooling (principle)

Figure 329
Annual air temperature for evaporative cooling

— Surrounding air
— Air cooled by evaporation

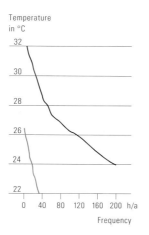

Temperature in °C

Frequency

Figure 331
Changes in diagram due to adiabatic cooling via 'evaporative wall'

ΔT Temperature reduction

Δx Increase in relative and absolute humidity

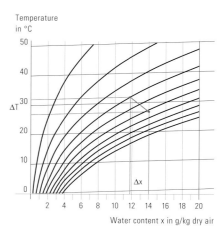

Temperature in °C

Water content x in g/kg dry air

14.
Deep and Shallow Geothermics

Unimaginable amounts of energy are stored inside the Earth, flowing in a continuous stream from the centre to the surface. About 30 % of this energy stems from original heat, i.e. from the formation of the Earth approx. 4.5 billion years ago, while the remaining 70 % is created by the decomposition of natural, radioactive isotopes. The resulting thermal temperatures increase by approx. 3 % per each additional 100 m of depth (Figure 332).

Geothermal energy can be harnessed to supply not only individual buildings but also and especially entire neighbourhoods and settlements, industry and manufacturing plants, agriculture, horticulture, etc. Geothermics is also used for electricity production (steam production). The storage of heat and cold energy in the soil is becoming increasingly important and, therefore, deserves a more thorough examination at this point.

Hydrothermal geothermics uses warm to hot deep waters for the direct heat supply of entire cities and settlements (e.g. thermal baths, utilization of heat energy in Iceland, etc.). Earth-connected heat pumps utilize shallow geothermics (earth coils, thermal labyrinths). Bore holes utilize the heat energy of the earth up to a depth of approx. 150 m. In the Hot-Dry-Rock process, heat energy is derived from hot deep-seated rock to produce electricity (steam or vapour turbines) and thermal energy.

Geothermics is a technology with guaranteed unlimited supply and availability. No emissions or waste products result from it, making it one of the most environmentally friendly and climatologically safe processes. The extraordinarily low operation costs (almost cost-free heat energy) are offset by investment costs, which must be studied in each case for economic viability to determine the optimal cost-benefit ratio. Although earth heat is not currently a leading energy source, it has practical application for district heating and heat-pump systems. Environmental problems will surely make geothermics more prominent and give it a much more important role than it has had. Geothermics may help solve future energy-supply problems, since a geothermally derived district heat supply places virtually no burden on the environment through combustion of contaminants. To improve the economic viability of corresponding installations, geothermal systems offer the option of utilizing thermal water or transported deep water.

Several current projects have received public funding to set up systems as research or utility facilities. However, one problem with geothermics must be mentioned – the risk that only every fourth boring will be successful.

14.1
Geothermal Power Stations
(Deep Geothermics)

Bore holes are a relatively new development, first implemented in Europe in Weggis, Switzerland. Bore holes, 2000–3000 m deep, are fitted with a production and an insulated transport pipe. The water circulating in this installation is heated in the earth and is usually a source for a heat pump. When temperatures of 100°C or higher are reached at a specific site, the energy can be used directly without an additional heat pump (heat exchange through plate or pipe heat exchanger).

A research installation currently in operation in Erding (near Munich; operated by ROM Rud. Otto Meyer, Hamburg/Munich) is a good example. In this installation, warm water is collected from the earth at a temperature of approx. 65°C. The Bavarian State Ministry for Water Management stipulated that thermal water be cooled to 20°C ± 3°C, to reach a district supply temperature of 110°C/ 45°C (intake/ return temperature). The thermal water is pre-cooled by direct heat exchange in this system (plate heat exchanger 3 K or pipe heat exchanger 5 K) and is then fed through an adapted heat pump where the remaining heat energy is drawn from the thermal water (55°C/20°C).

Figure 333 shows an installation using geothermal heat pump technology. The absorption heat pump is laid out as a two-step 'single-effect' absorption heat pump (two-step evaporator/ absorber).

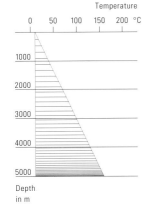

Temperature
0   50   100 150   200 °C

1000

2000

3000

4000

5000

Depth
in m

Figure 332
Temperature profile of lithosphere
In Central Europe thermal temperatures increase by 3°C per 100 m of depth. In regions with so-called 'geothermal anomalies' thermal temperatures increase more rapidly.

Figure 333
Diagram of geothermal heat
pump installation
(Entropie S. A./ROM)

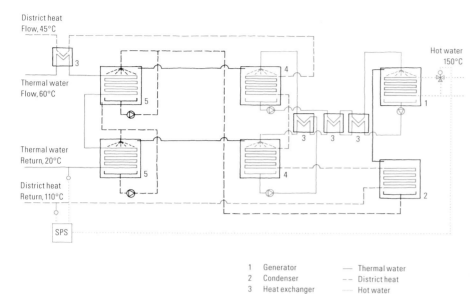

District heat
Flow, 45°C

Hot water
150°C

Thermal water
Flow, 60°C

Thermal water
Return, 20°C

District heat
Return, 110°C

SPS

1	Generator	——	Thermal water
2	Condenser	– –	District heat
3	Heat exchanger	⋯⋯	Hot water
4	Absorber	——	Steam
5	Evaporator	– –	Condensation
		——	Coolant/-mixture

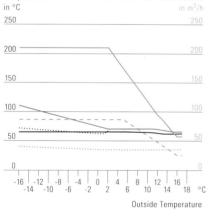

Temperature   Thermal and district heat water volume
in °C   in m³/h

Outside Temperature

Figure 334.1
Parameters of temperatures
and mass flux in a geothermal
heat pump, annual readings

⋯⋯ Exit (HP)
⋯⋯ District heat, recirculated
—— District heat, transmitted
—— Inlet temperature TW to HE
—— District heat volume
– – Thermal water volume

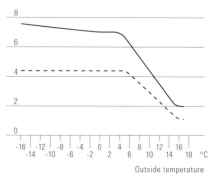

Output
in 1000 kW

Outside temperature

Figure 334.2
Efficiency curves of geothermal
heat pump installation, annual
readings (cooling of thermal
water to 20 ± 3°C)

Recirculated district heat
< 40°C

—— Output HE + HP + drive
– – Output from geo(thermal)
heat

There are two evaporators where the thermal
water is cooled to 20°C in a two-step process of
vaporizing distilled water. The low-temperature
steam created in the evaporators is absorbed
by a concentrated lithium bromide solution in
separate absorbers. To achieve a closed circuit,
the solution is constantly renewed in a generator
at a temperature of 150°C, generating pure
steam, which is cooled with the district heating
water. The absorption heat pump is fitted with
two internal heat exchangers to improve the
cooling ratio. On its path from the absorbers to
the hot generator, the solution is heated in the
exchanger, and cooled on its return respectively.

The total output of the district heat network is the
sum of the heat exchanger output, the cooling
perfomance of the heat pump and the generator
performance minus any heat loss factors (approx.
200 kW in the illustrated example). The output
yield, whose variables are the district heat mass
flow and its return temperature, determines the
outlet temperature of the transmitted district heat
at the absorption heat pump. The heat pump system must be protected from exposure to extreme
inlet temperatures (= return temperature of the
district heating system).

The output of the absorption heat pump is regulated through the outlet temperature of the district heating water (min. 65°C, max. 80°C). A
regulator valve at the generator (150°C) is used to
adjust the output as needed. The cooling performance of the evaporators (heat extracted from the
thermal water), as well as the generator output
and the heat transfer, are directly proportional.
In other words, the more heat is transferred from
the heat pump, the more heat is extracted.
Changes to the mass flow of the thermal water
thus regulate the outlet temperatures. The
parameter and efficiency curves are shown in
Figures 334.1–334.2.

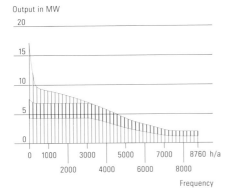

Output in MW

Figure 335
Annual output characteristics of the district heat supply in Erding (Geothermal water cooled to 20 ± 3°C, temperature of recirculated district heat < 4°C)

III	Output HE + HP + Generator + PB	HE	= Heat exchanger (geothermal)
III	Output HE + HP + Generator	HP	= Heat pump
III	Output HE + HP	Generator	= Hot water
		PB	= Peak boiler (gas driven)

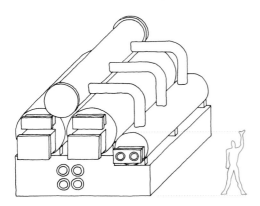

Figure 336
Comparative dimension of geothermal absorber heat pump (4.4 / 7.8 MW)

Figure 335 shows the annual output characteristics of the district heat supply in Erding based on geothermal heat utilization. The proportion of geothermal heat in the thermal output to the district heat network is 53 %, that of the primary heat is 35 % and that of the peak boiler is 12 %. Table 9 once again lists the individual data depending on the outside temperature for the layout of a correspondingly operated geothermal heat pump. Figure 336 gives an idea of the size of such a system.

Another option for deep geothermics, applicable for depths of 200 m to 1000 m and more, is a system developed by Geocalor AG in Switzerland. This open system uses a double-walled pipe (Ø approx. 150 mm) which is inserted into the bore hole and then filled with quartz shingle. When this system is used, e.g. to a depth of approx. 500 m, a pump is installed around the 200 m mark, which transports water from the deep. There, the water is cooled by a heat pump and then returned to the ground through two drain pipes (in the example, drainage at approx. 170 m depth). In the quartz shingle of the bore hole, the water drains down at a very low speed, heats up on its way down and reaches the bottom of the bore hole, from where it is quickly pumped to the surface (Figure 337). Numerous installations in Switzerland have been equipped with this system; the range of performance is 10 kW – 240 kW. One special feature of the system is the double-walled central pipe, which insulates heated water from the surrounding shingle and thus prevents heat loss via the colder soil or rock as the water moves towards the surface. The geothermal potential is thus efficiently utilized, yielding a heat pump efficiency quotient higher than 4. The specific potential quotient depends upon local geological conditions. Experience has shown that granite with a temperature increase of 4 – 5 K per 100 m offers the best conditions. The values for water-bearing sand or clay are 3 – 3.5 K per 100 m and for non-water-bearing clay 2 – 2.5 K per 100 m.

Table 9
Parameter table
(Recirculated temperature of district heat < 40°C)

	Thermal water (TW)			District heat (DH)			Heat-pump technology (HP)					Peak load boiler (PB)		
Outside temperature	Output	Incoming TW	Exit HP TW	TW mass flow	DH return	Exit HP DH	DH mass flow	Cold energy HP	Generator	Heat output HP + HE	Cooling factor	Output Geo	Output PB	DH flow
[°C]	[MW]	[°C]	[°C]	[kg/s]	[°C]	[°C]	[kg/s]	[kW]	[kW]	[kW]		[kW]	[kW]	[°C]
t_{Ou}	Q_{Net}	$T_{TW \cdot HE_i}$	$T_{TW \cdot HP_e}$	m_{TW}	T_{DHR}	$T_{DH \cdot HP_e}$	m_{DH}	Q_C	Q_G	Q_{HP+HE}	η_k	Q_{Geo}	Q_{PB}	T_{DH}
-16	17.0	65.0	20	24.0	40.0	72	58,0	2,307	3,353	7,668	0,69	4,414	9,320	110
-8	13.2	65.0	20	24.0	37.5	68	58.0	2,057	3,023	7,337	0.68	4,414	5,874	92
-3	10.8	65.0	20	24.0	35.9	65	58.0	1,900	2,816	7,131	0.67	4,414	3,719	81
-1	9.9	65.0	20	24.0	35.3	64	58.0	1,837	2,733	7,047	0.67	4,414	2,861	76
6	6.6	65.0	20	22.8	35.0	70	45.2	1,703	2,556	6,613	0.67	4,157	0	70
12	3.8	63.0	20	13.1	35.0	70	26.2	989	1,615	3,778	0.61	2,262	0	70
16	2.0	62.0	20	6.3	39.9	65	19.1	600	1,102	2,000	0.54	998	0	65

t_{Ou}	Outside temperature
Q_{Net}	Output
$T_{TW \cdot HE_i}$	Temperature thermal water, heat exchanger, inlet
$T_{TW \cdot HP_e}$	Temperature thermal water, heat pump, exit
m_{TW}	Mass flow thermal water
T_{DHR}	District heat recirculated temperature
$T_{DH \cdot HP_e}$	Temperature district heat, heat pump exit
m_{DH}	Mass flow district heat
Q_C	Cooling output, heat pump
Q_G	Generator output, heat pump
Q_{HP+HE}	Total geothermal heat output
η_k	Cooling factor
Q_{Geo}	Output Geo
Q_{PB}	Output peak boiler
T_{DH}	District heat temperature

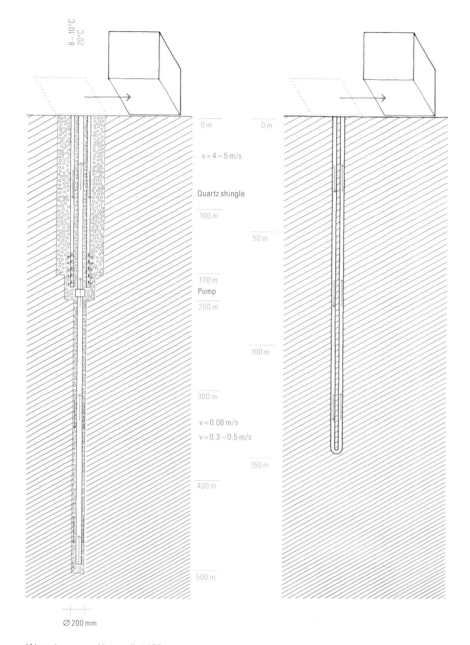

Figure 337
Structure of bore hole
for open system (Geocalor)

to Figure 338
Heat source circuit
Bore hole back-filled up
to 150 m mark

8 – 10°C
20°C

0 m

v = 4 – 5 m/s

Quartz shingle

100 m

170 m
Pump
200 m

v = 0.08 m/s
v = 0.3 – 0.5 m/s

300 m

400 m

500 m

∅ 200 mm

0 m

50 m

100 m

150 m

Water is pumped into soil at 100 m
depth and seeps through the quartz
shingle at approx. 0.08 m/s inside
the bore hole to the end of the pipe
(∅ ≅ 50 mm) absorbing heat from
the soil.

Above the pump the heated water is
brought to the surface in a thermal pipe.
The air-filled chambers of the thermal
pipe reduce heat loss to the surrounding
soil.
(Internal pipe diameter approx. 50 mm)

Figure 338
Diagram of geothermal bore hole
installation with three closed circuits:
Heat source circuit,
heat pump circuit
and heating circuit

14.2
Bore Holes, Earth Coils
(Shallow or Surface Geothermics)

Smaller installations and individual projects are
more suited to shallow or surface geothermics in
the form of bore holes or earth coils.

At a depth of 100 m, earth temperatures range
from approx. 10 – 14°C, depending upon the region
and the ground structure and consistency. This
heat can be used to heat buildings with the help of
bore holes combined with heat pumps, which
means that bore holes can be used economically
and be manufactured to satisfactory operational
specifications for depths up to a maximum
of 150 m.

Figure 338 shows the principle of a bore hole
installation with the various cycles (heat source,
refrigerating agent, heating cycle). Generally,
a U-shaped polyethylene pipe with a maximum
length of 150 m and a diameter of 3 – 10 cm is
inserted into the ground through a bore hole. This
pipe now functions as a heat source. Heat is extracted from the earth through the closed circuit
(heat source cycle) in the bore hole by transporting brine (water with approx. 25 – 35 % antifreeze
content) through the pipe into the depth, where
it rises again through a second pipe and flows to
the evaporator. The bore holes are back-filled to
ensure good contact between bore hole and earth
and to increase the heat transfer (backfill with
suspending agents mixed with cement compounds or silica).

The brine in the heat source cycle usually has a
temperature of -2°C to +5°C and is heated in the
earth by approx. 1.5 – 3 K, depending upon the
probe length. The maximum heat extraction is:

approx. 120 – 140 W/m in the groundwater,
approx. 50 – 70 W/m in the soil.

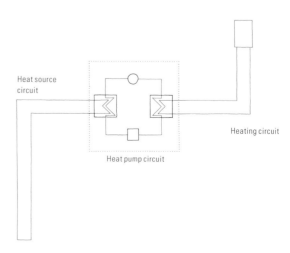

Heat source
circuit

Heating circuit

Heat pump circuit

Figure 339 records the temporal variation in earth temperatures at depths of 5 m, 50 m, and 85 m (bore hole installation in Elgg, near Zurich). As is evident from the graphs, earth temperatures at shallow depths drop by approx. 4 K more than at a depth of 85 m. The temperature fluctuation in the earth depending upon heat extraction is also clearly visible (degree days).

When bore holes are positioned, care must be taken to evaluate the temperature interaction between bore holes, because earth heat for more distant regions cannot quickly enough replenish the heat that has been extracted. In Figure 340.1, the cone of depression near the bore hole shows the radial temperature distribution around the hole. Immediately next to the bore hole, the earth is cooled by up to 8 K. At a 50 cm distance from the bore hole, the cooling drops to approx. 4 K, and at an approx. 2.5 m distance, the cooling drops to less than 1 K. When the heat pump is turned off, the cone of depression is replenished, although the temperatures cannot be expected to return to normal during a heating period. From Figure 340.1 it can be inferred that bore holes should be at least at a distance of 6 m, to prevent adverse inter-ference. Figure 340.2 lists supporting data and shows the decrease of the average source tem-perature (earth temperature), depending upon the distance between two bore holes. Other studies by RWE Energie AG in Essen on the increase of heat extraction have shown that fitting a bore hole with two pipe loops is the optimum solution and that installing four loops per bore hole does not yield any noticeable improvement.

Another potential application of bore holes is in the direct creation of cold energy (cooling heated water in the earth). Corresponding system sol-utions can be used for the direct and indirect cool-ing of building components previously mentioned.

It is important to ensure that the supply tempera-tures of relevant cool cycles are not much lower than +18°C and the return temperatures not far above +22°C. Utilizing earth cooling means reject-ing heat given off from the building to the soil. Therefore, it is necessary to ensure that the annual energy flow is well balanced, i.e. that the heat energy returned to the earth during the warm sea-son is balanced again during the cold season. Assuming a spatial heat energy flow of approx. 0.065 W/m² in the earth, an average distance of 6 m

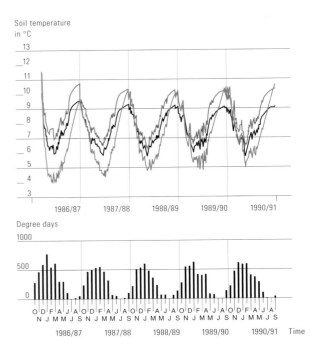

Figure 339
Temporal variation in earth temperatures at depths of 5 m, 50 m, and 85 m, and at 50 m distance from bore hole in Elgg, Switzerland, over a period of five years of operation
(Degree days 20 /12)

— 85 m
— 50 m
— 5 m

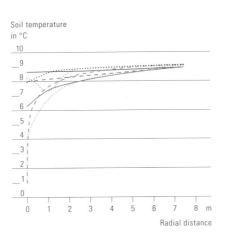

Figure 340.1
Dynamic of cone of depression. The graph shows the radial tem-perature distribution at the installation in Elgg for different times during 1988/89.

— OCT88
-- DEC88
...... FEB89
...... APR89
-- JUN89
— AUG89
...... OCT89

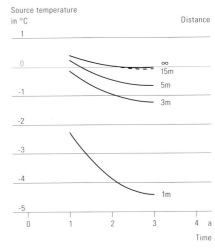

Figure 340.2
Reduction of average source temperatures dependent on distance between two bore holes

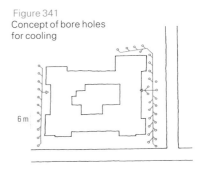

Figure 341
Concept of bore holes for cooling

6 m

between bore holes leads to a probe energy yield of approx. 30 W/m. The maximum probe depth should not exceed 100 m; otherwise, investment costs are disproportionately high. Figures 341 and 342 show the placement of bore holes for cooling an area in a building and the principal schematic of the cooling cycle, respectively.

Another form of heat extraction from the earth is the use of earth collectors (earth coils, underground horizontal pipe coils). Figure 343 shows the principle of a system of energy utilization with horizontally arranged earth heat exchangers. An important criterion for successfully applying this method is that the heat conduction quotient of the ground, its density and its specific heat capacity be suited to heat extraction, to achieve high efficiency coefficients. Experience shows that moisture content is in direct proportion to heat extraction (the more moisture, the higher the extraction rate). In a horizontal arrangement, corresponding earth collectors are placed at a depth of approx. 1–2 m. Depending upon the soil or ground consistency, approx. 20–40 m² of soil surface is required per kW of heat energy (clay-containing soils are better than gravel or sandy ground). Approx. 2 m² of earth surface is necessary per m² of living space in a monovalent operation (heating the building exclusively by earth heat pumps); and since large surfaces are often not available, horizontal earth collectors or coils have been superseded by bore holes.

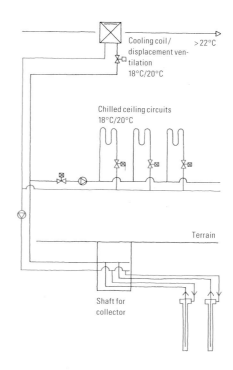

Figure 342
Principle of cooling cycle
Bore holes

Cooling coil/displacement ventilation
18°C/20°C
> 22°C

Chilled ceiling circuits
18°C/20°C

Terrain

Shaft for collector

Bore hole
max. depth 100 m
min. distance 6 m

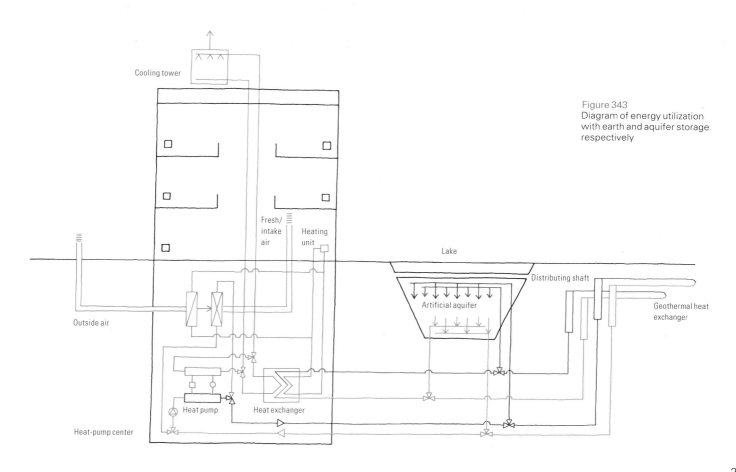

Figure 343
Diagram of energy utilization with earth and aquifer storage respectively

Cooling tower

Fresh/intake air

Heating unit

Lake

Distributing shaft

Artificial aquifer

Geothermal heat exchanger

Outside air

Heat pump

Heat exchanger

Heat-pump center

14.3
Aquifer Reservoir

Figure 343 shows, in addition to the earth heat exchangers, an aquifer reservoir in its basic form and integrated into a complete heating system. The soil and the aquifer can alternate as reservoirs. In this case, earth heat exchangers or aquifers extract heat energy from the soil with the help of heat pumps during a heating period (Figure 344). When the heat pumps are in operation for cooling (e.g. cooling a building), the condensor heat is stored in the soil.

During winter operation, and partially during the transitional season, heat energy is extracted from the soil, which grows increasingly cooler. The cooled soil thus presents, throughout summer and the transitional season, an energy potential which can be used to cool buildings. During the cooling period, the heat transfer medium (brine-water blend) is pumped through the earth heat exchanger, where it cools and can then be used directly for cooling air. When the soil has warmed again, because of the cold extraction, to such a degree that it can no longer be used for refrigerating energy, the cold cycles at the heat pumps are reversed and now function according to the usual cold operation cycle. At the same time, chillers can transfer their condensator heat to the soil, resulting in a heat storage parallel to cooling operation.

When artificial aquifers are installed, the earth is kept moist by creating water surfaces near the earth heat exchanger. This must, however, be carefully calculated to ensure that the water surfaces do not warm up so much as a result of heat storage that a high rate of evaporation ensues. Directing excess heat energy to aquifers and storing it there is, therefore, only possible to a limited extent.

Economical and efficient storage for heat at low temperatures in each location can be achieved by adapting the design of an aquifer reservoir to the soil available at the site. The options are shown in Figure 345. Aquifer reservoirs, i.e. heat storage in a moist gravel bed and water-bearing layers respectively, are an economical alternative to non-pressurized container reservoirs for larger capacities. Economy alone dictates that large heat-storage facilities should be located as near as possible to the consumer. This is, however generally made more difficult by the fact that

Figure 344
Diagram of heat pump installation

Operation in winter

Heating of building

Flow and return for heating by means of geothermal heat exchanger/aquifer reservoir

Fresh air

Operation in transitional season

Cooling of offices and work areas by means of geothermal heat exchanger/aquifer reservoir

Fresh air

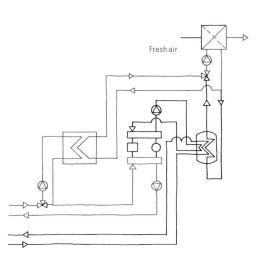

Operation in summer

Cooling of offices and work areas by means of heat pump

Flow and return of stored transfer heat in heat exchanger/aquifer reservoir

Fresh air

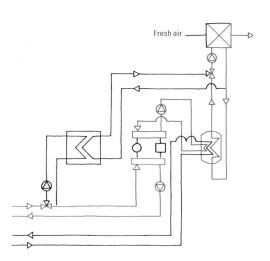

large open surfaces are usually not available in the densely built environments which have the highest energy requirements. Often the only available surfaces are open areas between buildings, which can then be used accordingly.

When aquifers are constructed, the relevant reservoirs must always be operated with oxygenated water, for hygienic reasons and to avoid anaerobic conditions. The bacteria infiltrated by air into the cycle water should never by sterilized with biocides but must instead be filtered out in a bypass cycle. Organic materials should be avoided and should not come into contact with the cycle water, where they would provide a breeding ground for bacteria. The groundwater surrounding the aquifer should be heated by only a few degrees. At the same time, the heat emission from the reservoir through the upper heat-insulating layers should be kept to a minimum, to prevent noticeable influences upon the urban climate or the microclimate near buildings.

Depending upon construction form, aquifer reservoirs can shift the temperature front horizontally or vertically. A vertical flow is predominant in the reservoirs shown on the following pages. During extraction, warm water is transported to the upper (extraction) system and the same amount of cold water is simultaneously taken from the lower section of the system. Buoyancy forces have a stabilizing effect on temperature distribution (water speed approx. 3 times the speed of the temperature front). Decisive criteria for the use of free convection are the permeability coefficient of the rock fabric (permeability factor k_F), the thermal expansion factor b and the temperature difference ΔT between reservoir and upper extraction system, characterized by the Rayleigh quotient. In Figure 346 it can be seen that free convection in undisturbed soil with a permeability coefficient less than 10^{-4} m/s is barely noticeable. Vertical storage is only possible when no convection occurs.

Figure 345.1
Aquifer reservoir in natural ground
Capacity 15,000 m³ equivalent to 8,800 m³ water volume

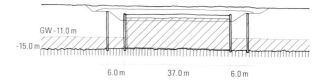

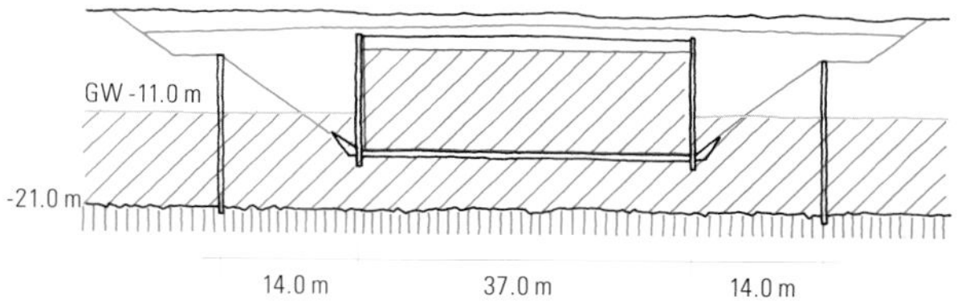

Figure 345.2
Form of aquifer reservoir with prepared ground
Capacity 15,000 m³ equivalent to 9,600 m³ water volume

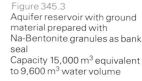

Figure 345.3
Aquifer reservoir with ground material prepared with Na-Bentonite granules as bank seal
Capacity 15,000 m³ equivalent to 9,600 m³ water volume

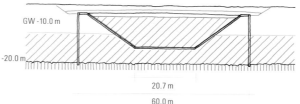

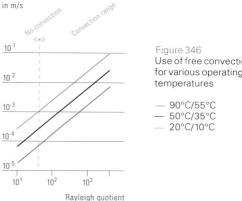

Figure 346
Use of free convection for various operating temperatures

— 90°C/55°C
— 50°C/35°C
— 20°C/10°C

The extraction performance of an aquifer reservoir is defined by the permeability of the ground and the filter surface (surface of storage and extraction system). Stable, horizontal temperature distribution can be ensured by selecting a filter speed low enough to balance the buoyancy forces of the pressure drop caused by the flow. For a temperature spread of 35 K, the density difference of the water results in a buoyancy force of approx. 10−2 mWs/m. The maximum allowable extraction or storage performance Q for this spread is defined by:

$$Q = 10^{-2} \cdot k_F \cdot F$$

Q = transported water volume in m³/s
F = filter surface in m²
k_F = permeability coefficient in m/s

The filter surface for utility heat-storage applications must be minimal to reduce volume utility losses through the heat transfer layer between warm and cold storage water.

An even countercurrent in the storage and efficient utilization of the storage volume can be created by designing the storage and extraction system, for financial reasons, with pipes which are not spread across a large area but are, instead, arranged in a parallel or star-shaped fashion (Figure 347)

As mentioned, heat loss through the surface cover should be minimal and certain covers are recommended. As an example, Figure 348 shows the temperature curve in a covering layer (U-value = 0.2 W/m²K). The same applies to the floor and to the walls separating the aquifer from its surroundings.

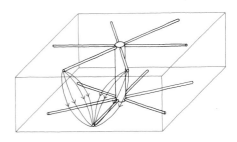

Figure 347
Flow in aquifer reservoir close to surface with horizontal fountain system

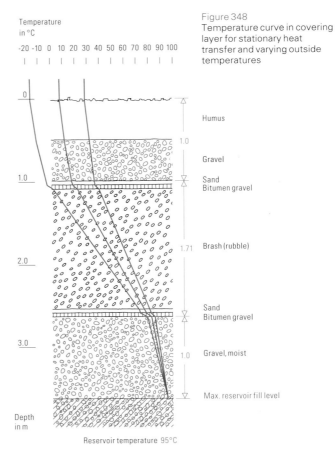

Temperature in °C

-20 -10 0 10 20 30 40 50 60 70 80 90 100

Depth in m

Reservoir temperature 95°C

Humus
Gravel
Sand
Bitumen gravel
Brash (rubble)
Sand
Bitumen gravel
Gravel, moist
Max. reservoir fill level

Figure 348
Temperature curve in covering layer for stationary heat transfer and varying outside temperatures

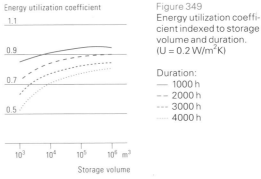

Energy utilization coefficient

Storage volume

Figure 349
Energy utilization coefficient indexed to storage volume and duration.
(U = 0.2 W/m²K)

Duration:
— 1000 h
-- 2000 h
--- 3000 h
······ 4000 h

The energy utilization coefficient of an aquifer reservoir is defined as the ratio of stored heat energy to utilized energy. It depends on several factors:

– the time during which the stored heat remains in the reservoir,

– the surface area A in relation to the volume,

– the geological conditions of the site (groundwater level, groundwater speed, conductivity and vapour permeability of the ground material, thickness of water-resistant layers),

– the water permeability of the separating walls and the vapour permeability of the bitumen gravel layers.

Figure 349 shows the energy utilization coefficient indexed to storage volume and duration. The layout of an aquifer and some details are shown in Figure 350. Aside from the previously described aquifer reservoirs, set in natural or specifically prepared natural ground, a reinforced concrete container could be inserted into the ground as storage or reservoir (Figure 351)

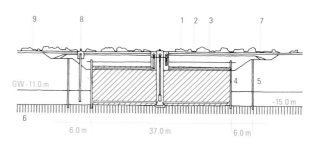

Figure 350
Cross-section of natural reservoir

1   Insulating layer
    2 cm sand, 4 cm bitumen gravel, 2 cm sand
2   Vapour screen
    2 cm sand, 4 cm bitumen gravel, 2 cm sand
3   Natural soil
4   Drainage wall
5   End wall
6   Water-bearing bottom
7   Binding material
8   Safety well
9   Humus

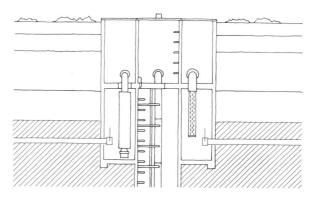

Figure 350.1
Detail
upper extraction system
('Warm water system')

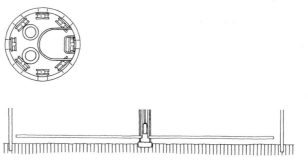

Figure 350.2
Detail
lower extraction system
('Cold water system')
and section of central shaft

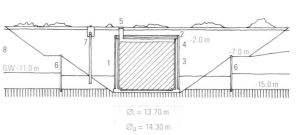

Figure 351
Reinforced concrete container (cylinder) as aquifer reservoir
V = 1750 m³, t_{max} = 95°C

1   Prestressed concrete
2   Reinforced concrete lid (beams + slabs)
3   Insulation (Foamglass d = 10 cm)
4   Inner coating
5   Access shaft
6   End wall
7   Safety well
8   Natural soil

245

Figure 352
Integration of an aquifer
reservoir into the heat-recovery
installation of a large heat-pump
system

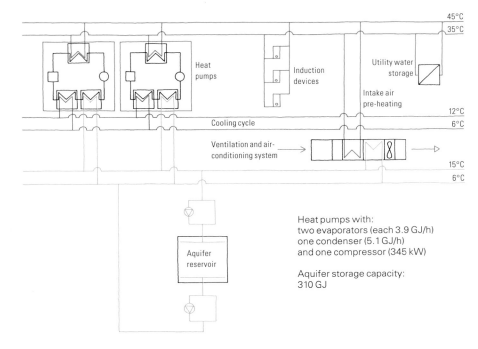

45°C
35°C

Heat
pumps

Induction
devices

Utility water
storage

Intake air
pre-heating

12°C

Cooling cycle

6°C

Ventilation and air-
conditioning system

15°C

6°C

Aquifer
reservoir

Heat pumps with:
two evaporators (each 3.9 GJ/h)
one condenser (5.1 GJ/h)
and one compressor (345 kW)

Aquifer storage capacity:
310 GJ

Figure 353
Loading and discharge amounts
of usable heat output for heat-
pump storage system during
December and February. The
usable heat performance of the
heat-pump in this example is
15.6 GJ/h for a full load.

— Loading
— Discharge

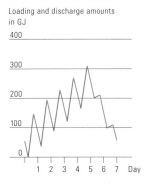

Loading and discharge amounts
in GJ

400

300

200

100

0

1 2 3 4 5 6 7 Day

A cost-benefit analysis of aquifer reservoirs and other storage options shows that upright, non-pressurized container reservoirs below 3000 m^3 are less expensive than aquifers or sub-surface concrete reservoirs. Above 3000 m^3 the natural aquifer reservoir and above 30.000 m^3 (water equivalence) the cast aquifer reservoir are more efficient than an above-ground container storage. Sub-surface concrete container reservoirs are four times as expensive as cast above-ground aquifer reservoirs, regardless of their storage volume. Each situation should be considered on its own merit, to determine the best economic solution.

Finally, Figure 352 shows the integration of an aquifer reservoir into the heat-recovery installation of a large heat-pump system and Figure 353 the schematic of the loading and discharge cycles for usable heat performance over the course of seven days.

14.4
Thermal Tunnel and Thermal Labyrinth

To cool fresh air in summer before it enters a building and to humidify it or to heat it in winter, it seems sensible to draw fresh air through pipes in the ground or through a concrete thermal labyrinth in the building itself – a solution very similar to that suggested and realized by the engineer P. Grove many years ago in his work on the Reichstag building in Berlin.

Thermal Tunnel (Earth Pipeline)

For smaller air volumes, e.g. for induction units in residential buildings, pipes with smaller dimensions (e.g. clay, concrete or plastic pipes) can be installed in the ground. The pipes should be at some distance from the building, because the impact of heat transmission from the building to the pipes would be too great when cooling is required. However, when heating energy is the primary goal, the heat lost through basement walls can naturally be captured in well-ventilated pipelines. In the planning of such installations, the pipe grid or the individual pipes must be deep enough in the ground to create either a noticeable heating or cooling effect. The graphs in Figures 354 to 357 can serve as a rough guide for dimen-

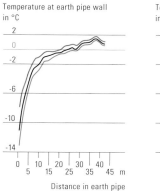

Temperature at earth pipe wall in °C

Distance in earth pipe

Figure 354
Temperature in the direction of the earth pipe wall, winter

— Values during max. outside temperature
— Daily average values
— Values during min. outside temperature

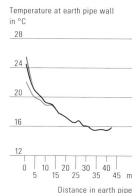

Temperature at earth pipe wall in °C

Distance in earth pipe

Figure 355
Temperature in the direction of the earth pipe wall, summer

Operation of earth pipe:
9 a.m. to 9 p.m.
— Values during max. outside temperature
— Daily average values
— Values during min. outside temperature

sioning. They show, on the one hand, the familiar funnel phenomenon of ground temperatures from top to bottom (surface to depth) and, on the other, the temperature curves in the direction of the earth pipe wall in winter and summer. Figure 356 shows the cone of depression in the ground surrounding an air-conducting earth pipe at 3 m depth, using the material values of a moist clay ground as an index. As has been established for bore holes, sub-surface earth pipes should have distances of at least 8–10 m, to minimize their influence on each other. Maximum heat gain for sub-surface pipes (earth heat exchangers) is achieved at a depth of 4–6 m, measuring a heat gain of 6–6.5 kWh/a per m³ of conducted air volume. In summer, the optimal depth for the earth heat exchanger pipe is approx. 4–6 m, and the cold energy gain approx. 7 kWh/a (assumed pipe length approx. 40 m).

The optimal pipe length may be defined by the necessity of having, in winter, an intake air temperature of 0°C at the end of the pipe, even when outside temperatures are at an extreme low for short periods of time, to prevent ice formation or freezing of the heat exchangers. Assuming an installation depth of 3 m, a pipe diameter of 127 mm and an air volume stream of 140 m³/h (ground as previously established), a steady state condition results only after the 100 m mark (Figures 358.1–358.2)

Figure 356
Cone of depression in ground surrounding earth pipe (Isothermal lines)

Earth surface: 0 °C
Pipe surface: 4.5 °C

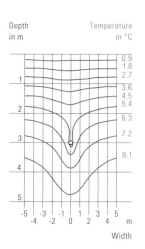

Depth in m   Temperature in °C

Width

Figure 357
Ground temperature

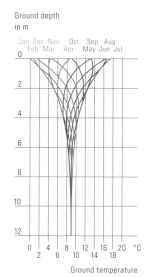

Ground depth in m

Ground temperature

Figure 358.1
Air temperatures in direction of earth pipe (winter) at 3 m depth (Ø 127 mm, V̇ = 140 m³/h) for various outside temperatures

— 0°C
--- -20°C

Air temperature in °C

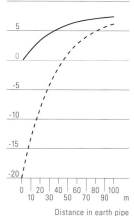

Distance in earth pipe

Figure 358.2
Air temperature in direction of earth pipe (summer) at 3 m depth (Ø 127 mm, V̇ = 140 m³/h) for various outside temperatures

— 35°C
--- 17.6°C

Air temperature in °C

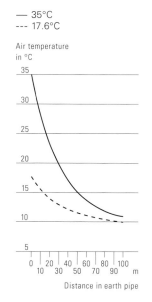

Distance in earth pipe

Thermal Labyrinth

In conclusion, here is an excerpt from a research study carried out by the Rud. Otto Meyer company (project leader: K. D. Laabs). A thermal labyrinth, consisting of 140-m-long concrete tunnels, was installed beneath the ground floor of the municipal theatre in Heilbronn (architects: Biste and Gerling, Heidelberg). Fresh air is drawn into these tunnels and conducted through the system below the building, where it is heated in winter or cooled in summer. Figure 359 shows the new theatre building, Figure 360 the thermal labyrinth in the basement during construction (with sketched-in air flow), and Figure 361 a cross-section with the schematic of the outside air flow, which reaches the air-conditioning and heating system either directly or by way of the labyrinth.

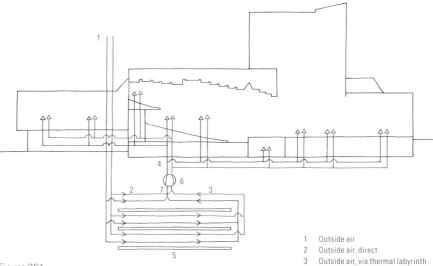

Figure 361
Diagram of outside air flow, reaching the air-conditioning system either directly or by way of the labyrinth.

1 Outside air
2 Outside air, direct
3 Outside air, via thermal labyrinth
4 Fresh air to rooms
5 Underground heat exchanger
   Concrete thermal canal
6 Fan
7 Dampers direct-thermal air

Figure 359
Municipal theatre in Heilbronn
(Architects: Biste and Gerling, Heidelberg)

Figure 360
Thermal labyrinth in new municipal theatre in Heilbronn, construction (with sketched-in air flow)

As the previous figures illustrate, fresh air is drawn directly into the building through a ground-level tunnel and conducted through the labyrinth. The ground surface of the concrete tunnel serves as heat exchanger, which is certainly not an optimal solution with regard to utilizing geothermal energy. In any case, this system yields definite heating and cooling effects (Figure 362.1 and 362.2 respectively). In winter, the outside air heats up in the thermal tunnel by approx. 2 K–4 K, and, in summer, it is cooled by approx. 1 K–8 K.

Figure 363.1 shows the energy balance indexed to a three-year period, showing also the required energies (heat and cold energy) and the savings potentials created by the thermal tunnel itself. It is evident that the greatest advantage of the thermal tunnel lies in saving refrigerating energy. However, due to its short utilization period, it is only partially efficient in saving heating energy. The specific maximum tunnel transmission rates are shown in Figure 363.2 in relation to the volume flow, which naturally fluctuates greatly in a theatre building, depending upon use and time frame. The specific maximum tunnel transmission rate is a result of the daily tunnel transmission rate and the effective transmission surface. When calculating the amortization for this research study, it was found that the additional investment necessary to construct the thermal labyrinth would pay back over a period of approx. 8–10 years, a finding that argues for further investigation and possibly implementation of related solutions.

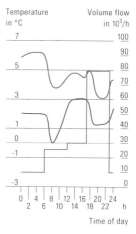

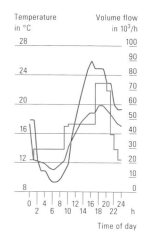

Figure 362.1
Recorded temperatures and analysis,
one day in Winter 1984

— Start of duct
— End of duct
— Volume flow

Figure 362.2
Recorded temperatures and analysis
Temperature increase and drop,
one day in May 1983

— Air shaft/entrance
— Air shaft/exit
— Volume flow

Figure 363.1
Energy balance
(Municipal theatre Heilbronn)
Averages over three years

Required energies
■ Cold energy
■ Heat energy

■ Savings potential through
  thermal labyrinth

Figure 363.2
Specific maximum tunnel transmission rates
(from representative values)

— Heat
— Cold (August, July)

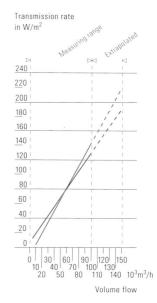

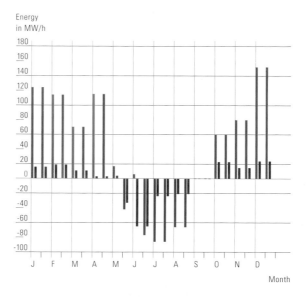

Active Measures
of Renewable Energy Usage

15

Various technical systems cause a noticeable reduction of contaminant emissions. If we are sincere in actively protecting the environment, we must use these technologies in the future even if they do not yet offer the payback rates required. An overview of the investment, operation and annual total costs of different system solutions shows the kind of payback we can expect.

16

Utilizing organic materials is not a primary topic for building design and technology. It is, however, of universal interest whenever energies from renewable resources are to be utilized.

15.
Other Active Thermal Systems

Active technical measures should combine maximum efficiency, e.g. integrated systems with the least possible primary-energy consumption, and minimum (environmental) contamination. This requirement applies equally to the production of electricity, heating energy and cooling energy. Minimizing heat requirements must also factor in building codes.

Using the new heating energy consumption code as a guide (Figure 364), a building should have a maximum heat requirement of approx. 50–100 kWh/m^2, corresponding to a requirement of approx. 30–50 W/m^2 heat loss or 8–15 W/m^3 per enclosed space. When this value is applied to a building with perimeter heating only, the resulting heat transfer coefficient for all wall and glass surfaces combined is approx. 1.8–1.9 W/m^{2}K (without taking 2- or 3-side glazing, roof areas and floor surfaces into consideration). For buildings with mechanical air-conditioning and heating systems in winter, the above-mentioned heat transfer coefficient is cut nearly in half to approx. 0.9 W/m^{2}K for wall and window surfaces. However, this last measurement includes heat gain in a building, e.g. from occupants, lighting, office machines, etc. In the future, average heat transfer coefficients for building surfaces (walls and windows) will be approx. 0.8–1.0 W/m^{2}K.

The heating requirements should be minimized largely through an integrated solution, avoiding over-insulation for operation in summer and the transitional season and offering, instead, variable heat insulation, which retains heat in the building when it is needed and allows heat to exit the building when cooling is required. Consequently, the heat transfer coefficient must be variable as well, i.e. the façade design must allow for a variable heat-transfer coefficient. Using high-insulation window units may produce the opposite effect. At the same time, minimizing window surfaces on a building does not satisfy the demand for maximum daylight quotients. A total energy balance sheet must be drawn up for the design of façades, to avoid incorrect and inappropriate solutions.

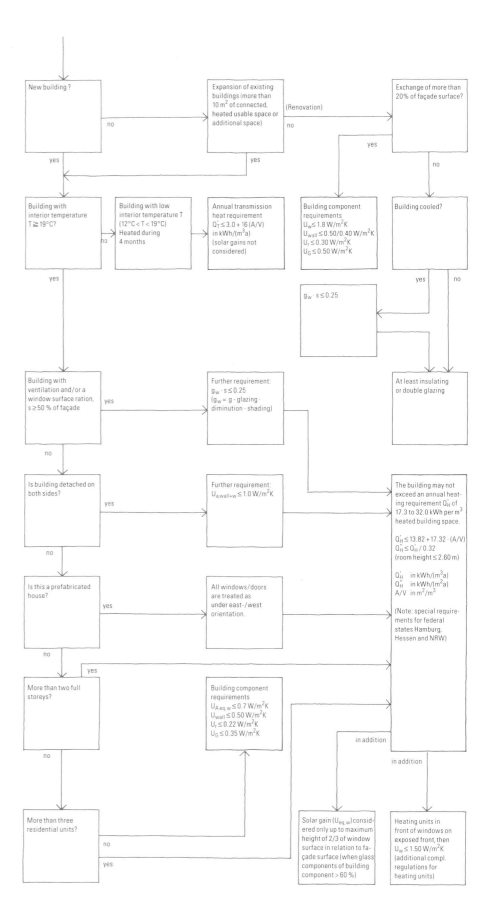

Figure 364
Flow chart for definition of requirements stated in new heating energy consumption code, 1.1.1995

U$_r$ U-value roof
U$_w$ U-value window
U$_{wall}$ U-value wall
U$_A$ Average U-value
U$_G$ U-value of wall touching ground

15.1
Condensing and Catalyzer Technology

Any use of fossil energy sources under the motto "less is more" must also ensure minimal environmental contamination while providing cost-efficient solutions. Figures 365.1 and 365.2 show the development of emission of nitric oxide (NO_X) for gas and oil combustion in the years preceding 1976 until ca. 1990. In Germany the steady rise in nitric oxide emissions was stopped by the air purity act and considerably reduced by the use of burners and catalyzer technology. The latter is explained in Figure 366. Utilizing the heat energy in flue gas is important for heating buildings (burner technology). The financial expenditure for boiler installations is higher than for conventional systems. However, it must be understood as an investment in the future and in promoting environmental protection. Greater efficiency in utilizing primary energy (oil/gas) and, in connection with it, a considerably higher efficiency quotient for the installation itself are a matter of course.

Figure 365.1
Development of emission of nitric oxide (NO_X) for gas combustion

Nitric oxide, added as NO_2 for 3% O_2 in mg/m³

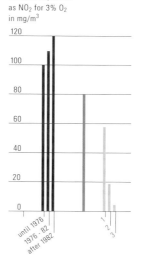

Figure 365.2
Development of emission of nitric oxide (NO_X) for oil combustion

Nitric oxide, added as NO_2 for 3% O_2 in mg/m³

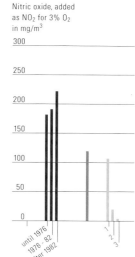

■ Existing installations
■ Air pollution regulation 92
■ Low-NO_X-installations:
1 Low-NO_X-burner
2 Conventional burner with catalyzer
3 Conventional burner with catalyzer and flue gas heat pump

Figure 366
Integration of catalyzer into flue gas flow

Catalyzer

1 SO_2 neutralization
2 Cat-element
3 NH_3 injection
4 Maintained high temperature
5 Control and monitor
6 Insulating material

*) dependant on system and layout

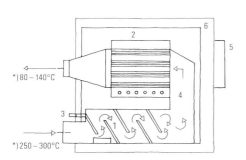

Condensing boiler

1 Boiler
2 Gas/oil burner
3 Flue gas
4 Heat recovery
5 Chimney
6 Bypass

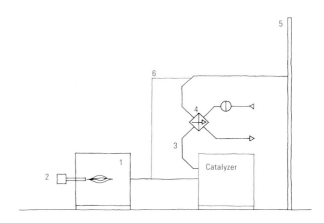

15.2
Emissions from Heat-Generating Stations

The environmental friendliness of heat-generating plants must be evaluated according to a range of criteria, and air purity is definitely at the top of the list. Primary-energy consumption, as well as CO_2 emissions resulting from production of the required energy, play important roles. To calculate the contaminant emissions of a heat-generating station, the energy consumption of the station is multiplied by an emission factor (Table 10).

Not all emissions are equally dangerous. An additional evaluation criterion is, therefore, necessary, which is given by the air purity act: The higher the polluting factor of a contaminant, the lower the emission limit for sulphur oxide (SO_2), nitrogen oxide (NO_X), carbon monoxide (CO) and solid waste.

Several technologies are comparable for their environmental qualities. The main systems are:

- condensing boilers with natural gas (annual utility efficiency 90 %, with Low-NO_X-burners),
- heating boilers with oil (annual utility efficiency 85 %, with Low-NO_X-burners),
- heating boilers for steam with oil (annual utility efficiency 85 %),
- gas motor CHP (annual utility efficiency 90 %, 3-way catalyzer, supplementary burner or heat pump for return heat from motor),
- gas turbine (annual utility efficiency 85 %, secondary nitrogen removal with ammonia or carbamide [urea]).

The evaluation of emissions shown in Figure 367 is based on the production of one Gigawatt hour (GWh) of heat energy. It takes into consideration that a gas motor has a higher specific emission rate than, for instance, the Low-NO_X-gas boiler, but also that it produces electricity in addition to thermal energy and has, therefore, a better total energy balance (electrical energy/thermal energy) than the boiler system.

Table 10 Emission factors for different heat generating systems	System	Fuel	NO_x (g/GJ))	CO (g/GJ)	HC^2 (g/GJ)	CO_2 (kg/GJ)	SO_2 (g/GJ)	Solids[4] (g/GJ)
	Gas motor[1]	Natural gas	10	30	8[5]	60	0[6]	0[6]
	Boiler	Natural gas	45	30	2[5]	60	0	0
	Boiler	Oil	55	50	15[3]	74	94	4
	Boiler Low-NO_x[7]	Natural gas	20	30	2[5]	60	0	0
	Boiler Low-NO_x[7]	Oil	30	50	15[3]	74	94	4
	Gas turbine[8]	Natural gas	30	50	5[5]	60	0	0

[1] with three-way catalyzer, steady state operation after 3000 to 4000 hours of operation

[2] Hydrocarbons without methane

[3] also higher hydrocarbons with higher risk potential

[4] Solids, risk varies depending on fuel

[5] only hydrocarbons to C_4H_x

[6] burnt lubricating oil residue

[7] no long-term experience

[8] with SCR catalyzer

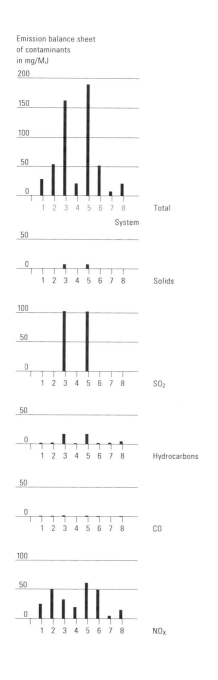

Emission balance sheet
of contaminants
in mg/MJ

Total / System

Solids

SO_2

Hydrocarbons

CO

NO_x

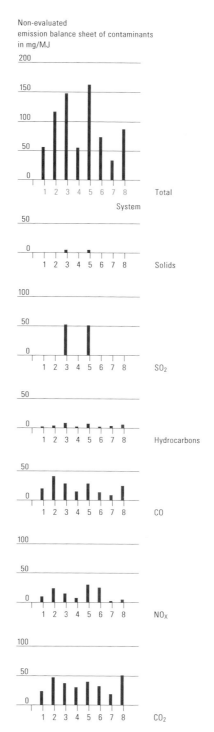

Non-evaluated
emission balance sheet of contaminants
in mg/MJ

Total / System

Solids

SO_2

Hydrocarbons

CO

NO_x

CO_2

The emission balance sheet shown in Figure 367 includes only 'conventional contaminants', i.e. not CO_2. A non-evaluated reading (Figure 368) includes the emission of CO_2. Here, too, gas-motor-driven systems combined with electric heat pumps are the least polluting installations. Although gas-motor-driven systems cost more to install than boiler systems, the higher investment costs may well be offset by lower energy consumption and lower emission rates and thus tip the scale in their favour.

In any case, heating and cooling, as well as electricity, should all be provided by system combinations which show good results for investment costs, energy consumption and contaminant emission.

Figure 367
Emission balance sheet
of various contaminants
(Evaluation based on:
primary energy and energy
gained)

Figure 368
Non-evaluated emission
balance sheet of various
contaminants (primary energy without consideration
of total efficiency quotient;
integration of catalyzer into
flue gas flow)

Systems:

1 Gas turbine, combined with electric heat-pump
2 Gas turbine
3 Boiler, Low-NO_x, oil
4 Boiler, Low-NO_x, natural gas
5 Boiler, oil
6 Boiler, natural gas
7 Gas motor, combined with electric heat pump
8 Gas motor

Figure 369 shows different servicing strategies, where the production of cooling energy is partially effected by sorptive air dehumidification and adiabatic cooling. Figure 370 plots the emission of SO_2, NO_X and CO_2 by conventional energy supply stations (district heat supply with electric and absorption chillers), compared to Option 1. The emissions in Option 1 (district heat supply with sorptive dehumidification and adiabatic cooling) are clearly lower.

Figure 369
Comparison of different
servicing strategies

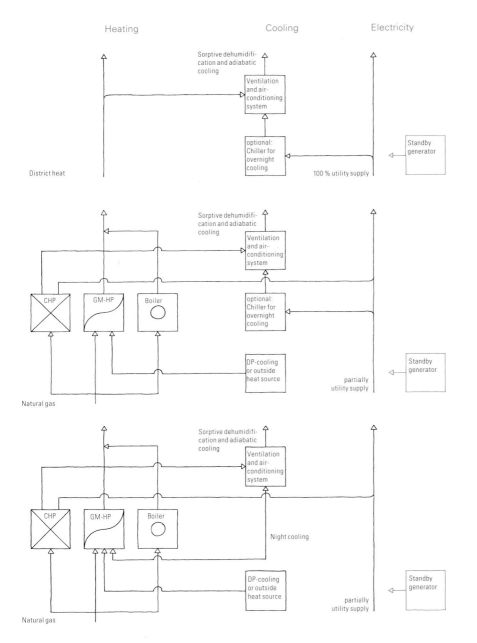

Heating   Cooling   Electricity

Option 1
District heat supply to building;
sorptive dehumidification
and adiabatic cooling of fresh air
(without chiller and cooling
tower)
Optional:
Small chiller for air cooling
for extreme outside
temperatures

100 % district electricity supply
Standby generator

Option 2
Waste heat recovery of CHP (=
standby sys.) and gas-motor-
driven heat pump for
– heating in winter
– dehumidification in
  summer

Gas boiler for peak requirements; DP waste heat used as
heat source for gas-motor-
driven heat pump, decentral
user power
Optional:
Small chiller for air cooling following extreme outside temperatures

No large cooling towers

Option 3
like option 2, but without small
chillers. Cooling when required
provided by gas-motor-driven
heat pump

No cooling towers

Figure 370
Emission of contaminants of
different servicing strategies
shown on the example of one
building

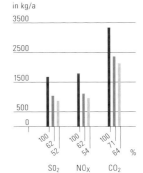

Emissions
in kg/a

■ District heat supply and
electric chiller
■ District heat supply and
absorption chillers
□ District heat supply with
sorptive dehumidification
and adiabatic cooling
(as in Option 1)

15.3
Heat Pumps – Absorber Surfaces

When façades are to be used for energy gain, absorber surfaces in combination with heat pumps are a good alternative. Cold water from the evaporator flows across the absorber surfaces on the façade, to utilize environmental energies and then be raised to a high temperature in a heat pump. Figure 371 compares the heat requirement and the heat gain from the environment through absorber surfaces and heat pump. It is assumed that from June to September a minimal heat requirement can be supplied in this manner without any difficulties. Absorber surfaces – in contrast to TIM façades – can reclaim energy on all sides of the building, since they harness environmental energy not only from solar radiation but also from rain and wind. Only in December and January is the efficiency coefficient of absorber surfaces zero, unless the absorber surfaces operate with brine solutions to continue reclaiming energy even when temperatures fall below 0°C. Figure 372 shows the working principle of an absorber surface connected to a heat pump.

15.4
Static Cooling, Free Cooling, Ice-Storage Installations

To cool outside air without dehumidification and absorb cooling loads in a room through cooling ceilings, energy is required, produced either through chillers with replacement refrigerants (H-CFC or, better, ammonia) or with heat energy (absorption cooling machines) or with free cooling or cooling energy from the ground.

Figure 373 lists the main groups of static cooling, i.e. cooling systems which operate by gravity and absorb heat energy in a room via convection and radiation. The chief cooling medium in these systems is water. The chilled water, as shown in Figure 374, is either created in a refrigerating machine or cooled in a cooling tower, capable of processing water at 14°C (approx.), with evaporation (free cooling).

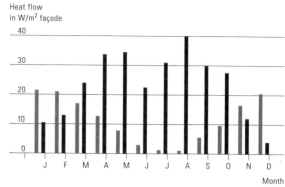

Figure 371
Heat gain via typical surface absorber (South façade U-value 4.5 W/m² K for 0.5 m² collector surface per 1 m² façade)

■ Heat requirement
■ Heat gain through absorber

Figure 372
Absorber surface for connection to heat pump
U-value $\cong$ 0.3 W/m²K

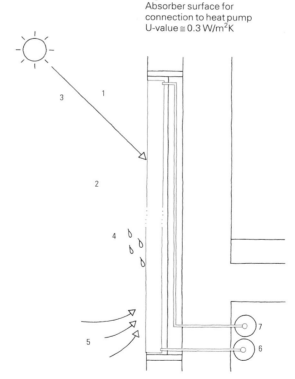

1 Insulation
2 Absorber
3 Radiation
4 Rain
5 Wind
6 Flow
7 Return

Figure 373
Main categories
of static cooling

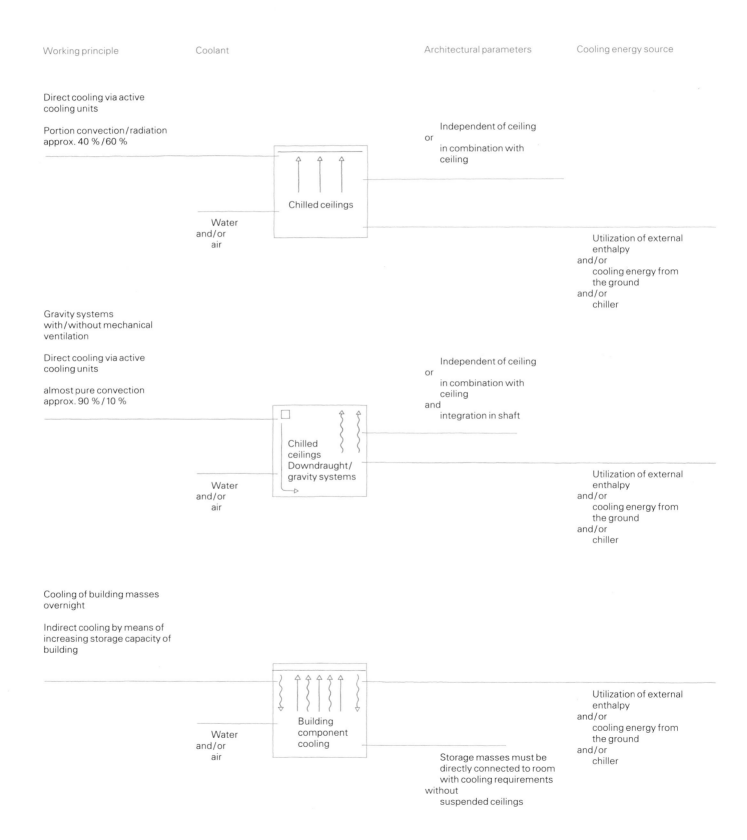

Working principle

Coolant

Architectural parameters

Cooling energy source

Direct cooling via active
cooling units

Portion convection/radiation
approx. 40 % / 60 %

Chilled ceilings

Water
and/or
air

Independent of ceiling
or
in combination with
ceiling

Utilization of external
enthalpy
and/or
cooling energy from
the ground
and/or
chiller

Gravity systems
with/without mechanical
ventilation

Direct cooling via active
cooling units

almost pure convection
approx. 90 % / 10 %

Chilled
ceilings
Downdraught/
gravity systems

Water
and/or
air

Independent of ceiling
or
in combination with
ceiling
and
integration in shaft

Utilization of external
enthalpy
and/or
cooling energy from
the ground
and/or
chiller

Cooling of building masses
overnight

Indirect cooling by means of
increasing storage capacity of
building

Building
component
cooling

Water
and/or
air

Storage masses must be
directly connected to room
with cooling requirements
without
suspended ceilings

Utilization of external
enthalpy
and/or
cooling energy from
the ground
and/or
chiller

To keep cooling plants relatively small and day-time power rates low, it is often advisable to use an ice-storage installation which is 'loaded' overnight and transfers stored cold energy to the integrated system during the day. This process helps reduce load peaks during the day, which, in turn, eases the burden of electricity suppliers and generally reduces user tarifs. With the integrated system shown in Figure 374, the standard total cooling energy requirement can be reduced by approx. 50 % (electricity supplied to chillers) while also reducing initial investment costs.

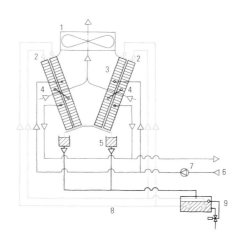

to Figure 374
Free cooling (hybrid cooling)
Air is drawn by the fans through the slanted chiller louvres, which are sprinkled from above with water. The water evaporates in the air flow, the evaporation heat is withdrawn from the chiller, whose medium – usually a water/glycol blend – is thus cooled.

Due to an optimal configuration of angle as well as air and water volumes, leakage as well as drainage of sprinkling water can be avoided.

1 Fans
2 Sprinkling water
3 Condenser units
4 Air
5 Water collection
6 Heat source
7 Primary cooling cycle
8 Secondary cooling cycle (Sprinkling water)
9 Water container with filter and automatic refill

Figure 374
Chilled ceiling with mechanical as well as free cooling (additional ice-storage installation is possible)

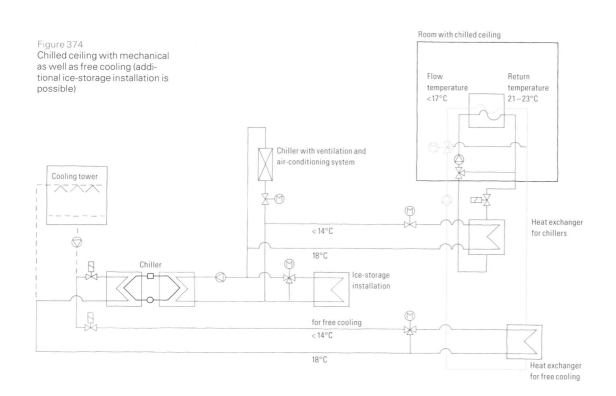

15.5
Desorption Process

The desorption process or air cooling via adsorptive dehumidification and adiabatic cooling is a system type for the creation of cooling energy with the help of heat energy. Figures 375.1 and 375.2 show the build up of such a system, indicating temperatures and humidities for a specific test case and relevant graphs in the chart.

Air cooling by means of adsorptive dehumidification and adiabatic cooling does not require a cooling plant in the usual sense, when dehumidification is not required. Cooling, e.g. with a gas-motor-driven heat pump, becomes necessary when the outside air is to be cooled and dehumidified. This cooling system requires neither H-CFC nor ammoniac or brine-cycles. Instead, it functions by spraying cold water on the supply and return air, thus creating adiabatic changes which cool and humidify at the same time. The outside air is initially dehumidified because the packing of the heated drying rotor (hygroscopic silica gel) contains very little moisture and is, therefore, able to absorb water vapour from the outside airflow.

Next, the outside air is cooled in a heat recovery unit. Further adiabatic cooling occurs by spraying cold water in the outside airflow, which then evaporates and lowers the supply air temperature while increasing the moisture content. Similar processes can be implemented, e.g. when excess heat from a manufacturing process is to be utilized or when thermal energy is created in collector installations, since it can be assumed that the greatest cooling energy is needed when high outside temperatures coincide with high thermal radiation.

Figure 375.2
Test curve of air for
sorptive dehumidification and
adiabatic cooling
(h-x diagram, corresponds to
psychrometric chart.)

Temperature
in °C

Water content x in g/kg dry air

Fresh air
1   Outside air condition
2   Air condition after
    dehumidification
3   Air condition after heat
    exchange
4   Air condition after
    adiabatic cooling

Return Air
5   Room air condition
6   after adiabatic cooling
7   after heat exchange
8   after additional heat gain
9   after sorption generator

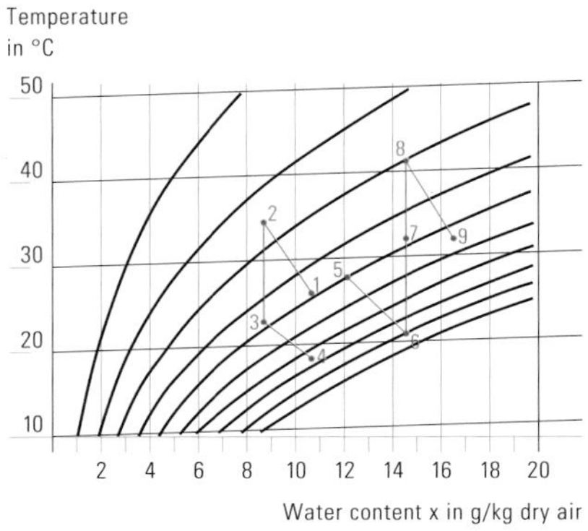

Figure 375.1
Air cooling by means of
adsorptive dehumidification
and adiabatic cooling with
different heat sources

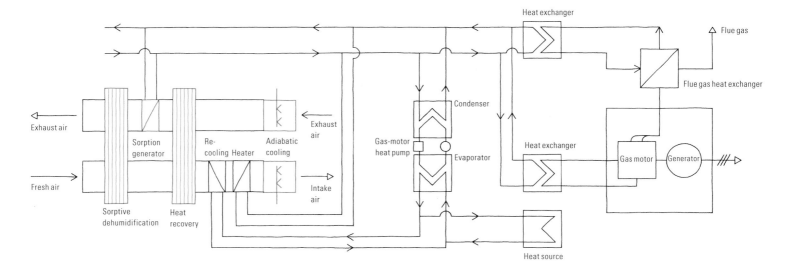

15.6
CHP – Combined Heat and Power Systems
(Total Energy Installation)

Combined heat and power systems (CHPs) are frequently gas-motor-driven installations, which produce thermal energy while creating electricity and supply either heat consumers in winter through a 'high-temperature line' or energy for refrigerating plants (absorption chillers) in summer. Figure 376 shows a simplified hydraulic network schematic of such an installation complete with a combined heat and power plant, absorption chillers, cooling towers, heat exchangers, pumps and consumer systems. The gas motor drives a generator for the production of electricity while also delivering heat via the flue gas heat exchanger and motor cooling-water heat exchanger for the supply of high- and low-temperature consumers. High-temperature consumers are consumers requiring a temperature of more than 100°C (e.g. for cooking); low-temperature consumers are, for instance, the absorption chillers shown in the schematic. The transformation rate of a primary energy (e.g. gas or oil) in these combined systems is approx. 32 % for electricity and 54 % as 'waste' heat for heating and cooling plants. Only 14 % of the primary energy is lost in the system itself.

In a combination of CHP systems and absorber installations, of the 100 % primary energy, 32 % is used directly to produce electricity and a further 12.6 % indirectly through reduction in electricity consumption. This yield of 44 % cannot be achieved with conventional systems. This system solution is

more energy-efficient for buildings with high electricity and cooling requirements than any other conventional and traditional system. It should be noted that this system, besides its excellent performance through the cooling process of the absorber, does not use any CFC's and is therefore environmentally friendly. The decisive advantage of motors with hot-water cooling lies in the fact that the cooling water of the motor and waste-gas heat can be used year-round because of the high temperatures. This improves the cost effectiveness of a system with hot-water cooling in summer and can be applied in many ways. CHP systems require higher investment costs than conventional solutions; amortization rates should be calculated before any choices are made. When the system is correctly sized and adapted to the specific electricity needs of a particular building, the additional investment costs are always more than justified and amortization periods may be as little as 2 – 5 years.

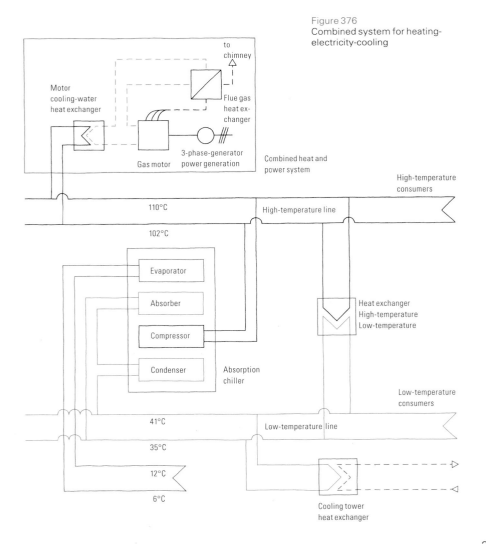

Figure 376
Combined system for heating-electricity-cooling

15.7
Wood Chip Combustion

In contrast to wood combustion in an open chimney or old wood-burning stoves, wood today is burned in chips for environmental reasons, attaining the level of automation required for large systems. Low polluting levels depend largely on complete combustion through very high temperatures and prolonged retention of the gases in the combustion zone. This requires considerable blending of gases and combustion air. Modern wood-chip-combustion systems, therefore, separate gasification combustion and heat utilization, as shown in Figure 377

The wood chips are transported to the pyrolysis chamber on a spiral conveyor and then slowly transported farther on a rotating grate. In the reduction chamber, the nitric oxides are reduced through preheating. The (combustion) gases created by this reduction enter a combustion chamber, where they are intensively mixed with fresh air to create complete combustion. The hot combustion gases then flow through a heat exchanger and an economiser and transfer thermal energy to the warm-water heat cycle.

When the wood is almost dry, very little carbon monoxide and carbon hydrogen are emitted. The temperature increase should be quite rapid; otherwise more contaminants are created. The problem in wood combustion is the burning not of new wood but rather of old pieces of wood which have often been treated or are completely impregnated. In these cases, the flue gas must be cleansed through catalyzers.

Great efforts are being made (especially at the ETH in Zurich) to develop clean-burning wood-chip-combustion plants, wood being an indigenous, plentiful and renewable resource in Central Europe.

Figure 377
Diagram of wood chip combustion installation

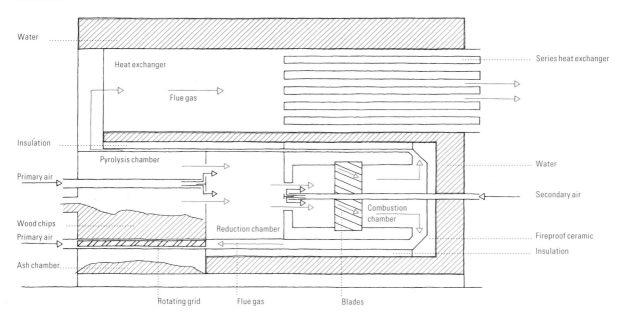

15.8
Fuel Cells

Fuel cells are truly a futuristic form of energy production. The high-temperature fuel cell is of particular interest for building technology. It transforms natural gas with an efficiency quotient greater than 50 % into electricity, producing waste gases with very high temperatures which can be used for heating purposes. The systems currently operating in pilot stations should be viewed as alternatives to combined heating and power stations. Unlike conventional motor-driven systems, this system does not set free any nitrogen oxide, operation is nearly noiseless and total efficiency quotients are in the range of other systems with power-heat-coupling.

The operating principle of fuel cell technology is flameless combustion of natural gas or hydrogen in a porous (hydro-) ceramic vessel. A cell consists of a ceramic electrolyte (0.2 mm ion-conducting zirconium oxide) and porous electrodes (0.03 mm) consisting of electroconductive metallic ceramics joined both ways (Figure 378.1). In the cathode, the oxygen of the supply air is ionized at temperatures of approx. 800°C, i.e. the oxygen absorbs electrons. Next, the oxygen diffuses, due to the resulting concentration quotient, through the electrolyte to the anode. There, the oxygen reacts on the blend of natural gas (CH_4), hydrogen (H_2) and carbon monoxide (CO), forming CO_2 and water at release of heat. The redundant electrons of the oxygen ion are also set free and return to the cathode via an external electric circuit. The direct-current voltage created between the two electrodes is less than 1 V, so that many cells must be connected in series to achieve sufficient output voltages. To do this, the fuel cells are stacked. Optimizing the current in a module makes it possible to utilize the released thermal energy for the preheating of supply air, for the processing of natural gas (reforming natural gas and water into CH_4, H_2 and CO), for the purposes of heating and for the post-combustion of the remaining natural gas (Figure 378.2), a process realized in the Hexis design (Sulzer Innotec, Winterthur). The schematic of such an installation is shown in Figure 378.3. The final cost of this kind of system, as regards mass production and introduction to the market, remains to be seen. The potential for rational energy utilization and environmental protection is, however, already established.

Figure 378.1
Principle of fuel cells

Oxygen ions from the air travel from the cathode via the electrolyte to the anode and react to the treated natural gas. This creates electricity and heat.

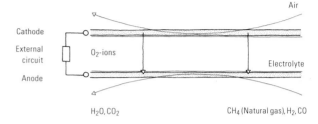

Figure 378.2
Section of cell stack

Only when several cells are stacked are units created which meet the required performance in the kW range.

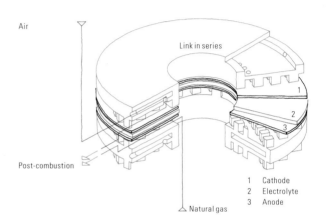

1   Cathode
2   Electrolyte
3   Anode

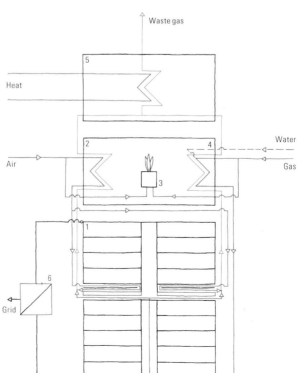

Figure 378.3
Diagram of fuel cell installation

1   Fuel cell stack
2   Air preheating chamber
3   Startup and auxiliary burner
4   Natural gas treatment
5   Flue gas heat exchanger
6   Controls, d.c./a.c. inverter

15.9
Cost

The economic viability of different technologies is a deciding factor in their application. The individual items determining viability are: investment costs (Figure 379.1), operating costs (primary energy + maintenance) (Figure 379.2) and annual total costs (operating costs + proportional cost of capital) (Figure 379.3). The values in these graphs are approximations, since local and market-driven factors often have a great effect on the actual cost. The same applies to the amortization rates for various systems shown in Figure 379.4. Generally, the following will apply to all considerations of cost:

depreciation period for technical installations	15 a
for builder's work (bore holes, etc.) (marked with *)	30 a
average interest	7 %/a
average annual energy cost increase	5 %/a
time base for all estimates	Dec. 94

Figure 379.4
Amortization rates for different technologies

1	District heat connection
2	Basic load CHP (+ boiler installation)
3	Heat-pump (el.) with bore hole
4	Heat-pump (el.) with earth pipe
5	Heat-pump (el.) with ground water utilization
6	Heat-pump (el.) with waste water utilization
7	Air collector with stone reservoir
8	Window collector
9	Flat plate collector (simple installation), single family house
10	Flat plate collector, multiple family house
11	Evacuated tube collector
12	Transparent insulating materials (TIM)
13	Chiller
14	Desorption installation
15	Chiller with ice-storage installation
16	Electricity supply
17	Photovoltaic installation (polymonocrystalline, amorphous)
18	Wind power installation (v > 5 m / s)
19	Small water power plant
20	Potable water connection
21	Grey water installation (flushing, household)
22	Grey water installation (reservoir)

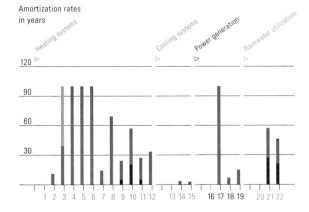

Amortization rates in years

■ Span of amortization rates for bore hole installations (depending on local conditions)
■ without subsidy
■ with subsidy

for rainwater utilization
■ without waste water cost
■ with waste water cost

Figure 379.1
Investment costs for different technologies

■ Upper limit
■ Lower limit

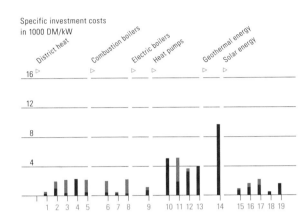

Specific investment costs in 1000 DM/kW

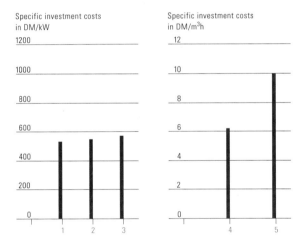

Specific investment costs in DM/kW

Specific investment costs in DM/m³h

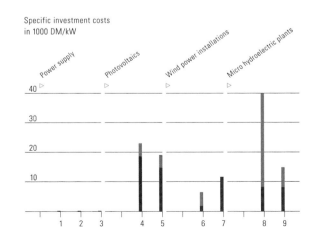

Specific investment costs in 1000 DM/kW

Figure 379.2
Operating costs for different technologies

(Primary energy + maintenance)

■ Upper limit (grey)
■ Lower limit (black)

Specific operating costs
in DM (Pfennig)/kWh

District heat | Combustion boilers | Electric boilers | Heat pumps | Geothermal energy | Solar energy

160 ▷

120

80

40

1 2 3 4 5 6 7 8 9 10 11 12 13 14 15 16 17 18 19

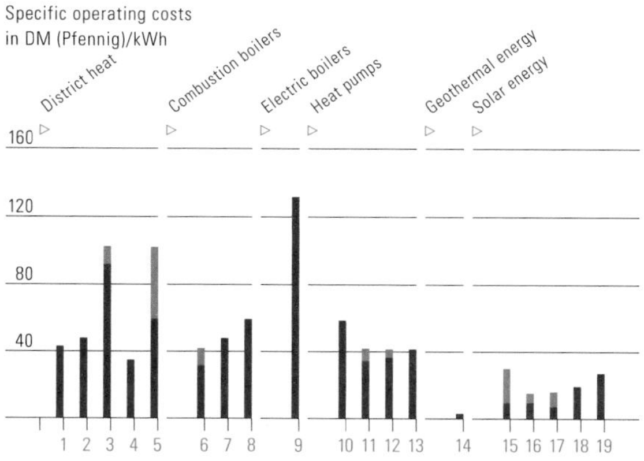

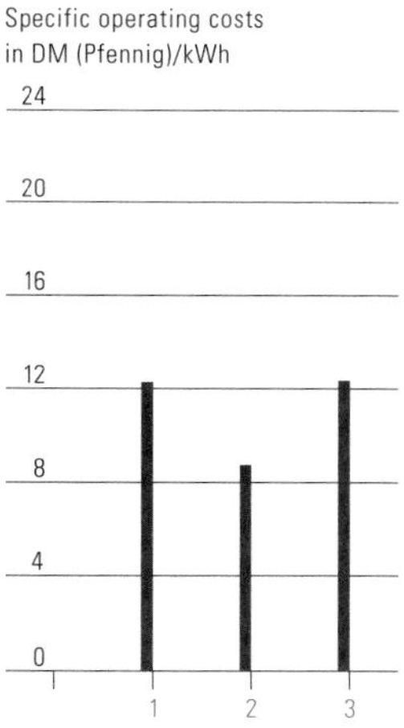

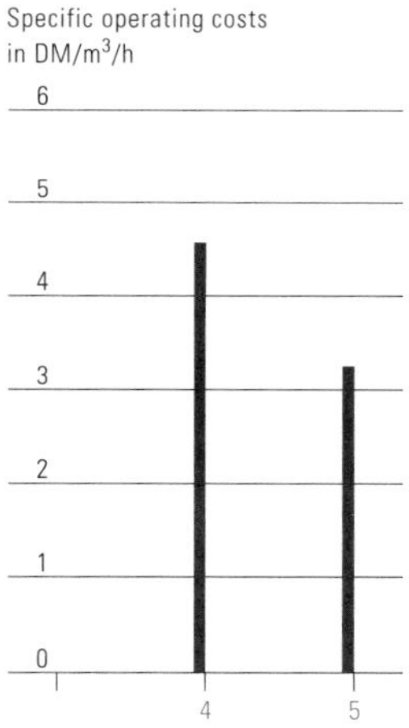

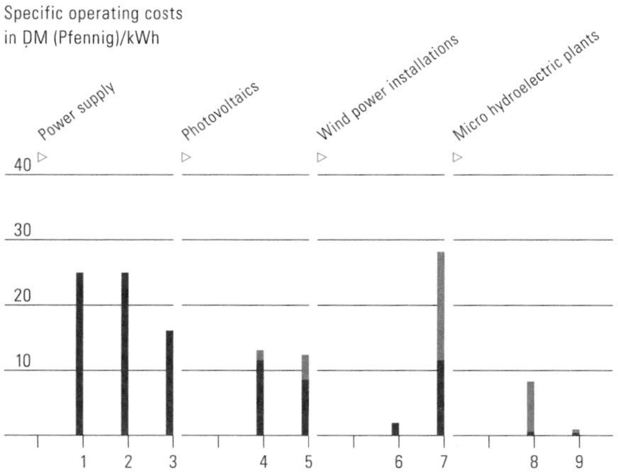

Figure 379.3
Annual total costs for different technologies

(Operating costs + capital costs)

■ Upper limit (grey)
■ Lower limit (black)

Specific total costs
in DM (Pfennig)/kWh

District heat | Combustion boilers | Electric boilers | Heat pumps | Geothermal energy | Solar energy

80 ▷

60

40

20

1 2 3 4 5 6 7 8 9 10 11 12 13 14 15 16 17 18 19

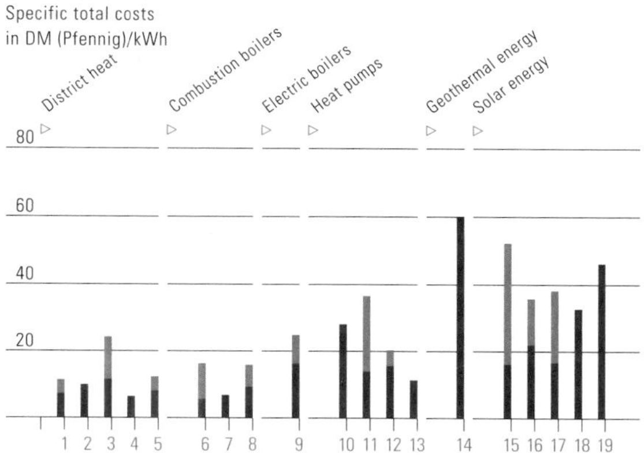

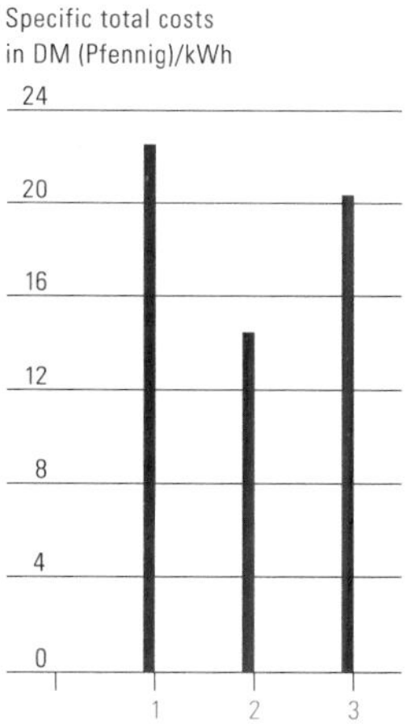

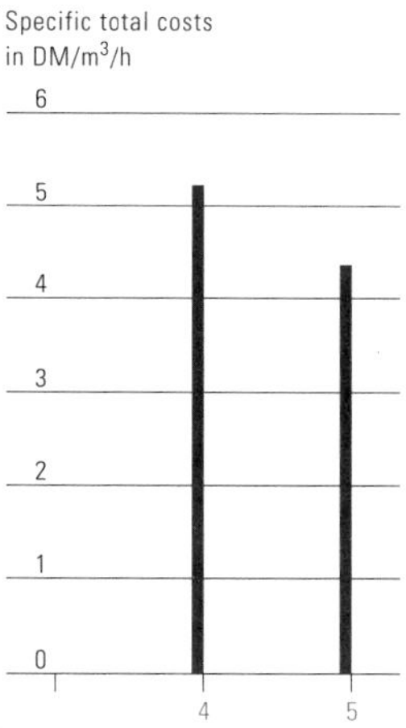

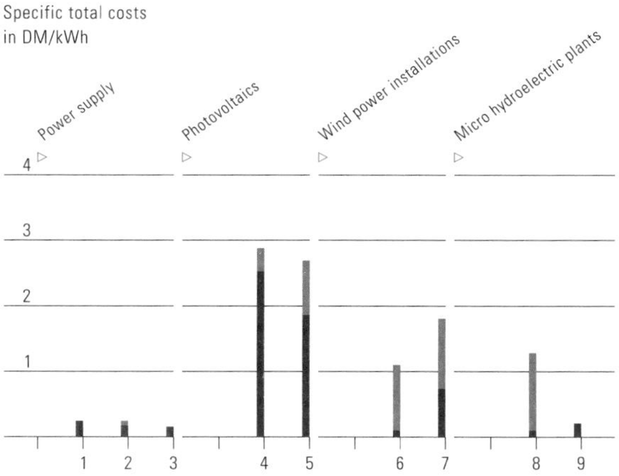

Heat supply systems

District heat
1 Waste incineration
2 CHP
3 Nuclear power station
4 Large power station, fossile
5 Wood incineration

Burners
6 Oil
7 Natural gas
8 Wood

Electric burners
9 Ceramic-/water boiler

Electric-driven heat pumps
10 with earth pipes
11 with bore holes *
12 with circulation fountain *
13 with waste water utilization

Geothermal
14 Direct utilization *

Solar energy [1]
15 Air collector
16 Flate plate collector
17 Evacuated tube collector
18 Transparent Insulating Material (TIM)[2] *
19 Balcony glazing *

([1]Investment costs in DM / m2 collector surface, for balcony glazing per m2 of balcony

[2]Operating costs in DM / kWh m2)

Specific operating costs
in DM (Pfennig)/kWh

24

20

16

12

8

4

0

1 2 3

Specific operating costs
in DM/m³/h

6

5

4

3

2

1

0

4 5

Specific total costs
in DM (Pfennig)/kWh

24

20

16

12

8

4

0

1 2 3

Specific total costs
in DM/m³/h

6

5

4

3

2

1

0

4 5

Cooling systems

1 Electric chiller (piston / turbo)
2 Absorption chiller with waste heat utilization
3 Electric chiller with ice-storage

Air-conditioning

4 Standard air-conditioning system
5 Desorption installation

All values are indexed to m³ / h treated, cooled air

Electricity generating systems

Net supply
1 Low voltage, household
2 Low voltage, industrial
3 Low voltage, renewable energies

Photovoltaic
4 Monocrystalline
5 Polycrystalline

Wind power stations
6 High-speed installations (w > 5 m/s)
7 Low-speed installations (w < 5 m/s)

Small water power stations
8 High-pressure installations (Fall height > 100 m)
9 Low-pressure installations (Fall height 5 – 10 m)

Specific operating costs
in DM (Pfennig)/kWh

Power supply | Photovoltaics | Wind power installations | Micro hydroelectric plants

40 ▷

30

20

10

1 2 3 4 5 6 7 8 9

Specific total costs
in DM/kWh

Power supply | Photovoltaics | Wind power installations | Micro hydroelectric plants

4 ▷

3

2

1

1 2 3 4 5 6 7 8 9

16.
Utilization of Organic Matter

Figure 380
Utilization of biomass

Figure 380 is an overview of the most important processes in the utilization of biomass. The energy source is the sun, which enables photosynthesis. This converts carbon dioxide from the atmosphere into different carbon compounds, such as sugar, cellulose or lignine, thereby releasing oxygen. Solar energy is latently stored in this process. All processes utilizing biomass ultimately set free CO_2 and energy, which means that materials harvested and used have to be planted again to maintain the CO_2 balance.

Biogas

Bacterial, anaerobic decomposition of organic matter with water and at temperatures ranging from 20°C to 55°C creates biogas. It is a combustible product of varying composition, depending upon origin. Biogas is created mostly from agricultural waste and animal husbandry. Its methane content fluctuates between 50 % and 75 %. It can, therefore, be used to produce heat or, combined with gas motors, for power-heat-production. To compensate for short-term fluctuations, biogas is stored in low- or medium-pressure reservoirs. Certain boiler- or gas-motor-driven installations can use biogas, as well as natural gas, as a secondary energy medium to ensure security of supply.

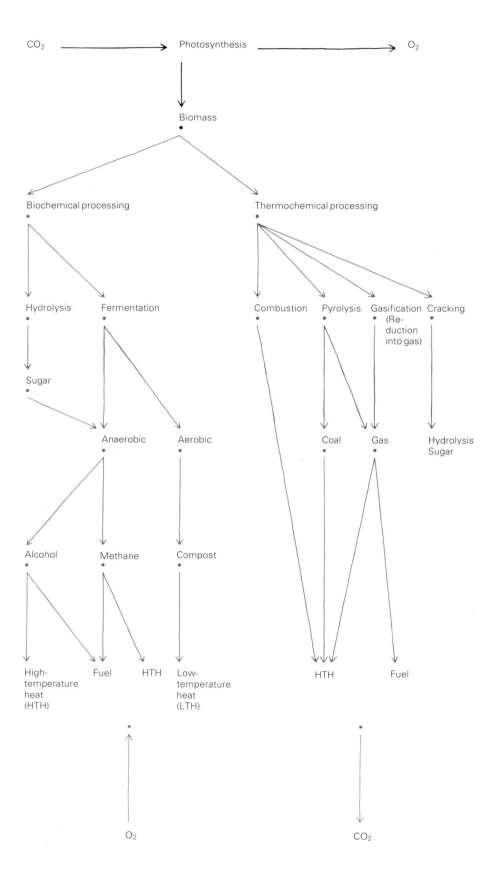

Methane Gas

Organic material ferments in garbage dumps, resulting in uncontrolled decomposition of organic refuse through bacteria. This process creates methane gas, which rises to the top layer of the dump and often permeates the atmosphere surrounding the dump site. The obvious disadvantages are bad smells, damage to vegetation and, possibly, spontaneous combustion, all of which can be prevented by exhausting the methane gas and storing it. Methane gas from garbage dumps consists of methane and CO_2 and, like biogas, can be used for heating or for creating electrical energy. Owing to the heterogenous nature of garbage, the actual composition and amount of methane gas will differ greatly from site to site. Hydrosulphides, higher carbon hydrogens and chlorinated hydrocarbons contained in methane gas make its utilization somewhat problematic. It can be gathered under pneumatic roofs (similar to a glass dome) and from there extracted and put into intermediate storage in suitable tanks. Figure 381 shows the roof covering a landfill currently under construction in Herford, Germany, by VBH GmbH Verbunddeponie Bielefeld-Herford (master plan: AEW Plan GmbH, Cologne; roof design: IPL Ingenieurplanung Leichtbau GmbH, Radolfzell). This project proves the technical practicability of pneumatic superstructures which could, with some restrictions, also be used for landfills containing organic waste.

Sewer Gas

Sewage treatment plants produce, as a by-product, materials which are also partially decomposed in anaerobic processes through bacteria. This creates sewage sludge and sewer gas with a high methane content (approx. 65 %). The sewer gas is often utilized in power-heat-combined stations, usually supplying most of the electricity needed for the sewage treatment plants. The resulting heat serves at the same time to heat the septic tanks.

Combustion of Biomass

Combustion of biomass (mostly wood) for energy production, as discussed in Section 15.7, requires a very exacting approach to combustion, which is largely guaranteed in modern installations. To ignite and feed the

combustion for high combustion temperatures (strongly fluctuating thermal value of biomass), natural gas or domestic heating oil is used. Besides wood and wood chips, garbage and straw are also used for combustion. In future, fast-growing species of 'energy plants' may be considered.

Reduction of Biomass into Gas

Reducing biomass into gas is a thermochemical process during which gas is created which has the combustible elements carbon monoxide and hydrogen. Out of these, another processing step can create such bioalcohols as methanol or ethanol which can, in turn, be used for energy production. High-temperature anaerobic pyrolysis of biomass produces a gas, usable in motors to generate electricity and thermal energy.

Figure 381
View of pneumatic roof covering a landfill in Herford, Germany (IPL Engineering Leichtbau GmbH)
Isometric drawing: south-east

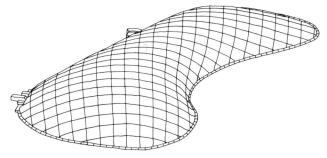

Active Measures
of Renewable Energy Usage

Active Measures
of Renewable Energy Usage

17

This last section introduces a selection of buildings, built or planned, which point to the future and are committed to integrated design while fulfilling a variety of utilization requirements.

Public utilities service building, Ettlingen, Germany

'Lightpark' project, Vilshofen

M. + G. Ricerche Laboratories, Venafro

Competition 'Photovoltaics on the Built Envelope'

Science and Research Park Gelsenkirchen, Germany

Tokyo-Nara Tower project

17.
Perspectives

Table 11 provides an overview of current, marketable, renewable energy technologies. It also clarifies which technologies are market-ready and which are ready but currently rarely implemented. It becomes clear that many of these technologies are still in the development phase and other fields require further research. Nevertheless, as architects and engineers, we live in an era which not only challenges us to develop new ideas but virtually cries out for innovative concepts. Therefore, a number of architects, engineers, and construction engineers are actively supporting significant trends for the development and design of future buildings. In conclusion, and to provide a glimpse of the future, here then are some groundbreaking projects for residential and office buildings.

Table 11
Market-ready regenerative
energy technologies

* technology ready for
market niche
**R&D required a.o. also for
environmental issues

	Technology ready for market (optimization requirements possible)	Insufficient application experience (e.g. lifespan)	R&D required for alternatives	Further development required	Further research required
Solar energy					
– Solar absorber	☐				
– Solar collectors (Low temperature)	☐		☐		
– Solar collectors (Processing heat)	☐	☐	☐		
– Solar thermal production of electricity (channel collector)	☐	☐			
– Solar thermal production of electricity (other technologies)				☐	
– Passive utilization in buildings	☐	☐	☐		
– Photovoltaic energy production (crystalline silicon)	☐	☐	☐		
– photovoltaic energy production* (amorphous silicon)				☐	☐
– other photovoltaic materials (e.g. connecting semi-conductors and tandem structures)				☐	☐
– Solar production of chemical energy carriers (e.g. hydrogen) Photochemistry					☐
Wind energy					
– Installations up to 400 kW	☐	☐	☐		
– Larger installations				☐	
Water energy					
– Large power stations	☐				
– Small power stations	☐				
– Tidal energy		☐			
– Wave energy				☐	
Biomass					
– Combustion	☐	☐**		☐	
– Gasification	☐	☐**		☐	
– Bio alcohol	☐	☐**			
– Plant alcohol		☐		☐	☐
– Other energy plants				☐	☐
Thermal energy from the earth					
– Geoscientific principles				☐	
– Utilization of hot springs	☐				
– Utilization of hydrothermal sources	☐	☐		☐	☐
– Utilization of Hot Dry Rock technology				☐	☐
Environmental heat					
– Electric heat pump	☐				
– Absorption heat pump	☐	☐	☐		
Applications and components					
– Photovoltaic application technology (e.g. water pump, lighting)	☐	☐		☐	
– Batteries, fuel cells	☐	☐	☐	☐	☐
– Control technology	☐			☐	
– Heat storage	☐		☐	☐	
– Hydrogen (Electrolysis, storage, handling)	☐		☐		

Public Utilities Service Building, Ettlingen

A public utilities service building, designed by
Prof. T. Wulf, Stuttgart, was recently completed
in Ettlingen. The administration building, integrating workshop and warehouse, forms an urban
complex in which all office areas face south-east.
A winter garden, along the south side of the building, is the central component of the built fabric
and functions as a climate buffer zone (passive
solar utilization), a recreational interior garden and
meeting place, and an experimental and exhibition space. The high-storage building is naturally
ventilated. In the transitional season, the warm air
from the winter garden is used to heat the shop
areas.

Figure 382.1
View into atrium and main
elevation of the New Municipal
Works building in Ettlingen,
Germany

Figure 382.2
Location plan

1   Photovoltaics
2   Solar collectors
3   Energy fence

Figure 382.3
Views of the building

The  Figure 382 series shows the buildings and details of how environmental energies are used. This building is a good example of various efficient and renewable energy technologies, which are visible to and experienced by visitors and occupants alike. A gas-fired condensing boiler system (performance approx. 450 kW) provides the first step towards an environmentally friendly and energy-conserving approach to heating the building. A 12-m^2-large collector surface with evacuated tube collectors further supplements the heating systems. The shop areas are heated by means of a heat pump system in combination with a massive absorber (the 'Ettlingen Energy Fence'), with embedded PV coils through which brine is pumped for gaining environmental energy even when outside temperatures are extremely low. This comprehensive system is completed by a photovoltaic installation for generating a portion of the electricity required in the building. The main focus in the design of this building was to improve the supply of energy and water management, to conserve as much energy and water as possible, to create the highest standard possible for environmental protection and to ensure effective and efficient supply.

Figure 382.4
Interior views of atrium and winter garden

Figure 382.5
Top:
Concrete massive absorber, 'Ettlingen Energy Fence'
Middle:
Photovoltaic installation
Bottom:
Collector field with evacuated tubes

The 'Lightpark' Project

Living in buildings of tomorrow means considerate cohabitation with nature and integration of nature into the design process. At the same time, building materials need to be minimized and used intelligently with a view to utilizing the energies provided by the environment.

The Figure 383 series shows a project by the Lichtpark GBR, Munich, a group of engineers in energy technology, framework design, open space design and planning, technical building services, architecture, and interior design led by the architect H. Mallmann, Munich, and by P. Marx in the area of design and interior design. The project envisions a combined living and working building design, where individual buildings consist of mostly pre-assembled wood and steel components. The 360 x 600 cm construction grid allows for identically sized rooms to be added at any time to fulfill a variety of functions. Furthermore, the grid principle facilitates modular, accessible, and hence easily exchangeable and expandable installation of all building services. The first lightpark project is currently under construction in Vilshofen/Lower Bavaria and will soon be presented to the public.

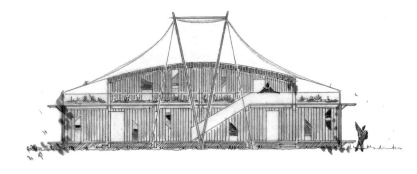

Figure 383.1
Lightpark Project, rear view

Living in a light-weight built structure integrating environment and living space

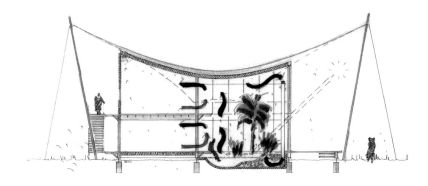

Figure 383.2
Wind-, sun- and thermal utilization in the living area

Figure 383.3
Direct and indirect utilization of environment

1 Collectors for warm water production
2 Decentralized warm air heating with warm water production
3 Return heat connection of central heating installation
4 Earth duct

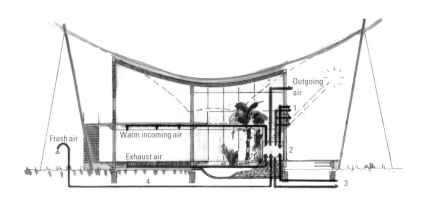

The flat roofs of the building are thermal roofs and can be used as planted water roofs. The main roof covering the entire building consists of white, textile membranes in the shape of four-cornered sails, creating not only a double curved membrane surface as a rigid form but also a rear ventilated cooling roof with a highly insulated inner roof surface. The walls and ceilings consist of a wood-layer louvre-system equipped with insulating components for sound and heat insulation. High insulating thermal glazing generates passive solar gain in the transitional season and in winter. Incident thermal energy is collected in large stone or water storage units. Interior foliage improves the microclimate and a decentralized heat pump installation heats the building, utilizing, in addition, heat recovery from exhaust air flow. In winter, the building is supplied with fresh air through pipes in the ground, where the air is preheated. The pipes also serve to minimally cool the supply air in summer.

Appropriate harmony between materials and human environment in extreme climates: North African nomad tents made of black goat wool provide shade and allow for the air to circulate in the heat. When it rains the material expands and becomes waterproof.

Figure 383.4
Model images of
Lightpark Project

The Lightpark is based on a concept whose aim it is to employ natural materials and to utilize environmental energies for the design of ecologically sound buildings adapted to the Central European climate.

M. + G. Ricerche Laboratories, Venafro

In 1994, the Constructec prize, the European Award for Industrial Architecture, was awarded to the research facility of the chemical company M.+G. Ricerche in Venafro in Southern Italy. Architects and engineers Samyn & Partners, Brussels, designed a building for chemical research which called for maximum flexibility and progressive development. Other project participants were A. Cermelli, Studio H, Tortona (works management), F. Invernizzi, Tober, Tortona (building services technology), the manufacturers of the tent construction Conobbio, Milan, and the IPL Ingenieurplanung Leichtbau GmbH, Radolfzell, Germany.

The principal feature of the design is a tent construction erected on an oval-shaped ground plan (85 x 32 m) covering the central area of the complex (Figure 384 series). The offices and laboratories are housed in container-like reinforced concrete buildings situated below the tent, also providing space for large-scale experiments. The tent construction is located at the centre of a large water basin, which serves to emphasize the futuristic character of the building and, above all, cools the outside air (adiabatic cooling) used to ventilate the building (office areas are air-conditioned). The construction consists of six steel trussed arches, across which a PVC-coated translucent polyester membrane is stretched.

Figure 384.1
M. + G. Ricerche laboratories,
Venafro (Italy)

In daytime, natural lighting is provided through the glazed sides, the fan-lights above the trusses, and the translucent membrane. At night, indirect lighting is provided. The heated interior air at the boundary layer to the underside of the membrane can create good ventilation by buoyancy through the fan-lights, whereby adiabatically cooled fresh air would enter the building from below. The architectural form, the site layout, and the cooperation of architect and engineer have led to an interesting overall solution open to further modifications.

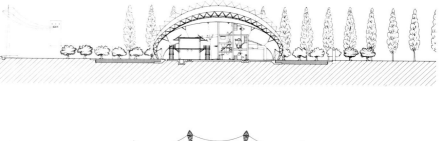

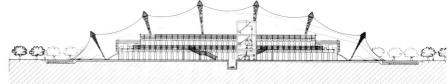

Figure 384.2
Sections of site and building

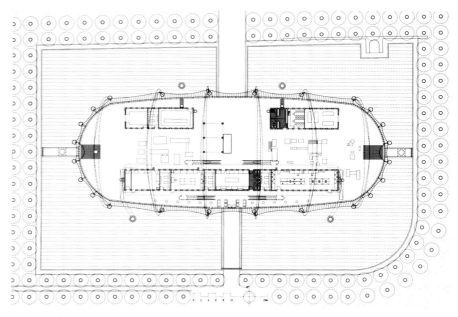

Figure 384.2
Floor plan (ground floor)

277

Competition 'Photovoltaics on the Built Envelope'

Schüco International held a competition for architecture students on the theme 'Photovoltaics on the Built Envelope'. The following award-winning design was entered by the Technical University, Berlin.

The competition called for the development of innovative concepts for a new metalworks building, taking into consideration higher building ecological requirements for new construction projects. The design by students S. Fuls, W. Hinsch, T. Ilskensmeier, and C. Klingbeil (Figure 385 series) features parallel, linear built fabrics, which are a continuation of the existing urban structure.

Furthermore, this design includes several approaches to utilize solar energy (Trombe wall with buffer zone), with south-east orientation in front of office zones and combined shading and photovoltaic elements on the roof of the manufacturing hall with simultaneous light penetration. Fixed and moveable service arms installed on the grid covering the entire hall serve to shift and orientate photovoltaic and shading elements, depending on daytime and season, in such a manner that the photovoltaic elements, especially, are always in the optimal sunpath position. The stunningly simple procedures for horizontal motion (only one moveable axis) have potential applications for other projects featuring flat roofs.

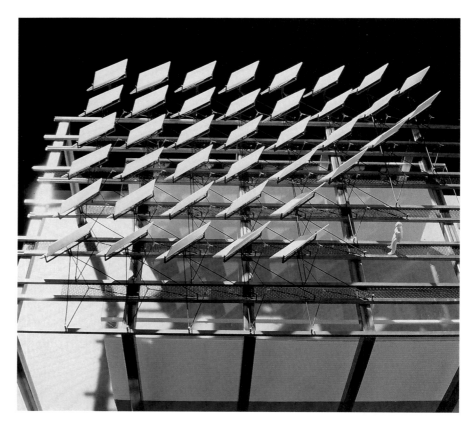

Figure 385.1
View of photovoltaic roof

Figure 385.2
Perspective of competition
design

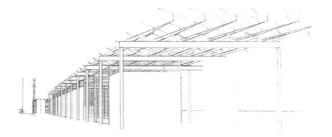

Figure 385.3
Bird's eye view of building

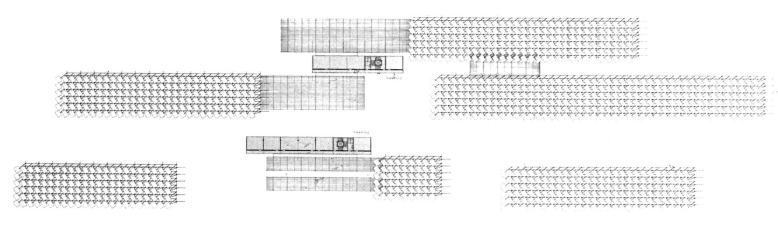

The design has been adapted
to the narrow site and the
layout of the built environment, structuring the site in a
south-west / north-east
direction.

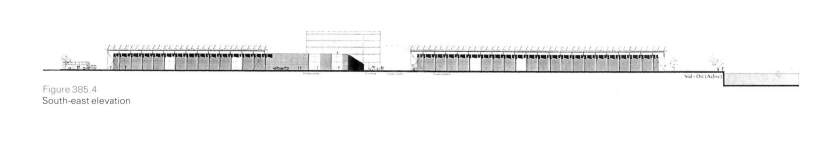

Figure 385.4
South-east elevation

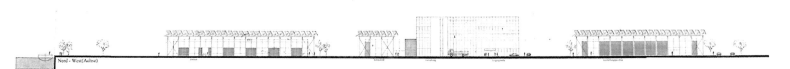

Figure 385.5
North-west elevation

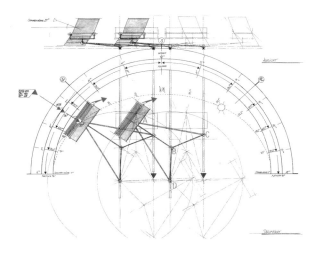

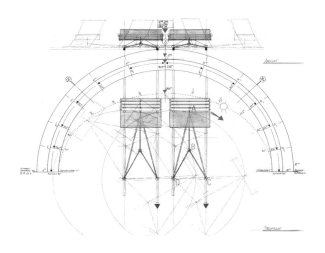

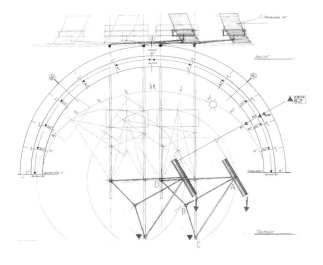

The shading unit and the adjustable axis AB are each mounted at the points of equilateral triangles, points A and B respectively. When the movable axis is shifted, these points rotate around point D. This change in angle enables the system to follow the sunpath by means of a simple movement of the axis. Looking at the movements over the course of a day, one observes that the shading units are angled away from the façade in the morning, thus shading the glass roof and the lightband from the flat angle of the morning sun. By noon the shading units have shifted to a position parallel to the atrium façades, the angle having changed in response to the sunpath shading the roof completely even at this time of day. As the day progresses, the shading units once again angle away from the façade, protecting the glass roof and the lightband as they did in the morning.

Figure 385.6
Schematic of environmentally responsive photovoltaic installation

Science and Research Park, Gelsenkirchen

The science and research park in Gelsenkirchen (architects: Kiessler and Partners, Munich), awarded the German Architecture Prize in 1995, is one of many projects by the IBA Emscher Park, whose goal is to restructure the Ruhr area, marked by decades of mining industry, since coal mining and steel production are no longer a viable employment basis for the resident population. Instead, the focus now is on future-oriented research and technology for workplace security.

Situated only a few hundred metres from the main train station, a science park was erected on the site of the former crucible steel works Rheinelbe, grouped around a central green park with a lake (Figure 386 series). To the east is a 300-m-long glass arcade directly linked to the three-storey gallery building and the nine pavilions. To the south is a round building housing conference and seminar facilities. On the north side the former administrative building has been transformed into a Labour Court. And on the west perimeter, in keeping with residences built during the nineteenth century, are city villas in a green setting. The arcade is the backbone of the whole complex. A public, weather-proof boulevard with cafés, restaurants and boutiques, it is, at the same time, the main access lane to the 300-m-long institute tract, to which it is attached with its slanted façade.

Figure 386.1
Science and Research Park,
Gelsenkirchen, Germany
Location plan and view into
glass arcade

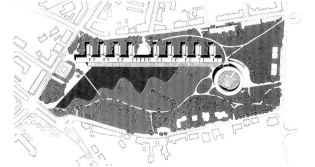

The façade of the institute tract is based on a grid
of 1.44 m in which glazed elements alternate with
elements consisting of openable wings, a kind
of french door design. To reduce the glass surface
and to avoid overheating in summer, vertical
elements with louvres were installed with an
attached insulated tilting unit. In summer, depending on weather, this unit can be used to take
advantage of cool night air, while maintaining the
building's security.

During the daytime in summer, there is a need for
protection against excessive solar radiation incidence. This is provided on the institute façade
and the slanted façade of the arcade with automatically controlled, external shading. To ensure a
draught-free environment, the consulting Fraunhofer Institut in Freiburg asked for the installation
of large fresh-air and small exhaust-air openings in
the arcade (top and bottom, respectively).
This request led to the creation of the 7 x 4.5 m^2
large openable panels, which are controlled by
electric motors. In summer, the arcade can thus
be opened along its whole length to the park. The
incoming fresh air is sufficiently cooled by the lake
to create comfortable conditions, even on warm
summer days. The smoke exhaust system of the
building can be used to further support this cool air
flow. Furthermore, the floor heating can be used
for cooling, by using the water for heating the service water via a heat pump. In winter, the arcade
remains closed towards the park and incident
energy is used in the arcade and in the offices for
heating. The installation of a large, spandrel-
braced photovoltaic power plant (220 kWp/a) on
the roof of the building is planned for the near
future.

Figure 386.2
Concept of natural ventilation

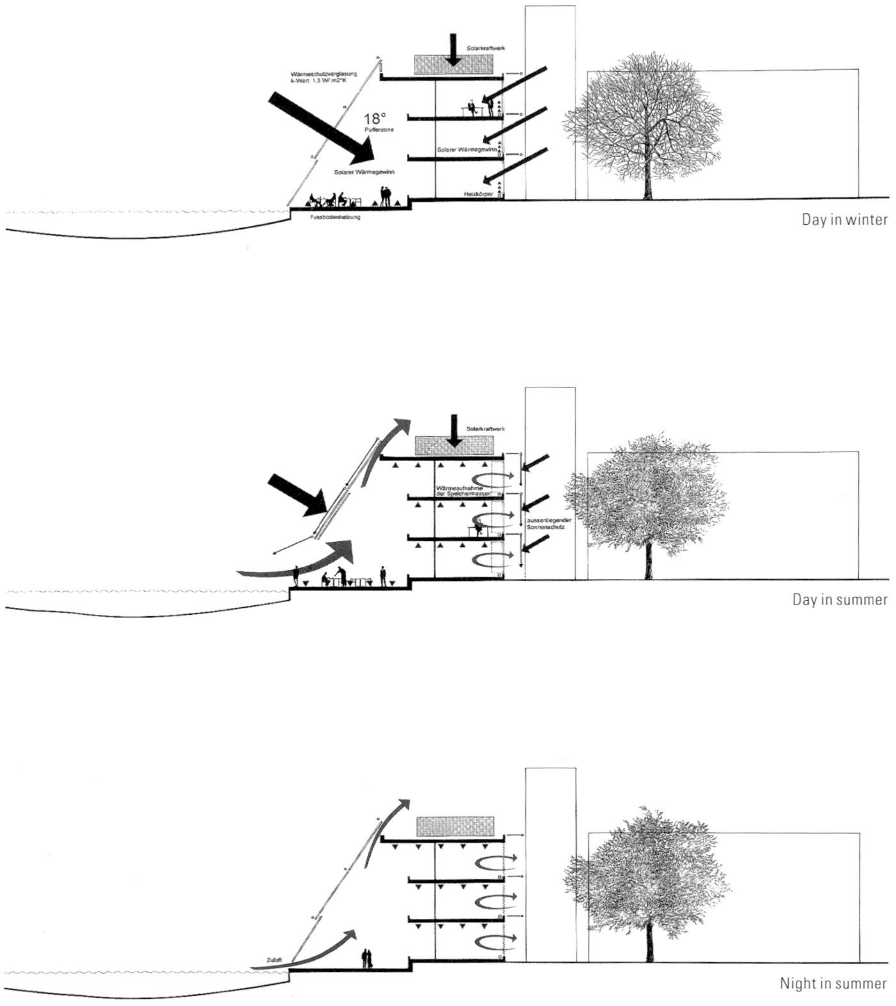

Day in winter

Day in summer

Night in summer

Figure 386.3
The openable arcade makes it
possible to cool the building with
the air rising from the lake. In
winter, the arcade is closed and
serves as a winter garden.

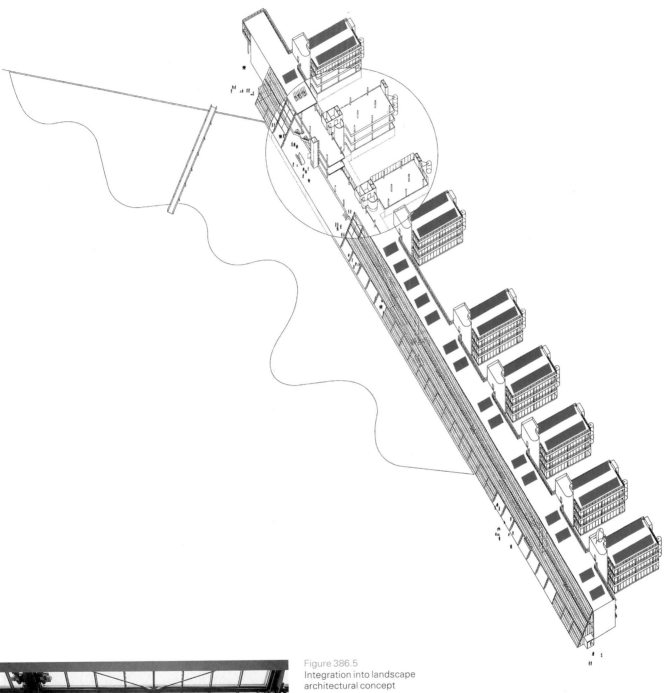

Figure 386.4
Isothermal drawing of photovoltaic installation

Figure 386.5
Integration into landscape
architectural concept

Tokyo-Nara Tower Project, Tokyo

The architect Ken Yeang, Kuala Lumpur, together with his team, has for many years focused intensively on ecologically orientated large projects. The ground plans and the model photograph shown in the Figure 387 series present an object which at first sight appears utopian. The design of this building has been shaped not only by concerns of natural ventilation but also by flexible shading measures, planted surfaces, and the utilization of rainwater.

The architect comments on his design as follows: (Quote)

"Vertical landscaping spirals around, through and inside the built form. The verdant foliage cools the building: the fringing of floors and atrial spaces allows careful planting to control air movements within the structure; the mass planting relative to the built structure means that the biosystems can act symbiotically with mechanical systems to provide a balanced environment. Specialized mechanical devices and cherry pickers on tracks maintain the vertical landscaping as well as the external fixtures, glazing and cladding panels. These are constructed in the form of multi-purpose robot arms on moveable trellises.

The radial/spiral movement of floor planes creates a particular built form that allows the floors to shade themselves as they spiral up. The displaced pattern exploits the benefits of hanging gardens, inter-floor bracing and ventilation systems and provides a constantly changing atrial space, articulated by terraces, internal courts and private gardens.

Regularly spaced skycourt oases provide inhabitants with environmentally sound breaks in the built structure. These green parks, suspended high above the city, act as the tower's lungs.

Atrial spaces, winding within the tower, are the arterial routes by which floors interact. The atrial network, bridged by walkways and flanked by stairwells, constitutes a microcosm of activity, within the tower (while open to the environment) and insulated from the city.

Lift and service cores are laid along the east-west axis. The cooler façades on the north-south axis are left open by clear glazing and atrial voids.

The sides of the building along the east-west axis are more solidly glazed, with cast and perforated metal cladding, than those on the north-south axis which have open louvres, tiered sun shades and clear glazing."
(End of quote)

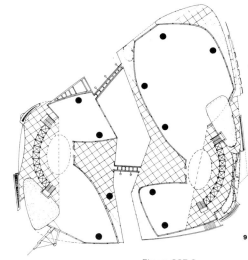

Figure 387.2
Typical floor plan

Figure 387.1
Tokyo-Nara Tower, location plan
Architekt: Ken Yeang, Kuala Lumpur, Malaysia

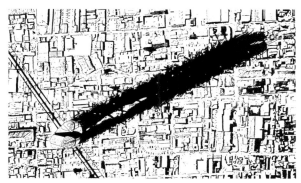

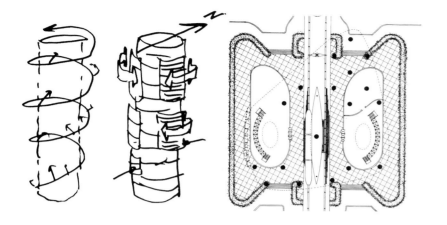

Figure 387.3
Model of 80-storey tower

The projects introduced on these last pages show the variety in approaches open to architecture and engineering to create designs committed to the central theme of this book. It can be expressed in a simple equation:

Ecologically correct building

=

crisis-proof buildings

=

pro-active environmental protection

=

improved perspectives for our children and grandchildren

Figure 387.4
Sunpath diagram

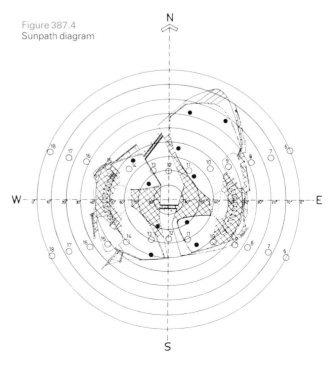

Acknowledgements

The creation of this book would not have been possible without the help of a number of experts contributing ideas and projects, as well as the many architects, some of whose projects are documented on these pages.

I am especially grateful to B. Eng. Ludwig Ilg and Bernhard Bauhofer (both of GfA, Gesellschaft für Aerophysik mbH, Munich) for their contributions to chapter 4.1.1 "Wind" and chapter 5 "Natural Ventilation of Buildings". I am also indebted to Dr. Eng. Joachim Stoll, Dr. Eng. Norbert Rosner, Dr. Eng. Gunter Pültz, B. Eng. Dieter Henze, B. Eng. Joachim Kast and, last but not least, B. Eng. Ulrich Behr (all HL-Technik AG, engineering consultants, Munich/Berlin).

Dr. Andreas Colli provided invaluable editorial help and authored the cost-benefit analyses for "alternative energy technologies".

These acknowledgements would not be complete without thanking the group which came together at Büro SchwaigerWinschermann with ideas and creativity for the design and production of this book, especially B.Eng. Andreas Alber for his drawings. They all helped to make the far reaching theme of this book clear and understandable.

Meyers Neues Lexikon,
1994

K. Daniels,
Werkbericht 9, Ökologie im Verwaltungsbau
HL-Technik AG, 1991

F. Gassmann,
„Was ist los mit dem Treibhaus Erde",
Verein der Fachverlage, Zurich,
BG Teubner-Verlag, 1994

Ken Yeang,
Bioclimatic Skyscrapers, Artemis,
London Ltd., 1994

K. Daniels,
Gebäudetechnik,
Verein der Fachverlage, Zurich,
R. Oldenbourg-Verlag, 1992

K. Daniels,
Werkbericht 12, Gebäudetechnik
für die Zukunft – „weniger ist mehr"
HL-Technik AG, 1994

DIN 1946, Raumlufttechnik
(Gesundheitstechnische Anforderungen),
Jan. 1994

Werkbericht 13,
Integrale Planungskonzepte –
ein Muß für die Zukunft
HL-Technik AG, 1994

L. Ilg, Bauhofer,
Windwirkungen an Fassaden,
Fassade 3/94

K.-J. Albers,
Untersuchungen zur Auslegung von
Erdwärmeaustauschern für die
Konditionierung der Zuluft für Wohngebäude,
Forschungsberichte des Deutschen
Kälte- und Klimatechnischen Vereins,
No. 32, 1991

Recknagel, Sprenger, Hönmann,
Taschenbuch für Heizung und Klimatechnik
Oldenbourg-Verlag, 1992/93

W. J. Eugster, R. J. Hopkirk,
B. Kälin, L. Rybach, P. Seifert,
Das Betriebsverhalten der Erdwärmesonden,
Schweizer Ingenieur + Architekt,
No. 46, 1992

K. Daniels,
Werkbericht 4,
Optimierte Technikkonzepte
für Hallenarchitektur
HL-Technik AG, 1990

K. Daniels, J. Stoll, G. Pültz, J. Schneider,
Werkbericht 11, Hochhäuser – natürlich
belüftet? – Neue Wege ökologischen Bauens
bei hohen Gebäuden
HL-Technik AG, 1992

M. Burg, H. Müller, D. Wüller,
Eine „intelligente Solarfassade",
HLH 44, 1993

T. Herzog,
Design Center, Linz,
Glasforum 4/94

K. Daniels,
Sonnenenergie,
Verlag C. F. Müller, 1975

R. Gasch,
Windkraftanlagen,
BG Teubner-Verlag, 1993

M. Grätzel,
Neue photovoltaische Zellen,
Schweizer Ingenieur + Architekt, 13, 1991

B. Strickler,
Water evaporation of 5 common indoor plants
under various climate conditions,
Proceedings 15th AIVC Conference, Buxton, GB

E. Maier, K.D. Laabs, E. Röber,
Erdwärmenutzung für die Raumklimatisierung
in Gebäuden, angewandt am Stadttheater
Heilbronn
BMFT-Forschungsbericht T 85-168

A. Harasim, B. Weissenbach,
Entwicklung eines Aquifer-Wärmespeichers
BMFT-Forschungsbericht T 82-032

Title image
H. Leiska, Hamburg
Design for exhibition pavilion,
Architects: von Gerkan, Marg und Partner,
Hamburg, 1987

1
Mauritius / Waldkirch

2
Mauritius / Rossenbach

3
based on drawing by H. Hooss, Stuttgart

to 3
Bernard Rudofsky, Architektur ohne
Architekten, Residenz Verlag, Salzburg, 1989

4
based on drawing by H. Hooss, Stuttgart

to 4
Adam und Partner, Munich

5
Stefan Moses, Munich

6.1, 6.2
HL-Technik archives

Page 28
K. Yeang, Kuala Lumpur

16 – 22
based on drawings by K. Yeang, Kuala Lumpur

33
Kessler Tech, Gießen

41
Deutsches Fernerkundungsdatenzentrum DFD,
DLR, Oberpfaffenhofen

55
top: W. Reuss, Berlin, and
bottom: U. Rau, Berlin, for the Senatsverwaltung
für Bau- und Wohnungswesen

56
Adam und Partner, Munich

57
Wolfrum, HOG Holzmann General-
unternehmungen

58
PFP-Planung Fahr Partner, Munich

61.2 – .4
G. Pfeifer, Lörrach

67
from Carlo Pedretti, exhibition catalogue,
Houston

69
L. Ilg, Zurich

70
top: Bernard Rudofsky, Architektur ohne
Architekten, Residenz Verlag, Salzburg, 1989,
bottom: Eamon O'Mahony, Limmerick, Ireland,
bottom left: R. Rogers Partnership, London

74, 75
from Cecil D. Elliott, Technics and Architecture,
MIT-Press

87.1, 87.2 and page 78
Gesellschaft für Aeropysik, Munich

88.1, 88.7 – 9
Tchibo Hamburg, Kühn

88.4, 88.5
ROM, Hamburg

89
L. Ilg and Gesellschaft für Aeropysik, Munich

92,93
Student groups as indicated in text

94
B. Strickler, Zurich

95–96,98,99
Sir Norman Foster + Partners, London

100, 107–110, 113
Schweger & Partner, Hamburg

122–128, 130–131, 136, 139
Kessler + Luch, Gießen

144–146, 149
Ingenhoven + Overdiek, Düsseldorf

161.2/.3
J. Weber, Munich

162.1
I. Nemec, Frankfurt

162.3
HL-Technik archives

163.1
Philipp Holzmann AG, Frankfurt a. M.

164.1, .4, .5
Struhk + Partner, Braunschweig

175.1, 175.3
H. Müller, Dortmund

176
HHS Planer + Architekten, Kassel

184
P. Bartenbach, Munich

187.1/.4/.5
Siemens AG, Traunreut

187.2/.3
HL-Technik archives

190
D. Leistner / Architekton

192–194
Okalux, Marktheidenfeld

202
from Alco - Systeme GmbH, Münster

203, 204
H.G. Esch, Cologne

205
Gartner & Co., Gundelfingen

206
M. Eschenlohr, Munich

208.1
Herzog + de Meuron, Basel

210
by M. Davis, London

212
Kessler + Luch, Gießen

213–215
von Gerkan, Marg + Partner, Hamburg,
K. Frahm, Hamburg

222
von Gerkan, Marg + Partner, Hamburg and
IBF, München

223, 224
HL-Technik archives

225, 226
burckhardt partner, Basel

227
Spaltenstein Immobilien AG, Zurich

234, 235
K. Frahm, Hamburg

236
von Gerkan, Marg + Partner, Hamburg

239–241
Auer + Weber, Munich

242
Auer + Weber, Munich and
HL-Technik AG, Munich

250
H. Leiska, Hamburg

251
Peter Cook, London and
Peake, Short + Partners, London

252.1
Pysall, Stahrenberg + Partner, Braunschweig and
D. Kruse, Hamburg

253.1
Kessler + Luch, Gießen

254.3
M. Zoll, Boymann Begrünungen, Glandorf

255, 256
S. Heuser, Ottobrunn

257
Lehrstuhl für Fluidmechanik, TU Munich

258
D. Siegert, Munich

259
Lehrstuhl A für Thermodynamik, TU Munich

265, 266
D. Leistner / Architekton

267–271, 273
Herzog + Partner, Munich

285, 286
based on maps by Stiebel-Eltron,
Holzminden

290
Alcan, Nuremberg

294
Solar-Energie-Technik, Altlußheim

296
Thermo-Solar, Regensburg

298
Stiebel- Eltron, Holzminden

303.1
HL-Technik archives

307
top: B. Strickler, Zurich
middle: Flachglas Solartechnik GmbH, Cologne
bottom: J. Reid & J. Peck

308
Solution AG, Härkingen, CH and
COLT International, Baar, CH

309
Solution AG, Härkingen, CH and
R. P. Miloni, Baden, CH

310
dpa

312
E. Rabe, Bundesbauamt Berlin

314–316, 319
drawings by Calatrava Valls SA, Zürich

317
HL-Technik archives

320
Dürschinger & Biefang, Ammerndorf

326, 327
HL-Technik archives

359
K. Gerling, Heidelberg

360
ROM, Hamburg

to 374
Jäggi AG, Bern, Zurich

381
IPL, Radolfzell

382.1, .3, .4
C.Kandzia

382.2
T. Wulf, Stuttgart

382.5
drücke fotostudio, Ettlingen

383.1 – .4
H. Mallmann, Munich

to 383.4
Bernard Rudofsky, Architektur ohne
Architekten, Residenz Verlag, Salzburg, 1989

384.1
Matteo Piazza

384.2, .3
Samyn + Partners, Brussels

385
Stanley Fuls, Wendelin Hinsch,
Tomas Ilskensmeier, Claudia Klingbeil, Berlin

386
Architekturphoto, Ralph Richter and
Kiessler + Partner, Munich

387
Ken Yeang, Kuala Lumpur, Malaysia

For some illustrations we were unable to
determine the copyrights. Any copyright holders
are requested to contact the author.

ABB

ABB Fläkt Produkte GmbH

ABB Fläkt Produkte GmbH
Schorbachstraße 9
35510 Butzbach
Germany
Phone +49/60 33/80-0
Fax   +49/60 33/80-5 86

– Ventilation- and air conditioning
  products
– Air handling units for hospitals
– Heat-recovery systems
– Fans
– Ventilators for air intake and air
  exhaust
– Fan-Coils
– Systems and components for
  controlled residential ventilation

ABB Fläkt Produkte GmbH is a European
supplier of high quality ventilation and
air- conditioning products.

The products are characterized by
progressive technology, high quality
standards, dependability and economy.
Nearly seventy years of experience
and numerous pioneered projects have
made ABB a leading company in the
area of air-conditioning products.

All components are developed and produced by ABB and are thus highly compatible. The product selection ranges
from central installation units, various
ventilation systems and radial- and axial
ventilators to different heat-recovery
installations, convector ventilators and
cooling convectors. Special mention
should be made of the new generation
of central air-conditioning units
EU-2000, a modular component which
has been given the RAL seal of quality.
It has been designed specifically for the
various requirements for air treatment
in the European countries. Development
and manufacture meet all quality assur-
ance criteria of ISO 9001.

ABB is a competent partner through first
class products, extensive know-how
and informed consulting.

IIIII   GARTNER

Josef Gartner & Co.
Werkstätten für Stahl- und
Metallkonstruktionen
Postfach 20/40
89421 Gundelfingen
Germany
Phone +49/90 73/84-0
Fax   +49/90 73/84-2100

Workshops for steel and metal
constructions

Gartner started in 1868 as a small
lock-smith workshop. Today the Gartner
company employs more than 1,700
people worldwide and is one of the big-
gest international curtain wall producers.

In its headquarters in Germany and the
subsidiaries in the Netherlands, the UK
and in Hong Kong, Gartner manufac-
tures mainly custom-made curtain walls
made of aluminium and steel. Further
products include special constructions
with integrated heating, ventilation,
cooling, sun protection and daylighting
technique, radiant cooling ceilings,
ventilated air flow façades and double-
skin façades, all types of aluminium
windows and doors made-to-measure.

GARTNER Quality

Gartner curtain walls and services
benefit from decades of experience and
the high demand for quality typical of
Gartner. Many current standards in curtain walling go back to Gartner developments. Even in times in which costs
seem to be the decisive criteria for the
award of a contract we refuse to reduce
our standards.

The quality of a product depends to a
high degree on the quality of its essential
components. To better control quality
and time schedules, Gartner started
many years ago the manufacture of aluminium extrusions, neoprene profiles,
panels and door closers as well as
anodising and powder coating. These
departments are managed as profit
centers which sell a considerable portion of their products to third parties,
including competitors.

Gartner worldwide

An efficient project management is
a significant pre-condition to fulfill ones
commitments. Big projects are run by
experienced project managers who
have proven their ability on important
international projects as far away as the
Far East. It is essential to involve competent partners from our various technical branches. The experience gained
benefits all new projects, including the
domestic ones.

HL⁄Technik

HL-Technik AG
beratende Ingenieure (VBI/VUBI/SIA)
Wolfratshauser Str. 54
81379 München
Germany
Phone +49/89/7 24 06-133
Fax   +49/89/7 24 06-139

HL-Technik develops techniques with
its origins out of the urban structure
up to a successful operation of a building
based on environmentally sensible
solutions.

Our goals are:

Progress through innovation, close
contact to our clients, integrated design
solutions and environmentally sound
technologies – for the client's benefit.

Our field of activities includes:

– Planning of infrastructure
– Thermal physics of buildings
– Building services
– Daylight and artificial lighting
– Service management

The HL-Technik team consists of:

HL-Technik AG, Munich, with central
design-consulting departments:
– Lighting design
– Information technologies
– Thermal physics

and regional offices in
– Berlin
– Dresden
– Düsseldorf
– Frankfurt
– Hamburg
– Munich
– Stuttgart

HL-Technik AG, Zurich

Gesellschaft für Aerophysik mbh
(Society for aerophysics), Munich

HL-Infrastrukturplanung GmbH, Berlin

HL-Service Management GmbH,
Siegen

KESSLER LUCH

KESSLER + LUCH GmbH

Rathenaustrasse 8
35394 Giessen
Germany
Phone +49/641/707-00
Fax   +49/641/707-316

Kessler+Luch GmbH is one of
Germany's leading contractors in the
field of building technical engineering
and is a subsidiary of the STEAG
Industrie AG, Essen.

Kessler+Luch's range of activities
includes design, engineering, procure-
ment, installation and maintenance of
air-conditioning, cooling, heating, cleanroom and environmental systems as
well as ventilation systems for power
stations.

Whilst in the comfort sector the most
important factor is the to create an
agreeable atmosphere for human
beings, in the area of industrial ventilation it is often necessary to protect
human beings from dangerous
emissions deriving from the production
process or, in turn, to protect the product itself. These differentiated tasks
demand adequate solutions.

Well known as an innovative company,
Kessler+Luch operates its own
Research and Development Laboratory,
where it is possible to optimally adjust
the architecture of a building to its scope
whilst at the same time perfectly integrating the necessary technical equipment.

To satisfy the different demands of the
customer testing methods ranging from
model room studies to numerical simulations are available.

Whilst numerical simulation provides
information on the temperature profiles
and the seasonal energy consumption,
air flow simulation offers the possibility
of determining the influence of wind or
other internal factors.

Model studies on the other hand make
it possible to adjust and optimize the
systems qualitatively and quantitatively
offering at the same time the possibility
of carrying out an optical evaluation of
the system on a 1:1 scale or a reduced
scale.

DEUTSCHE BABC●CK

KRANTZ-TKT

BDAG GROUP

H. KRANTZ-TKT GMBH

Am Stadion 18-24
51465 Bergisch Gladbach
Germany
Phone +49/2202/125-0
Fax   +49/2202/125-324

Projecting – Building – Managing

Investors, users and operators do more
and more realize that the individual
phases in the lifetime of a building must
not be contemplated as being isolated
units. At present, the trend is to see
a building as an integral product, as far
as economics are concerned. Such
thinking necessitates comprehensive
projecting schemes from developing to
retro-fitting. For only if architects, civil
contractors and mechanical contractors
set up and follow an interactive scheme,
aesthetic, functional and economical
aspects can be combined to achieve
optimum results. Comprehensive thinking and multi-disciplinary interaction of
all parties involved are prerequisite to
continual optimization, in the end leading to minimization of investment costs.
KRANTZ-TKT, one of the leading companies in the field of building services, is
your competent partner during the significant phases in the lifetime of a building. We have the know-how, pioneer
programs and technical equipment that
cover the entire range of projecting,
building, managing and retro-fitting.

Projecting: Our building simulation program outlines in figures what relationship exists between a building with its
physical properties and the projected
mechanical systems. Our R&D divisions
offer investors, architects, consultants
and engineers the opportunity to test
the planned systems and find new solutions together with us. Our equipment
design programs allow to select and
design adequate air distribution systems
under due consideration of functional
requirements, capacity and architectural
aspects in the earliest stage of projecting.

Building: Our CAD programs are qual-
ified aids to "live" integrated planning
since all building and related data determined during projecting and execution
can be transferred to be used for building operation. Our multi-disciplinary
experience as mechanical contractors is
the basis for integrated building services
planning and execution.

Managing: Our range of integrated facility management covers all activities in
connection with operation and maintenance as well as optimization of energy
efficiency and systems.

 SCHÜCO INTERNATIONAL

SCHÜCO International KG

Karolinenstraße 1–15
33609 Bielefeld
Germany
Phone +49/521/783-0
Fax   +49/521/783-451

For the sake of the environment

SCHÜCO is a company commited to a
wide range of interests and a market
leader in Europe for windows, doors and
façades which takes its responsibility
towards the environment particularly
seriously.

What, for many, has only recently become an issue as a result of an increase
in awareness of environmental factors,
has long been a matter of concern for
SCHÜCO and a permanent part of
SCHÜCO's policies on general and product development.

SCHÜCO has played a pioneering role in
many schemes for protecting the
environment – for example: resource-
saving recycling processes have been
set up right across the board for high
grade aluminium and uPVC profiles.

Furthermore, SCHÜCO has developed
a forward-looking logistics system for fittings which helps to avoid large quan-
tities of waste from packaging materials.

SCHÜCO has been making an important
contribution to environmentally friendly
building processes since 1991. After
an intensive research and development
programme, SCHÜCO was able to present a prototype of a synergy façade and
a first study into the use of photosensitive elements in façades.

In 1993 SCHÜCO was successful in integrating photosensitive cells in façades
both from a technical and an aesthetic
point of view. In the meantime, many
reference projects have been completed, proving without a shadow of a
doubt how synergy façades can help the
environment, save valuable resources
and still be of great architectural interest.
SCHÜCO has continued to develop synergy façades, introducing new photosensitive solar units and making even
more attractive and varied façades.
SCHÜCO can now offer a far greater
range of styles and systems using photosensitive elements. Far larger modules
can be designed, and their colours blend
in much more with the colour of aluminium façades and other infillings.

SCHÜCO International provides an
extensive support system to architects
and fabricators throughout the planning
and construction of synergy façades.
Of course, advice is also available on the
electrical engineering aspects of the
project – from the initial model stage
right through to completion.

SIEMENS

Siemens AG
Lighting Systems Division
Ohmstr. 50
83296 Traunreut
Germany
Phone +49/8669/33-1
Fax +49/8669/33-397

Light for People

Technical and representative, interior and exterior luminaires, street lighting, spotlights, downlights as well as office and industrial luminaires, also in combination with illumination electronics and daylight systems – our product range is as comprehensive as lighting requirements themselves.

In addition to producing luminaires we are primarily lighting experts: as in our philosophy "Light for People" we offer solutions tailored to every requirement.

Individual solutions

Light ensures safety, comfort and well-being. And light stimulates and motivates..... but only if it's not just bright, but good and proper. Good, proper lighting is our speciality.

When developing a lighting solution, we approach the individual illumination situation with flexibility – even if that sometimes means developing new luminaires. Over one third of our orders are custom solutions, which is appreciated by our customers.

High quality standard products.

We also specialize in the production of standard luminaires, whereby our strength in high product quality lies. The combination of wide ranging lighting engineering, different designs and colours as well as the use of modern illumination electronics means that the right product can always be found for the illumination situation.

Energy saving lighting systems

Energy saving illumination is our not inconsiderable contribution to conserving natural resources. With our energy saving program electricity costs for lighting can be cut by up to 75 % – that means less CO_2 as well.

Emphasis on innovation

Half of our product ranges are less than five years old. This shows how highly innovative our lighting is.

Planning, consulting and training

We offer a comprehensive range of planning assistance, consultation and training – and our customers profit from it – perhaps you too?

Sto AG
Ehrenbachstrasse 1
79780 Stühlingen
Germany
Phone +49/7744/57-0
Fax +49/7744/57-2177

Conventional composite systems for heat insulation provide passive protection for houses from loss of energy. This contrasts with the new StoTherm Solar transparent composite heat insulating system (TWDVS) which makes additional use of sunlight for an eco-friendly and economical source of heat. StoTherm Solar was developed by Sto AG in co-operation with the famous Fraunhofer Institutes for Building Physics in Stuttgart and for Solar Energy Systems in Freiburg. The Sto façade specialists were awarded the "Innovation Prize of the German Economy 1996" for this development.

StoTherm Solar significantly reduces energy consumption in old and new buildings. It consists of a light transmitting layer of polycarbonate of a capillary structure which allows the sunlight to pass through unimpeded so that it can be transformed into heat by a black absorber layer which simultaneously functions as adhesive for bonding with the outside wall element. A sealing and stabilizing glass fleece is bonded on the capillary plate. The final layer is formed by glass plaster.

The system functions selectively, i.e. its efficiency is highest during the winter and lowest in the summer. The lower sun during the winter months results in a flatter angle of incidence, thereby resulting in a much higher transmission rate than during the summer months when the sun is much higher in the sky so that only some of the rays pass through to the absorber layer. A large part of the sunlight is already reflected on the surface of the glass plaster. In this manner TWDVS insulated houses do not become overheated during the summer months, as is commonly the case in buildings with large glazed areas.

During the winter heating period up to 120 kWh are gained per square meter of TWDVS on the southern façade. The absorber layer achieves an efficiency of 95 per cent in the conversion of light into heat. The maximum possible temperatures within the absorber on the southern side cannot exceed 70°C, thereby excluding the possibility of damage to the masonry or system components. For instance, in winter the indoor temperature can be +20°C, and the temperature within the absorber +60°C, at an outside temperature of -10°C. The wall becomes a thermal store which then slowly releases the accumulated heat into the rooms with six to eight hours delay. The normal heat loss is now replaced by a flow of heat inside the wall from the outside to the inside.

ZANDER Klimatechnik AG
Rollnerstr. 111
90408 Nürnberg
Germany
Phone +49/911/3608-0
Fax +49/911/3608-162

Activity fields of
the ZANDER Group

1. Engineering of plants
Design and engineering of all kinds of plant for ventilation and air conditioning, coordination of the design with other technical services, drawing up tender documents, site management (during construction)

2. Technical contractor

2.1 Ventilation and air-conditioning plants
Comfort air-conditioning for administration buildings, hospitals, schools, universities, theatres, convention centres, indoor swimming pools, exhibition halls, department stores, shopping centres and industrial halls

Process air-conditioning, particularly in the following industrial areas: food industry, pharmaceutical industry, electronical industry, printing and paper industry, textile industry, car industry

2.2 Exhaust air decontamination

2.2.1 Mechanical separating plants for dusts and aerosols

2.2.2 Biological, thermal and chemico-physical exhaust air decontamination plants for gaseous contaminants like e.g. solvents and odours

2.3 Cleanroom technology

2.4 Refrigerating plants

2.5 Heating plants including thermal power stations and heat pump plants

2.6 Process measuring and control technology using DDC technology, Central control rooms

2.7 Energy management

3. Technical general contractor

4. Production
Ducts, cleanroom ceilings, special constructions for air-conditioning and ventilation systems

5. Service
All plants of the civil engineering: inspection, full and partial maintenance including process measuring and control technology plants and refrigerating plants, operating of plants

6. Facility management
Comprehensive service concept covering the entire needs of a property – from the operation of the technical facilities to infrastructural and commercial services

The contents of these company profiles are the responsibilty of the listed companies.

The author gratefully acknowledges the support of these firms.

Author
Klaus Daniels

Project consulting
Dr. Andreas Colli
Andreas Alber
Walter Schwaiger

Translation into English
Elizabeth Schwaiger, Toronto
(With thanks to
Malachy Neeson,
HL-Technik AG, Frankfurt)

Design and production
Büro SchwaigerWinschermann,
Munich
Walter Schwaiger
Alicja Kosmider
and
Christine Wagner
(English version)

Drawings by
Andreas Alber

Lithography, DTP consultation,
diagrams by
Christian Albrecht

Deutsche Bibliothek
Cataloging-in-Publication Data

Daniels, Klaus:
**The Technology of Ecological
Building**: Basic Principles,
Examples and Ideas / Klaus
Daniels. (Transl. from German
into Engl.: Elizabeth Schwaiger).
– Basel; Boston; Berlin:
Birkhäuser, 1997

Dt. Ausg. u.d.T.: Daniels, Klaus:
Technologie des ökologischen
Bauens
ISBN 3-7643-5461-5 (Basel...)
ISBN 0-8176-5461-5 (Boston)

© 1997 Birkhäuser –
Verlag für Architektur
P.O.Box 133,
CH-4010 Basel, Switzerland

Printed on acid-free paper produced from chlorine-free pulp.
TCF ∞

Printed in Germany
ISBN 3-7643-5461-5
ISBN 0-8176-5461-5

9 8 7 6 5 4 3 2 1